Off-Premise Catering Management

Off-Premise Catering Management

 Second Edition

Bill Hansen

Chris Thomas

WILEY

John Wiley & Sons, Inc.

Library of Congress Cataloging-in-Publication Data:

Hansen, Bill.
  Off-premise catering management / Bill Hansen, Chris Thomas.–2nd ed.
      p. cm.
      Includes index.
      ISBN 0-471-46424-4 (cloth)
  1. Caterers and catering–Management–Handbooks, manuals, etc. I. Thomas, Chris. II. Title.
    TX921.H36 2005
    642'.4–dc22   2004010499

Printed in the United States of America

10 9 8 7 6 5

I dedicate this book to my wife, Terry, who, for the past 21 years, has been there for me—whether it be writing this book, managing my catering business, or assisting me with administrative work while I teach Catering Management at Florida International University. She's always been there for me—and she's the love of my life.

She understands the pressures of catering, writing, and teaching, as well as the long hours and the incredible pressure involved in fulfilling client expectations. As I near what I hope to be semiretirement, Terry knows that I will make up for the lost time away from home as we travel, golf, and simply hang out together.

I love you, Sugar Girl,
Bill

Contents

✖ *Chapter 3*

Menu Planning   50

✖ *Chapter 4*

Beverage Service   76

✖ *Chapter 5*

Catering Equipment   117

■ *Chapter 6*

Logistics of Off-Premise Catering   149

■ *Chapter 7*

Human Resources   183

■ *Chapter 8*

The Show   228

Preface

It's an exciting time to be in the catering business—and I can still say that even after three decades! Competition is keen, but the sharp, personable caterer with good ideas, first-rate staff members, and an eye on the bottom line can build a very profitable business. There are more online sources than ever before for purchasing, vendors, and expert assistance. There are excellent professional organizations to be part of.

There is tragedy in the world, but there is also plenty of hope. People still want to enjoy their lives, marry, entertain friends, and impress clients. They turn to us in the catering industry to assist them. It is an honor to do so.

I began writing the first edition of this book back in 1990, and it was published in 1995. Today, with the keen eye, additional perspective, and attention to detail of my coauthor—longtime dining critic and food writer Chris Thomas—this second edition is much improved. Among other features, we have added:

- More time management tips
- Strategic planning techniques
- A far more extensive discussion on marketing
- Updated information on food safety and foodborne illness
- Updated laws and legal requirements, ranging from liquor laws to requirements for human resources management
- Staff recruiting and training ideas
- Ways to find unique and exciting catering venues
- Money-saving purchasing methods and product specs
- Trends in accessory services, ranging from photography, music, and wedding cakes to fireworks
- Leadership principles to ensure catering success
- A comprehensive "crash course" on wines from around the world

Of course, we've kept the handiest of features of the previous edition. There are lots of forms you can adapt to your own business to keep track of everything from rental equipment to specifics for each event. We've included plenty of lists for organizing front-of-the-house and back-of-the-house party requirements. And we often hear that the information on the wedding processional and positioning, presented in Chapter 13, has "saved the day" more than once. So it's included here too.

What we cannot put onto these printed pages is the passion and energy it takes to run a successful catering operation. That will have to come from you. We hope, however, that these attributes shine through all the sometimes mundane details in the chapters about legal and personnel issues, food storage, and budgeting. Stay the course.

Bill Hansen

Chapter 1

Introduction to Off-Premise Catering Management

Off-premise catering is serving food at a location away from the caterer's food production facility. One example of a food production facility is a freestanding commissary, which is a kitchen facility used exclusively for the preparation of foods to be served at other locations. Other examples of production facilities include, but are not limited to, hotel, restaurant, and club kitchens. In most cases there is no existing kitchen facility at the location where the food is served.

Caterers provide single-event foodservice, but not all caterers are created equal. They generally fall into one of three categories:

Party food caterers supply only the food for an event. They drop off cold foods and leave any last-minute preparation, plus service and cleanup, to others.

Hot buffet caterers provide hot foods that are delivered from their commissaries in insulated containers. They sometimes provide serving personnel at an additional charge.

Full-service caterers not only provide food, but frequently cook it to order on-site. They also provide service personnel at the event, plus all the necessary food-related equipment—china, glassware, flatware, tables and chairs, tents, and so forth. They can arrange for other services, like décor and music, as well. In short, a full-service caterer can plan an entire event, not just the food for it.

Off-premise catering can mean serving thousands of box lunches to a group of conventioneers; barbecuing chicken and ribs for fans before a big college game, serving an elegant dinner for two aboard a luxury yacht, or providing food, staff, and equipment for an upscale fundraiser with hundreds of guests. On a "degree of difficulty" scale from one to ten—one meaning "easy" and ten meaning "most challenging"—on-premise catering is a two, and off-premise would rank a ten!

Off-premise caterers meet the needs of all market segments, from the low-budget customer who looks for the greatest quantity and quality for the least amount of money, to the upscale client with an unlimited budget who wants the highest level of service, the ultimate in food quality, and the finest in appointments—crystal stemware, silver-plated flatware, and luxurious linens. Between these two extremes is the midscale market segment, which requires more quality than the low-budget sector, but less than the upscale.

Off-premise catering is an art and a science. The art is creating foods and moods, as the caterer and client together turn a vision into reality. The science is the business of measuring money, manpower, and material. Successful off-premise caterers recognize the importance of both aspects—art and science—and are able to work at both the creative and the financial levels.

In off-premise catering, there is only one chance to get it right. Many events, such as wedding receptions, occur only once in a lifetime. Other events are scheduled annually, quarterly, or on a regular basis, and the caterer who fails to execute all details of such an event to the satisfaction of the client will seldom have another chance.

Unfortunately for some, off-premise catering can be like living on the brink of disaster unless they are experienced. Uninitiated amateurs may not recognize a volatile situation until it becomes a problem, later realizing they should have recognized it earlier.

Catering off-premise is very similar to a sports team playing all of its games away from home, in unfamiliar surroundings, with none of the comforts of home to ease the way. There is no home field advantage, but there is a minefield disadvantage! As caterers plod their way toward the completion of a catered event, there are thousands of potential "land mines" that can ruin an otherwise successful affair. Some examples follow:

- Already running late for a catering delivery, the catering van driver discovers that all vehicle traffic around the party site is in gridlock. The traffic has been at a standstill for more than an hour, the police say it will be hours before the congestion can be eliminated, and the clients and their guests are anxiously awaiting dinner.
- The only freight elevator in a high-rise office building has been commandeered for the evening by moving and cleaning people, thus preventing access to the floor where a caterer is to stage an event scheduled to start in two hours.
- The wrong hot food truck is dispatched to a wedding reception. The error is not discovered until the truck has reached the reception and the bride and groom are ready for their guests to be served. It will take more than an hour to send the correct truck with the food that was ordered.
- A cook wheels a container filled with cooked prime ribs down a pier toward a yacht where the meat will be served to a group of 80 conventioneers in half an hour. Suddenly, the cook is distracted, and the prime rib container tumbles over the edge of the pier into 40 feet of water.
- The table numbers have vanished, and the guests are ready to be seated for dinner.

- The fire marshal arrives at a party site 20 minutes before a catered event and refuses to allow guests access to the party site because the space had not been authorized for party use.
- The catering crew arrives at the party site with a van full of food, cooked to order—exactly one week early.
- A new customer places an order and asks that the caterer deliver to a home where family members and guests will have gathered prior to a funeral service. The caterer sends the food and, upon arrival, is told that the person with the checkbook is at the funeral home and is asked to please stop back in an hour for the money. The delivery person leaves without obtaining a signature. Upon returning, there is no one home and no one from whom to collect payment.
- While using a garbage disposal in a client's home, the caterer suddenly hears a terrible noise and watches in horror as water and garbage spew from the disposal all over the floor. The irate customer refuses to pay the caterer and threatens to sue for the cost of replacing the garbage disposal that was ruined because of (in the customer's words) the caterer's "negligence."
- After catering a flawless party at a client's home and loading the catering truck to capacity, the caterer is shocked to learn from the client that all 15 bags of trash must be removed from the client's property because of the neighborhood's zoning ordinances.
- The caterer's rental company representative calls the caterer the morning after an event and advises the caterer that the $600 rented chafing dish is missing. It was there the night before, when the caterer left the client's home.

Get the picture? We could tell horror stories all day! Seasoned off-premise caterers agree, these are only a few of the thousands of obstacles that stand in the way of completing a catered event. This book addresses the various ways to professionally and successfully deal with difficult situations.

With all of these very real potential problems, why are there *more than 50,000* off-premise caterers in the United States? Why are more young people studying catering at two-year and four-year colleges and universities? Why are thousands of people starting their own catering companies, risking their savings on their dreams of future success? The reasons are numerous. They may love the adventure of working in new and exciting places. They look forward to the peaks and valleys of the business cycle. They love the intense feeling of satisfaction that comes after successfully catering a spectacular party. They love the myriad challenges of this very difficult profession. Many are their own bosses, with no one to answer to but the client. Many pick and choose the parties they wish to cater. Many make six-figure incomes each year, and others cater occasionally, just for the fun of it.

✗ Comparing Off-Premise and On-Premise Catering

What are the differences between off-premise catering and on-premise catering? Let's examine these differences, from both the client's and the caterer's viewpoints.

From the Client's Viewpoint

Most clients fail to consider the cost of the rental equipment such as tables, chairs, linens, china, glassware, and flatware when they consider engaging an off-premise caterer. They think it will be less expensive to entertain in their homes, or at unique off-premise sites, than in hotels. In fact, it can be more expensive, considering not only the cost of the rental equipment, but also other costs such as transportation of food and supplies to the site, the costs of special labor and décor, the need for tenting, air-conditioning and/or heating, and other expenses. Clients may save some money by buying their own liquor, but this can be insignificant as compared with the added costs. For many clients, the additional costs are far outweighed by the benefits of entertaining in the privacy of their own homes or the uniqueness of a special off-premise location such as a museum, state-of-the-art aquarium, antique car dealership, or historical site.

From the Caterer's Viewpoint

Off-premise caterers must plan menus that can be prepared successfully at the client's location. For example, foods to be fried should not be cooked in unventilated spaces, like small kitchens in high-rise office buildings. On-premise caterers are not as limited in this regard, and they are generally supported by built-in equipment that can support a wider variety of menus.

On-premise party personnel are more familiar with the party facilities than those who work at a variety of unfamiliar locations. Off-premise catering generally has greater seasonal and day-to-day swings in personnel needs, which can create a greater challenge for the off-premise caterer, who is constantly recruiting and training staff; turnover is usually high because such work is on an "as-needed basis."

There is definitely a greater potential for oversights in off-premise catering. Backup supplies, food, and equipment can be miles away or even inaccessible when catering, for instance, aboard a yacht miles from shore.

In spite of the uncertainties, off-premise catering offers the opportunity to work in a greater variety of interesting locations. The work is more likely to be different each day, resulting in less boredom and more excitement. For those looking for unlimited challenges and rewards, off-premise catering may be the answer.

✖ Advantages and Disadvantages of Off-Premise Catering

In his book *How to Manage a Successful Catering Business*, Manfred Ketterer mentions the numerous advantages of catering:[1]

Advance deposits
Limited start-up investment
Limited inventories
Controllable costs

Additional revenues
Business by contract
Direct payment
Advance forecasting
Free word-of-mouth advertising
Selectivity

Let's discuss a few of these items in more detail. First, most off-premise caterers require some form of advance deposit prior to an event. This deposit provides the caterer with some security if the event is canceled and also can be used to purchase some or all of the food and supplies for the party.

There is no need for large amounts of capital to get started, since most off-premise catering operations begin by using the existing kitchen facilities of a restaurant, club, hotel, church, or other licensed foodservice business. (It is common knowledge that many start their catering businesses in their home kitchens, but it is imperative to state that this is in direct violation of most local zoning ordinances.) In addition, all of the necessary catering foodservice equipment such as china, glassware, flatware, tables, chairs, and linens can usually be rented, thus avoiding having to invest in expensive equipment inventories.

Food and supply inventories, as well as operating costs, are much more easily controlled, because clients must advise the caterer in advance as to the number of guests that are expected. Off-premise caterers need buy only the amounts necessary to serve the event, unlike a restaurant where there is a large variation from day to day regarding the number of patrons and their menu selections.

Off-premise catering generates additional revenues for existing operations like hotels, clubs, and restaurants. They can generate even more profit by providing other services—rental equipment, flowers, décor, music, entertainment, and other accessory services.

Both the client and the caterer have expectations regarding the outcome of the party. These expectations should be clearly spelled out in a written contract. Payment for an event is normally made directly to a manager or owner, eliminating a middleman, whether it's a wedding planner, on-site food and beverage director, or one of the caterer's own staff members. This form of direct payment provides for better cash control and fewer folks to share the profit.

Advance forecasting is more accurate for off-premise caterers, because parties are generally booked weeks, months, or years in advance. Moreover, each part of the country has seasonal swings, which make revenue forecasting somewhat easier. For example, in the South the summer months are generally less busy, but in the North these are the busy months.

Off-premise events generate tremendous amounts of free word-of-mouth advertising, which can produce future business without the necessity of advertising. Many off-premise caterers feel that satisfied guests at one party will either directly or indirectly book another party by speaking favorably to friends and co-workers about the event and the caterer. In other words, one party can create future parties.

Caterers also have the advantage of being somewhat selective about their clients. There are no laws that require you to accept every request to cater. If the job doesn't meet your standards, politely decline. In sticky situations where you've already begun to work with a client but find that your communication styles just don't mesh—or, as sometimes happens with weddings, the client is not heeding your advice and you can't even decide who's really in charge—you can walk away, as long as you do so within the terms of your written agreement.

Off-premise catering does have some disadvantages too: Catering managers, owners, and staff undergo periods of high stress during very busy periods. Deadlines must be met. There are no excuses for missing a catering deadline. Stress is compounded because the workload is not evenly spread throughout the year. For most off-premise caterers, 80 percent of the events are scheduled in 20 percent of the time. For most, weekends are generally busier than weekdays. Certain seasons, including Christmas, are normally busier than others. Of course, caterers must maintain general business hours too!

Many have left the catering field, burned out by the constant stress and high energy demands. The seasonality of the business makes it difficult to find staff at certain times. Revenues are inconsistent, making cash management very difficult, particularly during the slower periods when expenses continue yet revenues do not.

For those caterers who operate hotels, restaurants, clubs, and other businesses, the time away from the main business—spent on the off-premise business—can hurt. It is difficult for even the most well-organized person to be in two places at the same time.

Many hoteliers and restaurateurs find the rigors of off-premise catering too great. Some quit after realizing the difficulty of catering away from their operations. They feel that the financial benefits are insufficient compared with the effort required to cater off-premise events.

✕ *Elements of Successful Off-Premise Catering*

What does it take to become a successful off-premise caterer? What experience is necessary, and what personality traits are desirable?

Work Experience. Prior experience in the catering profession or the foodservice industry is important. Experience in food preparation and foodservice (both back-of-the-house and front-of-the-house) helps caterers understand the procedures and problems in both areas and how the two areas interface. Those with a strong kitchen background, for example, would be wise to gain some front-of-house experience, and front-of-house personnel should learn the kitchen routine.

Many successful off-premise caterers began by working as accommodators. Accommodators are private chefs who are hired to prepare food for parties. Many assist the client with planning the menu, purchasing the food, and even arranging for kitchen and service staff. The food is prepared and served in the client's home or facility, eliminating the need for a catering commissary. Accommodators receive a fee for their services. The party staff is paid directly by the client.

Passion. Successful professionals are passionate about their work, and caterers are no exception. They love what they do! Clients and staff members will quickly detect a lack of passion, and it will cost you business and good workers. If you don't love what you do, move on and try something else.

An Entrepreneurial Nature. The desire to be an entrepreneur is a trait that is highly desirable for off-premise caterers. An entrepreneur must be willing to spend extraordinary amounts of time and energy to make the off-premise catering business successful, possess an inherent sense of what is right for the business, have the ability to view all aspects of the business at once rather than focusing only on one or two parts, and demonstrate a strong, incessant desire to be his or her own boss and become financially independent.

Basic Business Knowledge

- Accounting and bookkeeping skills are necessary to understand the financial aspects of operating a catering business. The ability to prepare and interpret financial statements is essential.
- Learn as much about computers as you can. You'll be amazed at how much you can accomplish by using e-mail, having a website, and using specialized programs for everything from budgeting to menu planning.
- It's also important to understand the legal aspects of catering. Laws that affect caterers include regulation of licensing, contracts, liability, labor, and alcoholic beverage service.
- A caterer, like any other businessperson, must have some human resource skills. Knowing how to recruit, train, motivate, and manage personnel is critical.
- Off-premise caterers should be knowledgeable about how to develop and implement a marketing plan.

Ability to Plan, Organize, Execute, and Control. These are the four basic functions of management. To plan, a caterer must visualize in advance all of the aspects of a catered event and document the plans so they are readily understood by the client and easily executed by the staff. Organizing is simply breaking down the party plans into groups of functions that can be executed in an efficient manner. Execution is the implementation of the organized plans by the party staff. Controlling is the supervisory aspect of the event. All well-organized and well-executed plans require control and supervision. The adage is, "It is not what you expect, but what you inspect." The premier off-premise catering firms in the United States insist on excellent supervision at each event.

Ability to Communicate with Clients and Staff. Listening is the key to good communication with clients and prospective clients. Off-premise caterers must listen carefully and attentively to determine what the client needs. A client who calls and asks, "Are you able to cater a party next Friday?" should be dealt with differently from one who calls and asks, "How much will it cost for a wedding reception?" The first caller is ready to buy your services, whereas the second caller is shopping. Astute caterers must be able to respond to client requests in such a manner that the client will immediately gain confidence in the caterer.

Communicating with staff is a complex issue. In simple terms, it can be reduced to the ability to tell staff what is expected so that they understand, and the ability to receive their feedback regarding problems, both actual and potential. The result of effective communication is an off-premise catering staff that professionally executes a well-planned party that meets or exceeds the client's expectations.

Willingness to Take Calculated Risks. Off-premise catering is a very risky business. It is not for the fainthearted who are afraid of the unknown. For example, it is more risky catering a corporate fund-raiser at the local zoo under a tent than serving the same group in a hotel ballroom. Off-premise caterers must know when the risk outweighs the gain. In this particular example, catering the event at the zoo without adequate cover in case of rain would probably be too risky. The event could be ruined. The tent makes the risk of rain a calculated one.

Sound Body and Mind. Off-premise catering requires working long hours without rest or sleep, lifting and moving heavy objects, intense pressure as deadlines near, and even long periods of little or no business, which can cause concern. Successful caterers should be in good physical shape, have a high energy level, and be able to mentally deal with seasonal business cycles that range from nonstop activity to slow periods with little or no business.

Off-premise caterers must be self-confident, but at the same time realize that they must always find ways to improve the quality of their food and services. In this profession a fondness for people and feeling comfortable in crowds is important. A "cool head" when under pressure will keep both staff and client calm while potential problems are resolved professionally and efficiently.

Creativity. This is the benchmark of all outstanding caterers. Creative caterers are able to turn a client's vision into reality by creating the appropriate look, feel, menu, service, and ambiance. Those who are not very creative can learn to be, or they can employ those who are creative.

Dependability. Dependability is a major cornerstone of success in off-premise catering. When a caterer fails to deliver what was promised, the negative word of mouth travels fast among clients and potential clients. Even in those situations where circumstances change, making it more difficult to perform as promised, the outstanding caterer will find a way to deliver rather than use the changed circumstances as an excuse not to deliver.

Open-Mindedness. Open-minded caterers read up on catering trends and try new recipes and menus. They are willing to prepare unfamiliar dishes requested by clients, after thoroughly testing and understanding the recipes. They discover and try new dishes. They are always learning better ways to run their businesses.

Ability to Meet the Needs of Clients. The needs of the client must always come first. Success in this business comes from identifying these needs and satisfying them. Unsuccessful off-premise caterers are those who get lost in trying to satisfy their own needs for money, equipment, and greater self-esteem. They forget that the primary goal is to serve the needs of the client. When a client's needs are met, the caterer's needs for revenues, profits, and positive feedback will automatically be met.

Ability to Project a Favorable Image. Prospective clients hire caterers based on their perceived image of the caterer and what the caterer will provide. In some sense, then, caterers are selling themselves more than their food. Off-premise caterers must be able to project a favorable image to the client, one that is in accord with the client's expectations. For example, a caterer whose image is sophisticated and upscale will be hard-pressed to sell a Little League banquet with a low budget. Successful caterers understand their projected images and target their marketing efforts at those clients who desire that image.

Sense of Humor. In this pressure-packed, deadline-oriented, and stressful business, it is easy to get carried away with the magnitude of the undertakings and become so tense and uptight that work ceases to be fun. Laughter at the right time can relieve that tension and stress, putting a renewed sense of fun into the work at hand.

How do caterers serve shrimps? They bend down!

✕ *Managing an Off-Premise Catering Operation*

Even those who possess the qualities that indicate off-premise catering success must know how to put these talents to use effectively. Off-premise caterers should be hands-on managers who are constantly customer focused. They must be able to lead staff and clients alike, while conducting business in a professional manner. They must be able to make timely, ethical decisions, while understanding what makes for a successful event. They must also avoid those situations that cause a business to fail.

Developing a Strategic Plan

Yogi Berra, the zany former New York Yankee catcher, is famous for his many witticisms, such as, "Nobody goes there anymore—it's too crowded." But his best quote may be this one: "If you don't know where you're going, you will wind up somewhere else."

That's the reason you need a strategic plan—a roadmap to help you determine the direction in which you wish to go, and the specific goals you'll need to accomplish to get there. A strategic plan starts with a statement of core values, which may include things like client satisfaction; ethical business practices; staff satisfaction, training, and motivation; community service; and operating an environmentally conscious business.

From these core values, a caterer can develop a Mission Statement—a succinct sentence that sums up the company's mission. Here's an example:

"To meet the catering needs of the corporate community, providing high levels of service and food quality that result in repeat business and vital growth."

After the Mission Statement comes the Vision Statement—a concise summary of where you want to be in the future. Again, an example:

"Within five years, our company will be the top-ranked catering firm in our area, with continuing sales and profit growth, while giving back to our community."

It's not enough to brainstorm about these statements. Writing them down is the first step to making a commitment—to make them a reality. Only after they are put in writing can you develop more specific objectives to increase sales and profits, measure customer satisfaction, size up your competitors, and plan the ways in which you will give back to the community.

Your Mission and Vision Statements lead naturally to the next step—to establish goals for the operation. You may have heard time management experts use the term "SMART" when describing goals. The acronym stands for:

Specific: The goals to be accomplished must be easily understood, concise, and unambiguous.

Measurable: There should be no question about whether one attains, or falls short of, a goal. It may be measured in terms of quality, cost, quantity, or time.

Attainable: The goals may be just out of reach, but they're not out of sight! The best goal challenges and motivates you and your team. If it's practically impossible, it may be too frustrating.

Relevant: The goals must fit well with your long-term mission and vision, your objectives, and the results you expect.

Time–bound: There must be a specific deadline for completion of each goal.

An example of a SMART goal might be to increase sales and profits by 20 percent each year for the next five years.

Once a caterer has set goals, there must be certain trade-offs. To increase sales, for instance, may require raising prices, hiring more staff to be able to cater more events, or spending money on advertising. The major goals can be broken into smaller, intermediate steps, with a time line to keep the company on track.

And remember, goals are not just for the owner of a company. The staff and other professionals employed by the company—tax preparer, banker, attorney—should also be well aware of the goals. You'll need their help to achieve them, and you want them on your side, committed to your goals. Too often, caterers believe they can do everything themselves. They fail to ask for or accept advice from outside consultants and colleagues. It is far more intelligent to ask for assistance when you need it. Someone familiar with your plans and your passion for them is far more likely to be helpful.

Finally, as soon as a goal is set, take some action on it.

The last part of a strategic management process is to reevaluate your mission, vision, and goals periodically. Times change, trends change, and you become aware of new information. Let's say a caterer's sales year showed a 50 percent increase, when he or she had set a 20 percent annual goal. In this case, the next year's goal might be more realistically revised to a 30 percent increase.

Hands-on Attention to Detail Management

The devil is in the details. Have you ever heard that old saying? Another way to put it: We've all been bitten by a mosquito or stung by a bee, but how many of us have been bitten by an elephant? It's always the little things that get us!

In catering, the details are virtually endless, a stream of tiny elements that might go wrong and result in a catastrophe. One thing forgotten, misheard, or misplaced can ruin an event. So it's important to check and recheck and to be prepared for last-minute emergencies.

It is simply not possible to run this kind of business from behind a desk, reading computer printouts and delegating all tasks. Off-premise catering companies must be managed from the center of the action, whether that is with the guests or preparing foods in the kitchen. It comes from checking and rechecking every detail to ensure that it meets the highest of standards. It comes from inspecting for the best and expecting the best. Some call this management style "management by walking around." In one sense that is true, but there is more to it than walking around. Astute off-premise caterers must:

- Obtain feedback from clients and guests regarding the food and service.
- Oversee the catering staff to ensure they are performing as directed and as expected.
- Help out when a table needs to be cleared or when the bar suddenly becomes very busy. Help in the kitchen during critical times such as hot food dish-up, and even help scrape, stack, and wash dirty dishes if that's what is necessary.

It's a roll-up-your-sleeves kind of profession, and you should never be totally satisfied with the way things are. Always look for new ways to present food and make it more flavorful, and for better and more efficient ways to do things.

Customer-Focused Management

An off-premise caterer's full-time mission must be to satisfy the needs of clients. Mike DeLuca, editor of *Restaurant Hospitality* magazine, puts it this way:

> Companies that are 100% customer focused make the customer's satisfaction their only goal. They do not have as goals, increasing sales by a certain percentage, raising a profit margin, or reducing debt. They believe . . . that if you strive to sell only the highest quality product and strive to please every customer, sales, profit and success will follow. This is a difficult concept for many of us to grasp. It means letting go of a financial accounting structure passed down from generation to generation of Harvard MBAs who've instilled in us that the only way to build your bottom line is to raise your top line and squeeze the middle. . . . That can work . . . but wouldn't you rather make the quality of your food, the dining experience and your customer's satisfaction your primary concern?[2]

The moral is simple: If you satisfy your customers while charging a fair price and controlling costs, profits will follow.

Managerial Decision Making

Off-premise catering managers must make decisions that keep their operations running smoothly. They realize that some decisions will be better than others, that there is no perfect solution to every problem, and that the best decision-making goal is to find the best possible solution with the least number of drawbacks.

Connie Sitterly, a management consultant and author, states that to be a good decision maker you should "plan ahead so when problems crop up, you're prepared to act, not react. Control circumstances, instead of allowing them to control you. Take the initiative by anticipating and solving business problems."

Although hundreds of books have been written about decision making, the following tips from Ms. Sitterly should be helpful. They're paraphrased from an article she wrote back in 1990 in *The Meeting Manager*, but they are still up-to-the-minute when it comes to making tough decisions successfully.

- Remember that there's seldom only one acceptable solution to the problem. Choose the best alternative.
- Make decisions that help achieve the company objectives.
- You need to consider feelings whenever people are involved. Even if you must make an unpopular decision, you can minimize repercussions . . . if workers know you have taken their feelings into account.
- Allow quality time for planning and decision making . . . pick a time when you are energetic and your mind is fresh.
- Realize that you'll never please everyone. Few decisions meet with unanimous approval . . . the appointed authority, not the majority, rules.
- Make time for making decisions . . . in business, delaying a decision can cost thousands of dollars.
- Put decision making in perspective. Every executive feels overwhelmed at times by either the enormity or the number of decisions made during a business day. . . . For peace of mind accept that you are doing the best job you can with the time, talent, and resources you have.
- Don't wait for a popular vote. Rallying your colleagues around your decision before you take action or waiting for their vote of confidence before deciding anything may cost too much in time. There are times when you just have to *do* something.[3]

Leadership

There are major differences between those who lead and those who manage. Catering companies need both types of executives, and some who can do both. If a catering company is earning seven- and eight-figure annual revenues, it is most definitely being led by people with leadership skills.

Leaders are able to get people to do things they don't necessarily like to do, but they do them and even enjoy them. You might say:

A MANAGER . . .	A LEADER . . .
Maintains	Develops
Administers	Innovates
Relies on systems	Relies on people
Counts on controls	Counts on trust
Does things right	Does the right things
Works within the system	Works on the system
Manages things	Leads people

A leader is more like a thermostat than a thermometer. A thermostat sets the standard temperature for the space it's in. A thermometer simply records the temperature; it can't change anything. And one more important trait: Leaders take a little more than their share of the blame and a little less than their share of the credit.

Professionalism and Common Business Courtesy

Off-premise caterers who are not professional in their business practices will never reach the pinnacle of success in the field. Before we address the technical aspects of catering in the succeeding chapters, it is of utmost importance that we define professionalism. The following guidelines are adapted from an article by Carol McKibben in *Special Events* magazine:

- Become known for doing what you say you are going to do.
- Give price quotes and commitments only when you know everything about the event.
- Treat clients and staff members with respect.
- Build relationships with clients. Do not look at them as accounts or projects.
- Be on time, or a bit early, for appointments. Be prepared for an appointment.
- Be honest; don't play games.
- Stand behind your work. If it is wrong, make it right.
- In the face of abuse from others, don't respond by becoming abusive. Try to detach yourself from it emotionally and handle it logically. Of course, do not use your position of power to abuse others.
- Dress professionally.
- Enjoy your work as an off-premise caterer. When work ceases to be enjoyable, it is time to quit and find a new career.[4]

Ethics in Management

The Roman philosopher Publilius Syrus said, "A good reputation is more valuable than money." This is as true today as it was in ancient times. And yet, lack of ethics is perhaps the most widely discussed topic in today's business world. We read and hear of illegalities, scandals, and other forms of questionable behavior bringing down some of the nation's largest corporations. Off-premise caterers are in no way exempt from ethical concerns. Even the smallest caterers deal in issues of fairness, legal requirements, and honesty on a daily basis. Examples include truth in menu, misleading advertising, unexpected and unjustified last-minute add-ons to the party price, and even underbidding a competitor when the client has disclosed your competitor's price.

The truly ethical caterer will assume responsibility for the host to ensure that the host plans an event in the best interest of the guests. A host who wishes to serve alcohol to underage guests or barbecued ribs to a group of elderly people (tough to eat with dentures) is out of line and needs to be advised that this will not work. In fact, an ethical caterer will refuse to cater an event that is clearly not being planned in the best interest of the host or guests.

There are times when a caterer is given a free hand in planning a menu. Perhaps a grieving client calls for food after the funeral of a loved one, saying, "Please send over food for 50 guests tomorrow night. You know what we like!" The ethical caterer will not take advantage of this situation by either providing too much food or overcharging the client.

Another temptation arises when the caterer is pressed to cater more events on a certain day or evening than he or she can reasonably accommodate. The extra money looks good. Unethical caterers will rationalize that they can handle all the events, even if an inexperienced supervisor or staff must oversee these events, or even if the kitchen staff will not be able to prepare the caterer's usual high-quality food because of lack of time and personnel. Caterers who take on more work than they can reasonably accommodate are greedy and are considered by many observers to be unethical.

In the foregoing situation the caterer should decline the work and perhaps recommend another caterer. Some caterers refuse to recommend another catering firm because they feel that if the client is not pleased with the other firm, the caterer who turned down the business will be blamed for the recommendation. Other caterers freely recommend one or more companies when unable to cater events.

There are times when it is very hard not to bad-mouth a competitor, but this is considered unethical as well as rude. Those who are ethical would rather point out their own strengths than downgrade the competition.

It can be very tempting for self-employed caterers to underreport income or overstate expenses. They rationalize that no one will know if they accept cash for a party, then fail to report it as income and pay the associated tax, or that no one will know if they happen to charge personal expenses now and then to the business. Some caterers who are licensed to sell liquor by the drink or by the bottle are tempted to bill clients for beverages that were not consumed. These practices are not only unethical—they are illegal.

Other ethical violations occur when caterers receive under-the-table cash "kickbacks" from suppliers, misrepresent their services to potential clients, or bid on party plans or ideas stolen from other caterers.

Caterers also soon learn that some clients are unethical. A few are masterful at finding fault with a wedding or other important event, then demanding a "discount" based on whatever flaw they feel they have uncovered. Some will refuse to pay for linens that were damaged by candles they lit on them! You'll find people who, mid-party, will ask you to stay "a couple hours of overtime, just to wrap things up"—then not show up to pay you for the extra time the next day, as agreed. Others will haggle over the tiniest details on an invoice or try to engage more than one caterer in a bidding war to lower prices. Caterers who deal with "middleman" organizations, like destination management firms or production companies, may find that a client of one of these companies will come back later to try to deal directly with you, thus cutting out the middleman who recommended you!

As a catering professional, you need to expect a certain amount of this behavior and must protect yourself if you suspect an ethical question may arise. Insisting on security deposits, having a valid and authorized credit card number on file for unforeseen charges, refusing to look at other caterers' written bids, and standing firm on your own invoice prices are just a few ways ethical problems can be avoided. And rather than cut out a legitimate middleman-type of vendor, you can either refuse to deal directly with a client who tries such a maneuver or suggest a commission be paid to the middleman.

You will also be put in some sticky situations as—during tough times, and even good times—certain clients will make unrealistic requests. They've often been good, regular clients too! But they'll promise you future business if you'll cater their party "at cost," or defer payment for them, or ask some other special favor "just this once."

These requests are unfair, and you're right to be squeamish about them. Off-premise caterers should be extremely wary when approached in this fashion. As a general rule, clients who do not pay their bills in a professional manner, or who are not willing to pay a fair price for catering services, are not worth the headaches they cause.

The Jefferson Center of Character Education has set forth a list of ten "universal values": honesty, integrity, promise keeping, fidelity, fairness, caring for others, respect for others, responsible citizenship, pursuit of excellence, and accountability.[5] These values should provide some solid guidance for any businessperson who considers him- or herself a true professional.

Separating Yourself from the Competition

Great caterers do more than imitate—they innovate. There are distinct advantages for those who offer a unique menu, a unique service, or perhaps a unique location. They may build and improve on someone else's concept, but they strive to take the idea to the next level. Rather than mimicking another's success, they imprint their own signature on their menus. To illustrate, let's take a look at two simple, self-service mashed potato bars:

THE TYPICAL APPROACH	THE UNIQUE APPROACH
Mashed potatoes	Sweet potatoes
Sour cream	Crème fraîche
Bacon bits	Canadian bacon
Chopped chives	Chopped fresh basil
Shredded cheddar cheese	Crumbled Stilton

The "Unique" bar may include all the traditional accompaniments too—but what a difference a little imagination makes! There might even be a bit of caviar to top the mashers at the Unique bar, and perhaps they'll be served in martini glasses. Why not have fun with it?

One of America's top chefs, Charlie Trotter, looks at food trends differently in his book *Lessons in Excellence.* Says Trotter, "It's important that you foster a company culture that spurs you and your employees to search for innovative opportunities. Innovations can satisfy needs that are unmet or offer solutions to time-worn problems, or they can be new ways of saving time, space and money."[6]

Trotter says he and his staff use input from their travels, readings, television, radio, and even hobbies to hit upon trends. They keep up on the latest changes in public opinion and demographics to search for interesting, potentially high-growth markets. Currently, they've identified ethnic cuisines such as Pan-Asian and Nuevo Latino as hot areas for menu innovation. The bottom line is that they create their own trends.

Similarly, as with any career, catering professionals need to reexamine their business strategies from time to time. Some caterers do what they do best, are well known for it, and never vary their formulas. Their clients love them and get exactly what they expect.

Other caterers blindly copy everybody else. They ricochet from one recipe to the other, never bothering to see if it meets their clients' needs. If they read about it in *Food Arts* magazine, they feel they *have* to serve it! But most caterers lie somewhere between these two extremes, blending the successful ideas of the past with new twists.

Great caterers also separate themselves from competitors by using the resources around them to build their businesses. In South Florida, for example, one caterer specializes in event planning for doctors, through his hospital foodservice management job. Another has an exclusive off-premise contract for a sports facility; a third was the on-premise caterer for a city club, which resulted in off-premise jobs for the club members. Capitalize on the audience you have—they're (almost) already yours!

✕ *Personal Management*

Off-premise caterers must learn how to deal with principles of stress management, time management, and personal organization if they are to manage at peak efficiency. Time is our most precious commodity, and to waste it because of being overstressed or disorganized will inevitably result in less-than-desirable results.

Stress Management

Stress comes from interaction with others, and from having to meet deadlines. A certain amount of stress and tension is necessary to achieve the best results—those who are too laid back generally do not maximize their potential—but too much stress causes chronic fatigue, irritability, cynicism, hostility, inflexibility, and difficulty in thinking clearly. Catering managers who are overstressed are unable to perform at maximum capability.

Stress can often be controlled through:

- Daily exercise such as brisk walking, running, or other aerobic pursuits that increase the pulse rate. Some folks purposefully take their minds off work when they exercise; for others, the daily walk or run is a time to get their day mentally organized.
- Relaxation techniques, including meditation and yoga.
- Writing down the issues that cause stress. Identify those issues in your life that can be controlled, and simply decide to make the best of those that cannot. List ways to deal with the controllable stress factors.
- Reading articles and books on stress reduction.

It is important to remember that some stress in catering is good. An arrow would not be propelled from a bow if the bow was not stressed. However, too much stress can break the bow, as well as ruin catered events.

Time Management

There are only 168 hours in each week, and the greatest rewards come to those who accomplish the most meaningful things during this fixed amount of time. Off-premise caterers realize that if they can accomplish more meaningful production in less time, they will have more time for things other than work. They also realize that working smarter, not harder, through the effective use of time will produce greater results.

The key to effective time management is to set goals for a lifetime, for five years, and for each year, month, week, and day. (Use some of the tips for putting SMART goals in writing—not just for "big picture" goals, but as part of your daily business.) Without written goals, off-premise caterers cannot effectively manage their time. Because time management involves choosing how to spend time, it is impossible to make proper choices without knowing your desired goals. The captain of a ship without a destination cannot choose the proper course. He will cruise aimlessly at sea, never reaching his port of call.

It is equally important to schedule "downtime" for yourself—for family, friends, hobbies, and interests other than work. You are guarding against burnout when you insist on some personal time.

Off-premise caterers can choose from an array of time-saving techniques and technical advances to help them in the quest to efficiently manage time:

- Make those daily, detailed lists of goals and objectives.
- Use technical advances to speed up paper handling, such as fax machines and computers with word processing, accounting, and menu-planning software.
- For heaven's sake, if you don't have a computer, get one! You can purchase one nowadays for a monthly payment of less than $40. You can take classes to learn how to use it or hire someone to teach you individually.
- Use cellular phones to stay in touch while away from the office. These are life-savers at off-premise catering locations when emergency and other calls are neces-

sary, and if you have downtime, a cellular phone can make it easy for you to use this time to return phone calls.

- Handle incoming papers only once. Here's the rule: Do it, delegate it, discard it, or file it. (Better yet, hire someone else to file it!)
- Do your most important work at times when you happen to be most alert. Most of us know whether we are "morning people" or "night owls." Take advantage of your peak energy periods to handle your most challenging tasks.
- Sign up for a seminar or course in time management to learn more tips.

One of the biggest time wasters for a caterer is also the source of much business—the prospective client who calls to ask questions—so it's an interruption that cannot be ignored, but can be controlled. Whoever answers the phone at your business should always qualify the incoming call by asking:

- The date of the event
- The location of the event
- The number of guests
- The budget for the event

Why? First of all, time can be wasted talking about an event before you ask the date and discover you're not able to do it in the first place because of a scheduling conflict. Perhaps the number of guests is too small or too large for your particular company, the budget is insufficient, or the proposed location is already booked for another event.

Always focus on results by asking yourself, "Will this activity help me achieve any of my goals?" Prioritize tasks in order of their importance and know when to delegate them to others. Most people waste countless hours, days, weeks, and years chitchatting on the phone, shuffling papers, running errands, and doing other things that are easy enough but offer little or no payoff. Learn to delegate these types of tasks whenever possible. Pay other people to do them, and don't tell yourself you can't afford it—you can always make more money, but you have only so much time. The true achievers—in catering and in other fields—minimize their time on low-priority, low-payoff tasks and turn their attention to those things that will bring the greatest rewards.

These tasks are often difficult to accomplish, take a great deal of time, and involve at least some risk. For example, a caterer could spend the entire day showing prospective clients numerous suitable locations for a major event. The caterer would then spend the next three days preparing a written proposal for an event at each of the locations, with no guarantee that the event will even take place. However, if the caterer is hired, there's a five-figure profit to be made. Worth the risk? Certainly!

Another high-payoff task might be to write a new catering menu. Both this and the aforementioned task require large chunks of time and involve some risk, but more than likely will produce major rewards in increased revenues and profits.

In summary, off-premise caterers who best manage their time in the long run will be the most successful. They become the leading caterers in their communities, in their states, and in the country.

Getting Organized

When projects, tasks, catering kitchens, and offices are organized, things run much more smoothly and efficiently. The time spent looking for things and jumping from job to job is wasted time that could be put to much better use. Many off-premise caterers have found various methods that work for them:

- Establish a filing system using hanging folders and manila folders. Categories can include upcoming events, projects to do, and projects pending. Files should be stored vertically, rather than stacked atop one another, for greater accessibility.
- Take a tip from event planners who start a separate notebook for each event they are working on. Into this three-ring binder go all notes, contracts, sketches, color samples—anything for that particular job.
- Consider hiring a professional organizer to come to your office and set up a filing and record-keeping system that works for your business.
- Keep those items that are used frequently close by.
- Focus on one project at a time, rather than jumping from one thing to another. This can be easily accomplished by blocking out some time during the day to work on major projects and arranging for no interruptions.
- Whenever possible, try to schedule time to return phone calls and/or e-mail messages. That way, you can handle them all at once, instead of scattering them (and your thoughts) in five-minute intervals throughout the day.
- Either at the end of each day or first thing in the morning, prepare a list of things to do for the day.

Summary of Personal Management

Those off-premise caterers who can effectively deal with stress, who properly manage their time, who learn to delegate and keep things organized will lead their peers into the future. They will set the standards for others to follow. They will accomplish more and will be in a position to receive the greatest rewards as a result.

✖ Looking Ahead—Catering in the Future

What does the future hold for caterers in this new century?

First of all, we know that catering is neither rocket science nor brain surgery. Change is inevitable in this business, but not at the same rate as, say, in molecular theory or medical technology. In fact, in catering, rediscovering foods of the previous century is trendy! Many caterers still feature the signature dishes—honey coconut shrimp, beef tenderloin, Caesar salad—that they've served for decades. Why? The customers demand, and enjoy, them.

This certainly doesn't mean things stay stagnant in our industry. Innovative buffet and food station décor will continue to evolve. Most catering companies will continue to build their reputations on elegant, "over-the-top" food presentations, and the healthy competition shows no signs of abating. Other caterers prize research, developing cutting-edge menu items to set them apart from the pack.

More women are entering the off-premise catering field. Paula LeDuc in the San Francisco Bay area, Katherine Farrell in Ann Arbor, Abigail Kirsch in New York, Mary Micucci in Los Angeles, and Joy Wallace in Miami are but a handful of enterprising women who have grown their companies into catering's elite.

Staffing woes will continue to be monumental, as hiring, training, and retraining get tougher. Foodservice has always been a somewhat transient industry. Astute caterers will use preemployment aptitude and personality testing, master online staff scheduling systems, and develop their own training programs. They will also realize, if they haven't already, that they must treat their employees at least as well as they treat their clients. Along the same lines, in a top-tier catering operation, the employees treat *each other* as well as they treat their clients.

Caterers of the future will come to realize that bigger is not necessarily better. Having a large volume of business is admirable—but only when the quality of your work rises to the same level. A company can grow to the point where quality slips, gross profit margins lag, more equipment is needed, overhead costs expand, and the bottom line shrinks proportionately. The intelligent caterer will downsize, watch margins and profits grow—and overall stress levels diminish—as they become more selective about the clientele they service.

Caterers are realizing that "high tech" will never replace personalized service, or "high touch"—but without high tech, they'll limit their *potential* for high touch. In an industry where, amazingly, some caterers still don't accept credit cards, the savvy businessperson is learning to embrace new technology, launching interactive websites and e-mail marketing campaigns. They're creating improved computer-generated proposals, rental orders, packing lists, staffing schedules, and instant financial statements. And they're realizing that computer-savvy business owners have more time to do what they love—which is run their business!

Competition will continue to increase. Sales will grow, but not without some dips, because economic woes, terrorist attacks, and the resulting fears cannot help but impact the catering profession. More caterers were hurt financially by the recession at the beginning of this century than by the September 11 terrorist attacks, but both left their marks on the industry. An increased use of security cameras at high-profile events (and in some cases, to thwart theft) is one result of the heightened awareness.

Mega-event catering is acknowledged as an excellent way to grow business—at golf and tennis tournaments, NASCAR races, air shows, boat shows, and more. In addition to being profitable events, they expose the caterer to a wider range of potential clients. Then again, a caterer from Augusta, Georgia, generates enough revenue from serving sandwiches and beverages at the Masters' Golf Tournament that he need not cater at all the rest of the year! The pressure experienced in servicing huge, multiday events is as big as the events themselves, but the rewards can be significant.

At the end of the 1900s, B. Joseph Pine II wrote *The Experience Economy*, a primer about the "new rules of engagement" for businesses.[7] Pine asserts that a new economic model is taking shape as we move from a service-based economy into an experience-based economy, where successful vendors literally create an "experience" for clients by using props and services to engage them in an "inherently personal way."

Pine claims that Walt Disney was the founding father of the "Experience Economy," and in today's restaurant industry there are plenty of examples—Rainforest Café, Planet Hollywood, Hard Rock Cafes, and other themed eateries that combine food, service, and atmosphere to create a more "complete" dining experience. This kind of trend is adaptable for off-premise caterers too, with elaborate themes, staff members who double as costumed performers, team-building events, and imaginative menu items presented in wild new ways to delight and entertain the crowd as well as feed them!

For those who love to have fun, and who are as adventurous as they are practical, it's a great time to be an off-premise caterer.

✕ The Seven Habits of Highly Successful Caterers

Let's examine some additional techniques, philosophies, and real-life ways to be successful in the challenging field of off-premise catering.

Habits are things we do automatically, like brushing our teeth, combing our hair, or straightening a tablecloth that's uneven. We hardly think about them, we just do them. Stephen R. Covey wrote *The Seven Habits of Highly Effective People*, which has been a bestseller for years—you should read it if you haven't already. But what are some habits that mark successful caterers? What separates star performers from the rest of the crowd? With a nod to Mr. Covey, here are seven key traits.

Willingness to Take Calculated Risks

One of our favorite sayings is, "A turtle goes nowhere until it sticks its neck out." In order to succeed, we must be continually growing and improving, and the only way to do this is to leave our comfort zones—and stick our necks out!

If you're right-handed, you feel quite comfortable writing with your right hand. Try writing with your left hand. You're definitely out of your comfort zone. But after a while, you'll find you can actually write with either hand. Successful caterers make things happen by taking calculated risks, whether it is trying new menu items, new buffet display concepts, or accepting a job in a new and challenging off-premise location. Caterers who refuse to take risks fail to grow and learn are left behind.

Sincere Concern for Others

Nobody cares how much you *know* until they know how much you *care*. Empathy and genuine concern for your clients and staff are paramount to long-term success. What are their needs, wishes, and desires? What are their concerns and their "hot buttons"? By putting ourselves in their positions, we can begin to show concern for others and understand them. When we do this, we develop meaningful relationships and, not coincidentally, loyalty. We give them what they want, and we get what we want.

Keeping Up with Current Trends

It's not just a matter of food and presentation and theme trends. Caterers who are not wired to do business online through the Internet and e-mail are missing out on huge opportunities.

The online catering referral service, Leading Caterers of America (founded by the book's co-author Bill Hansen), receives 5 to 20 inquiries per day from clients looking for catering services coast to coast, in Alaska, Hawaii, and occasionally overseas. People do shop for catering online, and the companies that lead the way have high-quality websites and diligently reply to e-mailed requests in a timely manner.

Caterers need to get in the habit of responding to e-mail correspondence as soon as possible, as well as providing e-mailed proposals to those clients who prefer to do business via their computers. Event planners who book caterers for their clients love receiving e-mailed proposals, because they are easy to copy-and-paste into their own proposals.

If you're not in the habit of working online, you're behind the times.

Excellent Priorities and Time Management

You get 20 percent of your sales and profits from 80 percent of your clients, and 80 percent of your sales and profits from 20 percent of your clients.

None of us ever go home at night thinking that all the work is done—it never is. It's simply a question of what's most important, as well as what's most urgent. Urgent things are never really an issue. There's no question that if you have a catered event today, it will get done. But what's most urgent is not necessarily what's most important. You must understand the difference.

For example, you could spend a day catering three small parties for 25 guests each, but fall behind on preparing a proposal for another job, in three months, for 500 guests—and lose it to a competitor whose proposal was simply submitted on time.

Successful caterers spend their time in those areas that generate the biggest paybacks in terms of money, quality, and other rewards. They make a habit of planning their days, leaving time for the most important, as well as the most urgent. At the start of each day they prepare an agenda that details both short-term objectives and long-term goals. If you're a student, you should already be using this technique to accomplish as much as you can in school.

Quality before Quantity

Bigger is not necessarily better. Still, many of us get caught up in that way of thinking. If our sales are $1 million, let's go for $2 million. If they're $2 million, what's wrong with $4 million? And if $4 million is good . . .

There's nothing wrong with building sales if quality does not suffer. However, when the quality of our products and services suffers so does the quality of our lifestyle. More business means more hours at work. And doctors will tell you they've never met a man or woman who, on a deathbed, expressed a wish that he or she had spent more time at work.

If we can grow our businesses with no adverse effects on the quality of our lives or our products, then we should go for it! But if we find profits slipping and clients complaining, and we need a letter of introduction when we stumble home at 3:00 A.M., then something's very wrong.

We need to make of habit of continually asking ourselves whether we might be better off with less business and more time for ourselves and for our families. We need to continually examine the quality of our work to ensure that it's not slipping because we've allowed ourselves to take on too much.

Being Detail Oriented

A baseball player who bats .250 gets three hits for every 12 times at bat. One who bats .333 gets four hits for every 12 times at bat. The difference—one more hit for every 12 times at bat—means the difference between an average major league ball player and a Hall of Fame inductee.

Do you make it a habit to continually look for the little things? A good caterer isn't nitpicky, but is forever finding something that needs to be tweaked, adjusted, redone, or improved—little things that most customers won't notice, but that greatly impact the overall professionalism of an event. Being aware of the details in flavors, looks, aromas, and tidiness separates the average caterers from the superstars. And, by all means, check the spelling, grammar, and punctuation in all your written materials, from brochures to contracts—or hire someone to do it. Again, the goal is to present a professional image. Remember? The devil is in the details.

Setting High Standards

If you refuse to accept anything but the very best, you very often get the best. Successful caterers set their standards high and expect excellence from themselves and their staff members. They're never happy with the status quo, always striving to make each party, wedding, or event better than the last. They debrief after an event, asking staff for input and improvements. They know that if they fail to improve, they're leaving the door open for their competitors to capture a good customer or a larger share of the market.

Successful caterers also make a habit of lifelong learning. They're forever reading, attending trade shows, and exploring areas that will help them improve their own businesses with new ideas. They challenge and reward their staff members for having the same attitude.

Vince Lombardi, the late NFL coach, who during his career coached the first team to ever win the Super Bowl, put it this way: "The quality of a person's life is in direct proportion to their commitment to excellence, regardless of their chosen field of endeavor."

How Does an Off-Premise Caterer Gauge Success?

There are a number of signs to look for when evaluating an existing off-premise catering business. Healthy companies rate highly in all of these areas. Those that are unhealthy, or even on the brink of failure, will not rate nearly as well.

- Management thoroughly plans, organizes, executes, and controls each catered event.
- Proper controls are in place for costs, accounts receivable and payable, and liquid assets such as cash and inventories. Theft prevention is also a priority.
- Food and service quality is well-controlled and meets or exceeds clients' approval.
- Pricing for food and services is fair and competitive with other firms in the marketplace. There is a spirit of healthy competition.
- The catering firm enjoys good working relationships with both clients and suppliers.
- Time and attention are given to food safety in storage, preparation, and display. Employees know the local health codes and follow them.
- There is sufficient working capital to operate the business. The firm can make loan payments as they become due. Excessive credit is not extended to clients.
- Budgets are prepared and followed. Business records, insurance coverage, and licenses are kept up to date. The information derived from these records is used to provide data to help manage the business.
- Sales growth is controlled. There are sufficient financial and personnel resources to operate as business steadily grows.
- Market trends are anticipated.
- Management and staff have a good working knowledge of the off-premise catering field.
- There are solid, trusting relationships between management and staff. Staff members are well trained and feel truly appreciated—because they are.
- Management works closely with a qualified accountant to plan for payment of taxes.
- And, finally, management is willing to seek qualified professional assistance if problems arise.

The Off-Premise Catering Model

Exhibit 1.1 is a diagram of all the factors that enter into the off-premise catering arena. It shows how managerial philosophies and techniques, as well as laws regarding personnel, business, alcoholic beverage service, and sanitation and safety, must all be interrelated to guide the company.

It then depicts how marketing efforts produce clients, which in turn creates needs for *site inspections* and *logistical plans,* including planning in these specific areas: menus, beverages, equipment, personnel, and any other related services.

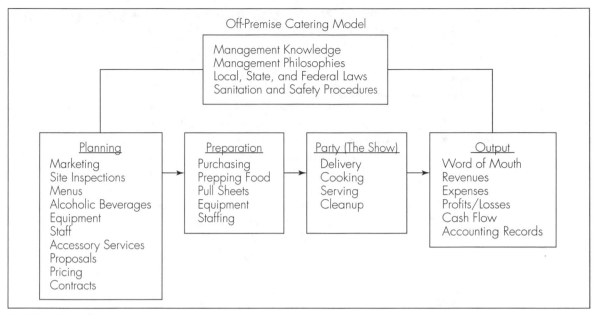

Exhibit 1.1 *Off-Premise Catering Model*

Once the planning is complete, it is possible to provide clients with *written proposals,* which include all the aforementioned plans along with pricing. Normally, proposals are modified somewhat. Once modification is complete and all provisions meet with the approval of both caterer and client, a contract is prepared that contains all the conditions outlined in the proposal.

As the party date approaches, certain *operational elements* are addressed, such as:

- Hiring and scheduling staff
- Purchasing and pre-preparation of menu items
- Ordering equipment as needed from party rental companies
- Obtaining licenses and permits, as needed, for use of the site, serving alcohol, etc.
- Preparing a "pull sheet" that details all items supplied by the commissary to produce the party.
- Coordinating all beverage and accessory services with the client and the vendors.

All the preplanning elements culminate on the day or night of "The Show." That's when staff, equipment, food, and other services arrive at the party site, and the event is executed.

After the event, there are certain *outcomes*, which include:

Positive and/or negative word of mouth about the event
Revenues, expenses, profits, and cash
Accounting records

By reading and studying this text, you will gain a thorough understanding of how all these elements combine to produce a successful off-premise event at the hands of a professional caterer.

✕ Conclusion

This book should provide all the necessary information to those who are motivated to start their own companies or to develop an off-premise catering division of an existing foodservice operation. Study hard, and, as an entrepreneurial and motivated student, you should be well on the way to a thorough understanding of the catering field.

We must warn you—catering is not an especially easy way to make a living. But it is an extremely rewarding and interesting field that combines interpersonal and organizational skills, societal trends, and financial acumen. If you do it well, your clients won't be the only ones celebrating at your events!

Notes

1. *How to Manage a Successful Catering Business,* Second Edition, by Manfred Ketterer, John Wiley & Sons, 1991.
2. Mike DeLuca, editor, *Restaurant Hospitality* magazine, copyright Penton Publishing, July 1992.
3. Connie Sitterly, president, Management Training Specialists and Sittcom., Inc., Fort Worth, Texas. (www.sittcom.com)
4. Carol McKibben, in *Special Events* magazine, November 1991.
5. Jefferson Center for Character Education, Mission Viejo, California. (www.jeffersoncenter. org)
6. *Lessons in Excellence,* by Charlie Trotter, Ten Speed Press, 1999.
7. *The Experience Economy,* by James H. Gilmore and B. Joseph Pine II, Harvard Business School Press, 1999.

Chapter 2

Getting Started— Laws, Locations, and Contracts

This chapter elaborates on the basic elements involved in starting an off-premise catering firm:

- Understanding legal aspects of the business and ensuring compliance
- Making decisions about the physical location of the business
- Researching funding alternatives
- Developing a catering contract that protects both the company and its customers

The first two points on the list—understanding the legal ramifications of operating a business and finding a suitable location—seem to be ignored regularly by would-be caterers. Many operate illegally from their homes, with neither licenses nor insurance. It is imperative that readers understand this is in violation of local and state statutes and that violators may be prosecuted and fined. Professional off-premise caterers follow the laws of the municipality, state, and federal government. Illegal caterers not only damage the reputation of our profession, but make it more difficult for licensed and insured caterers to compete with those who do not have the expenses of licenses and insurance.

The purpose of this chapter is to inform readers of the legal ways to establish an off-premise catering business in order to help elevate the standards for our fast-growing profession.

Each municipality, county, and state has specific regulations regarding the operation and licensing of businesses. It is impossible in this text to address specific laws for specific locations. Each prospective off-premise caterer is advised to contact local and state authorities first, before selecting a location or starting a business.

✖ Local and State Requirements

Zoning. Most municipalities require zoning permits to ensure that businesses conform to local laws. For example, zoning laws prohibit off-premise caterers from building catering commissaries in residential neighborhoods. Many require a certificate of use and occupancy before business may be conducted.

Businesses located in an existing structure previously used for similar purposes will usually have few zoning problems. Off-premise caterers who construct a new facility, convert an existing building used previously for other purposes, or extensively remodel an existing facility will need to carefully check zoning regulations. A zoning variance or conditional-use permit is required to operate a business on land not zoned for that purpose. Filing fees can exceed $1,200, and it can take 90 days or longer for a decision. To change zoning can take six months or longer and require extensive legal work.

Occupational License. After receiving a zoning permit, an off-premise caterer must apply for the appropriate occupational licenses required by the city, county, and state. In South Florida, for example, an off-premise caterer located in the City of Miami needs two occupational licenses, one for the City of Miami and one for Dade County.

License to Sell Food to the Public. Many states require this license, which normally is obtained through the state's Department of Business or Commerce.

Health Permit. A business dealing with food must have a health department permit. Prior to issuing a permit, the health department will inspect the off-premise caterer's facilities. Readers should refer to Chapter 12, "Sanitation and Safety," to gain an understanding of health department requirements.

Fictitious Name Registration. This is also commonly known as a "dba," short for "doing business as. . . ." A "fictitious" business name doesn't mean the business is not real. It means the company name that has been chosen either does not include the surname of the individual owner or partners, or the nature of the business is not clearly evident in the name. For example, doing business under a name like "Smith & Brown Associates" or "Young, Old and Sons" would require a fictitious business name to be registered even though the surnames of the owners are stated. The words following the surnames suggest that there are other owners who are not specifically named. However, doing business under a name like "Teresa Harrington Catering" would not require registering a fictitious business name, because the owner (Teresa Harrington) is conducting business under her legal name and the nature of the business is described. In the case of a corporation, a fictitious business name is "any name other than the exact corporate name as stated in the articles of incorporation."

Each state has rules about filing for a dba. It usually involves filling out a short application and paying a registration fee to the county clerk. Sometimes you have to give the clerk a copy of your Articles of Incorporation, if you are incorporated. Other states require the placement of a fictitious name ad in the local newspaper. Generally, the newspaper that prints the ad will file the necessary papers with the county for a fee. The easiest way to determine the procedure is to call a local bank and ask if it requires a fictitious name registry or certificate in order for you to open a business account.

State and Local Sales Tax. Off-premise caterers should contact the Department of Revenue and Taxation for their state and city for requirements. Sales taxes are further discussed in Chapter 10 of this book.

Worker's Compensation. This type of insurance is a state requirement for those who employ staff, including part-timers and corporate officers. This topic is discussed in Chapter 7, "Human Resources."

Other State and Local Permits and Taxes. Numerous other permits may be required—fire department permits, signage permits, and so forth. To avoid costly mistakes regarding signs, it is imperative to check local ordinances and to obtain written approval from the landlord before installing signage of any type. Many states have corporate income taxes, intangible asset taxes, personal property taxes, and unemployment taxes. There are a number of places where you can ask for state-specific details: your County Clerk's office, your Secretary of State's office, your state's Department of Commerce or Economic Development. It's also smart to talk with an attorney.

✖ *Federal Requirements*

Employer Identification Number. Off-premise caterers who employ staff must obtain an Employer Identification Number (EIN) using IRS Form SS-4. Employers are responsible for four types of federal payroll collections and payments:

1. Income taxes withheld from employee wages
2. Employer/employee Social Security tax (FICA)
3. Employer/employee Medicare tax (MICA)
4. Federal unemployment tax (FUTA)

Employment Taxes. Off-premise catering firms, as well as other businesses, are required by law to withhold federal income and Social Security taxes from wages paid to employees, and to file a quarterly return, IRS Form 941. Self-employed persons also pay more Social Security tax—the full 15 percent—because they are responsible for both the "employer's" and the "employee's" share of the tax (normally 7.5 percent each).

Monies withheld from employees must be paid when due to the federal government. New businesses with insufficient cash to pay all creditors may try deferring or underpaying their taxes so they can keep their suppliers paid, but penalties are severe. A $10,000 tax liability can increase to $14,050 in six months. Many businesspeople have found out the hard way that it is easier to take out a loan to pay the IRS than to deal with the consequences of paying late or not paying at all.

> A corporate officer who is held to be a responsible person and willfully fails to account for or pay the federal government the payroll taxes due will be personally liable for the unpaid taxes. . . . Payroll taxes can be a liability nightmare for the unsuspecting corporate officer or employee. However, careful planning before the business opens and while it is in operation can help minimize and reduce personal liability.[1]

Off-premise caterers should also be aware of federal reporting requirements for employees receiving tips. This subject is discussed in Chapter 7.

Unemployment Taxes. Off-premise caterers are also required to pay federal unemployment tax. IRS Form 940 is used for this purpose. In those states that require state unemployment taxes, the amount of federal unemployment tax required can be reduced.

If a worker's job is terminated (through no fault of his or her own), unemployment benefits provide a small amount of income for a given time period or until the person finds a new job. The system is funded by a tax levied on employers. Federal unemployment taxes are paid using IRS Form 940.

States normally require employers to pay unemployment taxes based on the amount of wages they pay, the amount they have already contributed to the state unemployment fund, and whether any of their discharged employees have been compensated from the fund. State taxes paid are credited against the federal tax.

Established caterers, with minimal unemployment claims, will play at a lesser rate than new caterers or those who have had more unemployment claims against their businesses.

Income Taxes. All off-premise catering firms are required to pay federal income tax, in addition to state and city taxes.

Immigration Requirements. All employers are required to verify the immigration status of all new hires on Form I-9. See Chapter 7 for more information.

Antidiscrimination Law Compliance. The Americans with Disabilities Act (ADA) of 1990 is a federal law that says companies with 15 or more employees cannot fire, or refuse to hire, persons with disabilities unless the impairment prevents a person from performing a particular job. Most citizens know the ADA as the law that requires companies to provide "handicapped" parking spaces, wheelchair-accessible entrances and restrooms, and the like. Refer to Chapter 7 for more information.

✖ *Legal Forms of Operation*

The four main legal forms of doing businesses are sole proprietorship, partnership, limited partnership, and corporation. Each of them has advantages and disadvantages.

Most businesses in the United States are sole proprietorships, owned and managed by one individual. A *sole proprietorship* requires no legal incorporation papers to be filed, although the business owner may need a city or state license for some types of business, and a dba or fictitious name filing. The major advantage of sole proprietorship is its simplicity. The disadvantage is that creditors can force the sale of personal property and liquidate bank accounts when the sole proprietor is unable to fulfill financial obligations—in other words, the company's debts are the owner's sole responsibility.

In a *partnership* (or *General Partnership*), two or more people are co-owners in a business. Again, no state filing of incorporation papers is necessary, but a dba may be required. Assets contributed by all partners become equity in the partnership, and both income and expenses are allocated to the partners. Each partner is legally responsible for the actions of the other partners. In a legal action, each partner will be sued personally. Each partner's share of the profits must be reported on that partner's individual tax return.

Limited partnerships are commonly used for real estate syndications and are used very infrequently for off-premise catering firms. The legal costs for starting a limited partnership can be quite high, because they are complex and involve a number of investors.

In a *Limited Liability Company* (LLC), the liability of each partner (or "member") is limited to the amount of his or her investment, and each partner is personally liable for his or her own negligent acts.

Most off-premise caterers choose incorporation as a realistic form of operation because the *corporation* is a separate legal entity from the caterer. The corporation alone is generally responsible for its own actions and debts. In a corporation, off-premise caterers are protected in most situations because, technically, they are employees of the corporation. A corporation must be operated in a correct legal manner, though, or this protection may be forfeited. There are two basic types of corporate structures, *C Corporations* and *S Corporations* (named after the IRS Code sections that govern them). The S (or "Subchapter S") form is recommended for most caterers, because only the corporation pays tax on its profits. In a C Corporation, the corporation pays tax on its profits and the owners also pay individual taxes on their income.

There are other, newer hybrid forms of incorporation, including Single Member Limited Liability Companies (SMLLCs) and Personal Service Corporations (PSCs). Each has its own unique tax laws, reporting requirements, and loopholes. It is advisable to consult with a tax attorney or accountant when making the decision to create a business, but ambitious off-premise caterers can complete the necessary paperwork and file for incorporation on their own, thereby saving the attorney fees for that portion of the work. Your Secretary of State's office will have all the required forms and instructions.

✕ The Family-Owned Business

Many catering businesses are family owned and operated, which can be both good and bad. When family members perform their jobs well, there are few problems—but when they don't perform up to standards, huge problems can arise.

According to Walter Sasiadek of Business Development Strategies, there are several practical tips to help maintain harmony in the family-owned workplace:

Have written contracts: Handshakes and verbal agreements are fine at a family dinner, but not in business. Hire an attorney to draw up an acceptable contract for everyone involved to sign.

Define job roles: If a family member doesn't want to accept the responsibilities and adhere to the professional standards that are expected in the industry, the individual shouldn't draw a paycheck, period.

Business is business: Don't allow favoritism to affect sound business judgment. Make sure that incompetence doesn't impact employee morale. Don't lie to employees about their advancement opportunities if the position is being saved for someone in the family.

Conduct weekly meetings: Meetings should be structured to be the same each and every time. Always begin with the same topic and progress according to plan. The structure will help keep everyone focused on the mission. *Example:* Start with profitability. Go over the Profit/Loss Statement item by item. Address every concern and then move on. If tempers get too hot, call for a ten-minute break.

✕ Finding a Facility

There are three basic options for off-premise caterers when considering facilities:

1. Operate an off-premise catering business from an existing foodservice operation where the caterer already works—a hotel, restaurant, club, or similar facility. This option is excellent because it minimizes start-up expenses.

Aspiring off-premise caterers may wish to look to the corporate world for start-up assistance. Since the tax deductibility of business meals has been whittled to only 50 percent, many companies have found it convenient and economical to hire their own chefs, upgrade their corporate foodservice, or bring in caterers for on-site meetings.

Start-up caterers may wish to affiliate with a corporation and, with its permission, use its facilities as a commissary for off-premise events. The added benefit in this scenario is that the corporate in-house diners will become off-premise catering clients.

2. Operate from a commissary already used exclusively for off-premise catering. This can be an expensive option and should be reserved for off-premise caterers who have a well-established business.

3. Find an existing facility that has an underutilized kitchen, and arrange to use it in exchange for a rental fee and/or providing the facility with needed foodservice. For example, a church kitchen that is used only occasionally would be an excellent option. The off-premise caterer would pay the church for the use of the kitchen on a monthly or "as-used" basis. Part or all of the rent could be paid for in services rendered. The off-premise caterer may cater some of the church functions at a reduced fee in exchange for rent credit.

In summary, the best and most cost-efficient facilities are those that require no initial investment and may even offer a built-in client base. A South Florida caterer developed a $2 million catering business with a small investment by offering catering services to a downtown businessmen's club. The caterer served lunch to the members at a reduced fee and, in exchange, was able to cater functions for club members, both at the club and off-premise, using the club's facilities. The profits were retained by the caterer.

✕ Selecting a Catering Commissary

This section is not for the off-premise caterer who is operating from a restaurant, hotel, club, or other regular foodservice operation, nor is it for the caterer who has set up operation in a church or other facility. This discussion is directed at those off-premise caterers who are evaluating commissary locations.

Ability to Pay

The best values are found in industrial areas located near expressways or major thoroughfares. Rents in these areas are fairly inexpensive, and access to major highways facilitates deliveries. The site should be clean and safe, but it need not have a prestigious storefront or be located in the center of town, since few (if any) clients will visit the commissary. Most off-premise catering sales are made with the client at the event site or in the client's home or office.

A good rule is that the total annual rent should not exceed 10 percent of projected annual sales. For example, a new off-premise caterer who expects to generate $100,000 in sales during the first year of operation should keep rent for the year at $10,000 or less.

Most small-to-medium off-premise caterers can operate well in facilities ranging in size from 1,000 to 2,000 square feet.

Key Points to Negotiate

The ideal leases are short-term contracts with renewal options. For example, a lease for one to two years with two five-year renewal options would be ideal for most off-premise caterers.

When inspecting a proposed site, look for:

Leaks in the roof or elsewhere
Sufficient staff parking arrangements
A delivery door for receiving and shipping foods
Adequate lighting
Adequate electrical and gas service
Sufficient exhaust venting over the hot line
Adequate storage
Adequate and accessible dumpster space
Good ventilation and air-conditioning
Insurance—what will the building owner pay for, and what are you responsible for as the tenant?

Overall security—good locks, night watchman, regular police patrols, etc.
Manageable traffic during rush hours

Other issues to discuss and/or negotiate are provisions for remodeling—if you
want some work done to the place, who pays? Sometimes a caterer can agree to
make improvements in lieu of rent payment for a few months, but if that is your
arrangement, be absolutely certain to get it in writing. Normally, leases include a requirement that you have the landlord's written permission to erect signage, land-
scape, paint, add exterior lighting, or change the structure in any noticeable way. If
improvements involve modifications to the roof, the original roofer should be hired
to make them; otherwise, any warranty will be void.

It seems as if it should go without saying, but you should also ask specifically
about what additional kind(s) of permission you'll have to get to operate a catering
company in this space. If the owner rents to you, and you then discover upon move-
in that the business park where the building sits has insurance limitations or covenants
that restrict you in some way, you'll have a problem. And if there are problems,
whom do you call? Is there a management company? Does the owner want to know
about and hire every handyman to fix every leaky faucet, or is it okay for you to
get it done and pass along the bill?

The lease should protect *you* as the tenant, not just the building owner. To that
end, it should include some "outs" in case of trouble. For instance, the lease should be:

- **Conditional,** meaning that you'll move in only if and when you obtain all the
  necessary licenses and permits to cater there. (And if, for some reason, you are de-
  nied one of the licenses or permits, that you can void the lease.)
- **Assignable,** meaning that if you want to move or close the business before it
  has expired, you can allow another party to move in and assume the lease.
- **Flexible** in case of emergency. This means that if you die, for example, your
  spouse or partner can terminate the lease without penalty. If the city condemns
  the building for some reason unrelated to your business, you can move without
  penalty. If you're moving in your own equipment, you have the right to remove it
  as long as you restore the building to its original shape (less "normal wear and
  tear"—a very important clause.)

One more important note: Without the owner of the space around, talk with
some of the neighboring businesses. Ask questions: How responsive is the management company? What do they know about the owner? Who were the last tenants?
How long did they stay, and why did they move? Meeting the neighbors can be a
real eye-opener! You may not even like them, which may ultimately be a factor in
your decision about whether to sign the lease.

Hiring an Attorney

You must always have an attorney review the lease to ensure compliance with all
legal requirements such as zoning, signage, and other matters. Above all, never commit to a lease agreement until all aspects of the lease have been thoroughly reviewed.
This is one area in which haste can result in huge financial obligations.

It's best to interview lawyers (and accountants too) before you ever need them. It is critical to find people who have experience with hospitality industry clients and are somewhat familiar with the industry. You also want someone who is dependable and will be available on short notice in case a problem arises. There are a number of on-line legal resources that you may wish to explore, such as www.hospitalitylawyer.com.

✕ *Funding Alternatives*

Many caterers have started their firms with little cash and plenty of "sweat equity." They have used clients' advance deposits to essentially fund their start-up costs. Others have invested considerable amounts in facilities and equipment. For most brand-new caterers, it is best to keep the initial investment conservative. One only needs to look at the thousands of restaurants that fail each year because of the huge investments required to open. Caterers, on the other hand, can start with substantially fewer up-front costs.

Funding can come from a variety of sources, including:

Your own savings
Family members
Investors
Credit cards
SBA loans
Bank loans and lines of credit
Equipment financing

Each of these sources has advantages and disadvantages. The ideal situation is, of course, to use your own funds to get started, as long this does not put your personal or family financial situation at risk. Bringing in outside investors or family members is an alternative, but with them come almost certain problems and disputes about how funds are being spent. Outside investors expect a return on their investment, which is a realistic outcome, and therefore feel they have some say in how their funds are being used. Most caterers prefer to cater rather than spend hours explaining their business decisions to disgruntled investors or family members.

Credit card debt is the largest single financial problem in the United States. Between 1992 and 2000, Americans' disposable personal income rose 47 percent—but their spending went up 61 percent, mostly on credit cards. The average household now owes at least $8,000 in credit card debt. Millions of people are unable to pay off these unpaid balances, thus incurring huge interest charges each month. Caterers should use credit cards only if they are able to pay them off each month in full. Otherwise, they should look for funding elsewhere.

Banks run hot and cold when it comes to financing catering businesses, mostly because of their lack of knowledge about the industry. Bank loans are generally short-term loans. Banks require personal guarantees and more equity than other funding sources, but their interest rates are generally the lowest of the available options. At a bank, sole proprietors can often use the value of their homes as collateral for a business Line of Credit, which also charges lower interest than most credit cards and requires monthly repayment. Lines of Credit are excellent tools for borrowing short-term amounts. You borrow only what you need and pay back some or all of it as funds become available. You pay interest only on funds that you use. A Line of Credit can be unsecured, or secured by assets like your accounts receivable, marketable securities, or real estate equity. It is usually extended for a year at a time and renewed after the lender reviews updated financial records each year.

The U.S. Small Business Administration (SBA) offers loans to small businesses, including an "Express Loan"—an expedited review process for loans of up to $250,000. SBA-guaranteed loans provide opportunities for those who may not otherwise qualify, although some feel their terms are very restrictive. Still, caterers are excellent candidates.

The SBA offers a variety of loan guarantee programs, which include:

- 7 (a) Loan Guarantee—Larger loans of up to $2 million
- Low Doc and SBA Express—Limited to loans of up to $150,000
- Micro Loans—Very small loans (up to $35,000) for start-up businesses

For more information visit www.sba.gov.

Home equity is another source of funds. A new, larger first mortgage or a second mortgage can provide a lump sum of cash that can be used to launch a catering business. Other forms of collateral such as stocks, bonds, or mutual fund shares can also be pledged as collateral for a business loan.

Catering equipment can be financed through companies that specialize in loans of this type. Local restaurant equipment dealers have relationships with firms that provide such loans. Their interest rates are generally higher than those of most bank loans, but lower than credit card interest rates. And you have the advantage of dealing with someone who is familiar with the equipment, its uses—and its problems, if any arise while you're paying it off.

✕ *Catering Contracts*

Off-premise caterers should develop a catering contract prior to accepting off-premise business, and an attorney should review the contract to ensure it meets basic requirements.

Before delving into the specific elements of this type of contract, note that there are some elements that are critical to an off-premise caterer's understanding of—and involvement with—contracts, according to Miami, Florida, attorney Donald A. Blackwell.[2]

1. "Have a working knowledge of what constitutes a binding contract and how a court is likely to construe its terms." A contract is a definite agreement between two or more competent people or parties to do, or refrain from doing, some lawful thing. The difference between a contract and pure negotiation is that there must be a meeting of the minds on all essential terms and obligations. For example, a caterer's proposal to perform service becomes a contract only when signed and agreed to by the client.

2. "Be specific." Each contract should be clear and unambiguous. No one should ever sign a contract that contains blanks. The failure to be specific about what an off-premise caterer plans to do could certainly be embarrassing the night of the event if the client expects something different. A roast beef dinner might mean "top round" to the caterer and "beef tenderloin" to the client. The caterer should be as specific as possible regarding quantity, quality, and method of preparation.

3. "Know the three general theories upon which caterers can be held liable."

- Breach of Contract: The caterer agrees to perform a service and does not perform the service.
- Third Party Liability: The caterers must use reasonable care or they can be charged with negligence. (In a dispute between guest and host of an event, the caterer and other vendors are considered "Third Parties.")
- Statutory Violations: The caterer fails to follow laws—adherence to fire codes or service of alcoholic beverages.

TOP TEN MOST ANNOYING THINGS CUSTOMERS DO TO CATERERS

1. Think they can postpone or even cancel an event without consequences
2. Fail to return telephone calls or letters
3. Fail to make promised or agreed-upon payments on time
4. Not agree to pay the minimum, predetermined cost figure
5. Allow significantly more guests to show up at an event and expect the caterer to produce the extra food and service to accommodate them—at no extra charge
6. Tell the caterer they won't be able to pay "all" of the money—and wait until the date it's due to make this announcement
7. Have completely unrealistic expectations
8. Expect the caterer to deal with issues beyond the scope of the written agreement
9. Claim they were "promised" something that is not in the contract, on any menu, or in any notes from conversations
10. Decide that they own all the surplus food that the caterer brought in just in case it was needed

Off-premise caterers may be involved in assisting clients with site selections, as well as subcontracting for certain accessory services—music, entertainment, flowers, décor, valet parking, and other services—for the party. As a general rule, off-premise caterers have a legal duty to exercise "reasonable care" for the safety and well-being of the guests attending an event. Although courts have not yet clearly defined the parameters of that duty, it can be safely assumed that they encompass:

- Investigating prospective party sites to determine that they are reasonably safe
- Investigating the service and safety records of prospective subcontractors of accessory services
- Warning clients and guests of known or reasonably foreseeable dangers

Off-premise caterers who fail to make a thorough safety inspection of a proposed party site before recommending its use—or who make the recommendation despite knowledge of potentially hazardous conditions—do so at their own risk. Similarly, caterers who fail to investigate the safety and service records of subcontracted suppliers substantially increase their risk of liability.

Proposal or Contract?

A catering contract is a blueprint for performance of a catered event. It creates an obligation on the part of the caterer to perform certain services, and an obligation on the part of the client to pay for these services. A contract requires a degree of trust, but it also provides for legal recourse in case either party violates (or is accused of violating) that trust. Signed contracts may even be used as loan collateral in some situations.

It is just common sense to draft a written catering proposal that spells out in detail all the services the caterer will provide at an event. Proposals are discussed in depth in Chapter 9, "Marketing." For the purpose of this chapter, suffice it to say that a proposal that has been agreed to and signed by both client and off-premise caterer is, for all practical and legal purposes, a contract. Some caterers use separate formats for proposals and contracts, but this is not necessary in most cases.

Components of an Off-Premise Catering Contract

The terms of off-premise catering contracts vary according to what is appropriate for the events, but they should include most of the following information:

1. The caterer's name, address, phone number(s), and fax number.

2. The client's name, address, phone, and fax numbers, plus any other pertinent phone numbers.

3. The date the contract was signed.

4. The date and day of the catered event.

5. Starting and ending times for the party, as well as other important times—what time a meal will be served or the specific times the band will start and end.

6. Minimum number of guests. This is the lowest number of guests to which this contract price will apply. When a caterer quotes a price per person for a minimum of 100 guests, this means that the per person price will apply for 100 guests. If there are fewer than 100 guests, this "minimum guarantee clause" gives the off-premise caterer the right to raise the price per person. An extreme example of this is a situation in which a client and caterer agree to a price per person for a group of 100, but one week prior to the event the client advises the caterer that there will be only 25 guests in attendance. Reasonably, the caterer cannot be expected to cater this party for the same price per person. This clause gives the caterer the right to charge more per person.

The number of guests attending an event is always an estimate. There are always last-minute changes that will affect the attendance. Approximate attendance figures may be determined by such factors as:

■ How many attended the same event last year?
■ Is it a business-related event where attendance is mandatory, or a purely social event?

- Will there be celebrities or prominent guest speakers?
- Are competing events being held at the same time or within 48 hours of this event?
- Is there a charge for attending?
- What types of food and beverages are to be served?
- What time of day is the event to be held—morning, afternoon, or evening?
- How long is the event expected to last?

7. Date for final "head count" guarantee. Four to seven days prior to the party date is standard for the off-premise caterer to require a guarantee of the number of guests to be paid for. Many caterers require that their clients provide this guarantee in writing, and the client is required to pay for at least that number even if fewer guests attend than were guaranteed. This clause is essential protection for the caterer, who should not have to suffer financially when the client overestimates guest counts.

8. Location of the event. This should include as much detail as possible—street address, building name, floor number, and any other information that will clarify the event's location. This may be the place to spell out who will make weather-related decisions for outdoor events (and how soon before the actual event) in case of inclement weather; and what the contingency plans are—an alternate site? A rented tent? Ponchos and galoshes for all? (Just kidding about the latter. . . .)

This section of the contract should specify the exact times the space will be available (for setup, event, and cleanup) and how long the space will be held without a deposit for this event.

9. Menu specifics. This section should include all menu details discussed with the client. Nothing should be left out or assumed. Major changes in menu or other elements should necessitate a new contract, and the existing contract should say so. Some caterers add a sentence stating that the menu must be finalized by a certain date and cannot be changed after that date; another option is a *substitution clause*, which states that if a certain item that was contracted for is not available, a suitable replacement may be substituted with the customer's approval.

Once in a while, you will have clients who insist on providing their own, special "family favorite dish" to commemorate an occasion. It's a nice idea, but be sure to include a disclaimer in the contract that you are not responsible for either the contents or preparation of food brought by anyone not employed by you. There are health, food safety, and liability issues to consider here. Some caterers charge a "service fee" for handling food that they do not provide.

10. Beverage arrangements. This section should include a complete listing of the nonalcoholic beverages provided by the caterers, as well as verification of whatever alcoholic beverages will be supplied by the client. In states where off-premise caterers may sell alcoholic beverages, this section would be modified appropriately.

11. Equipment. From candelabras to chafing dishes, this section contains a list of all equipment to be supplied by the caterer—tables, silver, chairs, linens, china, glassware, flatware, dance floors, stages, portable bars, and tenting. This section should also address who is responsible for loss or damage of items, as well as any rules about use of equipment to be provided by other sources (rental companies, the party site, etc.).

If there is anything specifically *not* allowed, this should also be mentioned. Whether it's rice or birdseed, lit candles, fireworks, flower petals, certain types of streamers or confetti (which many hotels and churches consider to be too messy), if the event site has a rule, it should be stated here.

12. Staffing. In this section, most off-premise caterers include the number of staff to be provided, the hours they will work, how they will be attired, and the applicable charges for their services. If other types of workers are needed (electricians, for instance), the contract should specify whether they are union workers and, if so, agree to pay prevailing union labor rates.

13. Floor plan and seating chart. Some events—weddings, business seminars with head tables, and the like—are complex enough that such items are necessary. The client should have final say about who is seated where, within the reasonable bounds of etiquette.

14. Vendors and accessory services. This area of the contract spells out important ancillary items and the vendors or contractors who will provide them: flowers and other decoration, music, audiovisual equipment, valet parking, and other details that may be arranged for by either the off-premise caterer or the client. The contract should state that any vendor hired by either the caterer or the client must cooperate fully with the caterer or event manager on-site, must provide proof of liability insurance, and must deliver and set up its wares at specified times.

15. Method for determining "head count." Exactly how do you gauge the number of people at an event? For billing purposes, you must be specific about how this is determined. There are a number of ways to do this—taking tickets, counting plates or napkin-rolled flatware, keeping track at the door with a handheld counter, or, at some larger events, with the use of a turnstile. For larger special events where this could be a sensitive issue, the method of determining the number of guests should be included in the contract.

16. Charges for additional guests above the guarantee. This is generally a per-person charge, which in some instances may be less per person than for those included in the base price. The rationale here is that the cost of serving these additional guests is generally less, since certain expenses (like rental equipment and number of kitchen staff) may be fixed whether there are 100 or 150 guests.

The real problems arise when a caterer suspects the client is underestimating the number of guests, only to raise the guarantee substantially on the day of, or day before, the event. This sends the caterer scurrying for more food, more staff, and so forth, which is technically unfair after an agreement has been reached. Professional caterers deal with this situation in two ways in the contract—they spell out a higher per-person charge for extra guests added within 48 hours (or 72 hours, or whatever time period) of the actual event; or they plan for a certain percentage over the guarantee, and again, they spell this out in the contract. In either case, the point is not so much to generate additional income as to discourage clients from making last-minute additions.

17. Deposit policy This is one of the most important parts of any catering agreement. Normally, off-premise caterers require an advance deposit upon signing the contract. The deposit amount, along with due dates and amounts of future payments, must be listed in the contract. Specifics may be found in the "Deposits, Cancellations, and Refunds" section of this chapter.

18. Charges for extra hours. Normally, the labor charges for extra hours are at a premium rate, since in many parts of the country, catering staff is paid at a higher "overtime" rate when parties go longer than planned. The astute off-premise caterer will always approach the client or person in charge of the event before this becomes a problem—a polite reminder that things should be wrapping up or the staff will be going into extra hours. Entertainers should be instructed by the client and/or caterer not to go past the specific times agreed to without first checking with one or the other.

However, a caterer who is slow in serving a meal through no fault of the client certainly cannot charge overtime. Common factors that impact overtime include the following:

■ Certain locations, like museums and historical sites, have curfews that may eliminate the problem of overtime.
■ Clients holding events in high-rise office buildings should be advised that overtime charges will apply if the off-premise caterer is significantly detained from leaving after the event when elevators are not available (usually cleaning or moving people use them exclusively in the evenings).

19. Special instructions. There is always something else that must be considered. This section can incorporate details such as:

■ It's a surprise party—use caution when calling the client!
■ Specific instructions for "the day of . . ." "Give special attention to Uncle Joe," "Serve Aunt Mabel light drinks," etc.
■ Specifications about whether the caterer will provide meals for the band and other persons working the event.
■ Policies about the disposition of any leftover food. Do you take it away? Does it belong to the client? Generally, raw ingredients are yours, but prepared foods are negotiable. However, consider your potential liability if someone takes home leftovers and becomes ill. This is a quality control issue, not a matter of being miserly!

20. Security. Who will ensure that alcohol is not served to minors or to anyone who already appears to be intoxicated? If it's a charitable event, such as an auction or dinner gala, there may be quite a bit of cash at the registration tables. Who keeps an eye on it? As a caterer, you are not responsible for the personal property of clients or guests. One of the ancillary services you may provide (through the building or site where the event will be held) is a certain number of paid security personnel, whose salaries are specified in the contract. It should be stated in the contract whether any security person will be carrying a firearm and that this person is licensed to do so.

21. Setup and cleanup. List exactly who is responsible for decorating and for tearing down afterward. Musicians will want to set up their own equipment, but otherwise some hotels, country clubs, and other facilities will have rules about using their personnel to do setup and cleanup. Find out what these rules are and include them in the contract.

22. Adherence to laws and ordinances. This is a broad statement indicating that you will abide by all the pertinent laws and ordinances of your area, and that you expect the clients and guests to do the same. When it comes to alcohol service, this section include certain specific statements: that bartenders will check IDs, that the client will also be vigilant about any liquor law violations and will assist the caterer in handling these situations tactfully, or that the caterer has the right to close the bar if there is a problem. The fire department also has concerns about too many persons in a space that is too small, so compare the guest list with the room capacity. Also check—and include in the contract—whether or not smoking is permitted in the space.

23. Taxes and gratuities. List the applicable taxes and who is responsible for paying them. If catering for a tax-exempt organization, add a line stating that you must be given a copy of its tax-exempt certificate or number prior to the event (which should be kept on file in case of a later audit). Even service charges are subject to your state's sales tax.

If the servers are going to be tipped (or not), this fact—and the amount—should be mentioned in the contract. If the only tips are for bartenders, who keep an empty bowl or jar at the bar for this purpose, it should still be stated in writing.

24. Insurance requirements. This clause should state that you, the caterer, have liability and worker's compensation insurance and that you require proof that your subcontractors, and any hired by the client, also have liability coverage.

On the topic of insurance, although it is certainly not a requirement, intelligent caterers suggest that clients obtain cancellation insurance, especially for weddings. In the sometimes stormy weeks and months before the nuptials, they're simply ensuring that in case the whole thing is called off, the caterer and vendors will be paid.

25. Legal statements. These are phrases that add some "teeth" to the contract. They establish *binding authority*—that the person signing this agreement is the one authorized to do so: "The client has read and fully understands the contract and is aware of its financial implications." You might also include an *assignment clause*. This restricts the client's ability to hand over his or her contract obligations to someone else without your knowledge and agreement and/or a whole new contract. In short, neither party should be able to make a change to the contract without the other's knowledge and written consent.

An *indemnification clause* states that the client agrees to hold the catering company, its employees, and its subcontractors "harmless" for losses, damages, and expenses related to the misconduct or negligence of the client, its subcontractors, or its guests. A *severability clause* states that even if a court finds part of the contract unenforceable, the rest remains valid.

Many companies specify a bad check charge in their contracts, as well as a clause that allows the caterer to tack on the additional cost of hiring a collection agency if it becomes necessary to do so.

26. Cancellation and refund policies. This topic is discussed in detail in the "Deposits, Cancellations, and Refunds" section of this chapter. Suffice it to say that the cancellation and refund policy should be clearly spelled out in the contract.

On the advice of your attorney, you might add a contract clause about *liquidated damages.* It means that both parties agree to a specific dollar amount to settle an obligation if it is impossible to assign a monetary value to the amount of financial harm the claimant (caterer) will suffer when an event is canceled. The amount of liquidated damages increases as the date of the event approaches. The rationale is that a caterer could have booked something else in that time slot, worked many hours on the planning, and lost business as a result of the client's decision to cancel. However, if the date is rebooked, the clause should also include a predetermined cancellation fee to be refunded to the client.

27. Detailed list of charges. This part of the contract should list, usually on a separate page, all charges pertinent to the agreement: for food, beverages, equipment, staff, accessory services, other charges, service charges, gratuities, sales taxes, and totals.

28. Dated signatures of both caterer and client(s). In the case of weddings where brides, grooms, and their families are involved, according to Elio Belluchi, professor of law at Florida International University, "It is advisable for off-premise caterers to obtain as many signatures as possible on the contract—from both sides of the family—in case it is necessary to proceed with legal collection procedures. Collections are much easier when contracts are in writing and when there are signatures."

Dr. Belluchi also advises that all changes in menu, other arrangements, and guaranteed head counts be made in writing. As he puts it, "If it is not in writing, it never happened. Oral agreements are not enforceable if they are over certain amounts, which are determined by state statutes."

In conclusion, an off-premise catering contract should contain all of the necessary details in order to execute the catered event. We realize we've provided a lot of detail here, and you should take care to use as much as you need without making your agreement into an intimidating "legalese" mess. A good contract should be reassuring, not off-putting, to the clients—who understand that, between the lines, catering an event does involve a high degree of mutual trust. However, in today's litigious society, it also involves a high degree of organization and the ability to thoroughly document plans.

✖ Deposits, Cancellations, and Refunds

Any of these topics can be the focus of some of the stickiest situations in the catering industry; here we discuss them one by one.

Deposits

First, do not be shy about asking for a deposit! It is an accepted practice in the social and corporate marketplace. A deposit assists cash flow and is especially helpful during the slower seasons when parties are minimal. Deposit policies vary from caterer to caterer. In general, the larger and more expensive the event, the larger the deposit. Moreover, a contract signed many months or years prior to the date of the event will require a smaller deposit than a contract signed only a few weeks or months in advance of the event.

Here's a basic deposit policy chart, adapted from South Florida's lavish catering facility, The Signature Grand.[3]

✖ Deposit Policy

Minimum $1,000 or amount listed below, whichever is greater				
MONTHS UNTIL PARTY OR EVENT	AMOUNT OF INITIAL DEPOSIT	NUMBER OF ADDITIONAL DEPOSITS	ADDITIONAL DEPOSITS AS A PERCENTAGE OF TOTAL AMOUNT	DEPOSITS SPACED BY NUMBER OF MONTHS APART
1	50%	Balance 3 days prior	0%	0
2	25%	1	35%	1
3	20%	2	25%	1
4	10%	2	30%	1
5	10%	3	20%	2
6	10%	3	20%	2
7	10%	3	20%	2
8	10%	3	20%	3
9	10%	3	20%	3
10	10%	3	20%	3
11–13	10%	3	20%	4
14–16	10%	3	20%	5
17–19	10%	3	20%	6
20–22	10%	3	20%	7
23–24	10%	3	20%	8

Clients are expected to make their deposits and payments on time. When they do not, without making other arrangements, they should be sent a letter mentioning that they are "in default under the terms of the agreement." This letter should include a deadline for the payment due date, stating that if it is not met, the contract will be canceled. Most clients pay immediately after receiving the letter. For those who do not, the event is canceled.

Cancellations and Refunds

A cancellation, for whatever reason and by any signatory, is a breach of the contract. Cancellation policies should be spelled out very carefully, and reviewed by an attorney. In some states there are laws about cancellations and deposit refunds. A cancellation should be handled like any other contract modification—*it must be made in writing and agreed to by both parties* before it is valid.

Most off-premise caterers at the time of a cancellation will have already received at least one of a client's deposits or payments. Should all, some, or none of the deposit be refunded? There are no clear answers, but there are some questions that can be asked on a case-by-case basis to lead to a reasonable solution:

■ What is the reason for the cancellation?
■ When is the cancellation occurring—how soon before the actual event date?
■ What are the actual losses to the caterer in terms of food, other costs, and turned-away business?
■ How much is the caterer's time worth for having planned the event?

The main objective should be to maintain future goodwill with the client. Most clients are understanding as long as they feel the caterer is fair and is not trying to take advantage of a situation. A good idea is to allow the client five to seven days after the contract is initially signed, to cancel without consequence. It's a good-faith gesture that allows the client to really read the agreement and think it over. (And, when you think about it, do you really want this person as a client if he or she is hesitant about the details from the beginning?)

In circumstances when the cancellation happens a year or more prior to the event, a good policy may be to refund the deposit as soon as the date is rebooked. In fact, a New York court ruled that unless the caterer could substantiate damages, the catering firm was obligated to return the advance deposit for an event more than three years away. The judge felt this was plenty of time for the caterer to rebook the date.

When bad weather threatens the event, the off-premise caterer should call the client two or three days beforehand and advise the client that it is necessary to procure and start preparing the food now. At this point, the caterer can give the client the option of canceling, changing the venue, or going ahead with the event with the realization that if it is canceled after the food has been purchased, the client will be charged the caterer's expenses for the food and related costs, with no markup. (Under no circumstances should the caterer charge more than his or her own costs in this situation.)

Occasionally, an event must be canceled at the last minute because of a tragedy involving one of the principals. In these cases, it is best to be gracious and wait a period of time before discussing refunds.

Finally, the off-premise caterer should also allow for his or her *own* right to cancel or postpone in extreme circumstances—labor strikes, acts of God (natural disasters), personal tragedies—anything beyond your control that would prevent you from performing your duties under the contract. Again, spell out a refund policy to cover this situation.

When the Caterer Blinks

It is inevitable that a caterer will sooner or later fail to live up to a client's expectations, creating a need for some form of refund or credit. When he or she makes a mistake, it is always good policy for the off-premise caterer to proactively bring it to the client's attention—rather than waiting for the client to bring it to the caterer's attention. We know a caterer who, during a busy holiday season, forgot to bring one of the eight hors d'oeuvres to be served at a Christmas party. In such a case, assuming there is no time to correct the situation, it would be best to simply advise the client of the problem prior to the party, offer some type of refund or credit, and make arrangements to augment the menu with another item that could be easily obtained, perhaps from a local supermarket. The worst course of action is to say nothing and hope the client does not notice—you'll almost surely lose future business with that client, as well as perhaps receive less money for the event, than you would by simply offering a credit in advance.

When faced with an irate customer, a caterer should:

- Let the customer vent his or her anger and displeasure without interrupting or offering excuses.
- Take notes and ask pertinent follow-up questions.
- Acknowledge that the customer has been heard and summarize to reinforce the fact that you understand their points.
- Let the customer know you empathize with his or her situation.
- Follow up on the complaint quickly and get back to the customer, preferably face-to-face and perhaps with a "peace offering"—a bottle of wine or freshly baked cookies.

When dealing with staff members who have been involved in such a situation, avoid the temptation to berate them! Recognize that this is an opportunity to improve staff performance, and remember to discuss the things that were done right too.

When real disaster strikes that is clearly the fault of the caterer, it might be worthwhile to mail a box of gourmet chocolates to everyone who attended the event, along with a bright note that exonerates the host.

Caterers should also be wary of those people who complain about everything. Many grouse solely because they suspect it will get them price concessions, even with bogus or trivial complaints. When something does go wrong, regardless of whose fault it is, most caterers feel terrible. However, catering contracts should be designed

CONTRACTUAL NIGHTMARES

Whenever there is a contract for an event, there is at least some chance that fate and circumstances will combine to either delay or cancel it. Postponement and cancellation are two different things, but they each involve a major commitment of time and resources, and the additional hassle of getting things changed or cancelled. The caterer's policy should depend largely on how much notice has been given.

Then again, we've heard of nightmare situations in which, for example, a fiftieth anniversary party was cancelled due to the husband's death. The banquet facility's policy—which is the norm—was that if the room is rebooked for that date, the deposit money is refunded; otherwise, no refund is given. And yes, most catering contracts do state that deposits are nonrefundable. So yes, it is a contractual issue, but in this case, what about compassion?

An additional, critical piece of advice gleaned from wedding consulting is to determine very early in the planning process exactly who the real decision-makers are. If there's a pre-event crisis—from a hurricane to a change of heart—who will have the last word? The catering company may be "hired" by the bride-to-be, but if her parents are paying the bill, they should be signing the contracts jointly with their daughter, and should be given the same information about postponement and cancellation policies.

Communications experts say most of us know up to 50 other people we share information with regularly by word of mouth. When a customer has had an unpleasant experience, they'll tell 9 to 10 other people; 13 percent will tell more than 20! Is keeping the deposit money worth that risk?

Common sense, courtesy, and compassion. All are necessary in unusual situations. No matter how long or how technical the contract, the bottom line should always be to treat each client with honor and respect when unfortunate things happen, as they sometimes will.

---

to limit liability to the actual value of the product or service for which the customer has contracted.

For example, if the client paid for a display of crudités and the caterer did not provide it, the caterer should be required to refund only the actual value of the display, without exorbitant additional amounts for embarrassment, pain, and suffering.

In fact, savvy caterers know how to make the most of customer complaints— by turning them into positives. In addition to providing a refund, many caterers provide the customers with a discount for future events that will ensure they return. Obviously, it is also important to give these customers very special attention when they do return, so that they will, in turn, spread your goodwill to others.

✖ How to Survive a Lawsuit

In today's litigious business climate, even top caterers who pay their insurance premiums, mind their operations, and train their staffs may end up being sued for anything from coffee being too hot, to someone's tripping over a cord. Smart caterers will handle customer complaints immediately, giving their clients what they want. Even if the caterer is not to blame, it's best to go overboard to avoid a lawsuit.

However, in the event that you, as a caterer, are sued, the first things that should be done to determine a course of action are:

- Quickly locate employees who may have been involved and ask for their cooperation.
- Contact an attorney.
- Contact your insurance company.
- Determine whether this is a "nuisance" suit or one with real potential for damages. The longer you wait, the higher the risks and the greater the legal fees.

We've seen suits that are filed years after an incident, making it virtually impossible to locate former employees to testify. However, you can often track down former employees through their Social Security numbers.

It is critical to keep good notes about adverse incidents. You might ask your attorney to draft an Incident Report, a simple sheet that you can photocopy and have on hand at every event along with the rest of the paperwork, to fill out just in case. It is also important to caution staff members to decline comments to news reporters or other guests and to inform you immediately. In those cases in which a supplier could be involved, contact that person or firm too.

Before rushing into court, it's advisable to consider types of Alternative Dispute Resolution (ADR). These include mediation and arbitration.

Mediation involves retaining an objective individual as a go-between, essentially a facilitator who attempts to resolve the issue. This process takes time, patience, and the ability to compromise. Mediation is a voluntary procedure, however, and discussions made during mediation are not admissible in court.

Arbitration takes place before a single person or a panel of three persons, who listens to both sides and makes a decision on the case. For more information on arbitration, visit the website of the American Arbitration Association (www.adr.org).

✖ Conclusion

An understanding of laws and contracts is essential for success in this business. One mistake in this area can cost a caterer his or her business and livelihood. This chapter advises readers of many legal requirements, but its intent is not to replace professional legal counsel—only to make readers aware the many legal ramifications in the off-premise catering arena. It is always smart to obtain professional legal advice before undertaking any business venture.

Notes

1. Darrell VanLoenen and Joseph W. Holland, "Payroll Taxes and Personal Liability," in *Florida International University Hospitality School Quarterly*, spring 1993.
2. Donald A. Blackwell, partner, Anania Bandklayder Blackwell Baumgarten Torricella & Stein, Miami, Florida. (www.anania-law.com)
3. Reproduced with permission of The Signature Grand Catering Mansions, Davie, Florida. (www.thesignaturegrand.com)

✕ Chapter 3
Menu Planning

According to Jerry Edwards, president of the National Association of Catering Executives, "Planning a menu that is creative, cost efficient, and a crowd pleaser is what subtly separates the great caterers from the good ones. To be a great caterer you must serve great tasting foods that can either be innovative or traditional."[1]

This chapter addresses the major considerations of off-premise menu planning for caterers—including basic rules for planning various types of menus and methods for determining food quantities and food costs.

A properly planned menu is a major part of the success of an event, and a badly planned menu can ruin an event. Caterers who serve only half a tea sandwich for lunch to a collegiate football team will more than likely find themselves being used as tackling dummies after the meager repast!

In this chapter the reader will learn ways to avoid such unfortunate situations, as well as gain a complete arsenal of menu planning principles and techniques.

It is important to note here that this textbook is not a cookbook. There are thousands of wonderful cookbooks available in libraries and bookstores, overflowing with recipes that can be adapted for use in off-premise catering. What this chapter can do is teach you what to look for when selecting recipes for use at off-premise events.

✕ Planning Principles

Before you begin asking menu-related questions, as we have already mentioned, it is important to qualify the client in terms of the date of the party, the number of guests, the location of the party, and the budget. By asking these questions first, the astute off-premise caterer will avoid wasting time discussing a menu for an event that is not feasible in the first place. Your time is better spent planning menus for those who are realistic prospects.

An off-premise catering menu cannot be planned until the caterer knows the event's location and the type of kitchen facilities, if any, available there. Lack of refrigeration, water, electricity, adequate cover, and ventilation will most definitely determine what type of cooking can be done on-site. For example, frying food to order in a high-rise office building, in an empty office without ventilation, will fill the whole floor with the smell of grease.

After prequalification and selection of the party site, the menu planning process begins. The menu and service style will determine all of the following:

Foods to be purchased
Staffing requirements
Equipment requirements
Off-premise facility layout and space utilization
Décor for buffets and food stations
Food production and preparation requirements
Beverages, both alcoholic and nonalcoholic

Menu planning involves asking the clients a lot of questions to determine what they perceive and want. Suggested questions include:

- "How many guests are you expecting?"
- "Is there a kitchen or other area for cooking?"
- "Who are your guests? Are they male, female, or couples?"
- "What are their ages? Where do they reside? Are they fairly sophisticated party go-ers? Are there any socioeconomic, ethnic, or religious factors that might affect the menu?"
- "Would you like your guests served while seated at a table, or would you prefer a buffet or food stations?"
- "Are there any foods that you particularly want (or do not want) to be served? Are there any special dietary needs?"
- "What is the purpose of the event?"
- "What will your guests be doing before and after this event?"
- "Have you had (or been to) this type of party or event in the past? If so, what did you like (and dislike) about the menu and the food?"
- "What would you like your guests to say about the menu and food after the event?"
- "Are there any association affiliations?" (You would not serve chicken, for instance, to a Cattlemen's Association.)
- "Are there any corporate affiliations that might determine menu items?" (You would not serve Pepsi products at a meeting of Coca-Cola executives.)
- "What are the budgetary considerations?"

By asking these and other related questions, the off-premise caterer should be able to spark a dialogue that begins the menu planning process. The end result is a menu for the event that combines the client's wishes with the caterer's food knowledge.

Menu planning can go from one extreme—when the client tells the caterer, "You know what I like; send me a menu"—to the other, when the client already has a desired menu and is simply asking the caterer to provide a price to prepare it. However, most menu planning falls between these two extremes, with clients who have some menu ideas but are looking for the caterer's opinion and advice.

✕ *Basic Menu Categories*

Catered foods can be served at any hour of the day or night. Off-premise caterers are asked to serve sunrise breakfasts, midday lunches and brunches, evening dinners, post-theater desserts, box lunches, and myriad other types of foodservice. Menus vary depending on the caterers and the markets they serve. Menus also vary depending on the style of service—buffet, stand-up, or seated. Service style is influenced by the purpose of the event, the allotted time for dining, and the location of the event, to name a few factors.

Here are some basic types of special event service:

Seated, served meals
Buffets
Food stations ("action stations")
"Stand-up" cocktail parties
Barbecues and picnics
Combinations of any of the preceding types

Seated, Served Meals. In planning menus for these events, caterers must serve foods that are suitable for serving at a table, either individually plated or from platters. Served meals may be preceded by cocktail receptions, which may or may not include various hors d'oeuvres passed by servers or appetizers presented at food stations and buffets.

The basic courses for a seated, served meal include:

Appetizer or soup
Salad
Sorbet ("intermezzo")
Main course—entrée, starch (optional), one or more vegetables, and garnish
Cheeses (with or without fruit, nuts)
Dessert
Coffee (regular and decaffeinated) and tea

There are endless variations to this format. In European-style menus, the salad is served after the main course, but prior to the cheese course. The appetizer course may be eliminated if the premeal hors d'oeuvres are plentiful. Some menus include a fish course in lieu of an appetizer or salad. A sorbet course should be served only if there are two or more courses served prior to it. Many main course menus eliminate the starch and include two or more vegetables. Dual entrées (also called "duets") feature two main courses, such as sliced tenderloin of beef with a fish or chicken dish. Portion sizes of each are roughly half a full-size portion. This works very well, as it satisfies the tastes of most people. If a guest asks for a plate of all fish or all beef, the request can easily be accommodated.

Many Americans are unfamiliar with the cheese course, unless they've spent time in Europe. It's a profitable addition to an upscale dinner menu and can also be fun to put together. (Learn more in the "Trends in Foodservice" section of this chapter.)

Some clients prefer a combination of served and buffet-style courses. For example, a chilled soup appetizer could be served or preset at the tables; the guests are then served the main course buffet-style. Another interesting variation is to serve all courses except the dessert and coffee at the table, allowing guests to get up for dessert and coffee and mingle with guests from other tables. In this situation, dessert selections should be bite-sized and/or easy to eat while standing, and coffee should be served in some type of attractive mug to eliminate the need for a saucer.

Buffets. In buffet service, the guests are directed to the buffet table(s) where a variety of foods may be selected. Guests either help themselves or are served by attendants. The advantages of offering a variety of foods, plus the need for fewer service staff, makes a buffet a very popular choice for off-premise events. When the client wants variety, this service system is more practical and cost-effective than providing a served meal that guests order à la carte from a menu.

One of the most frequently asked questions by clients is: "Which is more expensive, a buffet or a served meal?" The answer to this varies from caterer to caterer. Generally, buffets require less labor to serve the food, but greater food quantities. A buffet table should be continuously replenished during service so as not to be empty after the last guest eats. There is no simple answer, but you can truthfully say that the cost will depend on the menu choices, the level of service required, and other factors. A buffet table filled with expensive seafood and beef tenderloins will cost more than a simple three-course chicken dinner served by a waitstaff. A seven-course served meal that includes caviar, lobster tails, and desserts flamed at tableside will cost more than a buffet consisting of simple salads, a chicken dish, rice, and a basic vegetable.

Buffets may or may not be preceded by hors d'oeuvres. If the latter is the case, it is wise for the caterer to be prepared for guests to place more food on their plates than they would if they'd eaten a bit prior to the meal.

A minimum buffet selection would include one salad, one or two entrée choices, one starch (rice, potato, or pasta), one vegetable or a vegetable medley, bread or rolls, and butter. Desserts and coffee may be put on the same table or on a separate table or may be served directly at the dining tables.

Food Stations. Food stations work well when food needs to be offered on different floors within a building, when international foods are offered, when the client wants people to mingle and move about, or when the client simply wants something different.

> Using the station concept allows [the caterer] to divide the food presentation into smaller components and still have impact; each station can make a statement of its own with decoration, colors, and menu. The station concept makes it possible to offer diverse menu items that you might not be comfortable placing on a single buffet table. It also divides the space and the guests so that the traffic flows smoothly and there are shorter lines. And finally . . . using stations will give the party a more casual feel.[2]

Some popular food station concepts include:

Stir–fry. Raw and blanched vegetables, several types of marinated meats and sauces, cooked to order in a wok by a trained chef.

Fajitas. Thin strips of beef or chicken sautéed with green peppers and onions and served in a soft tortilla with salsa, sour cream, and other condiments.

Pasta. Various types and shapes of cooked pasta are heated on tabletop stoves and topped with a variety of sauces—marinara, pesto, and cream. Crusty Italian bread and Caesar salad go well with pasta.

Gourmet pizza. Pizzas with a variety of toppings are cooked to order in a small oven or pizza oven.

Meat carving. One or more meats are carved to order. Beef tenderloin, turkey breast, loin of pork, and rack of lamb are popular choices. Many caterers serve them on rolls or breads as sandwiches with appropriate sauces.

Dessert, coffee, and cordials. A variety of pastries, fresh fruits, tarts, éclairs, cookies, and chocolate desserts are served with a variety of coffees. Quality and flavor are more important here than size. Crème brûlée and chocolate are the most popular dessert items, and caterers can never go wrong serving high-quality ice creams and sorbets. Cordials and cognacs may also be served in accordance with state liquor laws.

These are but a few of hundreds of food station possibilities: Cajun foods, potato skins, fritters, Southwestern foods, Greek foods, Mexican foods, seafood bars, sushi, quesadillas, tempura, satay, Danish smorgasbord, crepes, ice cream and frozen yogurt, hot or cold soups, miniburgers and hot dogs, and large tables filled with cut and whole imported cheeses, fresh fruits, and vegetables.

It is always an option to use a limited number of food stations, in lieu of (or in addition to) passed hors d'oeuvres, prior to a served meal. Some prefer to offer station foods throughout the evening, which keeps a party less formal. Seating for all guests at a food station party is optional. Some clients prefer to have no seating, or seating for only a portion of the guests, which encourages more socialization. Others prefer that each guest has an assigned seat, with each place setting prepared with all of the necessary flatware and glassware.

"Stand-Up" Cocktail Parties.

In the United States, hors d'oeuvres are customarily served at cocktail parties, which may or may not precede lunch or dinner.

> Russians call them *zakuski*; Greeks, *mezze*; Spaniards, *tapas*; Italians, *antipasto*; Mexicans, *antojitos*; and Chinese, *dim sum*. Hors d'oeuvres is French for "outside of work," or food prepared "outside" of the main course. . . . Hors d'oeuvres should be a feast of flavor, color and texture to be savored in one or two bites. Selections range from savory canapés to lavish spreads of crudités (raw seasonal vegetables), accompanied by a dipping sauce.[3]

Hors d'oeuvres may either be passed by food servers or placed on buffets. They should be bite-sized and easy to eat. The location of the party will influence the hors d'oeuvre selection—for example, where cooking space is limited, cold selections are more practical. Honey coconut shrimp, which is a fried item, cannot be cooked to order in a building without sufficient ventilation. (Although a client once insisted on conch fritters for a cocktail party on an office building's 16th floor. The fritters were cooked to order on the loading dock, transported on the passenger elevators, and served within minutes!) Please note that with fried foods, it is important to serve them quickly, because they soon become dry, cold, and tasteless.

Ideally, off-premise caterers should make their own hors d'oeuvres in-house, but ready-made appetizers that were once seen as completely undesirable are now beginning to gain acceptance in the catering community. Some products are obviously better than others. Because making hors d'oeuvres from scratch is very time-consuming, caterers should at least consider paying a higher unit cost for a ready-made product, as long as the quality is there, and utilizing kitchen staff for other purposes.

Barbecues and Picnics. *Webster's New World Dictionary* defines a picnic as "a pleasure outing at which a meal is eaten outdoors." Many off-premise caterers make an excellent living catering outdoor events in public parks and other open-air locations. Menus can range from simple (or gourmet versions of) burgers and hot dogs, to chicken and ribs, to steaks and seafood kebabs. They can also include Maryland crab fests, New England clambakes, Caribbean barbecue, Southern fries, pork barbecues, oyster roasts, grilled pizza, and Louisiana shrimp boils—each with its own flavors, accompaniments, and décor. Popular wood chips include:

Hickory—Strong, pungent bacon-like flavor, used for pork or beef.
Mesquite—Sweeter than hickory, but still strong. Great for duck, lamb and beef.
Alder—Light, delicate flavor, excellent for salmon, chicken and pork.
Cherry or Apple—Sweet, fruity flavor, great for game birds, pork and poultry.[4]

For cutting-edge barbecues and picnics, try:

- Ancho chili–braised barbecued lamb shanks with black beans and red tomato
- Grilled elk loin with bourbon sauce
- Grilled ostrich with chipotle cream sauce
- Grilled Texas quail with Parmesan cheese grits and Smithfield ham sherry-maple glaze
- Wood-grilled wild Alaskan salmon with wild-rice pilaf and Zinfandel-cranberry sauce

✕ Catering Menus

Federal Truth-in-Menu laws require that caterers and other menu planners correctly describe and represent their menus. The major points to observe include:[5]

Brand names: A copyrighted or registered trademark must be used "as is" and may not be used to represent a generic product.
Means of preservation: You can't call something "fresh" if it has been previously frozen—ever! This includes items like shrimp.

Merchandising terms: Don't say anything served commercially is "homemade." It wasn't actually made in someone's home, and thank heavens! That would be an unlicensed facility! Use words like "home style" or "traditional" instead.

Point of origin: This refers to the original spot where the product was grown or harvested, such as Maine lobster or Florida stone crabs.

Price: Cover charges, service charges, and gratuities must all be contained in a contract or communicated by letter. They should never be hidden or go unmentioned in negotiations.

Product identification: Sometimes a product must be substituted at the last minute because what was ordered was not available, not delivered, too expensive, or otherwise impossible to use. Be certain to state the correct products being used, but reserve the right to substitute, with the customer's permission, under extraordinary circumstances.

Quality: Grades of meat and poultry products should refer strictly to USDA-recognized terminology (Prime, Choice, Select, Standard, and Commercial) or accepted variants thereof (Grade A, Good, Number One, Fancy, Grade AA, and Extra Standard).

Quantity (portion sizes): Steaks are often sold by weight, and *weight before cooking* is the generally accepted term.

Type of preparation: Use the proper terms for the cooking methods you are actually using on the particular food item—baked, broiled, fried, sautéed, smoked, roasted, and so on.

Verbal and Visual Presentation. Have you noticed that on most product packaging in supermarkets, the gorgeous food photo has a little caption? It says, "Serving Suggestion." This legally covers the food processor in case the end result doesn't look quite as perfect. Take a hint from that part of the industry and be certain that what is described by the waitstaff, or on the menu, or photographed for reproduction on menus or table tents, actually represents what the customer receives.

Exhibit 3.1 is an abbreviated version of Bill's Catering Menu.

⊠ *Exhibit 3.1* Bill's Catering Menu

This is just a sample from a couple of Bill's Catering Menu categories. The entire menu is 24 pages long! There are 23 soup selections, 15 salads, at least three dozen side dishes, and complete menus for Bill's signature "Floribbean Cookouts." The idea is not to overwhelm the clients, but to entice them to choose—perhaps even a bit more than they'd originally intended—from a variety of delicious dishes. Warning: DO NOT READ THIS when you are hungry!

HORS D'OEUVRES

Seafood Selections
Honey Coconut Shrimp
Key Lime Shrimp
Cooked, Chilled Large Shrimp with Cocktail Sauce

Maryland Crab Cakes with Orange Tarragon Sauce
Grilled Key West Shrimp Skewers
Cracked Conch Fritters with Bahamian Cocktail Sauce
Florida Lobster Fritters with Mustard Sauce

Spicy Pistachio Shrimp Fritters
Scallop Toasts with Wasabi Caviar
Smoked Trout Mousse on Bruschetta Rounds
Cajun Seafood in Pastry Cups
Asiago Cheese and Shrimp Puffs
Smoked Salmon Tarts
Catfish Spring Rolls with Southern Tartar Sauce
Shrimp Spring Rolls with Orange Chili Sauce
Roasted Shrimp, wrapped in Katif with Vanilla Rum
   Sauce
Asparagus wrapped in Smoked Salmon with
   Mustard Dill Sauce
Salmon Gravlax with Mustard Dill Sauce, served on
   Black Bread
California Sushi Rolls with Ginger and Wasabi
Seared Tuna on Won Ton Crisps with Ginger Pesto
Grilled Swordfish Skewers with Honey Ginger
   Sauce
Smoked Shrimp Salsa Tarts with Cilantro Cream
Almond-Coated Rock Shrimp Cakes with Coconut
   Dijon Cream
Jerk Tuna Burgers with Mango Salsa
Shrimp on a Stick, with Wasabi Cocktail Sauce
   and Papaya Mint Relish

Non-Seafood Selections
Crispy Florida Alligator Bites
Nicaraguan "Pastelitos" (rich, filled pastry patties)
Beef Negi-Maki with Ginger Teriyaki Sauce
Lamb Skewers with Fresh Mint Sauce
Mushroom Caps (choice of eight fillings)
Curried Chicken Spring Rolls with Apricot Dip
Smoked Chicken and Black Bean Mini Phyllo
   Burritos
Spinach and Feta Cheese wrapped in Phyllo Pastry
   Pillows
Bill's Special Quiche
Jerk Chicken Pizza with Mango Salsa
Pistachio-Crusted Smoked Gouda Bites
New Potatoes with Sour Cream and Caviar
Skewered Thai Peanut Chicken
Thai Pot Stickers
Bacon-Wrapped Chutney Bananas
Hearts of Artichoke Tempura with Bearnaise Sauce
Bruschetta with Tomato, Basil, Red Onion, Herbs,
   Parmesan, and Grilled Portobello Mushrooms
Beef Sirloin and Bleu Cheese Bruschetta
Sesame Chicken Kebabs with Peach Mustard Sauce
Smoked Duck Pot Stickers with Orange-Chili Plum
   Sauce
Sweet and Spicy Confetti Duckling Rolls

Samosas—Indian Beef, Chicken, or Vegetable
Duckling Empanadas with Ancho Chili Raspberry
   Reduction
Brie and Brown Sugar Puffs
Cheese Quesadillas with Mango Jicama Salsa
Beef Empanadas
Imported Cheeses (ten to choose from) with
   Pappadums
Crudites and Three Dips
Fresh Fruit with Yogurt Dips

DESSERTS

Individual Desserts
Bill's Chocolate Ganache Topped with Strawberries
   and Sabayon Sauce
Strawberries Sabayon, or Champagne Chocolate
   Sabayon
Poached Pears with Kirsch Sabayon or Gran
   Marnier Sauce
Chocolate Champagne Goblet with Strawberries
   Sabayon
Chocolate Seashell filled with Strawberry,
   Raspberry, Lemon, or Vodka Mousse
White Chocolate Cups filled with Chocolate
   Ganache, Strawberries Sabayon, or Fresh
   Raspberries and Blueberries
Lemon Flan with Candied Zest
Espresso Crunch Cannoli
White Chocolate Raspberry Cheesecake
Chocolate Truffle Cake with Belgian Chocolate
Cappuccino Mousse Cake
Brandied Pear Patisserie with Puff Pastry
Apple Almond Tart

Buffet Desserts
Sottobosco (a mixed berry tart)
Assorted Petit Fours
Tiramisu
Tri-Color Pâté (Layers of White, Dark, and Milk
   Belgian Chocolate)
Pistachio Pâté (White Belgian Chocolate and
   Pistachio Nuts)
Chocolate Decadence Cake
Chocolate Truffle Cake
Cappuccino Mousse Cake
Apple Almond Tart
Cheesecakes—ten flavors available
Ice Creams—all flavors available
Assorted Tartufos
Spumoni

✕ Dietary and Nutritional Claims

Dietary terms such as *fat-free* and *low-sodium* must be accurate and not misleading. Frequently, guests who are allergic to certain foods will ask a server about the ingredients in a particular dish, so it is extremely important that servers have the proper information about foods and ingredients. They should be instructed to ask the kitchen staff or management prior to answering questions about a food's ingredients, inasmuch as people may become ill, or even die, from eating certain ingredients. The most common food allergens, responsible for about 90 percent of all allergic reactions, are commonly known as the "Big 8":

- Eggs (including some egg substitutes, which contain egg whites, and some foaming products used to top specialty coffee drinks)
- Milk (from cows or goats, and in butter, yogurt, cheeses, lunchmeats containing casein or whey)
- Peanuts (or mandelonas, peanuts soaked in almond flavoring)
- Tree nuts (almonds, Brazil nuts, cashews, hazelnuts, filberts, pecans, macadamia nuts, pine nuts, pistachios, walnuts, etc.)
- Fish (crab, crayfish, lobster, shrimp, etc.)
- Shellfish (clams, mussels, oysters, scallops)
- Soy
- Wheat (some types of imitation crabmeat contain wheat)

BIRDS OF A FEATHER—UNDERSTANDING CHICKEN LABELS[6]

Free-range means chickens have free access to the outdoors for a significant portion of their lives. This is just a marketing tool, and anyone with a door on the chicken coop meets the technical definition of "free-range." There are no criteria for what the chickens eat, what antibiotics they receive, or the amount of free-range space.

Free-roaming chickens is a marketing label that means only that the chickens are allowed access to the outdoors. Most are kept in barns and are allowed outside occasionally.

Natural implies that chickens are fed antibiotic- and hormone-free grain, but currently there is no strict legal definition of "natural" chicken.

Organic means that the chickens were raised on land certified as "organic" by the U.S. Department of Agriculture (USDA). This means the land has been free of chemicals, pesticides, and herbicides for at least three years, and extensive bookkeeping records and inspections are required. Organic chickens are not fed antibiotics, as are some conventionally raised chickens. A USDA-approved third-party private or state certification program must certify organic foods. Caterers and restaurants do not have to be certified to serve organic foods; however, organic and nonorganic foods cannot be stored together and must be properly identified on the menu. Caterers also need to prove organic claims by keeping records that document the certification of whatever organic foods they serve.

In addition, sesame seeds and sulfites (a food preservative used in many types of cooked and processed foods, as well as a natural byproduct of beer- and wine-making) also cause allergic reactions in some people. For more information about food allergies and the Big 8, check the website of the Food Allergy and Anaphylaxis Network (foodallergy.org) and the U.S. Food and Drug Administration (FDA) (fda.gov).

Caterers who choose to make nutrition-content claims on menus must be able to support these claims in accordance with FDA guidelines. For example, if a caterer claims that a particular menu item is "light," the caterer should be able to prove that this particular menu item contains at least one-third fewer calories than the regular item. To support this claim, the caterer may need an expensive laboratory nutrient analysis. The lesson: Before making a claim, be aware of the costs that may be involved to support it.

✗ *Types of Menus*

Most off-premise caterers prepare some form of preprinted menu to share with customers. These may or may not include printed prices, depending on the caterer's market. Usually, those caterers who market to the budget-conscious, lower-priced market will preprint prices. Upscale caterers who prepare food at party locations and custom menus for each client will generally not preprice their menus, but provide price quotations for specific menus on request.

Preprinted menus offer some advantages:

1. The client can respond quickly by reading the menu and making selections without long consultations with the catering sales staff. It automatically gives clients menu ideas and minimizes the number of required sales staff.

2. These menus help "control" the client by giving him or her specific choices, rather than allowing the client the freedom to come up with items at will that you may not be familiar with—or that won't fit the off-premise preparation situation.

3. The kitchen staff will be familiar with the menu, thus making its work more efficient.

Before off-premise caterers decide whether to preprint a menu, they should also consider the printing cost. Printing can be very costly, and some customers may perceive preprinted information as being uninventive or not "personal" enough. Today's computers make it easy enough to prepare and print custom menus for individual occasions, if you have a staff person with enough time to do this. You can also put menu (and price) information on your own Internet website, along with photos of the dishes—showing beautifully styled food, of course! Either option makes it convenient to price items based on ever-fluctuating food costs, charging a bit more when food costs are high or when there is greater demand for catering services, such as during the Christmas holidays, and less during slower periods when food costs are less and demand is lower.

For caterers who wish to offer a preprinted menu with a personal touch, one alternative is to offer a simple menu that lists some of the most frequently served menu items (without prices), and then custom-create an additional, personalized menu with the client's input.

Whether it is in print or on a website, a menu should reflect the image the caterer wishes to project. Menus printed on inexpensive paper will convey a different image than those printed on 24-weight bond paper with gold inlays. A menu should not appear too "busy." The typeface must be large enough to read easily, with wide borders and space between listings. As much as 50 percent of the page can be white space. Menus should reflect a good balance of marketing and ingredient information. We've all had restaurant experiences in which we were disappointed when the food arrived at the table and didn't come close to matching the waiter's gushing description of it. It's also a good idea to include short descriptions of any items that may be unfamiliar to the reader.

An excellent resource for menu writing is *Webster's New World Dictionary of Culinary Arts.* In addition, the Official Food and Beverage Spell-Checker software program takes the guesswork out of spelling more than 17,000 culinary and beverage terms. For more information, visit restaurantconsult.com. Nothing says "unprofessional" like misspelled words on a menu, brochure, website, contract, or proposal.

The fact is, you're a caterer—not a writer. If you're not confident of your ability to draft appealing, thorough, and catchy menu copy, hire a food writer to do it for you. A good relationship with a local freelancer at a reasonable hourly cost will ensure you've got someone to take one last critical look at things before you send the menus out.

TERMS TO ENLIVEN YOUR MENU

What Do You Cook That You Might Describe As:
Hot, Icy, Zesty, Crisp, Tender, Velvety, Luscious, Juicy, Fluffy, Light, Sweet, Sizzling, Delicate, Garnished, Fresh, Smooth, Crusty, Silky, Creamy, Crunchy, Chilled, Tender, Plump, Saucy, Savory, Mellow, Soft, Warm

Use Terms Like:
Winter, Spring, Summer, Fall, New, Created, Seasonal, Chef's, Harvest, Rainbow, Bouquet, Prime, Choice, USDA Grade, Extra Large, Jumbo, Freshly, Natural, Whole, Original, Signature, 14-Ounce, One-Pound, Half-Pound

Words That Sell Include:
Affordable, Alluring, Aroma, Enticing, Exclusive, Exquisite, Exotic, Fabulous, Fascinating, Flawless, Genuine, Glistening, Impeccable, Irresistible, Lavish, Memorable, Mouth-Watering, Professional, Radiant, Spectacular, Striking, Substantial, Succulent, Sumptuous, Tantalizing, Tempting, Unforgettable, Unsurpassed, Upscale, Vivid

✕ *Basic Menu Planning Guidelines*

There are no strict, do-or-die rules for planning off-premise catering menus. There are always exceptions that result from regional preferences, the clients' desire for something innovative, and the capabilities of the caterer and staff. For example, most caterers would not advise serving chocolate soufflés to a group of 500 dignitaries at an off-premise location with no kitchen—but there are caterers who have perfected their techniques and organizational skills well enough to serve 500 soufflés at the peak of perfection. Toques (chef's hats) off to them!

As a rule, though, it is always better to keep off-premise catering menus as simple as possible. With client input, the off-premise caterer should strive to create menus with the following characteristics:

- They have worked well for past events.
- The staff has prepared them before, for groups of the same approximate size.

- They feature signature dishes for which the caterer is known.
- They feature locally grown and raised foods. In California, this might mean abalone and artichokes, or stone crabs and key lime pie in Florida.

Some clients request that their guests be offered a choice of entrées at a seated, served meal. For example, they will ask that a caterer offer the guest a choice of fish, beef, or chicken and that an order be taken from each guest at the function. It is also smart to offer a vegetarian alternative as well. Offering such choices may seem impractical, because it requires the caterer to have extra portions of each entrée, as well as the extra staff to take and serve the special orders. However, if the client's budget allows for the extra cost, the caterer should comply with the request. If the budget does not allow for the extra expense, it is far better to persuade the client to offer a buffet meal that allows guests to choose from a variety of entrées.

Another option is to offer a dual entrée—smaller portions of two of more entrées on each plate. If the client insists on the seated served meal with entrée choice, give the client the responsibility of taking entrée orders in advance (as part of the RSVP to the event), then providing a count to the caterer a few days prior to the event, along with the seat assignments for each guest.

Well-planned menus should consider the appropriateness of the food flavors, colors, textures, and shapes. Too much of any one of these components is not good. Flavors should be interesting, with some highlights, but not too tart or pungent. Natural colors—red, red-orange, peach, pink, tan, brown, butter yellow, light and dark greens—are good. Contrasting textures, as simple as crispy croutons in a salad, add interest and excitement to the course. Interesting shapes are always welcome, as long as they are not all the same. For example, a plate with round tomato slices, round sliced beef tenderloin, and round scoops of potato salad and coleslaw would not be as visually appealing one with the items presented differently: Layer the tenderloin slices on a bed of radicchio, cut the tomatoes into wedges, and serve the salads in bright hollowed-out vegetables.

Here are some additional guidelines for menu planning:

1. Serve foods that are popular. For example, prime ribs of beef will be better received by more guests than fillet of shark. Well-liked and trendy restaurant menu items can be varied and adapted to meet off-premise catering needs.

2. Butlered (passed) hors d'oeuvres should be one or two bites and not messy to eat. Passing hors d'oeuvres makes it much easier to control consumption, rather than holding them in chafing dishes where a few guests may overindulge and leave only scraps for the rest of the group. The quality of cooked-to-order, hot passed hors d'oeuvres is usually superior to that of those that are cooked in advance and held in chafing dishes.

3. Be careful not to duplicate items on the menu, such as by serving stuffed pea pods as an appetizer, and then again as the vegetable; or lobster bisque as the first course, and lobster tails as the entrée.

4. Develop menus that are compatible with the capabilities of your kitchen staff. A caterer who specializes in chicken and ribs does not need a five-star chef. A caterer who specializes in gourmet dinners will not be successful with a short-order cook as head chef.

SPECIAL DIETS

The Vegetarian Resource Group says it is difficult to reliably estimate how many people are vegetarians, but most surveys indicate that between 3 and 7 percent of Americans at least call themselves "vegetarians," although few are familiar with the strictest definition of the term—a person whose diet consists of vegetables, fruits, grains, and nuts. Many who use the term do not eat red meat, but will occasionally eat fish or chicken. As the population ages and becomes more health conscious, many families simply have a couple of "meatless meals" every week. Here are a few important subcategories:

Vegans are the strictest vegetarians. They do not eat anything from an animal source— this includes honey, since it's produced by bees.
Lacto-vegetarians eat no animal products except milk and dairy products.
Ovo-lacto-vegetarians eat no animal products, with the exception of eggs and milk products.

There are other types of special diets to be aware of, as they may be mentioned in meal planning:

Low-fat—Low fat from any source
Low-cholesterol—Low fat from animal sources
Anti-allergen—Prepared with no wheat, eggs, seafood, or nuts
Diabetic—No sugar
Kosher—Food that has been selected and prepared in accordance with Jewish dietary laws
Low-salt—For persons with high blood pressure or heart problems
No MSG—No monosodium glutamate, a flavor enhancer often used in Asian cooking

You may occasionally get a request for a dish that is prepared without garlic, onions, nuts, or a particular spice. This usually indicates a guest's allergy or digestion problems, which should always be taken seriously. The same goes for coffee service— you should always have alternatives to caffeinated coffee, since caffeine intake can be a problem for some people.

5. Astute caterers consult with their chefs when planning menus with clients. Off-premise caterers need to know when to say "no" to unusual client demands. There are two sides to this situation: If caterers say "no," they may lose the client, or at least appear uncooperative. If the caterer says "yes," the kitchen may have difficulty producing the food. Unusual requests should be honored when possible, particularly during slower seasons and for smaller-size groups. The busy holiday season is not a time to experiment.

6. There are no hard-and-fast rules for the number of items on a buffet, or the number of courses in a seated, served meal. The foods and courses can range from a few to several. Smart caterers always remember the "big picture" when planning courses. What is the purpose of the event, and what will satisfy the majority of the guests?

7. No menu is complete without including the appropriate beverages for the meal. This may mean a selection of wines to accompany particular courses, coffee with dessert, or perhaps imported vodka with caviar.

8. Garnishing food is an art that is frequently overlooked. When planning menus, presentation should always be considered. Many caterers garnish plates with herbs or other ingredients used in preparing the dish; others use items that add color and/or enhance the appearance of the plate.

9. Concentrate on what's good and fresh instead of what's new or hot. Local, seasonal ingredients will be at their peak, so take advantage of them to create your own take on regional culinary traditions. Buying in season is also smart for the budget, as your produce should cost less.

10. Be sure to always include vegetarian selections. Up to 7 percent of Americans now call themselves vegetarians, so give them a tasty alternative to meat!

A great way to sum it up comes from off-premise caterer Judy Lieberman, author of *The Complete Off-Premise Caterer*:

> A seated meal must be planned so that each course pleases the palate in such a way that, while each one is enjoyed, the next can be anticipated and savored in its turn. A well-prepared formal meal builds to a crescendo with the main course, then tapers gently off to a sweet finish at the end of the meal. Guests should feel beautifully fed, not overstuffed or glutted with too many rich courses. [Nor] should they feel bored by repetition or confused by a series of intense and conflicting tastes.[7]

Other thoughts on developing your menu include just keeping your eyes open and your own palate alive and curious. Ask your clients where they like to go when they dine out. Eat there too, and see what you think. Plan an occasional visit to a city known for its great food. Scan the latest cookbooks and food magazines. Attend a few of your competitors' events—not as a "spy," but as a legitimate guest when you're invited.

✗ Food Presentation

Consider all five senses in menu planning—sight, hearing, touch, smell, and taste. Texture, aroma, temperature, color, and spiciness are parts of the overall flavor of the foods you serve. Bright colors may indicate freshness or proper doneness. Steaming foods imply heat. You can "hear" the flavor in a sizzling fajita platter, the crunch of an apple, the fizz of Champagne being poured into an elegant flute.

Eating is a sensuous pastime, and the way the food is presented is as important as the way it tastes. Buffet and food station presentation can also make or break your reputation as a caterer. Everything matters—from the height of the buffet table, to the linens that drape it, to way foods are grouped, to the lighting that shows them off. It is important to remember that although the guests may never focus on these individual elements, they definitely notice and appreciate the overall presentation.

Let's take the imaginary food off of our mental buffet tables now, and look at the architecture beneath the food—what holds it and what keeps it warm.

Serving and Holding Options

Try elevating heat-resistant sturdy platters on glass blocks with canned heat (such as Sterno) underneath. This works best when all guests go through the line at once, but is not recommended for buffets that last for long periods of time.

Use polished aluminum platters elevated on wrought iron stands. Check out www.cheffield.com or www.regalinternational.com. The cost of nice-looking platters is quite modest, and you'll receive many compliments on the results.

The latest chafing dish innovation is a butane-fueled chafing dish that actually cooks. These state-of-the-art chafers burn for four hours on one can of butane. You can bring your food cold to an off-premise event and quickly reheat it. Visit www.hammerjack.com for more information.

Some caterers use large granite slabs raised on glass blocks with canned heat underneath. At chef stations, your crew can prepare foods to order in front of guests, to be served from woks, skillets, griddles, and sauté pans.

A simple and cost-effective way to display cold foods, such as bite-sized desserts, is to elevate two or more pieces of Plexiglas. Support them with martini glasses, or those old-fashioned, wide-rimmed Champagne glasses, adding loose floral buds for a final touch of color. This type of display works well with chocolate-dipped strawberries or mini fruit tarts.

Chilled ice displays are fun and dramatic. They can range from small pieces that chill and display fruit or seafood, to complete buffet tables carved out of ice. Molds are available that allow a caterer to make fairly simple ice displays; for custom or more complex designs (company logos, etc.), you should hire an ice sculptor.

Vancouver, British Columbia caterer Debra Lykkemark of Culinary Capers came up with her own "tiered table," using three or four round tables of successively smaller sizes. The bottom table is a 60-inch round, placed on the floor with legs extended. A large box is then placed on the table, and a 48-inch round table is placed on top of the box without the legs extended. On top of that, another box is placed, and then a 30-inch round. Linens are draped over the top, and the entire table looks like a gigantic wedding cake.

Visit stores like Home Depot, Target, and Pier One Imports for design inspiration. Some Pier One locations actually allow you to use their pieces and return them— undamaged, of course—for 20 percent of their purchase cost. And don't forget your local thrift stores for true inspirational bargains and unique period pieces. When designing buffets for ethnic meals, be sure to visit local stores that carry the particular cuisine's ingredients, where you'll also find indigenous (and often inexpensive) props.

Then again, be sure not to lose the food amid the props! We've all been to buffets that look great, but made us think, "Where's the beef?" In the words of the late, great caterer John Mossman, "The best advertisement is on the end of the fork." We all hear stories about buffets that looked beautiful, but the food wasn't hot enough, it simply lacked flavor, or the caterer ran out of food.

For plated foods, use different colors and shapes of china. Garnishes should accent and enhance, not hide, and those garnishes that are produced with an obvious "degree of difficulty" improve the presentation. There are a number of interesting garnishes:

Balsamic and red wine glazes
Lemon, lime, and orange slices
Champagne grapes
Crispy fried leeks, basil, or other herbs
Chocolate shavings
Cocoa powder and powdered sugar
Rice paper and flowers
Shiso sprouts and micro greens
Seeds—pumpkin, pine nuts, sesame
Mu fun noodles
Sun-dried lemon, orange, and fennel
Caramelized nuts, herbs, and seeds
Edible flowers
Lemon grass
Enoki mushrooms
Baby corn
Fresh bamboo
Ginger—roots or pickled
Cinnamon sticks
Hearts of palm
Exotic fruits—kumquat, mango, starfruit

The International Caterers Association suggests using small boxes or Styrofoam slabs to elevate foods. Or save Styrofoam packing peanuts, place them in plastic bags, tie them shut, and use them as "beanbags" to prop up salad bowls and platters at attractive angles. The Internet is an incredible resource for buffet design ideas. Type "buffet and food station presentations" on a search engine, and you'll find thousands of matches.

✖ Culinary Trends

Off-premise catering is an industry most definitely impacted by food trends. Some caterers simply refuse to acknowledge them and continue to operate by serving their own tried-and-true classics for decades. Others seem to want to be on the "cutting edge" of trendiness. There is room for both types of caterer—and for those who'd rather offer a little of both trends and traditions.

As time passes, it is evident that some things change and others stay the same. Yesterday's "comfort foods," like mashed potatoes and meatloaf, reemerge as today's trends. Budget is still a constant concern when it comes to planning menus. There is a strong demand for value, as well as quality. We see a continuing emphasis on diet and nutrition, yet most folks throw their dietary concerns to the wind when planning a once-in-a-lifetime celebration like a wedding. They'll include special meals for kosher or vegan guests, but for everyone else, it's prime beef, fresh seafood, and rich, calorie-laden desserts.

Labor-Saving Foods

For many caterers, finding, training, and retaining qualified culinary staff is a huge problem, so labor-saving foods are rapidly growing in popularity at all levels of the industry. High-end caterers can benefit from foods prepared by the *sous vide* method, which means "under vacuum." The food is cooked in advance, sealed in vacuum packaging, and quickly blast-frozen. It can then be warmed in boiling water or microwave ovens prior to serving. For more information on this method, visit www.cuisinesolutions.com.

A 2001 food industry survey published in *Restaurants & Institutions* magazine revealed that restaurateurs and chefs want more high-quality breads and baked products, grilled veggies, presliced meals of a better quality, fresher-tasting meat products that are grilled or broiled, flash-frozen, and shipped. They want flavored oils, seasoning blends that don't evaporate on the grill or in the oven, and more innovative sandwich spreads.

The survey also asked about the use of some labor-saving foods. Here they are, along with the survey percentages of respondents who use them.[8]

Prepared salad dressings	84%	Par-baked breads and rolls	59%
Frozen cakes, pies, and cookies	72%	Breaded fish portions	59%
Soup bases	72%	Ready-to-use croutons	59%
Portion-packed condiments	68%	Seasoned, coated fries	52%
Sauce and gravy concentrates, mixes	68%	Ready-to-use sauces	52%
Breaded chicken pieces	65%	Shelled eggs	48%
Precut, prewashed produce	64%	Precooked bacon, sausage	45%
Frozen potatoes	62%	Seasoned rice blends	45%
Prepared appetizers	62%	Dehydrated potatoes	42%
Bakery mixes	61%	Premarinated chicken pieces	42%
Preportioned steaks and chops	42%		

Trends in Foodservice

A number of trends in foodservice have emerged in the early years of this millennium.

Ethnic cuisines. These cuisines, of course, will always provide innovative additions to a smart caterer's arsenal of offerings. *Middle Eastern* items such as dolmas, Kasseri cheese, hummus, and tahini are used more frequently. Spices (anise, caraway seeds, black cumin) are popular and ingredients (chickpeas, eggplant, grape leaves, pine nuts, red lentils, and bulghur) enhance the aromas and flavors of these healthful dishes.

Pacific Rim, "Asian Fusion," and Pan-Asian cuisines. These cuisines have made their mark on catering menus from coast to coast. Dishes such as Szechwan Tuna with Soba Noodles, and Crispy Tempura Lobster with Ponzu and Caviar are representative of menu choices. Catering chefs are using such exotic ingredients such as palm sugar, Chinese celery, fresh water chestnuts, garlic shoots, lemongrass, mirin, ponzu, and other Asian ingredients to diversify and expand their menus.

Indian cuisine. We've also noticed renewed interest in this type of cuisine, as our clients' taste buds demand spicier and more European-fused dishes. Bright, moist Tandoori chicken, the wide variety of naan (Indian breads), aromatic spices like cardamom and curry, and jasmine rice make these foods as pretty as they are delicious.

Cheese courses. Popular in Europe, a cheese course is served after the main course, but before dessert (or sometimes in lieu of dessert). Limit the selection to no more than five types of cheese, and choose a variety of flavors, intensities, and textures. Take the cheeses out of refrigeration in time to reach room temperature by serving time. Garnish with fruit and nuts, and serve them with a good, crusty French bread.

Underutilized cuts of meat. High-flavor braises and stews made with so-called secondary cuts of meat are growing in popularity. These cuts often require slow cooking, but the results are delicious. Lamb shanks, duck drumettes, oxtail roulade, braised short ribs in beer, lamb shoulder roulade, braised veal shanks, roast beef hash, shepherd's pie of braised lamb, beef cheeks, char-grilled skirt steak, flank steaks, and top blade steaks are finding their way onto more menus.

"Street foods." This category includes anything traditionally served from carts or informal food stands—kebabs, fish and chips, and "walk-around" items like beignets and churros.

"Retro desserts." You can have fun at serving stations with luscious selections that can easily be flamed for effect— crêpes suzettes, Bananas Foster, or Cherries Jubilee.

Signature, "artisan," or specialty breads. Cornbread, popovers, flatbreads, and chapatti lead the way on progressive catering menus.

In addition to the foods themselves, the styles of service are changing.

Individual tableside ordering. This is a trend that progressive caterers use to draw clients away from their competitors. It is a somewhat risky and labor-intensive business when you allow guests to select from two, three, or even four different entrées. It's imperative to know your clients, keep excellent records from past events, and, of course, charge your approach accordingly.

Dessert buffets with seated, served meals. This type of buffet allows the guests to get up, mingle, and avoid the drowsiness and lethargy that comes after eating and sitting for a period of time. Caterers also incorporate coffee service and specialty coffee drinks, or after-dinner drinks, with the dessert buffet.

✕ *Computing Food Quantities*

After planning a proposed menu with a client, the next step for the off-premise caterer is to determine the various quantities and portion sizes for the menu items. This is necessary not only to be able to calculate the cost of the menu, but also to determine food quantities that are needed for purchasing, preparation, and production purposes.

Computing how much people will eat is guesswork to some degree, but with experience a caterer begins to develop certain standards for consumption. Astute caterers keep records of the food production and consumption of prior events, and by combining this information with current requirements, can better determine food quantities for future off-premise events.

Too much food is always better than too little. Caterers should never run out. Extra food is necessary for a number of sensible reasons:

■ Staff can make mistakes—spills, overcooking, miscounting food items.
■ A few extra guests always manage to show up.
■ Guests may be unusually hungry.
■ There may be special, unforeseen requests. It may be necessary, for instance, to feed the musicians or other people, at the last minute, at the client's request. In addition, most off-premise caterers, at their own expense, feed the catering staff.
■ There are few worse feelings than worrying during an event about whether there will be enough food to feed the guests. Every caterer at one time or another has had to reduce portion sizes during the dish-up period to ensure that there would be enough for everyone. For your own comfort, be sure there's enough.
■ And finally, heed the main rule for computing food quantities: Don't *guess* who is coming to dinner. *Know* who is coming to dinner!

There are many true stories about caterers who were expecting one type or size of group, only to be horrified—and unprepared—when another type arrived. The off-premise caterer who says to a client, "Don't worry! I know what your group will like!" may be asking for trouble, particularly if the caterer plans a decadent, high-cholesterol meal—for a group whose members are all on the Pritikin diet.

Some particulars to determine when planning food quantities harken back to the questions to ask clients indicated earlier in this chapter:

■ Average range of guests?
■ Male or female?
■ Where were they before, and where are they going after, the event?
■ Are they from out of town on holiday, or local?
■ Are they sophisticated party goers or occasional party goers?

Why ask these particulars? Well, the local, sophisticated party goer will eat less than the person from out of town who goes out infrequently. Guests who are active and have eaten little all day will be much hungrier at dinnertime than those who have been inactive after a heavy lunch. Guests will eat more if food is served buffet-style. They will eat less if the room is crowded, because it will be difficult for them to reach the food tables. And, usually, men eat more than women. Another factor: People eat more during cold weather.

Record keeping after each catered event will assist the off-premise caterer with determining future food quantities. A postparty report that includes the following information should be part of every client's file:

- Number of guests guaranteed and number who attended
- Quantity of each menu item prepared
- Leftover amount of each menu item
- Any unusual factors that may have affected consumption
- Recommended future changes to food quantities

Armed with these accurate records and a knowledge of the group, with each successive event you should be closer to correct planning and budgeting.

So how much is "enough"? Experienced caterers should provide between 5 and 20 percent extra for each menu item. The percentage varies based on the group's guaranteed head count, plus the potential for extra guests. The smaller the group, the larger the percentage overage; the larger the group, the smaller the percentage overage. Here's an example:

NUMBER OF GUESTS GUARANTEED	PERCENT OVERAGE	ORDER FOOD FOR
20	20	24
50	15	58
100	10	110
200	7.5	215
400	5	420

Note that these are general guidelines; the amounts may vary from caterer to caterer and region to region.

Who pays for this extra food? The client does, because it is important that the caterer include this extra food in the cost calculation for the particular event. Specific techniques for costing are discussed in Chapter 10.

The following are general guidelines regarding suggested food quantities per person for various food items. Please be advised that these are only guidelines. Once again, food portions may vary from region to region, and from caterer to caterer.

ITEM	PORTION PER PERSON
Assorted hors d'oeuvres	4–8 pieces if before dinner
	8–12 pieces if served with food stations
	18–24 if served all evening, with no dinner
Large shrimp	1–2 if passed as hors d'oeuvres
	4–12 if on a buffet
Soup (first course)	6–8 ounces
Salads	1–4 ounces
Main course	4–8 edible ounces
Starch, vegetables, side dishes	2–4 ounces
Desserts	Varies (the richer the dessert, the smaller the portion)

For the uninitiated, determining food quantities can be stressful and difficult. Inevitably, novice caterers will, at least once, err on the side of too little food, and they can only hope that there is a nearby store or a backup plan to fill the void before the guests notice.

Determining How Much Food to Order

After determining the portion sizes, the next step is to determine how much food to order. Most recipes are not written for the exact number of guests at an off-premise event. A knowledge of basic math is necessary in order to convert the recipe to serve the group size. Here is a simple example:

An off-premise caterer has booked a party for 100 guests. Allowing for a 10 percent overage, it will be necessary to prepare food for 110 guests. The caterer plans to serve four items, and the recipe for each one of these items is written to serve various numbers of guests—for 8, 12, 25, and 50 guests, respectively. The off-premise caterer needs to convert each of these to feed 110. The conversion formula is to divide the number of required servings by the number of servings in the recipe to determine a *factor* as follows:

$$\frac{110}{8} = 13.75 \qquad \frac{110}{12} = 9.2 \qquad \frac{110}{25} = 4.4 \qquad \frac{110}{50} = 2.2$$

The next step is to multiply the factor by the various items in the recipe to determine the quantities of each recipe ingredient. If the recipe for 50 calls for 2 gallons of milk, for 110 guests the caterer must multiply 2 gallons of milk by 2.2 to get 4.4 gallons of milk.

For some ingredients, such as baking powder, baking soda, yeast, and some seasonings, the factor method will not always work. So caterers need knowledge in quantity food preparation techniques. Otherwise, experimentation before the event occurs is mandatory.

Determining Yields

Determining food quantities becomes more complicated when dealing with foods that need to be trimmed, cut, and processed before preparing. An example is freshly cut fruit. How many strawberries, grapes, melons, and kiwis will it take to produce 10 pounds of fruit?

An excellent tool to help caterers determine yields—not only for fruits, but for all types of foods—is *The Book of Yields: Accuracy in Food Costing and Purchasing*, Sixth Edition, by Francis T. Lynch (John Wiley & Sons, 2005; available in paperback or as a CD-ROM). Also check www.chefdesk.com for ordering information and other yield-related resources.

Here are some specific yields for a few popular vegetables:

VEGETABLE	PERCENTAGE OF LOSS AFTER TRIMMING
Asparagus	45
Broccoli	20
Carrots	30
Onions, peeled	15
Potatoes, peeled	20
String beans	15
Tomatoes	5

A reliable formula for computing an amount to order is:

$$\frac{\text{Serving Size}}{\text{Yield}} = \text{Raw Portion Size}$$

For example, suppose a caterer wishes to serve 8-ounce sirloin steaks, which will be cut by the chef from top sirloin butts. The caterer knows that 50 percent of the top sirloin butt can be used for steaks after the fat is trimmed off. So, how much top sirloin butt is needed to prepare 110 steaks?

$$\frac{\text{Serving Size (8 oz.)}}{\text{Yield (50\%)}} = 16 \text{ oz. per steak before trimming}$$

For 110 steaks, 16 oz. each $= \dfrac{1{,}760 \text{ oz.}}{16 \text{ oz./lb.}} = 110$ pounds of top sirloin butt

Sirloin butts average 15 pounds each, so if the caterer is ordering them only for this event, the total number of pieces needed can be calculated by dividing 110 (total pounds needed) by 15 (pounds each), which equals 7.33 sirloin butts. You should always round up, so this order would be 8 sirloin butts, a total of about 120 pounds.

✖ Calculating Food Cost

The food cost for each menu item can be determined by multiplying the amount of each ingredient by the cost per unit for the ingredient. In the preceding example, if the top sirloin butt costs $2.50 per pound, the total cost for the top sirloin butt is:

$$120.00 \text{ lb.} \times \$2.50 = \$300.00$$

To determine the cost per steak, simply divide $300 by 110 steaks, to get $2.73 per steak).

The cost of the meal can be determined by simply adding the costs of all menu items to be served, including:

Hors d'oeuvres
Appetizer(s)
Soup(s)
Salad(s)
Intermezzo course
Entrée(s)
Starch(es)
Vegetable(s)
Garnish(es)
Rolls/bread/butter
Dessert(s)
Coffee/decaf/tea/cream/sugar/low-calorie sweetener
Any other food costs (spices, frying oil for cooking, etc.)

Later chapters in this book deal with the ramifications of food cost, as well as various methods for pricing menus.

✗ Leftovers

Obviously, there are no leftover foods if the caterer runs out of food—but good caterers do not run out of food! There may be an exceptional situation in which extra guests are fed, but normally there are leftovers. Buffets and food stations usually generate more leftovers than seated, served events because the buffet and food stations need to look full even as the last guests are served.

Most leftovers result from guests not showing up. Less often, they are the result of extra food that the caterer brings to serve extra guests over the guaranteed amount.

The disposition of leftovers can be a major problem for off-premise caterers. Do they leave them with the client? Do they reuse them? Do they throw them out, or perhaps donate them to a charity? Most off-premise caterers have established policies for disposition of leftovers, and there are several options.

Throw Out

"When in doubt, throw it out." This rule should apply to any foods that have not been stored at temperatures below 40 degrees Fahrenheit or above 135 degrees Fahrenheit. There is no need to risk food poisoning. Foods that have been left out on buffets and foods that do not clearly appear fresh should be discarded.

Foods that have been exposed to contamination should never be used again. Individual unwrapped portions of food that have been served to customers may not be used again.

It is important to note that it is not always possible to identify food spoilage by appearance, smell, or taste. Food may appear to be safe even when it contains toxins or large numbers of harmful microorganisms. To repeat: When in doubt, throw it out.

Give to Client

Normally, clients who have an in-home or small business party ask for the leftovers, and this is understandable—they paid for them! Some caterers comply with these requests, and others refuse. Those who refuse to leave leftovers take the position that they have no control over how the food will be handled after they leave. Perhaps the client may leave potato salad out for hours before refrigerating it, only to eat it the next day and become violently ill. Of course, the caterer gets the blame. Some caterers advise the client that the local health department prohibits them from leaving food behind. This makes the health department the villain, not the caterer.

Many caterers bring foods, such as large cheeses, that are used for display purposes at a number of parties. These are not the client's property, since the cost is not normally charged in full to a particular client, but prorated over a number of events.

Many off-premise caterers who cater wedding receptions will prepare a "goody basket" for the bride and groom to take to their hotel. Corporate clients for upscale events are usually not interested in keeping the leftovers; however, an exception may be company picnics, where most clients ask that their employees be able to take home the extra food. (Bring plenty of aluminum foil and carryout containers to these events, but use caution—never package food for take-home if there is any doubt as to its freshness or how it will be handled.) There are caterers who ask that their clients sign disclaimers in case anyone becomes ill from leftover food. An attorney should be consulted prior to preparing a disclaimer form.

Reuse

Reusing leftover foods can be risky for those who are unfamiliar with various foods. For example, some caterers may reuse large blocks of cheese that have been on display, or meats that have been braised and kept cool, but they know not to reuse mayonnaise-based salads that have been left out or other foods that spoil quickly.

If leftovers may be reused, the staff should do the following:

■ Store them in well-covered, well-sealed containers. Shallow containers are best to facilitate quick cooling of foods.
■ Store cooked and processed foods away from raw foods, to minimize the dangers of cross contamination.
■ Quickly cool hot foods to 45 degrees Fahrenheit, then cover.
■ Clearly label containers to indicate their contents and preparation dates.

Give to Homeless Shelters or a Local Charity

The Good Samaritan Food Donation Act of 1996 encourages food donations to nonprofit organizations by protecting the food donors from civil and criminal liability. This legislation makes it much easier for caterers and their clients to put leftover foods to good use in charitable feeding programs. Food donors still must comply with any state or local regulations. In addition, a food donor is liable only when acting with the knowledge that the donated food might harm another person.

Many agencies will pick up food either at the party site or at the caterer's commissary the day after the event. For large events, some caterers schedule a food pickup at the party site, knowing that more than likely there will be leftovers. This can reduce the extra work of taking the food back to the commissary for storage until disposition. Contact the food bank in your community, or check the website of Second Harvest, a national nonprofit organization that has long championed the cause of using food overages for charitable purposes (www.secondharvest.org).

Some caterers erroneously think that food given to a nonprofit organization can be written off as a charitable contribution. This is not the case, because the food originally was charged to the caterer's operation as an expense when it was purchased. Deducting it again would be a violation of federal tax law. The same holds true for corporate clients who deduct the caterer's bill as a business expense. They cannot "double-deduct" it, claiming it again as a contribution.

Those clients who are not deducting the cost of the party may perhaps receive some tax credit if the food is donated to a charity, but questions of this type are better clarified by a professional accountant.

Staff Meals

Many caterers allow their staff members to eat the leftovers before they leave the party. Others bring special food for their employees, particularly if they eat before the party begins. Most off-premise caterers do not permit their staff to take home extra food, feeling that it may prompt them to also take home things other than legitimate leftovers. Food for thought. . . .

Use at Other Facilities

Some off-premise caterers operate other facilities where leftovers may be reused. For example, a caterer who operates a restaurant may be able to resell leftover roast beef as a "barbecued beef sandwich special" the next day. Extreme caution must be used when doing this, to ensure that the food has been properly handled. One way a caterer may do this is to keep any extra food packed under refrigeration or in coolers. This food is usually the "extra"—sometimes referred to as "insurance"—that was brought for unusual situations. It is kept out of the client's view, because often the cost of this food has not been added into the overall costs of the party and the food is only there for emergencies in case extra guests arrive. Because this food is truly the caterer's property, it can very well be reused as long as it is properly handled.

Reward Helpful People

Those who are behind the scenes at the event site and who assist the caterer are good candidates to receive food. The helpful security guard, the loading dock attendant who assists the caterer while entering and leaving the building, or the building engineer who helps out when a fuse blows should be rewarded. Food is always a welcome reward, and giving it away is less expensive to the caterer than giving money.

Return to Vendor

Under certain conditions, if prearranged with a supplier, unused food can be returned if it has been held at proper temperatures and remains unopened. For example, a caterer who is serving expensive Beluga caviar might arrange with the supplier to return any that was unopened and kept on ice. Some wine suppliers will also allow returns of unopened bottles, if state law permits it.

As you see, there are plenty of options for leftover food other than letting it go to waste. It is extremely important that, as an off-premise caterer, you establish a leftover policy in advance of events, and you must advise the clients of this policy as part of your contract negotiations. This prevents any misunderstandings about the disposition of leftovers after an event. There have been plenty of perfectly catered parties with unhappy clients who blamed their caterers the next day for "taking off with" leftover food "that I paid good money for!" Don't let it happen to you.

✕ Conclusion

Menu planning for an event involves a lot more than sitting down and making a list of a client's favorite foods or those that you enjoy preparing. Everything from the time of day and purpose of the event, to the client's budget, to the limitations of the site itself, will help dictate what you serve and how you serve it. Part of intelligent menu planning also involves what to do with any leftover food you have the day of the event. In short, the term "menu planning" is probably more "planning" than it is "menu"!

Notes

1. Jerry Edwards, president, National Association of Catering Executives, Columbia, Maryland. (www.nace.net)
2. Joyce Piotrowski, in *Catering Business*, May 1990.
3. *Restaurants & Institutions*, © 1992. A publication of Reed Business Information, a division of Reed Elsevier, Inc. All rights reserved.
4. *Table Topics*, newsletter of the International Caterers Association, June 2001.
5. National Restaurant Association, Chicago, Illinois.
6. *Sante*, The Magazine for Restaurant Professionals, September 2001. (www.santemagazine.com)
7. *The Complete Off-Premise Caterer*, by Judy Lieberman, Van Nostrand Reinhold, 1991.
8. *Restaurants & Institutions*, © 2001. A publication of Reed Business Information, a division of Reed Elsevier, Inc. All rights reserved.

✖ Chapter 4

Beverage Service

Off-premise caterers must be knowledgeable about alcoholic beverages, as well as the laws that affect their sale and service. Most full-service off-premise caterers serve alcoholic beverages and, in some states, sell them at various locations. Caterers who are licensed to sell off-premise not only earn profits from the drink sales, but they generate additional profit by selling mixers and ice and providing bar service personnel.

Off-premise caterers are frequently asked by clients for advice on how much and what types of alcoholic beverages to serve. The caterer who is uninformed in this area certainly can't inspire much confidence in the client, particularly when other caterers' proposals include beverage recommendations. Expertise in this area can mean the difference between being hired or not.

Off-premise caterers are often asked to provide bartenders for functions, which can result in certain legal implications. It is imperative that your bartending staffers are knowledgeable about proper bar service techniques. Some off-premise caterers even turn down business if clients want to provide their own bartenders, since they may not perform up to the caterer's standards and may therefore reflect poorly on the event—and the caterer.

So astute off-premise caterers will learn as much as possible about beverage service for two primary reasons: It can be a real moneymaker; and it can also be an incredible legal headache if not operated in accordance with state and federal liquor laws and the principles of responsible alcohol service.

✖ State and Local Liquor Laws

Each state, county, and city has its own laws for the sale of alcoholic beverages. These laws do not always make sense to folks in the foodservice industry, but they must be followed nonetheless. A standard that applies in every state is that if an alcoholic beverage is sold, the vendor must have a license to sell it. The definition of the word "sold" is that money must change hands as a required condition of accessibility to the alcohol.

The process of obtaining a liquor license can range from "very easy" to "extremely difficult." The application process often involves a background check of the catering company owners, including disclosure of the company's financial records. It may take anywhere from 30 to 120 days from application to approval. It may be complicated by the location of the business—many cities have ordinances about alcohol service within a certain distance from schools or churches, although off-premise caterers can typically work around this restriction because their service sites vary. In some states, a caterer must buy the license from someone else, rather than directly from the state. In addition to licenses, special alcohol permits are often required by cities or counties for single events.

The details vary by state, but here are five basic scenarios for the sale and dispensing of alcoholic beverages:

1. Off-premise caterers are permitted to serve, but not sell, alcoholic beverages. They cannot charge the client for the alcohol itself, but they may charge for mixers, ice, glassware, and other items needed to serve it. In this case, the caterer may pick up the beverages from a liquor vendor, but the caterer may not "front" the money for the alcohol. Instead, payment must be made with the client's check or credit card, payable to the liquor vendor and for the exact amount of the purchase.

2. Off-premise caterers or their clients may obtain a special or temporary permit that allows them to sell liquor at a specific event, at a specific time, in a specific place. This type of permit is almost always sold for charitable events, not regular corporate or social functions.

3. In a limited number of states, the off-premise caterer can obtain a license to sell and serve alcoholic beverages off-premise on a regular basis. The off-premise caterer must already possess a license to sell alcohol at an on-premise location. For example, a restaurant owner, licensed to sell alcohol at the restaurant, may apply for a license to sell it at off-premise events that the restaurant caters.

4. In a growing number of states (including Florida) off-premise caterers may purchase a license to sell alcoholic beverages at off-premise events, but they must purchase the alcohol from a retail liquor outlet and cannot buy directly from a wholesale distributor.

5. Many states have different licensing requirements for selling liquor, versus selling only beer and wine.

As you can see, not knowing the legal licensing and permitting requirements in an area can get you in trouble. The first step is to contact the department in your state that controls the sale of alcoholic beverages.

✖ *Liquor Laws and Legal Liability*

There is an additional challenge in today's litigious society, and that is the question of liability. Who is responsible for damage, injury, or death that results from someone's drinking too much and acting irresponsibly?

In states that follow so-called common law, the responsibility for intoxication rests with the consumer of the alcohol, rather than the person who tended bar or sold the drinks to the consumer. However, the increasing social concern with alcohol abuse (and its impact on innocent victims) has prompted most states to pass some sort of *dramshop law*. The word is a combination of *dram*, originally meaning a small drink of liquor, and *shop*, meaning the place where it is sold. The term comes from England, where in the 1800s laws penalized pub owners who continued to serve "habitual drunkards" after being warned of their intoxication by their families or employers.

Today, even where common law is in force, courts often use the dramshop law concept, holding that those who serve alcohol must take some responsibility for its downside; that it is unacceptable for a business to provide drinks to a person who is, for instance, underage, already intoxicated, or has a known drinking problem. They say "reasonable care" must be used by servers, who should do whatever is normal and prudent to foresee possible harm and protect others from it. (This idea, in legal terms, is called *foreseeability*.) This situation has prompted any number of "Responsible Alcohol Service" training programs and certifications for servers and bartenders, which is a good thing no matter what the legal wrangling over liability. You'll learn more about such programs later in this chapter.

Interestingly, dramshop laws may not apply to a catering staff serving alcohol that was purchased by a client, rather than by the catering company. However, there are plenty of other laws that do apply. There are several types of legal liability when it comes to alcohol service:

Third-party liability. An overall concept that the server or seller of the alcohol is just as much a part of the incident as the person who was harmed or the person who did the harm. A "third party" can be a bar, restaurant or caterer, individual server or bartender, among others.

Administrative liability. This applies to the holder of the liquor license. This is the penalty for breaking an alcohol-related law. It may result in a fine, a temporary suspension of a license, or even its complete revocation. The penalty is always levied against the third party.

Social host liability. This term is used in some states. It means that when an off-premise catering staff person serves a party guest, and that guest then injures or kills him- or herself or someone else, if the guest is deemed intoxicated under state law, the staff person, catering company, and party host could be named in lawsuits and be liable for a portion of the damages.

Criminal liability. This means the alcohol server has broken the law by being negligent or selling alcohol irresponsibly. Criminal charges can be filed against a licensed business, the individuals it employs, or even the host of a social gathering at which alcohol was served. Being found guilty of criminal liability usually means serving jail time in addition to paying fines.

Sometimes both civil and criminal cases are filed in the same incident. If so, they are decided independently. One court, or both, may convict.

It is the responsibility of off-premise caterers in each state to know the laws and follow them. Off-premise caterers should remember that there are legal costs even to prove noninvolvement and even when there is no liability on the part of the off-premise caterer or staff. Before you ever need it, it is wise to have a discussion with an attorney about these issues. He or she may also suggest additions (or a separate addendum) to your catering contracts to alert clients about your responsibilities—and theirs—when alcohol is served at functions that you cater. You should include a clause stating that your workers will refuse to serve minors or guests who are either intoxicated or clearly at risk of becoming intoxicated.

You can also purchase liquor liability insurance. Your insurance provider should have some valuable insight about your business risks and should explain exactly what is covered by your insurance policies.

Legal Definitions of Intoxication

As with liability laws, states also vary in their definitions of intoxication and how allegedly intoxicated persons are tested and charged. In any state, a person is considered "drunk" when his or her blood alcohol level is higher than the level permitted by law in that area. *Blood alcohol content (BAC) laws* varied quite a bit between states until 1999, when Congress passed a law that no state would receive federal dollars for highway maintenance unless its BAC level was at least .08. Today, almost all the states have set the level at .08; only a few use the .10 level.

What does this mean? The BAC figure is a percentage of the amount of alcohol in a person's bloodstream at the time he or she is tested. At a BAC level of .08, there is one drop of alcohol for every 80 drops of blood. At a BAC level of .10, there is one drop of alcohol for every 100 drops of blood. That may not sound like a lot, but alcohol is potent enough that a BAC of .30 could put someone into a coma, and higher levels can result in death.

The debate about acceptable BAC levels has been long and heated because so many factors determine how any particular human body will absorb alcohol. Gender, age, overall health and mental state, weight, medications, the type of alcohol, and whether it is ingested with food all have an impact on how quickly it is absorbed into the bloodstream.

BAC levels are used to determine convictions for drunken driving, usually known as DUI (driving under the influence) or DWI (driving while intoxicated). About half the states also have *per se laws* (from the Latin *per se*, meaning "by itself"). A per se law says a blood alcohol test is the only evidence needed to convict a person of a charge like drunken driving or public intoxication. An *administrative per se law* goes a little further, giving a law enforcement officer the power to immediately arrest or revoke the driver's license of anyone who refuses to take, or fails to pass, an alcohol breath test. In some states there are *presumptive laws*, which allow an arresting officer to make his or her own decision about a person's sobriety after the officer has administered a test at the scene. (You've seen these tests in movies, no doubt: An officer makes a person walk a straight line, touch a finger to the nose, answer questions, etc.) Drunken driving penalties vary widely among states, but one thing is certain—in the last 20 years, they've gotten a lot more stringent.

The other two types of laws that concern caterers and their staff members are drinking age laws and so-called *open container laws*. Every state's legal drinking age is 21, and there are severe penalties for serving alcohol to minors, even when they've evaded the law with fake identification. Most states also have a law that prohibits drinking while driving, or having open containers of alcohol in a vehicle. Remember this when someone wants to cork a partial bottle of wine and take it home from a party you are catering.

✕ *Responsible Alcohol Service*

The food and hospitality industries have been very active in promoting responsible service and consumption of alcohol. To be able to serve alcohol, your staff members are required in most states to take a course and pass a responsible beverage service test. Even if it's not a requirement, it's a good idea, and this type of training is readily available. Liquor distributors, insurance companies, law enforcement agencies, and state restaurant associations may offer courses or can recommend a video version. Encourage anyone who works for you, part-time or full-time, to take such a course and to sign a statement that they have completed it.

Many of the solutions offered in these courses are common sense:

- Encourage shorter cocktail hours. Rather than a one-hour cocktail time, serve drinks for half an hour, then immediately serve the meal.
- Be sure to serve plenty of attractive hors d'oeuvres at cocktail receptions. Cheeses, fried foods, and other hors d'oeuvres that are high in fat content are excellent choices because they help reduce the amount of alcohol that is absorbed into the system.
- Have plenty of delicious, attractive nonalcoholic beverages available, such as soft drinks, fresh juices, still and sparkling waters, a tropical punch, and/or nonalcoholic wines, beers, and champagnes. Make them look just as refreshing as the alcoholic drinks.
- Have servers pour wines for the guests, rather than placing the bottles on the table, and have servers tap beer kegs and do the pouring. This helps control the rate of consumption.
- Close the bars well before an event is over; schedule "last call" up to an hour before the official ending time of the party. This is already an accepted practice at most sporting events and concerts, and it's easier on your staff too.
- Serve plenty of coffee and pastries toward the end of an event. Coffee will not "sober up" a person who is already tipsy, but it will help slow the absorption of alcohol and is an alternative to drinking more.
- Instruct staff members never to allow guests to pour their own drinks, no matter how busy the bar area gets.
- Never pour double shots, and do not serve mixed drinks that contain two or more spirits (Cosmopolitan, Long Island Tea, Manhattan, Martini) at "last call." A person's BAC level can continue to rise even after he or she has stopped drinking, as the body processes the alcohol the person has already consumed.

Responsible service also means being vigilant and recognizing when someone appears to have been overserved. A good server or bartender will keep an eye on how many drinks a person has ordered and how those drinks appear to have impacted the drinker's personality. Everyone socializes differently, but there are a few common signs of intoxication:

- Alcohol almost always impairs motor skills. People who've had too much to drink may stagger, bump into things, fumble with objects, and just seem awkward. This inability to control balance and coordination is known as *ataxia*.
- A related effect is that the drinker's reaction time is slower. Words are slurred, sentences go unfinished, or the person can't remember what he or she was trying to say. At times a person can look and act sleepy.
- Alcohol causes most people to relax their inhibitions. They may become louder, more animated, boisterous, or affectionate; they may swear more or become argumentative. For many people, drinking brings emotions to the forefront—they laugh or cry more easily and without embarrassment.
- Judgment is impaired when a person drinks too much. At this point, people are less cautious—buying drinks for strangers, switching to a stronger drink, guzzling drinks instead of savoring them. A typical lapse in judgment is evident when they argue with anyone who tries to take their car keys from them: "I'm fine! Of course I can drive!"

The Beverage Law Institute in Tallahassee, Florida, is an organization that provides training and consulting services for selling alcoholic beverages. Here are just a few of its smart service tips:[1]

- Count drinks, but be aware that the guests may have been drinking elsewhere before they arrived.
- Chat briefly with people when they order their drinks.
- Purposely slow down the speed of service when guests are drinking and ordering rapidly.
- Delay service when there is already more than one drink per person on the table.
- Respect the wishes of those who indicate they do not want another drink. Suggest some nonalcoholic alternatives.
- Suggest foods and snack items when appropriate. At catered events, this is easy— the guest isn't paying extra for them!

Management Responsibilities

As a caterer, do not forget that it is not just the guests you are watching, but your staff members as well. Part of their work agreement with your company should include a signed statement that *they* will abide by the alcohol sales and service laws of your area, that they will not show up for work after drinking alcoholic beverages themselves, and that if caught drinking on the job or pilfering extra liquor meant for client functions, they will be terminated immediately.

In addition to overseeing the servers, there is plenty that a caterer/company owner can do to limit his or her liability on a job site. Simply being visible, or having a manager in the area where guests are being served, exhibits a sense of responsibility—that things are being taken care of. Understaffing big events is a serious mistake when alcohol is being served. It is far better to hire more workers than needed, so that identification can be checked and there are more "eyes" to watch for potential problems related to drinking.

At functions like weddings and family reunions, enlist the help of the hosts in a discreet way. Ask in advance (politely, of course) whether there is anyone about whom the host or family has a particular concern, and they will probably tell you, candidly, that Aunt Mabel or Uncle John may need some extra "watching." Assign someone to do this.

The other part of being a manager is being available to staff members who have a problem drinker on their hands and may need your assistance in dealing with the person directly or asking the host to assist in this role with an invited guest. The off-premise catering owner, manager, or supervisor should generally handle the actual "cut-off" procedure, with the support of the party host if possible. According to the "Learn2Serve" program created by HotelTraining.com, when refusing to serve someone, caterers should be diplomatic, avoid an audience, make direct eye contact, and be sure to have the support of security or other staff members in case of an altercation. It is also important to use nonjudgmental statements:

"I am sorry. I have served you as much as I am allowed."
"I am sorry. I am not allowed to serve people under age 21."
"I am sorry, but if I serve you another drink, we might lose our license" (or, "I might lose my job)."[2]

Do not allow the guest to bargain, intimidate, or argue with you. You have made a decision to refuse further service for good reasons, and you must stick with it. It is best to leave the table or immediate area after you have made your statement, which prevents your being drawn into explanations or arguments. You must also inform co-workers when a guest has been cut off, to prevent the person from simply ordering more alcohol from an unsuspecting staff member.

In rare cases an unruly guest must be asked to leave. It may be advisable to make the necessary transportation arrangements—call a taxi or arrange for the person to ride with another party guest. (Note that a guest cannot legally be detained.) In the event that an intoxicated guest drives away, notify the police with the make and model of the car, its license number, and the direction in which it was traveling. Just because the guest has left the party does not excuse you, or the party host, from liability if something terrible happens.

Each situation is different, and your presence as an owner or manager lends automatic authority in getting a problem solved. Trust your staff members. Back them up if they are challenged by a belligerent guest who wants more to drink when he or she is clearly overserved.

A caterer should always maintain a diary or log of alcohol-related incidents that includes significant details: date and time of the occurrence, action taken by management, witnesses to the occurrence, and any other significant details that may be supportive if the caterer is required to appear in court at a later time.

✕ *An Introduction to Beverages*

Off-premise caterers frequently assist with the service of alcoholic beverages. It is not necessary for off-premise caterers to be as knowledgeable about beverages as, for instance, a hotel bar manager, but some knowledge is necessary—the ingredients in a martini, a few basic drink recipes, and how to stock a typical off-premise catering bar. This section offers basic knowledge in regard to beverage types and ingredients.

Basic Beverage Vocabulary

This list is just an introduction to a highly technical industry. It includes major types of distilled spirits, terms for measuring and serving, and a few wine terms and definitions of common bar accessories and condiments.[3]

After dinner drink—A dessert drink, often sweet and creamy, with a liqueur base, ordered after a meal. People enjoy a liqueur by itself or with coffee or brandy, as an after-dinner drink.

Aperitif—A wine typically served before a meal to whet the appetite. It is usually a fortified wine, flavored with herbs and spices.

Bar sugar—Superfine sugar.

Bitters—Spirits flavored with tree bark, herbs, fruits (but never sugar). They are used in small quantities—just a few drops—in some mixed drinks. Examples: Campari, Angostura.

Blended whiskey—A blend must contain at least 20 percent straight whiskey, plus neutral spirits. The blend may be made of two whiskies and a neutral spirit. Blended whiskies do not have to be aged. Example: Seagram's 7 Crown. (See also *Scotch.*)

Bourbon—Whiskey distilled at not more than 160 proof, from a fermented mash of at least 51 percent corn (and usually other grains as well). It must be aged at least two years in new charred oak barrels. Examples: Jack Daniels, Jim Beam, Maker's Mark, Knob Creek, Wild Turkey.

Brandy—A distilled spirit that is made from wine or other fermented fruit juice. Examples: Armagnac, Calvados.

Brown goods—Industry nickname for spirits that are dark in color and have hearty flavors, like whiskies and brandies.

Call brand—A brand of liquor (usually a bit more upscale than the *well brands*) "called for" or requested by customers when they order a drink.

Canadian whisky—Imported from Canada, it is usually a blended whisky, aged at least three years, and has a reputation for being smooth and light-bodied. Examples: Canadian Club and Seagram's VO. (Note that whiskey with an "e" is usually a product of the United States or Ireland; Canada and Scotland spell it without the "e." A few American brands with Scottish heritage also remove the "e.")

Chaser—A liquid served at the same time as a shot of alcohol, to be drunk immediately after taking the shot. Usually, a chaser is ice water or beer.

Coarse salt—A "chunkier" type of salt used for putting on the rims of glasses for drinks like Margaritas and Bloody Marys. Also called *Margarita salt* or *kosher salt.*

Cognac—Brandy produced in the Cognac region of France. Examples: Courvoisier, Hine, Martell.

Dash—A measurement of about 10 drops, equal to one-eighth teaspoon.

Dasher—A dispenser on the neck of a bottle of bitters, Tabasco, etc., that limits their output when poured to only a few drops at a time.

Dry—This term varies, depending on the type of alcohol being referred to. A "dry" Martini means one that contains very little dry vermouth. A "dry" Manhattan or Rob Roy means using dry vermouth instead of sweet vermouth. A "dry" wine means one that is not sweet.

Free-pour—A method of preparing cocktails without exactly measuring the ingredients. Only truly experienced bartenders should be allowed to free-pour, because it can be wasteful and result in drinks of inconsistent strength and flavor.

Gin—A neutral spirit flavored with juniper berries for a strong, aromatic taste. Examples: Gordon's, Beefeater, Bombay, Tanqueray.

Irish whiskey—Grain spirits made in Ireland from malted and unmalted barley in copper pot stills. These whiskeys are triple-distilled, making an extremely smooth drink that appeals to whiskey connoisseurs. Examples: Black Bush, Bushmill's Original, Jameson, John Power & Son.

Jigger—The glass or stainless steel cup used to measure liquor. The size varies, but $7/8$ ounce is the most popular. This size allows the bartender to pour a little extra, yet still keep the alcohol at 1 ounce.

Liqueur—A brandy or other spirit, sweetened and infused with natural flavors (often fruits and spices). Liqueurs are usually strong, sweet, and syrupy. Examples: Drambuie, Kahlua, Galliano, Grappa.

Neat—A term for whiskey or Scotch served undiluted, at room temperature, usually in a small glass (or shot glass) with a separate glass of ice water. Also called "straight."

On the rocks—Served over ice.

Pourer—An opened bottle of liquor is capped with this stainless steel spout, which reduces the flow of liquor to a controllable speed or a pre-set amount for the convenience of the bartender. Pourers must be cleaned regularly by soaking them in water.

Rum—Liquor distilled from the fermented juice of sugar cane, sugar cane syrup, sugar cane molasses, or other sugar cane product. Examples: Bacardi, Appleton Estate, Mount Gay, Captain Morgan, Ron Rico.

Rye—A type of whiskey distilled at not more than 160 proof from a fermented mash of at least 51 percent rye (a grain) and aged at least two years in new charred oak barrels. Example: Old Overholt.

Scotch—Whiskey that is imported from Scotland. It is usually blended, and very distinctively flavored because the grains from which it is made are dried over peat fires, giving them a unique, smoky taste. Examples: Ballantine's, Cutty Sark, Dewar's White Label, Chivas Regal, Johnnie Walker.

Simple syrup—A sweetener for mixed drinks, made of 1 part sugar and 1 part water. Bartenders generally make their own simple syrup.

Single malt Scotch—Unblended whisky made in Scotland from malted barley. Flavors range from soft and light, to full-bodied and soft. The most exclusive (and expensive) of these are the single malt, single cask scotches, which come from one barrel and are unblended, even with other barrels at the same distillery. Examples of single malts: Glenfiddich, Glenlivet, Glenfarclas, Laphroiag. (Connoisseurs could list them for days!)

Sparkling wine—A wine that bubbles when it is poured, because it contains carbon dioxide. In inexpensive wines, the carbon dioxide is injected into still wine; in expensive French Champagnes (and other wines made in the Champagne method), the carbon dioxide builds naturally in the bottle as the wine ferments.

Splash—A slang term for a unit of measure equal to about one-quarter ounce; or a request that a drink be mixed with water.

Squeeze—Refers to a small piece of lemon or lime which, when served as a garnish, is first "squeezed" before being dropped into the drink. Also see *Twist*.

Still wine—Wine that does not contain carbonation. Most wines are "still wines."

Straight—Undiluted. See *Neat*.

Tequila—A distinctively flavored, relatively low-proof spirit made in Mexico from the fermented juices of the blue agave plant. The tequila made from 100 percent blue agave is known as tequila puro; there is also *mixto* (at least 51 percent blue agave, with sugars and spices added) and *mescal* (made from other types of agave, or not made in one of the five government-sanctioned growing regions for tequila). Examples: Jose Cuervo, Sauza.

Top shelf—The term used for the highest-quality (and usually most expensive) liquor that the bar stocks. Also known as *premium call*.

Twist—A garnish made from a slice of citrus fruit peel, which is "twisted" over the top of the drink to release a hint of zest before being dropped into the glass.

Vodka—A neutral spirit, which is not aged, has no color, and has been filtered (usually through activated carbon) to remove any aroma or taste. Examples: Absolut, Aquavit, Grey Goose, Smirnoff, Stolichnaya.

Well brand—What the bar pours as its "standard" spirit when a customer does not ask for a specific brand. Also called *house brand* or *pouring brand*.

White goods—Industry nickname for colorless spirits: gin, rum, vodka, tequila.

Which Brands to Stock?

Off-premise caterers are frequently asked to recommend to clients those items that should be provided at bars. Preferences vary, depending on locale and the trendiness of particular drinks. Bourbon is more popular in Kentucky than in the northern United States; wines are more popular in California than in West Virginia. Therefore, our suggestions are intended to be generic guidelines. Regional differences (and clients' budgets, of course) will play a major role in any caterer's final recommendations.

Basic liquors for any bar in the United States are the "building blocks" for most mixed drinks: bourbon, gin, rum, vodka, tequila, plus Scotch and Canadian whiskies. Within each of these types, there are three "categories" of items:

■ A relatively inexpensive "well brand"
■ A medium-priced "call brand" with a good reputation
■ A more exclusive "top shelf" or premium brand

Any liquor retailer or wholesaler will be glad to share information about which brand belongs in which category, but an experienced bartender should certainly know that much already. An interesting trend in recent years is that people tend to drink less, but drink better quality liquors. This means growth for the "super-premium brands," and the rarer "boutique" Scotches, gins, and so forth. Ask about the preferences of the host and his or her intended guests before stocking the bar. The sophistication of the clientele will also alert you to the need for stocking specialty items like cordials, brandies and Cognacs, and liqueurs.

There are also common mixers that will vary with the drink menu you develop—seltzer, bottled water, 7UP, Coca-Cola, tonic water, Bloody Mary mix, orange juice, and others. Garnishes and types of glassware will also be determined by your drink menu.

Basic Wine Terminology

A knowledge of wine can be a tremendous help in satisfying clients' needs. Off-premise caterers should learn all they can about wines, especially how to pair wines with food selections. A knowledge of wine is easy and fun to obtain. There are numerous wine-tasting groups around the country that meet for meals and discussions, and they welcome enthusiastic newcomers. Newspapers and magazines frequently print articles about wine, and there are also excellent specialty journals you can subscribe to—*Wine Spectator, Spirit Journal, Food and Wine, Gourmet*—to name just a few.

Remember, your clients often know next to nothing about wine. They are depending on you to make selections that their guests will enjoy, and that will fit the budget for the event. If you lack a knowledge of wine or are just beginning to learn, at least be wise enough to ask if your clients have any preferences. You'll have an easier time discussing wine with clients when you know a few of the basic terms. The following list of terms is by no means all-inclusive. For the most part, we discuss actual wine (and grape) names later in this chapter. We've made exceptions here for a few French wine terms and regions that may otherwise cause some confusion.[4]

Acidity—The tartness or sharpness of a wine's flavor; a very necessary characteristic of wine.

Aging—All wine ages (grows older) in the bottle. Most red wines, and many whites, will improve, becoming deeper in color and richer in flavor as they age if they are stored correctly. Some wines are made specifically to be aged several years before drinking; others are not.

Alcohol—The alcohol content of a wine intensifies its other characteristics and makes the wine taste smooth and full-bodied. Most wines are 10–13 percent alcohol by volume; by law in the United States, wine cannot exceed 14 percent alcohol unless it is labeled "fortified."

Appellation—An area of France in which a specific type of grape is grown and used to make a specific type of wine.

Aroma—The fruity or flowery scent of a wine.

Balance—The term for a wine's overall mixture of acid, alcohol, tannin, and natural sweetness.

Big—A wine described as "big" usually has a powerful flavor.

Blush—A wine that is pink or salmon in color. Rosés, Tavels, and white zinfandels are examples of "blush wines."

Body—The "feel" of the wine in the mouth, which is a result of its alcohol, sugar, and glycerin content. You'll see wines referred to as light-bodied, medium-bodied, and full-bodied.

Bordeaux—One of the five major wine-producing regions of France—and here's where it gets complicated. Within Bordeaux, there are more than 50 regions, each with its own unique wines that bear the names of the towns where they are made. Some of the most famous red Bordeaux areas are Medoc, Pomerol, and St.-Émilion. A wine that is labeled "Bordeaux" is a red wine, and it's usually a blend of grapes (Cabernet, Cabernet Franc, and Merlot). There are also white Bordeaux wines. Some of the most famous whites are Graves and Sauternes, and they are made from Sémillon or Sauvignon grapes.

Bouquet—Similar to aroma, this term refers to the more complex, interesting scent of a wine. A wine's bouquet can be fruity, flowery, smoky, "forward," "clean," earthy, and so on. The terms are as colorful as the wine labels themselves, and there is no "right" or "wrong" in describing what you smell.

Breathe—Wines come in contact with air when they are opened. This slight oxidation, occurring from the time the bottle is opened and poured until it is sipped, is known as "breathing." It's also called *aeration*. Some people feel that letting an older wine (especially a red) sit for a few minutes after opening gets rid of any musty odor it may have as a result of sitting in the bottle for years, but it is really not necessary. The wine gets plenty of air as it is poured into glasses. (If your clients are wine aficionados, you may ask if they'd like the wines to breathe before serving. It will, if nothing else, impress them that you asked!)

Brut—A French word that indicates the driest (not sweet) style of Champagne.

Burgundy—Another of the famous French wine-growing regions, Burgundy is best known for the wine that bears its name, a red made from Pinot Noir grapes. Other famous wines from the Burgundy region include Côte de Nuits, Côte Chalonnais, and two wines made from the Gamay grape—Beaujolais and Nouveau Beaujolais. Dry white Burgundies are made from the Chardonnay grape and named for their specific areas: Côte de Beaune, Maconnais, and Chablis are just a few. In the United States, the term "Burgundy" has unfortunately come to mean a generic red wine. The "real things" are anything but.

Capsule—The protective sheath of metal or plastic over the cork and neck of a wine bottle. It helps keep the cork from drying out.

Carafe—A clear glass container for serving wines. Available in several sizes, the most popular being the liter and half-liter sizes.

Chablis—A true Chablis is a lovely, dry white wine from the French Burgundy region. However, in the United States, the term has been used for years to refer to a generic white wine. When most guests order "Chablis," they may simply mean the house white wine.

Champagne—Although the term is used for any sparkling wine in the United States, it legally (and rightly) belongs to sparkling wines made in the Champagne district of France, and the word is capitalized when written.

Charmat process—Also called the "Charmat bulk process," this is the way to make inexpensive sparkling wine by sidestepping the lengthy aging process of true Champagne production. The second fermentation (that makes the wine bubbly) occurs in a large tank instead of individual bottles, as a result of injecting the wine with carbon dioxide before bottling it.

Claret—The British term for a red Bordeaux wine.

Classified growths—The French don't just legislate wine regions, they also have a sophisticated system for "classifying" some wines based on their overall quality and reputation. The classification information can be found on the wine label. (See the following section, "Appellation Systems.")

Corkage fee—The amount charged by a restaurant to open bottles that have been brought in but not purchased from the restaurant. A caterer may charge a corkage fee (a few dollars per bottle) to open wines provided by the customer.

Corked—A description of a wine that has gone bad, usually because some bacteria on (or in) the cork have caused the wine to have a "musty" or otherwise unpleasant odor.

Cru—The French word for "growth." (See the following section, "Appellation Systems.")

Decant—A very old wine often contains sediment. It should be poured slowly and gently from the bottle into a glass decanter or carafe, to leave the sediment in the bottle. Decanting is a rather showy process. It's sometimes done over a lit candle so that the pourer can clearly see inside the neck of the bottle and stop pouring before the sediment is poured.

Dessert wine—Any sweet wine served at the end of a meal may be considered a dessert wine, but the name also refers to a class of fortified wines that includes port, sherry, marsala, and others.

Dosage—When Champagne is being made, it is stored cork-down so that the sediment created in the bottle is collected at the top. It is "popped out" before the final cork and wire cage are put on, and a bit more liquid must be added to bring the wine back up to full-bottle level. This liquid, called the *dosage*, may be wine with a bit of sugar added, or brandy.

Dry—A term that means the opposite of sweet. It *does not* mean sour!

Finish—The aftertaste of a wine.

Flinty—A term you may hear that describes the taste of a very dry wine, such as a true Chablis from France, or a dry-style Riesling from the Mosel area of Germany.

Fortified—Wines to which brandy or other spirits have been added (which increases their alcohol content). Ports and sherries are examples of fortified wines.

Jug wine—A simple, inexpensive table wine nicknamed for its large "jug" bottle.

Late harvest—Very sweet wines made from grapes that have been allowed to overripen on their vines and even be affected by a mold called *Botrytis cinerea* ("noble rot").

Legs—When a wine is swirled in the glass, the streams that run down the sides of glass indicate the presence of glycerin. A wine "with legs" is usually smooth and full-bodied.

Maderized—This term refers primarily to white or rosé wines that have oxidized, or passed their prime, and are turning slightly brown or orange. You don't want to serve a maderized wine.

Magnum—A wine bottle holding twice the amount of a full (750 millimeter) bottle of wine. Magnums are showy and fun to open on festive occasions.

Meritage—A wine that has been blended from different types of grapes instead of a single, predominant varietal.

Methode champenoise—The traditional French method of making Champagne, in which the wine is made, then yeast and sugar are added to prompt a secondary fermentation (inside the bottle) that creates the bubbles (carbon dioxide) as a byproduct.

Non–Vintage (NV)—A term used for wines (usually Champagnes) made from grapes grown in different years, so a single year cannot be used on the label.

Port—This is the "national wine" of Portugal, a fortified blend to which neutral grape brandy is added during fermentation. The resulting wine is sweet and alcoholic (about 20 percent alcohol) and generally served as a dessert wine.

Punt—The indentation in the bottom of a wine bottle. Its shape adds strength to the bottle, and wine is correctly served when the server places his or her thumb in the punt and bends the bottle forward.

Rosé—A pink, peach, or rose-colored wine. Rosé is made from red grapes, but the skins (which give wine its color) are separated from the juice shortly after the grapes are crushed, before they have time to impart their rich, red color. (Also see *Blush.*)

Sangria—A wine-based drink concocted of wine, fruit juice, and sugar water or soda water, served chilled.

Sec—The French word for "dry," which, in Champagnes, means a slight sweetness.

Sediment—Some types of wine, especially older reds, contain natural deposits of solids that drift to the bottom of the bottle. Sediment is harmless but unsightly and may require that the wine be decanted.

Sekt—The German term for sparking wine.

Sherry—A rich, often amber-colored wine served as an aperitif. Sherry is made by letting air oxidize the wine as it is aging, then adding brandy to it after fermentation. True sherries are always imported from Spain. Their flavors range from very dry to very sweet, and they are high in alcohol content (about 18 percent).

Sommelier—A person who has been trained to serve wine; the "wine steward" in a restaurant.

Split—An individual-size bottle (usually of Champagne), 6 ounces in volume.

Spumante—The Italian term for sparkling wine.

Still wine—Wine without carbon dioxide bubbles.

Structure—A description of the four main components of a wine's flavor: acidity, alcohol, tannin, and sugar (or sweetness).

Sulfites—A byproduct as grapes ferment into wine is *sulfur dioxide.* It does a lot of good things for the winemaking process, including killing bacteria and preventing spoilage; however, a small number of people are sensitive to these sulfites or have allergic reactions to them. Hence, the government warning label on wine bottles.

"Swirl and spit"—A term describing what is done at wine tastings; the taster swirls the wine around to aerate it by moving the glass in a circular motion; after it is tasted, the wine is spit into a "dump bucket" rather than being swallowed by the taster. This enables people at tasting events to try many wines without imbibing too much.

Tannin—The component in wine that gives an astringent or slightly bitter taste. It comes from the skins and stems of the grapes when they are crushed and adds to the overall character of the wine. Tannins also help preserve the wine. They mellow, or become less harsh, as the wine ages. (A wine that is opened too young and is still "big" and bitter may be referred to as "tannic.")

Tartrates—These are tiny, clear crystals (of tartaric acid) that form naturally in some wines as they age, or in white wines that have been stored in very cold conditions. You usually see them at the bottom of the bottle or clinging to the cork. They are harmless, but many consumers assume there are bits of glass in the bottle and refuse it.

Tastevin—The small silver cup a sommelier wears around his or her neck, usually on a ribbon. It is used mostly "for show." A bit of wine is poured into it so that the color and clarity of the wine can be observed before it is served.

Varietal—A type of grape. A "varietal wine" is a wine made primarily of a certain variety (type) of grape. In most European countries, in order to legally use a varietal name, the wine must contain at least 85 percent of that particular grape. In France, it's 100 percent; in the United States, it's 75 percent.

Vin—French for "wine." Pronounced "van."

Vino—The Spanish and Italian word for "wine." Pronounced "VEE-noh."

Vintage—The year in which the grapes are picked is its "vintage," which is put on the label.

Vintner—A winemaker.

Wein—The German word for "wine." Pronounced "vine."

Yeast—This is the microorganism that causes grapes to ferment and become wine. Yeast is found naturally on grape skins, but winemakers would rather control their own products by adding the types of yeast they prefer.

At this writing, we can also recommend two extensive and useful "wine dictionaries" available on-line at no charge: the "Wine Glossary" at www.virtualitalia.com, and "The Living Wine Dictionary" (where you can hear voices pronounce the terms) at www.stratsplace.com. The latter is also a good site for overall information on wine from different countries—shots of labels, maps and descriptions of regions, and so on.

A great overall reference book for caterers is *The Wine Bible* by Karen MacNeil, (Workman Publishing Company, 2001). This reference text of more than 900 pages covers everything from assessing and tasting wines to winemaking, grape varietals, and an in-depth analysis of all the world's great wine-growing countries and regions. This is a "must read" for any caterer who is serious about learning more about wines.

✕ *Appellation Systems*

Every country that makes any amount of wine has its own minimum legal requirements for making and accurately labeling wines. These are usually known as *appellation systems*, after the original French laws. Even if you know little about the specific wines, the appellation information on their labels will give you a clue about their overall quality—where their own country "rates" them among its native wines or, at least, that the wine meets the country's legal standards. Here are just a few of the appellation rules and terms for five popular winemaking nations—there are lots of others.

France

Appellation Contrôlée—(Or Appellation d'Origine Contrôlée; you can refer to it in the wine trade as "AOC.") This phrase on a French wine label indicates that the wine meets the government standards for that type of wine. The standards specify alcohol content, type of grapes used to make the wine, how long it must be aged, and so forth, and that the grapes were grown and the wine was made in that specific geographic area.

In descending order from top-of-the-line to pleasant table wines, there are several classifications, but these are the most common:

- Grand Premier (gronn PREM-ee-ay) Cru
- Grand (gronn) Cru
- Premier (PREM-ee-ay) Cru
- Villages (vill-AZH)

In addition, the famous Bordeaux wines from Medoc are officially classified according to a complex system that was created in 1855 when top wine brokers were asked to "rate" each winemaking chateau by their perception of its quality. Times have changed, but this venerable system is still used to describe these wineries as "First Growth," "Second Growth," and so on, down to "Fifth Growth."

Rather than memorize the rankings, you can check a Bordeaux label to see if it contains one of these less confusing terms:

- **Château**—means the wine is a product of an individual vineyard, made and bottled at the winery (chateau) whose name is on the label. "Mis en bouitelles au Château" means "bottled at the winery." Like "estate-bottled" Californians, these are usually the top-quality Bordeaux wines.
- **Proprietary**—means you're getting a table wine of good enough and consistent enough quality that it carries a specific winery name.
- **Regional**—means the wine comes from a particular region. It's the least expensive, locally made wine.

Another French word you'll note on some wine labels is *monopole*. It's like a brand name—it means a single vineyard or exporter owns the particular name of the wine and/or winery and is responsible for the quality of wines produced there.

Germany

The German law was passed in 1971. It classifies wines as follows:

QmP—*Qualitatswein mit Pradikat* is the top quality designation. The winemaker is not allowed to chapitalize (add sugar during fermentation).

QbA—*Qualitatswein bestimmer Anbaugebiete* (no, you'll never have to *say* it!) indicates that this is a "quality wine" that comes from one of Germany's 11 wine districts.

Landwein—A table wine that is a little better than average in quality. This designation is seldom seen.

Tafelwein—The German version of jug wine, which is usually not exported and does not have a winery name on the label.

QmP wines are subclassified as follows:

- **Kabinett—**A wine made from grapes that have ripened normally.
- **Spatlese—**Translated as "late picking." These wines are made from grapes left on the vines longer than a normal harvest, resulting in a more intense sweetness.
- **Auslese—**Translated as "out picked," this means the grapes were left on the vines longer than normal, *and* handpicked bunch by bunch.
- **Beerenauslese—**Translated as "berries out picked," this means that individual grapes were picked at the peak of overripeness to create a sweet, rich wine. These wines are not made very often, and they're quite expensive.
- **Trockenbeerenauslese—**The added term *trocken* (dried) indicates that the resulting handpicked grapes make even richer, sweeter (and more expensive) wines when they're practically raisins. It doesn't mean the *wine* is dry; it means the *grapes* were dried—an important difference!
- **Eiswein—**Translated as "ice wine." This wine is made by letting the overripe grapes freeze on the vine and crushing them while still frozen. This process produces a real flavor intensity.

Italy

Italian wine standards went into effect in 1963 and are called "DOC" and "DOCG." Here's the difference—the original *Denominazione di Origine Controllata* spells out the usual parameters: the boundaries of each wine-growing region, a maximum amount that can be harvested per acre, the types of grapes and percentages that must be used to label a wine with a varietal name, and some minimum requirements for aging and alcohol content. Then a slightly more stringent set of rules was added, with the word "*Guarantita*" after the "DOC." This means a tasting board checks the finer wines and "guarantees" their quality. Thus, a DOCG wine will probably cost more than a DOC wine.

Interestingly, Italian wineries can choose not to participate in the system, so there may be some that don't have these designations but are still excellent wines. A new appellation created in the 1990s, called *Indicazione Geografica Tipica* (IGT), is not nearly as stringent as the other designations and was established to bring some of the non-participating wineries back into the fold.

For most Italian vinos, quality clues on the labels include these terms:

- **Classico Superiore—**means the wine comes from a specific wine-producing region (not a neighboring area), that it has been aged longer than the standard mini-

mums required by law, and that it may have a higher alcohol content than the lesser-quality wines of its type.
- **Classico**—means the wine comes from a specific wine-producing region.
- **Riserva**—means "reserve," indicating that the wine has been aged longer than the minimum time required by law.

Only a few types of the many Italian wines are tasted by the DOCG tasting boards: Albana di Romagna (the only white on the list), Barbaresco, Barolo, Brunello di Montalcino, Chianti, and Vino Nobile di Montepulciano.

Spain

The Spanish wine appellation system has more than 50 DOs, or *Denominacions de Origen*. The wine label terms that offer quality-related meaning relate only to red wines. They are:

- **Gran Reserva**—means the wine is aged in oak barrels at least two years, and in the bottle for at least three years. Top quality; in some years, no wines are selected for this designation.
- **Reserva**—means the wine has been in oak barrels for a year, then in the bottle for at least two, before being sold.
- **Crianza**—means the wine has been in oak barrels for one year and in the bottle for one year. This designation usually refers to inexpensive Spanish table wines.

Other common terms you'll see on Spanish wine labels are *bodegas* (which means "winery") and *cosecha* (which means "harvest").

United States

U.S. winemaking regions are called American Viticultural Areas, or AVAs for short. Many AVA rules are related to percentages, as you'll see in this quick overview:

- To label a wine with a varietal (grape) name, it must contain at least 75 percent of that type of grape.
- At least 85 percent of the grapes must come from a specific AVA for the wine-maker to include the name of the AVA ("Napa Valley," "Sonoma Valley," etc.) on the label.
- If the winery wants to include the name of an individual vineyard, 95 percent of the grapes must be from that vineyard.
- When a wine is vintage-dated (specifies a year on the label), 95 percent of the grapes must have been grown in that year.

Marketing terms like "Reserve" or "Vintner's Reserve" are often used on American wine labels, but they don't have any legal meaning. Wines sold in America also require government warning labels that caution about drinking while pregnant, that drinking alcohol impairs one's ability to drive a car or operate machinery, and that drinking alcoholic beverages may cause "health problems."

✕ *Wines of the World—A (Very) Short Course*

Wine appreciation is one of those topics that make it clear that the more you know, the more there is to know. The next few pages are an attempt to simplify and highlight. Of the 24,000 or so names for grape varietals, these nine are considered "classics":

WHITE GRAPES	RED GRAPES
Chardonnay	Cabernet Sauvignon
Chenin Blanc	Merlot
Riesling	Pinot Noir
Sauvignon Blanc	Syrah
Sémillon	

France

The major wine-producing regions of France, in order of most prominent to least prominent, are:

Bordeaux
Champagne
Burgundy
Beaujolais
The Rhone
The Loire
Alsace
Languedoc-Roussillon
Provence

Bordeaux. Although the very top Bordeaux wines are renowned worldwide (Château Margaux, Château Lafite, etc.), these make up only a small percentage of the region's output. Most Bordeaux are neither famous nor expensive, but instead are good dinner wines for everyday use. They are about elegance and intensity of flavor, rarely massive or powerful. The leading appellations (grape-growing areas) are:

APPELLATION	WINE STYLE
Barsac	White, both dry and sweet
Graves	White and red
Margaux	Red
Pauillac	Red
Pessac-Leognan	White and red
Pomerol	Red
St.-Èmilion	Red
St.-Estèphe	Red
St.-Julien	Red
Sauternes	White, both dry and sweet

Names to know: A few of the Bordeaux wines to taste and become familiar with are:

WINERY NAME	WINE TYPE
Château Carbonnieux	Classic white graves
Château La Louviere	White graves
Château Laville Haut-Brion	White, very elegant
Château de Pez	St.-Estèphe
Château Gruaud-Larose	St.-Julien
Château Petrus	Pomerol, elegant and rich
Château Pichon-Longueville	Pauillac
Château d'Yquem	Sauternes, France's most exalted dessert wines

Champagne. True Champagne comes only from one region, also called Champagne, about 90 miles northeast of Paris. Champagnes are blends of many still wines. They are produced by a complex process involving the addition of yeast and a bit of sugar to wine that has already been bottled, to prompt a secondary fermentation in which natural carbon dioxide is created and trapped inside each bottle to become the bubbles in the "bubbly."

On their labels, Champagnes are categorized by sweetness. The words don't literally match the actual descriptions of the flavor, but they are traditional.

LABEL TERM	WHICH MEANS
Extra Brut	Very, very dry
Brut	Dry
Extra Dry	Off-dry
Sec	Slightly sweet
Demi-Sec	Sweet
Doux	Very sweet

Most Champagne is clear to straw or light golden in color and is made from Chardonnay, Pinot Noir, and Pinot Meunier grapes. Blanc de Blancs Champagne ("white from whites") is made entirely from Chardonnay grapes. Rosé champagnes, with their beautiful colors and luscious flavors, are considered prizes among those who know their Champagnes.

Names to know: Some of the best known and most readily available Champagnes include Bollinger, Dom Perignon, Krug, Laurent-Perrier, Louis Rodederer, Moet & Chandon, Mumm, Perrier-Jouet, Piper-Heidsieck, Pol Roger, Pommery, Taittinger, and Veuve Cliquot. Also, for great value, try Billecart-Salmon if you can find it.

Burgundy. Burgundy is a fairly small wine region in central eastern France, which makes some of the most sought-after (read "expensive") and exquisite wines. Top white Burgundies are all made from the Chardonnay grape, and the top reds come from the Pinot Noir grape.

The term *domaine,* used in Burgundy, is not precisely equivalent to the term *château,* used in Bordeaux. In Bordeaux, a château is a single estate composed of vineyards surrounding a building or a house. In Burgundy, a *domaine* is a collection of vineyard parcels, often extremely small and scattered throughout many villages. The winery will, in fact, make a separate wine from each. Burgundy's wine regions include:

APPELLATION	WINE STYLE
Chablis	Whites
Côte d'Or	Whites and reds, both renowned (famous producer Domaine de la Romanée-Conti)
	Cote de Nuits reds (famous producers Gevrey-Chambertin, Nuits-St.-Georges, Vosne-Romanée)
Côte de Beaune	Reds (famous producers Aloxe-Corton, Chassagne-Montrachet, Pommard, Santenay)
Côte Chalonnaise	Mostly reds; good bargain wines
Maconnais	Inexpensive whites (famous producer Pouilly Fuisse)

Beaujolais

Beaujolais is part of Burgundy, but it's farther south than the other regions, the climates are dissimilar, and the grapes are different. Beaujolais is as lighthearted as Burgundy is serious. All Beaujolais is made from Gamay, a grape that produces light, soft, fruity wines.

Beaujolais Nouveau is different from its cousin. It is the youthful, grapey, slightly spritzy first wine of the Beaujolais harvest, bottled specifically to drink promptly in celebration of the harvest. Many restaurants and caterers hold parties each November (the third Thursday of the month) when the first cases of "Nouveau" arrive from France.

Wine labeled "Beaujolais" is the basic wine. The next level is Beaujolais-Villages, which is a notch better in quality and comes from 39 villages in the hilly midsection of the region. Beaujolais Crus is the best; it comes from 10 special villages located on steep granite hills in the northern part of Beaujolais.

Names to know: Bouchard, Drouhin, Georges Duboeuf, Janin, Jadot, and Kermit Lynch.

The Rhône. The Rhône Valley in southeast France is divided into two parts, northern and southern. Red wines dominate the region, although whites and rosés are made there too. The most famous northern Rhône reds are Côte-Rotie, Hermitage, and Croze-Hermitage, all made from the Syrah grape. The most famous southern red is Châteauneuf-du-Pape ("Château of the Pope"), which is also the wine type with the highest alcohol content (a minimum of 13 percent by French DOC regulation). Southern Rhône wines are made from lesser-known grapes—Grenache, Mourvedre, and Cinsault—blended with some Syrah. The southern Rhône is also the home of Tavel, a dry rosé wine made from Grenache.

Names to know: M. Chapoutier, E. Guigal, Alain Graillot, and Paul Jaboulet. In recent years, a younger "crop" of California winemakers have experimented with great success with Rhône-style wines and grape varietals. You may hear them referred to as the "Rhône Rangers," but the true Rhône wines are still French in origin.

The Loire. The Loire is one of the largest and most diverse winemaking regions in France. Virtually every type of wine is made there—still and sparkling, dry and sweet, red, white, and rosé. The signature characteristic of all Loire wines is their zesty acidity. The leading white grapes of the Loire—Chenin Blanc and Sauvignon Blanc—make wines so extraordinary that they are the world's standard-bearers for these grapes.

Loire wines to know are:

APPELLATION	WINE STYLE
Pouilly-Fumé	Sauvignon Blanc, crisp and concentrated in flavor
Muscadet	Melon (unusual grape), dry and light
Sancerre	Sauvignon Blanc, with characteristics of both Pouilly-Fumé and Muscadet
Vouvray	Chenin Blanc, from semidry to sweet; some Sparkling Vouvrays

Alsace. The wines of Alsace are predominantly rich, dry whites. This region grows some of the same grape varietals grown in Germany—Riesling, Gewürztraminer, and Pinot Blanc—but the resulting French wines are big-bodied, concentrated in flavor, and higher in alcohol content than their German counterparts. Alsace wines often contain a dramatic streak of acidity and are not meant to be aged more than five years.

Almost all Alsatian wines are blends of wines from many tiny vineyards. Most grape growers have only a few acres and sell their wares to shippers who produce, bottle, and market the wines under the shipper's name.

Names to know: Domaine Marcel Deiss, Domaine Weinbach, Hugel & Fils, and F.E. Trimbach.

Languedoc-Roussillon. The wines of Languedoc-Roussillon are among the most exciting and best wine values in France (possibly because the name of the region trips people up). At any rate, the Languedoc produces about 40 percent of all French wine, more than in the entire United States. A wide variety of grapes are grown, from Mediterranean varietals like Syrah and Grenache, to internationally known varietals like Cabernet Sauvignon and Chardonnay, to lesser-known but interesting grapes like Carignan and Oeillade.

The area is in far southern France and includes 34 appellations. Roussillon, the closest appellation to Spain, produces some of the same types of wine, including an unusual dessert wine called Banyuls from a village of the same name. It's made from late-harvest Grenache grapes and, by law, must contain at least 15 percent alcohol.

Names to know: Abbaye de Valmagne, Château de Beaulieu, Château Pech Celeyran, Domaine Rosés, Jeanjean, Maison Guinot.

Provence. Provence is in the far southeastern corner of France along the Mediterranean Sea and has only recently emerged as a serious wine-producing region. The two main winemaking areas here are Bandol and Côtes de Provence.

Only about 5 percent of the wines in Bandol are white, but they are prized by collectors for their excellence. The area is known for its big, dramatic red wines.

More than half the output in Côtes de Provence are zesty, refreshing rosés, perfect for warm-weather meals. The reds in this part of France are just passable.

Three Provençal wines to try are Routas Coquelicot Vin de Pays du Var (white); Domaine Ott Château de Selle, La Deesse (rosé); and Domaine de Trevallon Vin de Pays des Bouches du Rhône (red).

Italy

There are 900,000 registered vineyards in Italy and more than 1,000 documented grape varieties grown here. Italy is the source of almost half of all the table wines imported to the United States; much of it is "cheap and cheerful," of good value, and great to drink with casual cuisine. However, the Italian wines that knowledgeable wine drinkers get excited about tend to come from Piedmont, Tuscany, and three northeastern regions known collectively as Tre Venezie.

Piedmont. Two of Italy's DOCG-rated wines—the majestic reds Barolo and Barbaresco—come from Piedmont. Like great red Bordeaux, they can be aged a decade or more. They are made from the luscious Nebbiolo grape, and they're "big," with high alcohol contents (13 percent).

There are also lighter and equally sophisticated reds made here, from the Barbera and Dolcetto varietals. The Dolcetto wines may be compared to the French Beaujolais style, and they're usually bargain priced; the Barberas are more like the Côtes du Rhone style.

Names to know: Antoniolo, Bersano, Fontanafredda, Gaja, B. Giacosa, and Marcarini.

Tre Venezie. Together, the three regions of northeast Italy that make up Tre Venezie (Veneto, Trentino-Alto Adige, and Friuli-Venezia Giulia) produce mostly red wines, but they are known worldwide for their vibrant and racy whites. This area is also renowned for its sophisticated, modern winemaking techniques and high standards. The wines for which each region is best known are:

REGION	VARIETAL
Veneto	Bardolino
	Soave
	Valpolicella
Trentino-Alto Adige	Shiava
	Teroldego
	Chardonnay
	Pinot Blanc
	Sauvignon Blanc
Friuli-Venezia Giulia	Pinot Grigio
	Chardonnay
	Tocai (Tokay)

Tre Venezie is located on the sunny side of the Alps, which makes for perfect grape-growing conditions. It is also the home of two of Italy's leading wine schools and the country's most important wine trade show, Vinitaly, held every spring.

Names to know: Allegrini, Belisario, Bolla, Colonnara, Lenotti, Mancini, Tommasi, Zonin.

Tuscany. Tuscany is the home of three of Italy's most important red wines: Chianti, Bunello di Montalciano, and Vino Nobile di Montepulciano.

Chianti used to be that inexpensive red wine found in straw-bottomed bottles—and yes, they're still around—but it has done a complete turnaround in recent years to offer some of Italy's best reds at wonderful values. In 1984, Chianti was added to the DOCG designation. There are three "grades" of Chianti, which you'll find right on the labels:

- Chianti Classico Riserva is the top quality and has been aged for at least three years.
- Chianti Classico is from the actual Chianti area, not a nearby village.
- Chianti is the "table wine" designation for simpler, less pricey wines.

Most Chiantis are made from a blend of red and white grapes. Sangiovese is the primary red grape—in fact, by law, it must be 80 percent of the Chianti blend. A lesser-known red blending grape called Canaiolo may be added for fruitiness, and the rest is usually one of the popular white grapes, Trebbiano or Malvasia.

Sangiovese is also used to make Brunello and Vino Nobile de Montepulciano. Brunellos are very big wines that may be aged for a decade or more from their vintage dates.

From this region also come the "Super Tuscans," a group of avant-garde and rather expensive wines prized for, shall we say, their nontraditional upbringing. Starting in the 1980s, some very well respected Tuscan winemakers began using varietals (notably Cabernet Sauvignon and Merlot) that disqualified them from "official" DOCG designation, but produced some incredible reds. This shook up the appellation system in Italy and resulted in the new IGT designation and new appellations for the Tuscan reds.

You'll impress wine-knowledgeable customers (if budget is absolutely no object) when you offer to pour a "Sassicaia" (Tenuta San Guido Sassicaia) or "Galatrona" (Fattoria Petrolo Galatrona) for their next elegant dinner.

Names to know: Antinori, Castellare, Piccini, Ruffino, Fattoria, Villa Banfi.

Spain

The most famous Spanish red, Rioja, is named for its greatest wine-producing region. **Rioja** is usually made from Tempranillo, a fresh and interesting varietal that seems to combine all the punch of a big Cabernet with the more delicate Pinot Noirs. Garnacha (the Spanish version of the French Grenache grape) is also used, primarily for blending Rioja wines.

Names to know (of reliable Rioja producers): Marqués de Cáceres, Marqués de Riscal, Federico Paternina, Pedro Domecq.

From the same grapes, but in a different region, **Ribera del Duero** is more deeply concentrated, richly textured, and among the longest lived of all Spanish red. And the Penedes and Navarra regions are known for making above-average table wines, both whites and reds. **Penedés** makes an inexpensive (but Methode Champenoise) sparkling wine known as *Cava*. Popular names seen in U.S. supermarkets are Codorniu and Freixenet; other still wine producers who seem to dominate the scene in the area are Torres and Jean Leon. The **Navarra** area produces some excellent rosés, called *Rosado*.

The Spanish state of **Jerez** is world-famous for making Sherry, a fortified wine. Sherry is made in multiple styles, ranging from bone-dry to extremely sweet. Top Sherry producers include Hidalgo, Pedro Domecq, Sandeman, and Valdespino.

Portugal

Portugal's appellation system is known as "IPR," for *Indicacao da Proveniencia Regulamentada* (translated, "Indication of Regulated Provenance"). The nation is known for three types of wines: Port, Madeira, and rosé.

Sweet, fortified *Port* is the foremost wine of Portugal and is considered one of the most unique, delicious dessert wines in the world. It is made by adding brandy (also made from grapes) to the wine during fermentation, which leaves a lot of residual sugar in the wine. To protect its reputation for quality, Portugal now labels its products "Porto" or "Oporto" to distinguish them from copycats. There are ten different styles of Port, the most common of which are:

- **Ruby Port**—Aged in wood, dark, fruity, and blended from up to half dozen types of nonvintage wines. It is generally inexpensive.
- **Tawny Port**—A blend of finer, vintage wines, its name refers to its light, delicate color. It is aged up to 20 years in wooden casks and is moderately expensive.
- **Vintage Port**—After a couple of years in wooden casks, this very fine Port will age in the bottle for two or three decades. This is the most expensive style of Port, and you'll probably want to decant it before serving.

Portugal's other outstanding fortified wine is Madeira, the wine drunk by our founding fathers to toast the signing of the Declaration of Independence.

Names to know: Cockburn, Dow, Fonseca, Niepoort & Company, Sandeman, and Taylor Fladgate.

The regular red and rosé wines of Portugal are usually of excellent quality and value. Look on the labels for the terms *Vinho Verde* (well-made, usually inexpensive) and *Quinta* (similar to the term "Château" in France).

Germany

Germany is considered one of the world's top producers of elegant white wines, the best of which are clear and delicate, with beautiful floral bouquets. Despite the cloying, sweet inexpensive Riesling wines that make it to U.S. supermarket shelves, the majority of fine German wines are not especially sweet. The two best-known varietals are Riesling and Gewürztraminer, and there are other excellent buys made from grape varietals called Muller-Thurgau, or Silvaner.

Germany has 11 winemaking regions, but the 4 "prime" ones are:

The **Mosel–Saar–Ruwer** area is considered the greatest of the German wine regions. Named for the Mosel River and two of its tributaries, the whites from this area are outstanding—pale, fragrant Rieslings with lively, fruity acidity and just a hint of effervescence. Because German wine labels include the name of the village where the wine was made, you'll want to look for Bernkasteler Doktor (from Bernkastel), Piesporter Goldtropfchen (from Piesporter); and Wehlener Sonnenuhr (from Wehlen), to name a few.

The **Rheingau** in central Germany has the longest history of quality family-owned wineries of any region in the country. Towns that may be mentioned on labels include Erbach, Rudesheim, Hochheim, and Johannisberg. Famous vineyards of the Rheingau are Schloss Johannisberg and Schloss Vollrads ("Schloss" means castle). The Rheingau is also known for its Rieslings and late-harvest Rieslings and for full-bodied reds made from the Pinot Noir grape, which is called *"Spätburgunder"* in German.

The **Pfalz** (the word means "palace," and the area is also called **Rheinpfalz**), just north of France, is considered the most inventive, modern German winemaking region today. Again, Rieslings are the standouts here, but there are also pleasant, mild whites (and very good values) made from Muller-Thurgau, Silvaner, and a couple of lesser-known varietals, Kerner and Morio-Muskat. A smooth, fruity red wine is also produced, from the Portugieser grape. Villages to look for on wine labels include Diedesheim, Ruppertsberg, and Wachenheim.

The **Rheinhessen** is Germany's largest wine-producing area, spreading out over 65,000 acres. The grapes used are the same varietals used in the Pfalz area. Village names include Alzey, Bingen, Mainz, Nierstein, and Worms (pronounced "vurms"), and you'll taste some decent Spätburgunders (Pinot Noirs) from Ingelheim.

Austria

Like that of Germany, the Austrian wine industry is devoted primarily to crisp, dry white wines and magnificent late-harvest sweet wines. In general, Austrian wines are fuller bodied than German wines.

Whites worth noting are made from the tart Gruner Veltliner grape, which are difficult to find on store shelves but go well with seafood, plus Pinot Blanc, Chardonnay (called *Morillon* in Austria), and Riesling. For its dessert wines, Austria uses the same labeling system as Germany for quality and sweetness (spätlese, auslese, etc.) with one more designation—*ausbruch*. The dessert Rieslings are expensive, but worth the cost.

Austrian reds, even harder to find than the whites in the United States, include *Blauberger* (the Austrian term for Pinot Noir), *Blaufrankish* (the Austrian term for the Limberger grape), and *Zweigelt* (a hybrid red grape that produces delicious, fruity wines).

Names to know: (for whites) Malat, Nigl, F.X. Pichler, Prager, Solomon; (for reds) Fritsch, Gesellmann, Glatzer, Umathum. Learn more at austrian-wines.com.

Hungary

Hungary has 22 grape-growing regions, and about 75 percent of its production is white wine. It has had a lot of "catching up" to do in the wine world, inasmuch as the industry was very much neglected during the decades of Communist rule. However, investors are now showing a real interest in building an exciting viticulture trade.

Wines here show an amazing range. There are classic whites, rosés, and full-bodied reds, as well as the world-famous dessert wine Tokay Aszu, made from Botrytis-infected grapes of the varietal *Furmint*. Hungary makes lively, spicy Gewürztraminers and Muscats and an easy-to-drink, inexpensive red—Egri Bikaver ("Bull's Blood")—from a native Balkan grape called *Kadarka*. Find out more at winesofhungary.com.

Greece

If you think Greek wine is thick and golden and takes like perfume, think again! You've probably experienced *Retsina*, the big, sweet traditional wine that is flavored with pine resin. (Modern producers have toned it down in recent decades, adding a bit less resin for the tourist's palate.)

The wines of Greece were the most important wines in antiquity, and some of the grape varietals here are not found anywhere else in the world. However, since the 1980s Greek winemakers have also been experimenting with all the big-name international varietals. They produce Cabernet Sauvignon and Chardonnay in addition to their historic favorites. There's been a real revolution in quality and innovation.

The wine industry is regulated by VQPRD laws—translated, the Greek words mean "Quality Wine Produced in a Well-Defined Region." Interesting grapes you'll see on Greek labels are *Assyrtiko* (a fruity, acidic white), *Moshofilero* (a spicy, fruity white, similar to Gewürztraminer), and *Savatiano* (the grape used to make most Retsina). *Aghiorgitiko* and *Xynomavro* varietals both produce brightly colored reds with high acidity and lots of body. Learn more at greekwines.gr or stratsplace.com/greece.

United States and Canada

Wine lovers will argue about any "Top 10" list of regions, grapes, wineries, or anything else. However, almost all the wine made in the United States is made on the West Coast—more than 90 percent of it in California, because of the state's incredibly diverse and grape-friendly climate and geography. In the following paragraphs we focus on the key regions within California.

Napa Valley. About 50 miles northeast of San Francisco, the Napa Valley is perhaps California's best-known and (arguably, of course!) most renowned wine region. The valley is only a few miles wide and 25 miles long, but it contains seven different appellations. Grapes grown here include the reds Cabernet Sauvignon, Merlot, Zinfandel, Pinot Noir, and some Sangiovese; whites are also produced here, which include Chardonnay and Sauvignon Blanc and, to a lesser extent, Riesling, and Sémillon.

Names to know: Beaulieu Vineyards, Château Montelena, Duckhorn, Frog's Leap, Stag's Leap.

Sonoma County.

Sonoma County is directly north of San Francisco and has one million acres of land, making it more than twice as large as Napa. It's a patchwork of six different valleys with microclimates perfect for grape growing. At least 15 varietals are planted here. Until the 1960s, Sonoma was an area known for growing blending grapes and producing decent jug wines, but not for "serious" winemaking. That certainly has changed!

Names to know: Adler Fels, Benzinger, Buena Vista, Chalk Hill, Château St. Jean, DeLoach, Preston, Ravenswood, Sebastiani, Simi.

Central Coast.

Just north of Napa and Sonoma, the California coastal area can be divided into two basic subregions: Northern and Middle/South. Cities associated with the Central Coast are Livermore, Monterey (home of the famous Monterey Wine Festival), Carmel, and Paso Robles.

North includes eight different American Viticultural Areas, or AVAs. The most well known are probably Mendocino County, Lake County, and Monterey. The area also encompasses the Santa Cruz mountains and the Santa Clara and Carmel Valleys. The most famous growing region here is Mendocino.

Middle/South includes Paso Robles, the Edna Valley, Arroyo Grande, and the Santa Maria and Santa Ynez Valleys.

The Central Coast includes six counties, with more than 200,000 of vineyards in about dozen varietals—all the "big names," plus some interesting blending grapes, like Carignan, Grenache, and Cabernet Franc. Historically home to inexpensive, easy-drinking wines, in the past decade the Central Coast has seen a real surge in quality, especially with Barbera, Chenin Blanc, Chardonnay, and Pinot Noir.

Names to know: Au Bon Climat, Byron, Calera, Concannon, Edna Valley, Firestone, Jekel, J. Lohr, Sanford, Wente Brothers, Wild Horse, Zaca Mesa.

Washington State.

Washington State is considered one of the top producers of Merlot and Cabernet Sauvignon in the United States, but it also produces some very fine white wines, including Gewürtraminer and Sauvignon Blanc. Virtually all of this state's vineyards are in the dry, warm eastern part of the state, in the Columbia and Yakima Valleys. Winemakers in neighboring Idaho, like Ste. Chappelle, also buy some of their grapes from Washington growers.

Names to know: Arbor Crest, Canoe Ridge, Chateau Ste.-Michelle, Covey Run, Hogue Cellars, Quail Run.

Oregon.

Oregon produces about half as much wine as Washington State, but has every bit the solid reputation of its neighbor to the north. Oregon's specialty is Pinot Noir, a delicate and temperamental grape considered by many to make the most sensuous red wine in the world. Growers also plant their share of whites, including Pinot Gris, Riesling, and Chardonnay. The primary growing areas are the Willamette, Rogue, and Umpqua Valleys, all in the western half of the state.

Oregon's wine laws are very strict, to benefit the consumer. For instance, an Oregon wine cannot be labeled as a varietal unless it contains 90 percent of that type of grape—except for Cabernet Sauvignon, which has to contain only 75 percent Cabernet.

Names to know: Adelsheim, Amity, Eyrie Vineyards, Knudsen Erath, Ponzi, Springhill Estate, Tualatin, Witness Tree.

Other States, Other Wines. So many wines, so little time . . . ! Almost every state has a winemaking industry now, and it would be impractical to describe them all here. We've covered those along the West Coast, which are the primary producers in terms of volume. If your catering business will operate in a state that produces wines, it will be to your benefit to get to know these products—and even the people who make them. Visiting a winery is fun and interesting, and your clients will benefit from your "insider's knowledge."

Here are just a few websites to get you started:

General information: mywinetutor.com (basic info, with maps and some winery recommendations).

vino.com (listings and links to the individual wineries of all major wine-producing countries. Invaluable!).

Winespectator.com (search the archives of *Wine Spectator* magazine).

Wine.about.com (very readable site, written by self-taught Massachusetts-based wine expert Lisa Shea).

STATE OR REGION	WEBSITE ADDRESS
Arizona	arizonawines.com
Canada—British Columbia	bcwine.com
Missouri	missouriwine.org
New Mexico	winesofnewmexico.com
	nmwine.net (New Mexico Wine Growers Association)
New York	nywine.com/winelocator
	nywinecork.com
Canada—Ontario	wineroute.com
Pennsylvania	pennsylvaniawine.com
Rhode Island	visitrhodeisland.com/arts/vineyards
Texas	twgga.org (Texas Wine and Grape Growers Association)
Virginia	virginiawines.org

Australia

Australia is known for big, supple, mouth-filling white and red wines, many of which are terrific values. Names like Yellowtail and Rosemount Estate are often seen as restaurants' "house wines" because of their reliable quality and good prices.

The most renowned and best-loved red grape is Shiraz (the Aussie name for the Syrah grape of France). The majority of Australia's vineyards are clustered in the southeastern part of the continent relatively near Sydney, Melbourne, and Adelaide.

Names to know: Lindeman's, Penfold's, Rosemount Estate, Seppelt, Wynn's Coonawarra Estate. Learn more at australianwines.com.

New Zealand

New Zealand is best known for its crisp white Sauvignon Blancs and Chardonnays. Recently, in response to the world's natural cork shortage, New Zealand began requiring its wineries to use screw caps instead of corks. It's a daring experiment, because screw-off caps are traditionally seen only on very inexpensive jug wines. But don't let them fool you with these—New Zealand makes some excellent wines.

Names to know: Alexandra, Barncott Vineyards, Cooks Landing, Dry River, Grove Mill, Kumeu River, Marlborough Valley, Montana Wines. Find out more online at nzwine.com.

South Africa

Most South African wine is made by large cooperatives, but the best-known wine comes from several dozen small private estates. Wine-growing areas are divided into regions, and the regions are divided into smaller "wards." The government provides some financial subsidies to grape growers, making it possible to export their wines very inexpensively. Consumers are the winners, because the South African wines are great bargains.

Names to know: Boschendal, Kanonkop, KWV, Nederberg. (The KWV cooperative also makes a very well-respected brandy). Find out more at wine.co.sa.

Chile

Chile makes the most consistently good wines from the South American continent. Much of the Chilean wine is exported to the United States, also with government subsidies, so that it can often be found at bargain-basement prices. However, there are also moderate and expensive wines of very high quality that make it to U.S. store shelves.

Names to know: Reliable and inexpensive labels include Gato Negro and Gato Blanco, Caliterra, Concha y Toro, and Santa Rita. Also look for Casa Lapostolle, Villa Carmen, and Vina Errazuriz. Learn more at vino.com.

Argentina

Since the mid-1990s, Argentina has been developing a fine wine industry, which has become known for its luscious reds. Perhaps the most interesting is Malbec, which is more delicious when made in Argentina than in its native Bordeaux.

WINE BOTTLE SIZES

Some wines, especially Champagnes and sparkling wines, may be obtained in sizes other than standard 750-milliliter bottles. These can be especially festive at weddings and big events. These bottles have specific names, which you'll need to know to order them:

NAME	SIZE	NUMBER OF GLASSES
Split	187.5 mL	1.5
Half-bottle	375 mL	2.5
Bottle	750 mL	4 to 5
Magnum	2 bottles	10
Jeroboam	4 bottles	20
Methuselah	8 bottles	40
Salmanazar	12 bottles	60
Balthazar	16 bottles	80
Nebuchadnezzar	20 bottles	100

The term *bodega* on the label means "house" (château).

Names to know: Bodegas Lopez, Bodega Norton, Bodega y Cavas De Weinert, Felipe Rutini, San Telmo, Vina Amalia. The vino.com website also has excellent information on Argentine wine.

✕ *Beer*

Americans spend more money on beer than on milk, juice, coffee, and wine combined! It is a multibillion-dollar market. Major brands such as Budweiser, Coors, and Miller, as well as popular imports like Corona and Heineken, account for the major share of the market. But there are hundreds of smaller, regional microbreweries that produce beers for those with sophisticated palates, and plenty of interesting imports that may go well with certain types of foods: Tsingtao or Kirin with Asian cuisine, a good Belgian or German Bock (strong, dark lager—Beck's is the top German import) with German food, and so on.

For most off-premise events, caterers can play it safe by offering the "mainstream beers"—Budweiser, Coors, and Miller, and their "Light" cousins—and a couple of imports. This selection will appease most clients. However, you may be surprised at how many "beer aficionados" there are, many of them also home brewers. So it's good to know something about the local and regional microbrews that are available and to be prepared to offer them at an additional cost. Always ask if clients have a preference.

In addition, it is smart to offer a nonalcoholic beer, such as O'Douls's, Buckler, Kaliber, or Haake Beck. Plenty of people wish to enjoy the flavor of beer, but without the alcohol.

Beer from a keg is less expensive than cans or bottles, but can be more difficult to handle because of the size, weight, and setup process. Kegs come in two sizes for foodservice use, the half-barrel (15.5 gallons) and the quarter-barrel (7.75 gallons). The *beer system* for use with a keg includes a cylinder of carbon dioxide (CO_2), with a pressure gauge, a faucet (called a *tap*), and hoses (called *lines*) that run from the CO_2 cylinder to the keg, and from the keg to the tap, using *couplings*. The carbon dioxide is necessary to keep the beer carbonated and to create just enough pressure to get it from the keg through the lines and into the beer glass. Optimum pressure (which you check using the gauge) is 12 to 15 pounds per square inch (psi). It would be wise to let your local beer distributor perform a little demonstration of keg setup and tapping for your bartending staff.

If keg beer isn't cold enough or has been jostled before being tapped, it may come out too foamy. Under no circumstances should you let customers draw their own beer from a keg. It not only increases potential liquor liability problems, but many people do not know how to properly draw the beer. The biggest money-wasting "tradition" is promoted by folks who (mistakenly) believe you should fully open the tap for a couple of seconds and let the beer run, then put the glass beneath it. Instead, put the glass under the spigot first, fully open the tap, and keep the glass tilted so that the beer flows down the side of the glass. This usually avoids creating a large, foamy head on the beer.

For upscale catered events, beer from cans or bottles should be poured into the glasses to avoid the unsightliness of beer containers around the room. Some brides are adamant about this, as they do not wish to look at beer bottles and cans in their wedding pictures. Another way to avoid this problem is to pour beer from quart bottles at the bar, thus eliminating the need for kegs or individual bottles and cans.

✗ *Water*

Bottled water is a staple at catered functions, and little wonder. It makes a better mixed drink than tap water, and nondrinkers also like to have something stylish in their glasses. Fully one-third of the U.S. adult population does not drink alcohol, and bottled water is a classy and healthful alternative. Smart wine drinkers also know they should drink as much water as they do wine at an event, to help slow the absorption of alcohol into their systems.

Even the major soft drink companies have gotten into the bottled water business, as sales continue to climb. From 2002 to 2003, bottled water consumption increased 7.5 percent. As a caterer, you will want to be familiar with the various types of waters available. The U.S. Food and Drug Administration's product definitions for bottled water (and, therefore, the terms you'll see on the labels) include:[5]

- **Artesian water/artesian well water:** Bottled water from a well that taps a confined aquifer (a water-bearing underground layer of rock or sand) in which the water level stands at some height above the top of the aquifer.
- **Drinking water:** Drinking water is another name for bottled water. It is water sold for human consumption in sanitary containers that contains no added sweeteners or chemical additives (other than flavors, extracts, or essences). It must be calorie-free and sugar-free. Flavors, extracts, or essences may be added to drinking water, but they must comprise less than 1 percent by weight of the final product (or it is otherwise considered a "soft drink"). Drinking water may be sodium-free or contain very low amounts of sodium.
- **Mineral water:** Bottled water containing not less than 250 parts per million (ppm) total dissolved solids. Mineral water is distinguished from other types of bottled water by its constant level and relative proportions of mineral and trace elements at the point of emergence from the source. No minerals can be added to this product.
- **Purified water:** Water that has been produced by distillation, deionization, reverse osmosis, or other suitable processes, and that meets the definition of "purified water" in the *United States Pharmacopoeia*. Other suitable product names are:
  - "Distilled water," if produced by distillation
  - "Deionized water," if produced by deionization
  - "Reverse osmosis water" if produced by reverse osmosis.
  - "_____ drinking water" may be used, with the blank filled in with one of the terms defined in this paragraph, such as "purified drinking water" or "distilled drinking water."

- **Sparkling water:** Water that, after treatment and possible replacement of carbon dioxide, contains the same amount of carbon dioxide that it had at emergence from the source. (*An important note:* Soda water, seltzer water, and tonic water are not considered bottled waters. They are regulated separately, may contain sugar and calories, and are legally considered "soft drinks.")
- **Spring water:** Bottled water derived from an underground formation from which water flows naturally to the surface of the earth. Spring water must be collected only at the spring, or through a borehole tapping the underground formation at the spring. Spring water collected with the use of an "external force" must be from the same underground stratum as the actual spring and must have all the physical properties, before treatment, and be of the same composition and quality as the water that flows naturally to the surface of the earth.
- **Well water:** Bottled water from a hole bored, drilled, or otherwise constructed in the ground, that taps the water of an aquifer.

For catering use, we tend to include tonics, seltzers, and club sodas with our water orders when creating a bar setup.

- **Club soda** is filtered and artificially carbonated water, with mineral salts added.
- **Seltzer water** is also filtered and artificially carbonated, but without the added mineral salts.
- **Tonic water** is filtered and artificially carbonated, and flavored with small amounts of citrus juice and quinine (a mineral salt made from the bark of the chinchona tree that gives tonic water its slightly bitter taste).

✖ Soft Drinks

After years of steady increases in soft drink consumption, it is now on the decline in the United States, with a couple of notable exceptions—the "flavors" categories (like orange and root beer) and the diet soft drink category, as people tend to watch their weight. Colas and lemon–limes are still quite popular; they're just not experiencing the double-digit growth of the past.

Soft drinks are absolutely necessary to meet the needs of nondrinkers and the underage crowd at most events. A basic lineup should include:

- At least one major brand of cola
- At least one major brand of diet cola
- A noncaffeinated cola
- Several "non-colas" (orange, lemon-lime, ginger ale), both regular and diet
- A couple of "non-carbs" (lemonade, bottled teas)

For large, informal events, most soft drink distributors will provide fountain–style beverage service stations using 5-gallon tanks of syrup mixed with carbon dioxide and water, dispensed from spigots. This is the most economical way to serve to large gatherings. Two-liter bottles are more economical than the 12-ounce cans and assorted smaller bottle sizes, but the smaller bottles and cans present a more upscale image, as the guests perceive a "fresher" product. Always have plenty of ice on hand and, whatever you serve, make sure it has been well chilled.

✕ Figuring Beverage Quantities

Clients typically leave it up to the caterer to suggest the necessary amounts of liquor, wine, and beer for an event. Knowing the quantity of beverages to purchase (or to recommend that your client purchase) for a catered wedding, party, or event is one of the hallmarks of a professional caterer.

When suggesting quantities, it is always better to recommend too much, rather than too little, to be sure there is enough for the event, knowing that any excess can be returned or consumed later. Many beverage retailers and wholesalers will take back and credit you for any unopened, undamaged bottles of liquor and wine you return—another reason to have good relationships with your local vendors. Even bottled and canned beer can be returned if it has not been chilled and is still in its original packaging. Everyone is aware that it may be very difficult to go out and forage for more when you run out of something mid-party. Avoid the problem by ordering plenty.

Local customs often help determine quantity. In South Florida, for example, the major alcoholic beverages served are Scotch, vodka, white wine, and beer. Bourbon, Canadian Whisky and gin are not nearly as popular. Rum is a favorite with younger crowds and those from out of town. What are the trends in your area?

The next factors to consider are the length of the party, the type and purpose of the event, the time of day it is being held, and the temperature—especially if it is an outdoor event. Consumption will most always be greater at a Saturday night wedding reception lasting five hours than at a one-hour corporate reception held at 5:00 P.M. on a weeknight.

It is true that most folks are drinking less alcohol, for a combination of health, religious, and safety reasons. It is no longer considered "cool" to drink a lot. As a general rule, guests will drink the following number of beverages, on average:

LENGTH OF PARTY	NUMBER OF DRINKS
One hour	Two
Two hours	Three
Three hours	Three to four
Four hours	Four to five

It is important to note that from a 1-liter bottle of liquor (33.8 fluid ounces) you can pour about:

- 33 1-ounce drinks
- 27 $1^{1}/_{4}$-ounce drinks
- 22 $1^{1}/_{2}$-ounce drinks

In a standard bottle of wine (750 milliliters), there are 25.3 ounces and, depending on how generous your portion, that means four to five glasses per bottle.

Most beer is in 12-ounce bottles, and this is considered one serving.

A 1-liter soft drink bottle will provide five to seven servings, depending on the size of the glass and the amount of ice (and size of cubes) used.

A Word about Ice

When determining the amount of ice needed for an event, off-premise caterers need to consider the length of the party, the need for chilling wines, beers, and Champagne, the necessity to fill water glasses, and the temperature at the party site. A five-hour outdoor wedding reception with temperatures in the 80s can require as much as five pounds of ice per person! There are wine and Champagne to chill, water glasses to keep filled, and so on. A one-hour indoor cocktail reception, however, may require only 1 pound of ice per person. Again, it is best to err on the safe side by having too much ice. Extra ice can always be used to ice down leftover food.

The size and shape of the ice cubes are an important consideration in making drinks. Rectangular cubes stack better than round ones, but round ones fill the glass better overall. Smaller cubes fit better in most glasses, but larger ones melt more slowly (a consideration in extremely hot weather). But the most important thing about ice is that it be clean and clear.

Quantity Recommendations

Exhibit 4.1 provides some very general recommendations regarding liquor, wine, beer, and mixer quantities. Local customs, other extenuating circumstances, and your own knowledge over time will certainly modify these recommendations. Suggested quantities are rather liberal, taking into account the facts that mixers can be reused and that unopened, unchilled alcohol can be returned if desired.

Exhibit 4.1 does not take into account dinner wine served at the table. Off-premise caterers who provide table wine service can expect to serve another one to two glasses of wine per person. Consumption will be greater if there is no preceding cocktail party. Therefore, off-premise caterers can estimate an additional one-quarter to one-half bottle of wine per guest. Caterers should insist that wine bottles be opened only at the direction of the host or caterer so as to avoid having excessive amounts of opened wine left at the end of the event.

✖ Basic Drink Recipes for Off-Premise Caterers

Of necessity, most off-premise caterers serve a simple array of popular cocktails—no fancy multiliquor concoctions or specific Martini-afficionado instructions. Most drink orders are self-explanatory: "Scotch and water." To prepare this drink, simply put ice in a highball glass, pour the prescribed portion amount of Scotch, and then add bottled water. The following is a summary of recipes for the most popular drinks served at an off-premise catering bar.

⊠ Exhibit 4.1 *Liquor, Wine, Beer, and Mixer Quantities*

LIQUOR—LITERS

	50 GUESTS				100 GUESTS			
	1 HR	2 HR	3 HR	4 HR	1 HR	2 HR	3 HR	4 HR
SCOTCH	2	3	3	4	4	5	5	6
VODKA	2	3	3	4	4	5	5	6
GIN	1	2	2	2	2	3	3	3
BLEND	1	2	2	2	2	3	3	3
BOURBON	1	2	2	2	2	3	3	3
RUM	1	2	2	2	3	3	4	4
BEER, CASE	1/2	3/4	1	1	1	1 1/2	2	2
LITE BEER, CASE	1/2	3/4	1	1	1	1 1/2	2	2
WHITE WINE, 5TH	6	9	12	12	12	18	24	24
RED WINE, 5TH	2	3	4	4	4	6	8	8

SOFT DRINKS—LITERS

	50 GUESTS				100 GUESTS			
	1 HR	2 HR	3 HR	4 HR	1 HR	2 HR	3 HR	4 HR
COLA	4	6	7	8	8	10	12	14
DIET COLA	4	5	6	7	8	9	10	11
DIET LEMON-LIME	2	2	3	4	4	5	6	7
LEMON-LIME	2	2	3	4	4	5	6	7
GINGER ALE	2	2	3	4	4	5	6	7
CLUB SODA	3	4	5	6	6	7	8	9
TONIC	3	4	5	6	6	7	8	9
SPARKLING WATER	3	4	5	6	6	7	8	9

FRESH JUICES—ORANGE, GRAPEFRUIT, AND CRANBERRY JUICES—QUARTS

50 GUESTS				100 GUESTS			
1 HR	2 HR	3 HR	4 HR	1 HR	2 HR	3 HR	4 HR
2	3	3	4	4	5	6	7

LIMES (165 COUNT)—CUT INTO 16 WEDGES

50 GUESTS				100 GUESTS			
1 HR	2 HR	3 HR	4 HR	1 HR	2 HR	3 HR	4 HR
3	4	5	5	5	8	9	9

LEMON TWISTS—ONE LEMON PER FIFTY GUESTS—REGARDLESS OF LENGTH OF THE EVENT. FIVE ONION SKEWERS AND FIVE OLIVE SKEWERS PER EACH FIFTY GUESTS IS ADEQUATE. EACH BARTENDER SHOULD HAVE ONE BOTTLE OF SWEET VERMOUTH AND ONE BOTTLE OF DRY VERMOUTH. THIS WILL SUFFICE FOR MOST PARTIES OF ANY LENGTH.

BLOODY MARY MIX IS NEEDED FOR MOST BARS. FOR DAYTIME EVENTS, SIX QUARTS PER ONE HUNDRED GUESTS SHOULD BE ADEQUATE. FOR EVENING EVENTS, TWO QUARTS PER ONE HUNDRED GUESTS IS AMPLE.

DRINK NAME	GLASS TYPE	INGREDIENTS	GARNISH
Bay Breeze	Highball	$1^1/_2$ oz. vodka $^1/_2$ oz. cranberry juice $^1/_2$ oz. pineapple juice	
Bloody Mary	Highball	$1^1/_4$ oz. vodka Bloody Mary mix	Lime wedge, celery stick
Blue Martini	Martini	$1^1/_2$ oz. vodka Splash Blue Curacao Splash pineapple juice	Pineapple
Cosmopolitan	Martini	$1^1/_2$ oz. Absolut Citron vodka $^1/_4$ oz. Cointreau Dash Rose's Lime Juice Dash cranberry juice	Lemon twist or lime garnish
Madras (Matras)	Highball	$1^1/_2$ oz. vodka $^1/_2$ oz. cranberry juice $^1/_2$ oz. orange juice	
Manhattan	Rocks/cocktail	$1^1/_4$ oz. bourbon or blend $^3/_4$ oz. sweet vermouth	Stem cherry
Margarita	Rocks/cocktail	$^1/_2$ oz. tequila $^1/_2$ oz. Triple Sec Margarita mix	Lime wedge, salt rim
Martini	Rocks/cocktail	$1^1/_4$ oz. gin Dash dry vermouth	Green olive
Rob Roy	Rocks/cocktail	$1^1/_4$ oz. Scotch $^3/_4$ oz. sweet vermouth	
Screwdriver	Highball	$1^1/_4$ oz. vodka Orange juice	
Vodka Martini	Rocks/cocktail	$1^1/_4$ oz. vodka Dash dry vermouth	

A few years ago off-premise caterers would not have bothered to offer frozen drinks, as the use, care, and cleaning of blenders off-site (let alone finding someplace to plug them in) would have been considered a hassle. Today, however, the frozen drink is so popular that you might rethink their use. And, of course, frozen drink machines ("Margarita machines") are also available for rent.

A few easy recipes for frozen drinks are listed here:

Frozen Strawberry Daquiri
$1^1/_2$ oz. light rum
Strawberry mix
Blend
Serve in a rocks/cocktail glass with a strawberry garnish.

Frozen Rum Runner
1 oz. 151 rum
$^1/_2$ oz. crème de banana
$^1/_2$ oz. blackberry brandy

Dash grenadine
Fill with orange juice or bar mix.
Serve in a cocktail glass.

Frozen Pina Colada
$1^1/_2$ oz. light rum
Pina Colada mix
Blend.
Serve in a cocktail glass with a cherry garnish.

✕ *Beverage Stations (Bars)*

Off-premise caterers frequently provide "service bars" for clients, along with mixers, ice, and glasses. Portable service bars take much physical abuse as they are moved from event to event, and they also provide only a limited amount of storage space. Therefore, many caterers prefer to use skirted banquet tables for beverage service. These provide more working space, there is plenty of storage space for backup supplies underneath the tables, and, overall, they generally look better than service bars.

Exhibit 4.2 is a diagram of a service bar for a single bartender, using a table that is 6 feet long and 30 inches wide.

Exhibit 4.3 is a listing of all equipment, supplies, and liquor necessary to set up and equip this single service bar.

Eight-foot banquet tables may be used to set up beverage stations for two bartenders. It is best that each bartender have his or her own supply of liquor, soda, and glasses to eliminate reaching. They generally can share ice and cold beers and wines, provided the chests are strategically placed between them.

Bar Service Procedures

Here are a few tips to make the bartenders' jobs easier at catered events: The caterer should always check with the client regarding whether to serve alcoholic beverages to band members, photographers, floral designers, and others engaged to work at the event. As a general rule, serving alcoholic beverages to people "working the party" is not advisable. Under no circumstances should the caterer permit any of his or her own staff members to consume alcoholic beverages while working a catered event.

Caterers should establish a clear policy with staff members as to how much wine and liquor to open prior to the event. Opening too little will result in wasted time during the event; opening too much will result in wine that cannot be returned for credit. A good policy is for the caterer to prohibit any staff member from opening wine and liquor without first asking an on-site supervisor or manager.

Near the conclusion of a party where glassware is used, it is always good policy to station a catering staff person near the exit to ensure that guests do not leave with glassware. In most states, it is illegal for persons to have open containers of alcoholic beverages in vehicles, so giving a plastic cup to those who have not yet finished their drinks is simply not proper—and probably not legal—unless the guests

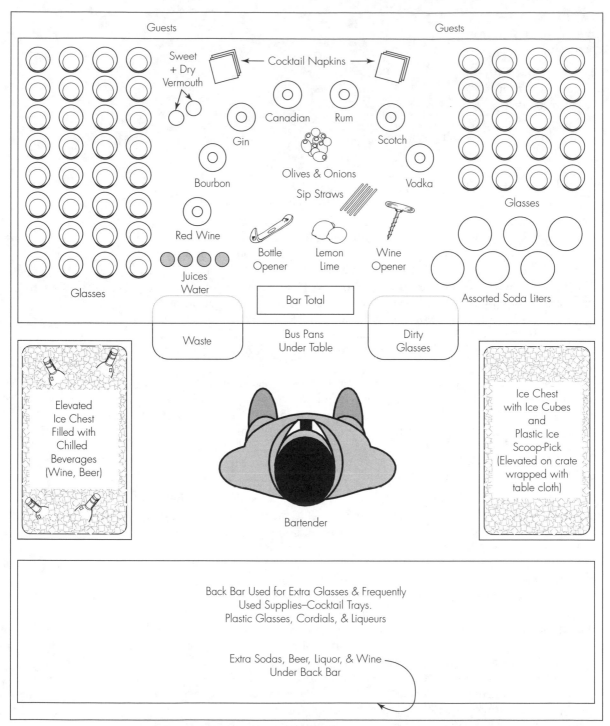

Exhibit 4.2 *Beverage Station (Bar)*

⊠ Exhibit 4.3 *Beverage Station Setup—Equipment and Supplies*

Two 6-foot by 30-inch tables
One 13-foot skirt for front bar (leave a four-foot opening at rear of bar for easy access underneath by bartender)
One 17-foot skirt for back bar
Two banquet cloths, or two 90-inch by 90-inch cloths (the color of the cloths and skirts should tie in with the color scheme of the event)
Clips to attach the skirts to the tables
Bowls for cut fruits, garnish, olives, onions, cherries, etc.
Stir straws
Sword picks (for onions and olives)
Ice chest for chilled beverages such as beers, wines, bottled waters, Champagne, etc.
Ice chest filled with ice for drinks
Plastic ice scoops
Wine openers
Bottle openers
Bus boxes for trash and dirty glasses
Matches
Cocktail napkins
Cocktail trays
Plastic glasses
Basic bar glasses (balloon wine glasses are good all-purpose glasses)
Specialty glasses (brandy snifters/cordial glasses)
Plastic pourers for liquor
Ice pick
Bar towels
Empty plastic crates (to elevate ice chests)
Small tablecloths to wrap around plastic crates

LIQUOR
A selection of basic liquors such as vodka, Scotch, gin, blended whiskey, rum, bourbon, and other requested brands
Wines and beers
At least one regular and one light beer, plus a white wine and a red wine. Please note that in some locations, blush, or rosé wine is a must, and that some facilities prohibit red wine due to the possibility of staining carpeting and furniture.

SOFT DRINKS, JUICES, AND MISCELLANEOUS
Cola
Lemon-lime
Diet cola
Diet lemon-lime
Ginger ale
Club soda
Tonic
Sparkling water
Orange juice
Grapefruit juice
Cranberry juice
Water
Sweet vermouth
Dry vermouth
Bloody Mary mix

AFTER-DINNER DRINKS (OPTIONAL)
Kahlua
B&B
Bailey's Irish Cream
Cointreau
Drambuie
Tia Maria
Courvoisier
White Crème de Menthe
Green Crème de Menthe
Other local favorites

GARNISHES
Lemon twists
Lime wedges
Cocktail olives
Cocktail onions

are leaving by motor coach, limousine, or taxi. Of course, it is permissible to provide plastic cups for nonalcoholic beverages.

✕ Conclusion

Serving alcohol at events is too profitable an option for a catering company to ignore, and it is pretty much expected—at least, as an option—from today's catering companies. So you might as well be informed and confident about your own (and your staff's) ability to provide it. This includes having the proper licenses and permits (and knowing how to obtain them, sometimes on short notice), servers that are trained in responsible alcohol service, the know-how to sufficiently stock beer, wine, and liquor stations with products the clients will enjoy and the correct glassware, mixers, garnishes, and utensils to serve them correctly.

For the catering company owner, it also means an ongoing commitment to stay current on state and federal liquor laws, and on trends and knowledge of wines and spirits, and to have a strict inventory control system for your beverage department. We'll talk more about inventories in Chapter 14.

Notes

1. Responsible Vendor Training Program, the Beverage Law Institute, Inc., Tallahassee, Florida (www.beveragelawinstitute.com).
2. Learn2Serve, HotelTraining.com, Dallas, Texas (www.HotelTraining.com).
3. Definitions adapted from *The Bar and Beverage Book*, Third Edition, by Costas Katsigris, Mary Porter, and Chris Thomas, John Wiley & Sons, 2003, Hoboken, New Jersey.
4. Definitions adapted from *The Bar and Beverage Book*, Third Edition, by Costas Katsigris, Mary Porter, and Chris Thomas, John Wiley & Sons, 2003, Hoboken, New Jersey.
5. International Bottled Water Association, Alexandria, Virginia. (www.bottledwater.org)

✂ Chapter 5

Catering Equipment

In this chapter you'll learn about the equipment that is necessary to operate an off-premise catering business—not only the items you'll require for food preparation and service, but commissary equipment and transportation equipment as well. We'll discuss ways to determine equipment needs and examine the option of renting rather than buying equipment. Your relationship with rental equipment companies is an extremely important one in the off-premise catering world, and we'll cover that, too.

An understanding of commissary equipment is essential for success in this field. This is the equipment you have in your kitchen facility for food production and is typically not portable. You need to be familiar with it, including how to buy it—and whether to buy it at all. Millions of dollars are wasted annually by inexperienced operators buying expensive equipment they just don't need. This chapter will show you how to make intelligent equipment purchases, including vehicles for transporting your wares.

Smart caterers also know that owning certain types of equipment is an excellent way to generate additional profit. The off-premise caterer can rent or provide equipment for events, offering a valuable service for clients who would otherwise have to look elsewhere for these items.

✂ Determining Equipment Needs

The types of required off-premise catering equipment are determined by analyzing a number of factors.

Menu. The foods you will serve greatly influence equipment selection. For example, a caterer who plans to serve a variety of deep-fried hors d'oeuvres will require more *fryolator* (deep-fryer) capacity than one who plans to simply offer assortments of cold canapés. The cold canapés will require rolling racks and refrigerated storage, whereas the caterer serving deep-fried hors d'oeuvres could store them before cooking in plastic containers that could be keep cold in ice chests at the party site, in accordance with local health department regulations.

Beverage Service. Will your company offer service of alcoholic and nonalcoholic beverages? If so, glassware, bar utensils, and beverage stations (portable bars) will be necessary.

Style of Service. How fancy will your parties be? A caterer specializing in barbecues will more than likely require only plastic ware, whereas an upscale caterer will need plenty of silver-plated flatware, crystal stemware, fine linens, and other first-class equipment.

Existing Equipment. This category includes both the commissary equipment and whatever is available at the event site. An off-premise caterer who leases a fully equipped commissary will have little need for additional commissary equipment. If you work frequently at party sites where there are existing bars, you won't need to be concerned with purchasing or renting bars for events. In short, don't spend money when you don't really need to.

Number of Guests. What is the maximum number of guests you will most likely serve? Off-premise caterers who specialize in home parties for 30 or fewer guests will require substantially less equipment than those who cater mega-events with thousands of guests.

Other Factors. These could include regional influences—clambake equipment in New England, portable meat-smokers for Southern barbecues. The specific equipment needs for each party are best determined by analyzing the party contract, then preparing a layout of the event. Include the guest seating area, the cocktail area, the food preparation and staging preparation areas, and all buffet tables and/or food stations. Such diagrams require detailed planning, which will help you "think through" what is necessary for an event. Make lists pertinent to each area, including everything from tables and chairs to the smallest details like toothpicks, cutting boards, and buffet spoons.

✕ *Equipping a Catering Commissary*

In Chapter 2 we discussed various methods of selecting a commissary location. This section covers key factors in planning a catering commissary, including basic equipment types.

Our first suggestion may sound difficult if you're on a budget, but, in the long run, it will save you money. If possible, hire a professional planner who knows how to lay out a kitchen efficiently. Almost all restaurant supply companies employ planners, and although you should take advantage of their suggestions, remember they are trained to sell as much equipment as possible, of the particular brands they happen to market. That's understandable, but doesn't help you as much as an independent planner who will have your best interests in mind and can negotiate with multiple suppliers to get the best deals.

Exhibit 5.1 is a generic layout for a 1,500-square-foot off-premise catering commissary, provided by Hugh Cunningham, a professional independent designer in Fort Lauderdale, Florida.

A professional planner will properly lay out an off-premise catering commissary, ensuring that the following major areas are arranged for maximum efficiency:

Receiving and loading
Storage
Refrigeration and freezer space
Preparation
Main cooking ("hot line")
Bakery
Pot washing and dishwashing

We've mentioned that the menu will dictate the necessary equipment, so have the menu well developed before you hire a space planner. Most commissaries will require ovens, broilers, and steamers but may not require deep-fat fryers, particularly if frying is to be done at the event site. Most fried foods, other than fried chicken, do not store well and are best cooked and served immediately. Solicit the opinions of your staff members, especially those who will be working in the commissary. These folks often have years of experience working in other operations, dealing with good and bad equipment and designs, and you can benefit from their knowledge.

Before you start planning a catering commissary, you should also have a general idea of the projected sales volume. A caterer content with sales of $250,000 per year definitely will not need a commissary capable of producing $5,000,000 per year in sales. *The most important guideline: It is usually better to err on the smaller size, with the option of expanding.* A facility that is overly large will require extra upkeep and maintenance and is simply not as efficient as a more compact facility in which distances between storage and work areas are less.

In creating the design—and you should have a hand in it, even when you do hire a professional—equipment should be placed so that:

- Excessive walking (and carrying of heavy supplies) is reduced.
- It is close to major utility connections.
- Multipurpose equipment is close to all staff.
- Equipment used most often is close at hand.
- Employees shouldn't have to walk more than 10 feet to a sink.

It is always advisable to order movable equipment on sturdy casters (wheels). This makes it easier to clean, allows different areas to share dual-purpose items, and allows for future flexibility if the layout changes.

Equipment mounted on walls is another big plus as far as cleaning is concerned. In addition, equipment equipped with floor grates for spillage, as well as stainless steel backdrops behind ovens and deep fryers, make cleaning easier and improve fire safety.

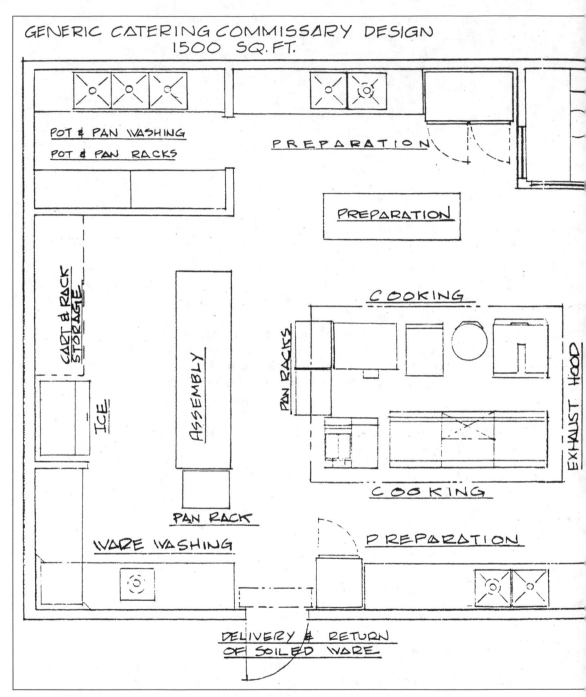

Exhibit 5.1 Generic Catering Commissary Design

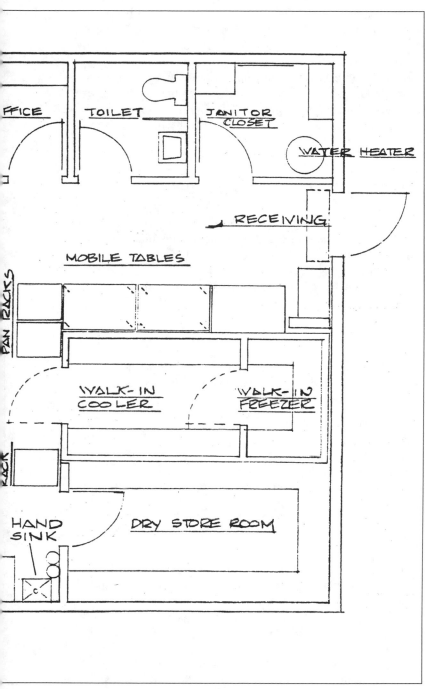

Exhibit 5.1 *(continued)*

It is imperative to have separate areas for incoming products, and finished products that are being shipped to clients. Another consideration is the overall appearance of the commissary. As part of your sales pitch, you may be required to show the kitchen to clients, who often want to see it, so make it clean and well lit.

Caterers should also think twice before automating. Highly automated equipment purchased to decrease labor and minimize tasks often ends up requiring more labor to maintain and to keep clean than the amount of labor saved! If you serve only two small buffets each weekday, for instance, you don't really need a computerized, automated slicing machine.

✖ *Basic Commissary Equipment*

A discussion of all basic commissary equipment follows, along with the criteria for purchase. Off-premise caterers should be aware that each catering operation requires a different equipment mix and perhaps a unique layout, as each will have different menu requirements and constraints. Use this discussion as a basic checklist and a guide. It's divided into cooking appliances, other types of appliances, and food holding equipment.

Cooking Appliances

Range Top. The most often used piece of commercial kitchen equipment is the range top, the heated cooking surface commonly known in home use as a stove. Range tops can be ordered:

- With individual burners, gas or electric—these are often known as *open top* or *grate top*, indicating the open-flame (gas) burners and metal grates over each burner on which the cookware sits.
- As a smooth, single-surfaced *flat top* or *hot top*. Flat top ranges are best to accommodate various large pots and pans, but they take more time to heat up and cool down than open top ranges.
- A combination of both.

There are also three basic types of ranges:

- The *restaurant range*, also called a *café range*, is popular for smaller foodservice businesses, or places where it is not going to be used constantly. It usually contains between six and ten open burners.
- The *heavy-duty range* is more of a workhorse, made of heavier materials, with burners that cook hotter and faster than restaurant ranges. It is designed for frequent and high-volume cooking.
- The *specialty range* is any one of several types of "custom" ranges outfitted for specific types of cooking—Asian, Mexican, soups and stocks, and so on.

Most chefs prefer gas ranges, and gas is usually the most readily available heat source in a commercial kitchen, but all appliances are also made in electric configurations.

Range Oven. Most kitchens want to make the best use of their space, so they order ranges with single or double ovens below. An oven with more than one cavity and set of controls is called a *stack oven*, because up to three of these ovens can actually be stacked, one on top of the other, to save space.

A main concern is the power source for these kitchen workhorses. Based on the specific location of the commissary, an experienced designer can determine the best power source: gas, electricity, or both. The floor of the oven is called the *deck*—that's why it's sometimes called a *deck oven*—and it's made of either stainless steel or ceramic. (The ceramic ones are best for bread baking.) Most ovens also have at least one metal rack to hold pans, but you can order more. Some models have steam injection capability for crusting breads and rolls.

Convection Oven. A popular alternative to the conventional oven is the convection oven. It uses internal fans to circulate the air inside the oven cavity, which results in 25 percent less cooking time and temperatures that can be 20 percent lower. It also requires a shorter warmup period. Convection ovens tend to dry out the food, so many caterers select a convection steam oven to introduce moisture into the cooking process. These ovens can do double duty as pressureless steamers. Many are computerized to provide different types of heat for different purposes. For example, they can first steam a duck to seal the pores, then roast it, and, finally, at the end of the cooking cycle, circulate hot air to brown the bird before serving.

Combination Oven/Steamer. This piece of equipment can bake and roast like a convection oven, steam and poach like a steamer, and cook or reheat food without drying it out. With three operating modes, it can:

- Cook with pressureless steam at 212 degrees.
- Convection cook at temperatures up to 500 degrees.
- Use a combination of steam and heat to provide typically faster cooking than dry heat alone, while browning the product and limiting shrinkage.

These versatile units are available in all sizes, from small-volume countertop units to floor-mounted rolling units with large capacities for banquets and institutional use.

Cook-and-Hold Oven. This type of oven roasts at low temperatures for many hours, resulting in greater moisture retention and better portion yields than conventional ovens. Most manufacturers claim 7 to 10 percent shrinkage, as compared with 25 percent for meats cooked in traditional ovens. A 14-pound prime rib, for instance, yields 11 servings when cooked in a convection oven, versus 15 servings produced by a cook-and-hold oven.

Microwave Oven. Don't think microwave ovens are just for home use! They come in very handy in commercial settings, to thaw and reheat small amounts of food quickly, and can also be purchased with a special attachment for browning. It is important to buy a commercial-grade microwave—the home-use models are not sturdy enough.

Fryer. Often called *deep fryers* or *deep-fat fryers*, these appliances come in countertop and freestanding floor models with capacities of anywhere from 15 to 130 pounds. A standard rule for calculating fryer size is that it takes six times as much fryer oil (the "fat") by pound as the item to be fried. For example, a 15-pound fryer will fry 2.5 pounds of food at a time (15 divided by 6). A caterer who specializes in fried chicken will need a larger-capacity fryer than one who does little frying. There are gas, electric, and infrared models.

Griddle. This cooking surface can be smooth, or grooved for frying hamburgers and other meats. It is typically used in commercial settings for frying or scrambling eggs, making pancakes, grilling sandwich surfaces, and sautéing. The griddle surface is called its *plate*, and most surfaces are sectioned into two or three separate plates with separate heat controls, so you don't always have to heat the whole surface.

Tilting Braising Pan. This flat-bottomed appliance looks like a griddle with raised sides, and, indeed, it can be used as a griddle, kettle, frying pan, or even a grill. It's a very handy workhorse that can reduce preparation time by as much as 25 percent simply because it tilts easily (with a hand crank or, for larger models, an electric motor) to remove the cooked foods.

Broiler. This appliance cooks food by bringing it into close proximity with intense, radiant heat, from either below or above. It browns the surface while keeping the inside of the product tender and moist—and it's not just for meats. When the heat surface is above the food, it's known as an *overhead* or *overfired* broiler, for obvious reasons. When the heat comes from below, it's an *underfired broiler* or *charbroiler*. Broilers may be heated with gas or electricity or by burning wood.

Barbecue Grill. This appliance comes in handy if your menu includes barbecued foods. Its heat source is either charcoal or propane gas. Charcoal grills are less expensive and produce excellent flavors, particularly with the addition of various types of wood chips. Gas grills provide a quick start, controllable heat, and a fast cool-down.

Steam-Jacketed Kettle. Kettles range in size from 20 quarts to 300 gallons and come in table-mounted and freestanding floor models. The steam-jacketed kettle is like a big bowl within a bowl; between the bowls, the empty space fills with steam, and the pressure of the steam can be adjusted higher (to cook foods quickly) or lower (to cook them slowly). Smaller models tilt to ease the removal of food. They are extremely versatile and excellent for preparing soups, stocks, and sauces.

Compartment Steamer. Also known as a *pressure cooker*, this appliance cooks food by transferring heat from steam onto the food—in this case, building pressure inside the cavity of the appliance. High-pressure steamers will cook small quantities of food very quickly, and low-pressure steamers will cook larger amounts of food, but not as quickly. They run on either gas or electricity, but a key consideration is to determine whether there is an existing steam source in the commissary. Otherwise, having steam appliances will mean ordering them with a self-contained steam generator.

Other Appliances and Needs

Coffeemaker. Most commercial coffee companies provide coffee-making equipment in exchange for using their coffee products. These units are installed in catering commissaries, where the coffee is prepared, then transferred to thermal containers and delivered to the party site.

The three main types of coffee-brewing apparatus are urns, satellites, and bottles. *Urns* are still the traditional means of brewing coffee in large batches—you've seen them in commercial businesses for years, made of stainless steel with a tap at the bottom to serve from. *Satellites* brew coffee directly into insulated containers for distribution to points of service. *Bottles* are used for producing smaller batches of coffee. *Air pots* are insulated containers, handy for holding and transporting coffee in small quantities. Many caterers now purchase espresso-brewing equipment, and even coffee grinders to roast their own beans.

For brewing coffee at an event site, you can use standard plug-in coffeemakers or portable urns. Farberware's brewer is highly polished stainless steel, suitable for placement on most buffets. At very high-end events, however, silver-plated samovars are necessary.

Food Mixer. Technically, this item is called a *vertical mixer* or *planetary mixer*, and it is used for mixing, blending, kneading, whipping, and emulsifying. In addition to the standard beaters (or *agitators*), stainless steel attachments such as whips, dough hooks, and pastry knives can be used. They are more expensive than aluminum attachments, but will last longer and not react with (and discolor) food products.

Almost every kitchen has a 5-quart mixer, and often a couple of larger ones too. Countertop mixers are called bench model mixers because of the stainless steel bench (table) they sit on. These come in capacities of 5 to 20 quarts; larger floor models range from 20 to 80 quarts. A 20-quart mixer can handle most mixing jobs for a small- to medium-sized caterer; the largest mixers are used by operations that make a lot of dough (no, not money!), like commercial bakeries and pizzerias.

There are lots of nifty attachments for mixers—for cutting and chopping, as well as bowl adapters to use smaller bowls with larger mixers, bowl guards (to cover the bowl during mixing, protecting the user's hands), bowl dollys (to roll big, heavy bowls instead of lifting them), and more.

Handheld Mixer. This is an absolute requirement for caterers doing small-batch cooking, because of its portability. Many models are cordless and can be recharged in three hours or less. They can be fitted with agitators to blend, beat, stir, and knead dough, and their mixing shafts are detachable for easy cleaning.

Food Processor. There are two standard types of food processors, used for cutting, chopping, and mincing foods quickly. The *bowl-style processor* has a rotating bowl and two blades (sometimes called *plates*) to do the work—different types of blades make different cuts. The food is placed in the bowl, which is then sealed; the chopping is done; and the food is removed.

There are also *continuous-feed processors;* the food is placed in a chute at the top and comes out another chute, sliced, or chopped, or otherwise processed. Home-use food processors just won't hold up under commercial rigors. For catering, a minimum of $^1/_2$ horsepower is required, and a 5-quart capacity bowl is minimum. Some models come with larger bowls and more horsepower. Processors are sold with a variety of options, including slicing disks for vegetables and fruits, shredding disks for making julienne vegetables and grating hard cheeses, and so on. A *Buffalo chopper* may also be used in off-premise catering operations, with a bowl that turns as the blade cuts soft foods like cooked vegetables.

Food Slicer. In addition to its ease of use for various tasks, as opposed to hand-slicing meats, cheeses, onions, and so on, a food slicer cuts more accurately than a knife. This means better portion control, a more uniform product, and cost savings. Slicers may be manual or automatic; both types involve moving the food back and forth on a carriage that slides it across a revolving blade. Slicers are usually identified by the diameter of the cutting blade, and the thickness per slice can be adjusted by setting a gauge plate on the equipment.

Refrigerator and Freezer. You'll need a number of these, and there are several basic types of refrigerated appliances:

- Walk-ins (or roll-ins) are large enough to stand in or to roll carts into. These can be either refrigerators or freezers and are used for bulk storage.
- Reach-ins are refrigerators installed near the work areas. They look the most like home refrigerators, but they may be kept colder because they're "reached into" very often, which affects the inside temperature. Some commercial reach-ins have several compartments with a separate door for each.
- Pass-through refrigerators are a type of reach-in, with doors on two sides, opposite each other, so they can be shared by two work areas. Food can be placed in one side and taken out of the other—salads made in a prep area, for instance, can be taken from the other side as needed by the wait staff.

Walk-in refrigerators and freezers should be installed flush with the floor, so it's easy to roll heavy items inside. They should have doors with handles that open from both inside and outside (to avoid shutting anyone in accidentally) and a door closer that works automatically when employees forget to shut it. Some have heavy-duty plastic strip curtains inside the big door, which can save energy by holding cold air in even when the door is open. Most commercial freezers and refrigerators have a safety light or buzzer that signals when the internal temperature is too high, and exterior-mounted thermometers so you can check the temperature without having to open the door or enter the unit.

Ice Machine. Ice-making equipment is rated by the number of pounds of ice it can produce in 24 hours. However, this rating is based on an incoming water temperature of 60 degrees Fahrenheit and an air temperature of 70 degrees Fahrenheit. A 10-degree increase in air temperature will reduce capacity by as much as 10 percent.

Your choice of ice machine will also depend on the types of cubes you need— you may wish to buy more than one machine, for cubed ice and crushed or flaked ice. Water-cooled ice machines are good for indoor use because they reduce the amount of heat generated within the kitchen.

To determine the best capacity for an ice maker, estimate the amount of ice needed for the busiest week. Multiply that amount by 1.2, then divide by 7. This will give you an amount you can then compare with the manufacturer's rating of the machine. The bin that stores the ice should normally hold twice as much ice as the machine can make in 24 hours. If your catering company has heavy weekend demands, you may wish to obtain bins with even larger capacity.

Ice machines require good drainage in addition to a water source. You should also install a water filter on the water line that feeds the machine. This will extend its life, as well as improving the taste of the ice and avoiding "off" odors. Many machines have self-cleaning capabilities and rust-free features.

Dish Machine. The type of dish-washing system you'll need depends on the volume of dishes (and pots and pans) to be washed and the amount of space you have. Commercial dish washing must be done at certain temperatures for sanitation reasons, and the heat generated makes ventilation a must in your dish room. (The dish room must also include space to stack and scrape dirty dishes and to dry clean ones.)

The basic machines require dishes to be placed into dish racks for washing. The racks are either placed inside the machine or placed on a conveyor belt that runs through the machine. (The latter type is called a *flight machine* or *rack conveyor*.) Many dishwashers require a *booster heater* to bring the rinse water temperature to 180 degrees for sanitation purposes, but some of the newer models are equipped with low-temperature, chemical sanitizing units. You can hire a chemical company to provide detergent for the machine, as well as parts and preventive maintenance services.

Garbage Disposal. A garbage disposal is installed as part of the dish-washing system, usually at the "dirty end" of the dish machine. It grinds up food scraps, which end up as part of the kitchen's overall waste output. Disposals are usually rated according to their horsepower. Other points to consider are the type and volume of the food waste and its physical size, the ability to reverse the flywheel that grinds the waste (to free it up when it jams), the availability of parts and service, and local health department regulations.

Kitchen Knives. The higher the percentage of carbon steel in a knife blade, the better it can hold its edge and stay sharp. The best knives are made of forged steel, shaped and ground from hot steel under pressure; lesser-quality knives are stamped from thin sheets of steel, in cookie-cutter fashion. A good chef's knife should have sufficient heft, but its weight must also be balanced between handle and blade, and it should feel comfortable in the hand.

Sinks. Heavy-duty kitchen sinks should be made of stainless steel, have coved corners (rounded, not sharp), and be wall mounted whenever possible to make them easier to clean underneath. A *three-compartment sink* is used for pot washing and is almost always required by local health departments. Each part of the sink should have an overflow drain, both hot and cold water, and a faucet that can swivel to reach all three compartments.

Separate *hand sinks* for hand washing are also required by health codes. They don't have to be very big, but they do have to be convenient to kitchen workers.

Ventilation Equipment. Local health departments require that exhaust hoods (or *canopies*) and grease filters be placed above all commercial cooking equipment (your "hot line") in order to remove the heat from the commissary as well as filter out the grease, which becomes a fire hazard. There are building codes that will specify how well the system must work; the industry norm is that the ventilation system must exhaust a total of 4 cubic feet of air per minute per 1 foot of floor space in the room. And, of course, ventilation hoods must be cleaned regularly, and their filters changed, to reduce the chance of fire.

Fire and Security Systems. Fire-retardant systems are required in new commissaries, and security systems will help keep insurance rates lower and deter criminal activity. Local police and fire departments can provide excellent advice on these concerns.

Receiving Scale. A receiving scale is a must for all off-premise caterers. Incoming supplies bought in bulk should be weighed to make sure you're not being short-changed. There are several types of scales for this purpose, ranging from countertop scales (to measure goods of 50 to 200 pounds) to beam scales that can roll on casters (wheels) and weigh objects from 100 to 1,000 pounds. Another option: Digital electronic scales are precise as well as compact.

Stainless Steel Preparation Table. Prep tables should be conveniently located throughout the commissary and include adequate storage space underneath and above them. Their edges should be rolled or coved (not sharp), and the table height should be about 4 inches below the worker's elbow, for comfort.

Rolling Baker's Racks. These are aluminum-frame racks on wheels that hold sheet pans. They can be used to store food and supplies or may be wheeled directly into walk-in and some reach-in refrigerators, and even into high-volume ovens in commercial bakeries.

Shelving. The width of the shelves should be determined by the items to be stored in the area. For #10 cans, 18- or 24-inch shelves work well, and 21-inch shelves are good for steam table pans. The best shelving lengths are 4 and 5 feet. Shelving is often purchased in four-tier units, but an optional fifth tier can expand capacity by an additional 25 percent.

A few other considerations: Vinyl-coated steel gives a nonskid surface; open-grid wire shelves allow air circulation and make it easier to see the wares; solid stainless steel shelves contain spills the best and are easy to clean, but need to be dusted occasionally.

Food Holding Equipment

In all cases, the best food transportation equipment is lightweight, rugged, and leakproof. It can be secured; it has wheels or can be easily transported on dollies.

For Hot Foods. This equipment should hold food at a desired temperature and the proper consistency, without cooking it further or drying it out. Infrared heat is best for holding food that is to be served within 15 minutes, and heats only the food, not its surroundings. For up to one hour, medium-term holding equipment, such as steam tables and insulated cabinets, works fine. For holding times of more than an hour, cook-and-hold ovens are excellent.

Numerous manufacturers offer metal warming cabinets that keep preplated foods and bulk food hot. Some models include humidity controls. They come in various sizes and heights and are also excellent for packing items upright in transit. Sheet pans filled with food slip directly into the cabinets, which can be wheeled directly into refrigerated trucks.

The past decade has seen the development of the portable and insulated pizza, food, and catering bags, many of which come with adjustable shelves to fit various size pans and handles that can be separated, allowing two people to carry them.

Hot foods can be transported to party sites in steam table pans, half- and full-size sheet pans, and food boxes. Rubbermaid and Cambro manufacture insulated food transportation carriers ranging in size from single-pan to multiple-pan carts. On the Internet, visit www.rubbermaidcommercial.com and www.cambro.com for some examples.

For seated, served dinners with guest counts in the hundreds, some caterers use banquet carts, which are often called *hot boxes* or *carters*. A banquet cart serves two primary functions—the first is to hold plated meals hot and safe while the kitchen staff is dishing up additional plates; the second is to transport the meals from commissary to the dining site. With the use of these carts, hundreds of guests can be served in a manner of minutes.

Look for a banquet cart capable of holding plated meals and that has quick heat recovery, inasmuch as the door will be open and closed a lot. Most carts use a minimum of 1,500 watts of electricity and are very well insulated. Also look for a heavy-duty base to support the weight of the food as it is transported over various (frequently uneven) surfaces. Look for durable hinges and latches that do no protrude from the cart.

For Cold Foods. Cold foods can be held in refrigeration, freezers, or ice chests. For transporting, refrigerated trucks are excellent, because baker's racks can be rolled right into the back of the truck. You can also pack the food into well-sealed plastic containers and chill it in ice chests with ice, but only if this is approved by your local health department. It is important that the food is sealed and that it never makes direct contact with either the ice or water from melted ice, for sanitation reasons. The website www.igloocommercial.com has some good samples of what's available for cold food storage and transport.

When transporting cold beverages like iced tea or lemonade in bulk quantities, caterers use insulated beverage carriers. When selecting these containers, be sure that they can be stacked easily and conveniently, retain temperature for up to five hours, seal securely, are rustproof, and have dripproof spigots that are recessed or protected from being accidentally flipped open when the carriers are stacked close together.

✖ Transporting Food and Equipment

Most caterers will need at least one vehicle for transporting food and supplies to event sites. Some smaller off-premise caterers can transport everything they need in an SUV, and larger operators may require a fleet of regular and refrigerated trucks.

Before investing in a vehicle, most caterers should rent vehicles of various sizes and try them out. Will a van be sufficient, or is it necessary to invest in a larger truck? Some caterers have installed portable, propane-powered cooking equipment in vehicles. Others have invested tens of thousands of dollars in elaborate "kitchens on wheels." Here we consider a few of the options.

Vans are very practical and quite economical for small- to medium-sized caterers who generally rent tables and chairs for events, rather than supply these items themselves. It is recommended to always use a van with heavy-duty suspension—for example, in the Ford line of vans, the 350 model would be preferable to the 150, because it carries more weight better. Caterers who have purchased the 150 (or other lightweight models) and wish to carry heavier loads with more stability should look into upgrades like heavy-duty shock absorbers, larger tires, and additional leaves in the springs.

Refrigerated trucks are not cheap. New models cost $25,000 or more, depending on size and features. After selecting a truck chassis, you can hire a local refrigeration or fabrication company to refrigerate and customize the vehicle. The best option is a self-contained refrigeration unit with a built-in generator; another option is a refrigeration unit that can be plugged into an outside power source.

Many caterers find it more cost-effective to rent trucks, and others believe in leasing or owning to ensure guaranteed access during busy periods. Some caterers purchase their smaller vehicles that travel more miles and lease the larger vehicles that are not driven more than 12,000 miles per year.

A few caterers have invested in *mobile kitchens* built into tractor-trailers, converted buses, and mobile homes. The leading manufacturer of mobile kitchens is Carlin Manufacturing, whose line includes sizes from portable "special event kitchens" that can be towed by SUVs, to huge self-contained trailers. Visit www.carlinmfg.com for a closer look at some of the options.

Whether you buy, lease, or rent, think about these things when you're selecting a truck:

1. Is it a reliable make and model that is easy to maintain?
2. The size should normally be no longer than 22 feet for driving ease and ability to turn corners in residential neighborhoods. Will the height of the truck allow it to enter areas where overhead clearances are limited?
3. Dual wheels in the back offer more stability and the ability to carry a heavier load.
4. Avoid trucks with wheel wells that cut into the cubic space available inside. At times, you'll need every bit of it!
5. Side doors are handy for loading and unloading items.
6. Lift gates are very desirable if you'll be transporting very heavy items such as ovens, dollies filled with chairs, or baker's racks filled with food.
7. Is there adequate lighting in the carrying compartment?
8. Is the truck insulated to protect the contents from extreme heat and cold?
9. Guardrails are handy on the inside walls.
10. Is there a drain for easy cleaning?
11. Look at the safety features of the vehicle, not only to secure the loads but to protect your drivers and other employees as well.
12. Is there an audible backup alarm that sounds when the truck is in reverse gear?

Design your catering fleet to meet the needs of busy periods, but also to minimize the time the vehicles must sit idle during slow periods.

As with any other vehicle, be sure to invest in regular preventive maintenance by either a reliable in-house mechanic or a trusted nearby service station. Another sound investment is a safety program for your drivers, which will help keep insurance premiums as low as possible.

Transporting food offers its own unique set of challenges, and off-premise caterers can be amazingly adaptable when it comes to getting food safely to its final destination. Of course, they take advantage of every possible tool and piece of equipment to do so!

For instance, none are without a two-wheel *hand truck* (or *dolly*) to easily transport full ice chests, cases of sodas, and other heavy items that are easily stacked. Dollies have four wheels and are good for transporting heavy loads over level surfaces, but are impractical at sites with steps or staircases to navigate.

Pieces of equipment like coffeemakers are best transported in custom-made plywood boxes, which offer more protection than their original cardboard box packaging. Plastic crates and containers are a must for transporting items of various sizes. Breakable items can be wrapped in old linens or plastic bubble wrap and packed in plastic crates. Bus boxes—those plastic tubs used to clear dishes from tables—with lids are also good for packing smaller items. Take hints from your local rental companies; notice how they pack things in bulk, and adapt their techniques.

✕ *Back-of-the-House Equipment*

Exhibit 5.2 is a listing of the miscellaneous equipment necessary for most off-premise catering operations. These items, used for mixing, measuring, and so on, are known collectively as *smallware*. The list is not meant to be all-inclusive, but may be used as a guideline or checklist for caterers who are just getting started in business.

⊠ **Exhibit 5.2** Back-of-House Equipment and Smallwares

Worktables with folding legs (4, 6, 8 and 10 feet)
Portable propane ovens
Portable fryers
Portable grill
Propane gas tanks
Electric coffeemakers
Electric tabletop convection ovens
Heat lamps
Electric countertop grill
Tabletop cassette au feu stoves
Electric hot plates
Rolling baker's racks
Warming cabinets
Chafing dishes for keeping food hot in kitchen
Stockpots (3, 6 and 10 gallon)
Woks
Sautée pans (8, 10, 12 and 14 inch)
Sauce pans, straight and slope-sided, nonstick (1.5,
    2.75, 3.75, 5.5, 7 and 10 quarts)
Sauce pots (14 and 26 quarts)
Steam table pans (full and half size)
Sheet pans (full and half size)
Smaller baking pans to fit in convection and home ovens
Roasting pans with locking lids
Baking pans for pies, cakes, cookies, muffins, and
    spring pans
Bread pans
Double boilers (8 and 12 quarts)
Brazier pots
Egg poacher
Blender
Stainless steel bowls (assorted sizes)
Cutting boards, composition plastic (assorted sizes)
Skimmers
Fry baskets
Ice cream scoops (assorted sizes)
Wire whips (assorted sizes)
Piping bags with assorted tips
Ladles (assorted sizes)
Tongs (assorted sizes)
Knives (French, carving, cheese, bread, paring, boning,
    cleaver, etc.)
Knife sharpener
Steels
Cook's forks
Funnels (assorted sizes)
Serving spoons (regular, slotted, perforated)
Spatulas (assorted sizes)

Rubber spatulas (assorted sizes)
Spaghetti servers
Pie servers
Pie markers
Egg beater
Rolling pin
Can openers
Vegetable peelers
Melon ballers
Garnishing tools (zesters, strippers)
Pastry brushes
Garlic press
Parmesan cheese grater
Paddles (30 and 49 inches)
Juice extractor
Box grater
Broiler scraper
Fruit corers
Poultry shears
Clam and oyster knives
Colanders
China caps
Sieves
Food mills
Thermometers (meat, candy, and deep fat)
Bus boxes with lids
Portion scales
Plastic food containers with lids (assorted sizes)
Beverage urns for holding cold and hot beverages
Ice chests
Garbage cans
Dollies
Hand trucks
Mop, bucket, and wringer
Brooms
Dust pans
Floor squeegee
Carton opener
Ingredient bins
Rubber floor matting
Oven and freezer mittens
First aid kits
Fire extinguishers
Extension cords
Hoses
Large funnel and metal containers for used cooking oil
Nonslip rubber floor mats

✕ *Front-of-the-House Equipment*

The front of the house means the areas that guests will see. Front-of-the-house equipment can be classified as follows:

Tables	Glassware
Chairs	Flatware
Linens	Tenting
China	Miscellaneous equipment

Tables. For off-premise catering, tables are generally classified in one of four types:

- Banquet tables are used for seated dining, buffets, food stations, and bars. The three most frequently used sizes are 8 feet by 30 inches (seats 8 to 10), 6 feet by 30 inches (seats 6 to 8), and 4 feet by 30 inches (seats 4 to 6). Of course, longer tables can be created by placing smaller ones end-to-end.
- Round tables are used for food stations and buffets, as well as for guest dining at catered events. They're considered to be more "upscale" and to foster conversation better than long banquet tables. Sizes are identified by diameter in inches, as follows: 72-inch (seats 10 to 12), 60- or 66-inch (seats 8 to 10), 48-inch (seats 6 to 8). The smaller sizes—36-inch (seats 4) and 30-, 24-, and 18-inch (all seat 2 to 4)—are used primarily for cocktail party setups.
- Conference tables are narrower than regular banquet tables (18 inches wide versus 30 inches) and are effectively used when space is limited. For example, when working in a narrow hallway, a conference table may fit, whereas a banquet table will be too wide. They also can be set up parallel to a banquet table to create an executive (wider) table. The most common conference table lengths are 6 and 8 feet.
- Special tables are used primarily for buffets and food stations to create various shapes other than simply straight lines. These include arc–shaped *serpentine tables*, which can be placed together to make semicircles and "S" shapes; trapezoids that create (when two are placed together) a six-sided table; quarter-rounds (8 or 10 feet in diameter), half-rounds (5 feet in diameter) or quarter-pies (30 inches in diameter), which can be used to "round out" the corners of square or rectangular tables and create a little extra seating. *Highboy tables* are those that are 42 inches high and are generally 36 inches in diameter. Guests can stand next to them or sit on stools. There are also *cake tables* on wheels, which come in diameters of 36 and 48 inches.

Chairs. The type of chair used at off-premise catering events varies depending on the type of event. Simple wooden folding chairs, usually in brown, are the least expensive, used when cost is a major concern. Folding Samsonite chairs, available in various colors, are good when a "classier" look is required. The wooden chair with a padded seat is a very popular and versatile style, and it comes in virtually any color—white, black, hunter green, natural wood, and more. The most expensive chair used at off-premise events is the *ballroom chair,* also with a padded seat. For upscale events, the Chiavari ballroom chair is an excellent choice. Originally introduced in the 1980s by Regal Rents of Los Angeles, it's now the industry standard and is available in silver, copper, gold, white, black, and natural. The mahogany Versailles chair looks similar to a wooden chair found in home dining and also features a padded seat.

For more information on some of the latest chair styles—including bamboo folding, bamboo rattan, the Black Queen chair, covered bar stools—and the latest colors in Chiavari ballroom chairs (raspberry, Montana blue, orange, amethyst, daffodil yellow, and sea green), visit www.panachepartyrental.com.

Regal International (www.regalinternational.com) has modified the original Chiavari chair by painting it with duotone finishes such as "Tuscan"—a rustic white with gold brush strokes—and copper patina with copper and green. Regal also offers a "Chameleon" chair, so named because it has four different removable backs.

Chair covers are available for most chair styles in various colors, fabrics, and sizes and can add an elegant look to a catered affair. Some of the most innovative and contemporary chair covers are manufactured by SculptChair (www.sculptchair.com). This company's line of stretch-to-fit covers has set the pace for innovative looks in this very trendy field.

When renting chair covers, be absolutely sure that they fit the chairs to be used at the event, because many covers are made exclusively for stackable chairs used in hotels, restaurants, and banquet halls.

Linens. An integral part of most parties, linens are noticed by the guests as soon as they enter the room. They should blend with the atmosphere, have no wrinkles, and be placed evenly on each table so that the bottom edges are parallel to the floor (except, of course, on the corners of rectangular tables topped with rectangular cloths). For upscale events, linens should reach the floor; for others, they should fall at least 12 inches from the top of the table on all sides.

When purchasing linens, off-premise caterers should look for the following things:

Are stains easily removed during washing?
Will the linens fade?
Do they easily resist mildew damage?
Are they fire retardant?
Do they require pressing?
What is the useful life span?
Can the napkins accommodate fancy folds?
How absorbent is the fabric?
Will it shrink?

Most linens are either cotton, cotton and polyester ("Visa"), or all polyester. Cotton linens are considered more elegant, but they do tend to fade and shrink and they require pressing before use. Polyester linens are more colorfast, and many do not require pressing if properly washed and dried. The main disadvantage to polyester linens is that they are nonabsorbent, which is an undesirable quality, particularly for napkins. Blends of polyester and cotton combine the advantages and disadvantages of both.

Round tablecloths, like round tables, are classified by inches in diameter. When ordering round tablecloths to cover round tables, you should add 60 inches to the diameter of the table if you wish the cloth to reach the floor. For example, a 120-inch cloth will reach the floor on a 60-inch round table. A 90-inch round cloth will cover a 60-inch round table, but it will not reach the floor—it falls about 15 inches, all around. Frequently requested round tablecloth sizes are 90, 108, 120, and 132 inches.

Cloths for rectangular tables are available in assorted sizes, such as:

60 by 120 inches	Covers 8-foot by 30-inch table
60 by 90 inches	Covers 6-foot by 30-inch table

Other sizes are dictated by local preference.

Linen trends change from year to year, so many caterers choose to rent linens to create a specific look for a specific event. Most linen suppliers recommend purchasing the basic solids—black, white, wine, ivory—and renting the trendy linens only as needed. Caterers should consider their client base before purchasing linens. For corporate events, under-the-sea prints and tropical motifs are fine, but for weddings, sheers, brocades, and satins are best. Sheer overlays are always in style. *Table skins* are two pieces of fabric that cover cocktail tables and highboys. They are manufactured exclusively by Affairs by Design (www.affairsbydesign.com). Some of the major linen suppliers are:

Artex International	www.artex-int.com
Milliken Napery Fabrics	www.milliken.com
Riegel Linen Supply	www.riegellinen.com
Tablecloth Co. Inc.	www.tablecloth.com

For linen rentals, caterers can contact:

A-1 Tablecloth Company	a1@a1tablecloth.com
BBJ Linen	www.bbjlinen.com
Cloth Connection	www.clothconnection.com
Got'cha Covered Linen Rental	www.gotchacovered.org
Party Arts	www.party-arts.com
Table Toppings	www.tabletoppings.com

Table skirting is available in virtually any color imaginable. Most are made from polyester fabrics for long life and resistance to wrinkling. Common sizes are 8, 13, 17, and 21 feet. Skirting should be used for all buffet tables, food stations, and head tables where guests are seated on one side. To determine the amount of necessary skirting, measure the linear feet to be skirted. For example, to completely skirt an 8-foot table, 30 inches wide, will require a 21-foot table skirt. This is computed by adding the dimensions of all four sides of the table: 8 feet + 8 feet + $2\frac{1}{2}$ feet (30 inches) + $2\frac{1}{2}$ feet = 21 feet.

Many rental companies also offer custom-made covers for banquet tables. These will fit over the table, covering to the floor, thus eliminating the use of skirting, top cloths, clips, pins, and labor.

China. The best china for use at off-premise catered events is simple, durable, and lightweight. The pattern should be in keeping with the caterer's image, the menu, and the caliber of the event. Plain white china is the most popular, followed by china with silver or gold trim; black china can be an interesting and distinctive touch. Some foods, such as smoked salmon, can be very elegantly presented on black plates. Coffee cups should have sufficiently large handles to avoid burning one's fingers.

When ordering china, it is imperative to consider both the menu and the type of event. Basic china items include:

Platters
Show plates
Dinner plates
Salad plates
Bread and butter plates
Dessert plates
Soup and cereal bowls
Bouillon cup and underliner
Vegetable dishes ("monkey dishes")
Coffee cups and saucers
Coffee mugs
Demitasse cups and saucers (for espresso)
Sugar and cream sets
Gravy or sauce boats
Salt and pepper shakers

As with linens, trendy new styles are always being added to tabletop lines. New geometric shapes and colors continually emerge, including square and triangle-shaped dinnerware. For an up-to-date look at some of the latest trends in dinnerware, keep an eye on these websites: www.tenstrawberrystreet.com and www.fortessa.com.

Glassware. The quality of the glassware must be in line with the overall caliber of the event. Plastic ware is adequate for picnics and barbecues. For parties around swimming pools, and in certain public places that simply don't allow glass to be used, the use of plastic is a necessity. Stemware is used for more upscale and elegant affairs, whereas tumblers suffice for many midscale events.

Annealed glassware is the least expensive. *Tempered* glassware is more durable, because there is an additional step in its manufacturing process that gives it greater strength than annealed glass. *Leaded* glassware (also called *crystal*) is manufactured by adding lead oxide and potassium silicate to the molten glass, making a very clear glass that produces a distinctive ring when struck lightly.

When selecting glassware, remember that:

■ The thicker the glass, the more durable it is.
■ A straight-sided glass has less strength than one with curves or bulges.
■ Glasses with rounded edges are easiest to clean.
■ A flared glass has a greater tendency to chip, crack, and break.
■ Crystal carries the highest price tag and has the least durability, but also offers the finest and most delicate appearance.

■ The two most likely reasons glasses break are impact (hitting something else) and thermal shock (fast temperature change).

Many caterers use a 13-ounce balloon-style wineglass as an all-purpose glass for water, wine, and most bar drinks except Champagne, brandy, and cordials served straight up. Tulip- and flute-shaped Champagne glasses are often used for upscale events. The saucer-style Champagne glass continues to be used by some caterers, although it is not recommended. The wide rim of this type of glass allows the bubbles to dissipate rapidly, so the Champagne goes flat too quickly.

To check glassware trends, contact some of the leading manufacturers:

Arcoroc (www.arc-international.com)
Cardinal International (www.cardinalglass.com)
Christofle Hotel (www.christofle-hotel.com)
Libbey Glass (www.libbey.com)
Riedel Crystal of America (www.riedelcrystal.com)

Flatware. Place settings reflect a caterer's image as much as any other detail and signal to guests the number of courses to be served. The weight of the flatware is probably its most important characteristic. The heavier the flatware, the higher the perceived value. Flatware should be comfortable to touch, hold, and use. Balance is essential. Basic flatware is either silver plated, stainless steel, or chrome. Gold-plated flatware is also available and can be used for an elegant touch, but it is very difficult to maintain because it chips easily. Silver plate is more expensive, more formal, and harder to maintain than stainless steel because it needs to be burnished regularly. Stainless comes in a broader range of prices and is generally more casual. Chrome is the least expensive.

Silver plate is a base metal electro-plated with silver to cover. The least expensive is silver over stainless. More durable, however, is an alloy of nickel, copper and zinc known as 70/30 brass or nickel silver. Since there is no standard for the amount of silver coating, the reputation of the manufacturer is important. Some manufacturers even add an extra coating to points of wear. Stainless steel varies in quality and price with the metals used in the mix. At the top of the line is 18/10. This is 18 percent chrome and 10 percent nickel. Nickel adds a warm silverlike luster. Chrome helps resist corrosion. Slightly below 18/10 is the most popular grade, 18/8, which is 18 percent chrome and 8 percent nickel. What is known as chrome is really stainless steel without nickel and either 18 or 13 percent chrome.[1]

Basic flatware pieces for catered events include:

Dinner knife
Butter knife
Dinner fork
Dessert or salad fork
Oyster fork
Teaspoon
Iced tea spoon
Soup spoon

Bouillon spoon
Serving spoon
Demi teaspoon
Dessert spoon

For more information on the latest trends in flatware, visit the websites of Corby Hall (www.corbyhall.com) and Oneida Foodservice, Inc. (www.oneida.com).

Tenting. The main purpose of tenting at an off-premise event is to protect the guests from rain and other elements. Other purposes include augmentation of an existing structure, as in placing a tent alongside a building to add room for the guests, or simply to create a more festive mood and enliven an otherwise uninteresting space.

There are several basic types of tents and canopies on the market:

- **Rope and pole tents.** These are commercial-grade tents, supported by poles and pulled tight using guy ropes attached to stakes. These tents have center poles and range in size from 20 to 150 feet wide, with expandable lengths. They must be installed by professionals.
- **Frame–supported tents.** The fabric of these tents is strapped or buckled to an aluminum frame. Sizes range from 10 to 40 feet in width, with expandable lengths. These tents have no center poles.
- **Marquees or walkways.** These long, narrow tent structures are used mainly for sheltering walkways or defining an entry into a tent. Widths are from 6 to 10 feet, with expandable lengths.
- **Canopy tents.** These are residential-grade, pole-supported tents that are pulled tight using guy ropes attached to stakes. Sizes range from 10 by 10 feet to 30 by 40 feet.
- **Tension structures.** These are commercial grades of pole-supported tents that utilize the strength of the vinyl-laminated fabric instead of the web or rope superstructure. Sizes range from widths of 30 to 80 feet, with expandable lengths.
- **Clear–span structures.** These are aluminum I-beam structures with fabric panels between the beams. Sizes range from 30 to 100 feet in width, with expandable lengths.
- **Quick–up framed canopies.** These are accordion-like canopies with collapsible legs that assemble quickly. Sizes range from 8 foot squares, to 10 by 15 feet.
- **Economy canopies.** These are inexpensive frame-supported canopies, usually 10 by 10 feet.

The formulas for determining tent sizes are covered in Chapter 6. As an off-premise caterer, you should be knowledgeable about tents, as you will use them often. For instance, many rental companies do not provide sides with tents unless sides are specifically requested. When ordering sides, it is important to specify whether they are to be clear, opaque, or opaque with windows. For events held after dark, and whenever opaque sides are used, lighting is essential. Theatrical-style lights are popular, as are elegant chandelier lamps that hang from the tent frame.

For the tent floor, off-premise caterers can choose from astroturf, wooden floors (for dancing or to provide for firm, even footing), or a combination of both. Frequently, flooring is installed over swimming pools to provide additional party space. Leave the floor installation to experts, and insist that they are fully insured. An installation mistake could result in disaster.

Platforms are used to elevate musicians, guest speakers, head tables, and bridal party tables. The risers to create platforms usually are available in 4- by 8-foot sections and can be installed at heights of either 12 or 24 inches. Railings and steps are excellent safety precautions, and skirting can be attached to the platforms to improve their appearance.

Tent poles are necessary in some cases, but unsightly. To disguise them, caterers may wish to place trees or shrubs next to the poles, or to use canvas pole covers. For very elegant affairs, fire-retardant tent liners may be used to completely cover the interior framework and poles.

Temperature control inside a tent is critical, particularly in very warm or cold climates or whenever it is necessary for all tent sides to be closed. Overhead or floor fans create air movement for cooling, but air-conditioning is usually required for comfort in a truly hot, humid climate. Costs for air-conditioning are very high, unlike the cost of portable heaters, which are rather economical.

Finally, you must be knowledgeable about any local regulations concerning the use of a tent. Many cities require a special permit for tenting, which must be obtained before the tent is set up. Tent rental companies can assist in this area, but it is your responsibility as the off-premise caterer to ensure this technicality has been taken care of before the event—and to get written proof of it. The last person you want to see at the party is an inspector who asks to see the permit—that was never obtained.

Leading tent manufacturers in the United States include:

Academy Tent and Canvas	www.academytent.com
DeBoer Structures USA	www.deboer.com
Eureka! Tents & Seasonal Structures	www.eurekatents.com
KD Kanopy, Inc.	www.kdkanopy.com
Olympic Tent/S.E.C. Sales Group	www.secsalesgroup.com
Tentnology	www.tentnology.com

✖ *Miscellaneous Other Equipment and Supplies*

Exhibit 5.3 lists the major front-of-the-house items used at off-premise catered events. Exhibit 5.4 includes other types of items, often used but disposable—that is, not reusable. Both lists are meant as guidelines; your own requirements will vary.

No current discussion of disposable products would be complete without addressing the topic of recycling. "Recycling within the special events industry can and should become an integral part of an industry that by nature produces an abundance of waste."[2] According to Tara Rosier, operations manager, Ambrosia Production in Santa Monica, California, off-premise events generate huge amounts of waste, and she suggests some tips for recycling on the following page:

☒ *Exhibit 5.3* *Miscellaneous Front-of-House Equipment*

Chafing dishes (stainless steel, silver-plated, one and two gallon)
Serving trays and platters
Serving bowls
Serving spoons, forks, knives, ladles and tongs
Cake and pie servers
Assorted baskets for buffet items
Assorted buffet decor items (shells, nets, blocks, mirrors, etc.)
Water pitchers
Samovars (urn for holding hot beverages)
Coffee pots
Water pitchers
Champagne fountains
Champagne and wine buckets
Candelabras
Bread baskets
Carving boards with warming lights
Carving knives, carving forks, and sharpening steels
Cassette au feu stoves for warming and cooking
Punch bowls
Ashtrays
Plate covers
Votive candles (small candles in glass cups)
Glo-ice trays (used for raw bars, ice carvings, and cold food displays)
Ice chests for ice for water glasses and chilling dinner wine
Oval waiter trays
Tray stands
Cocktail trays
Bus boxes and lids
Trash cans
Staple gun
Fire extinguishers
Machines for popcorn, sno-kones, cotton candy, and hot dogs
Wedding props (please refer to wedding section of text)

---

1. For bars, place empty beverage containers back into their original boxes, which naturally separates glass by color and also works well for plastic.
2. Aluminum cans should be placed in clear trash bags.
3. For casual events, trash containers should be placed around the site, with signs denoting the type of trash to be collected therein.
4. In the off-premise kitchen and commissary, cardboard boxes, wood produce crates, glass bottles, plastic containers, steel and tin cans all can be recycled. Training and labeling waste receptacles will help promote recycling and reduce trash collection bills.

⊠ **Exhibit 5.4** Catering Supplies

Disposable steam table pans
Cold cups (cold drinks, wine, Champagne)
Hot cups
Lids for cold and hot cups
Plastic plates (assorted sizes)
Plastic knives, forks, and teaspoons
Paper dinner napkins
Paper cocktail napkins
Doilies for trays and underliner plates for soups, etc.
Beverage stir sticks
Coffee stirrers
Swordpicks and skewers for skewering foods
Drinking straws
Film wrap
Aluminum foil
Heavy-duty tape such as duct tape
Plastic baggies
Wet-naps
Fuel for cassette an feu stoves
Sterno
Plastic gloves
Bug spray for flying insects and crawling insects (outdoor events)
Charcoal and charcoal lighter fluid
Business cards
Dish soap, silver polish, sponges, and scrubbing pads
Plastic for covering tables
Plastic table covers for kitchen worktables
Heavy-duty plastic for covering floors and carpets (like that used in homes and
    offices on which equipment is placed)
Paper liners for sheet pans
Disposable bowls, platters, and utensils
Garbage can liners
Disposable portion cups in various sizes
Disposable chef's caps
Wooden corn-on-the-cob skewers

Lo Tech Industries (www.lotechinc.com) makes a line of reusable tongs, servers, scoops, spoons, knives, ladles, and spatulas that are excellent products for caterers. Another very good resource for disposable packing is the Foodservice and Packaging Institute (www.fpi.org/jahia/Jahia).

Paper products made from recycled materials are available, but are not generally suited for off-premise events. Why not? The paper products used at catered events are already destined to go directly into landfills—they cannot be recycled because of the food waste on them. There is some recycling of polystyrene plastics if they are rinsed and sorted by type, which is impractical most of the time. So, from the standpoint of the environment, it is always better to use china dishes, glassware, and flatware.

✕ *Equipment Decisions: To Buy or to Rent?*

One of the questions most frequently asked by students of catering management, as well as newcomers to the business, is: "Is it better to rent or buy equipment?" The answer is, "It depends." A variety of factors influence this decision. Nearly all off-premise caterers own some and rent some equipment. Most off-premise caterers will purchase back-of-the-house equipment first, in their business-building phase. One way to make the rent-or-own decision is to ask yourself if you'll use any particular piece of equipment six or more times per year. If the answer is yes, consider buying it. Otherwise, rent it.

Another philosophy is that providing equipment—ranging from on-site food preparation appliances to salt and pepper shakers for tables—is simply part of being a service business, which is, of course, what off-premise catering is. The corollary, then, is that you're the expert. You're responsible for producing the successful wedding, party, or other event, and you deserve to make a profit for your work. Do you make more profit by renting, or by buying, particular types of items?

First, let's examine the advantages of renting equipment:

1. There is no capital investment.
2. There is no need to maintain the equipment.
3. As long as the caterer satisfies the "minimum order for delivery requirements" of the rental company, the rental company is responsible for delivering the equipment to the event site. However, it is still the caterer's responsibility to see that the rental company does deliver, on time, and the correct items.
4. There is no need to store rental equipment, thereby saving space and avoiding inventory hassles.
5. Many rental companies require only that dishes and equipment be "rinsed free of food" when you return them after an event. They wash the dishes and equipment.
6. The caterer has automatic access to a much wider variety of items, because rental companies have a wide assortment and the caterer is free to rent from more than one company.
7. Rental companies have much larger inventories than an individual caterer and can even subrent from a competitor to provide very large quantities of items. It's difficult for an individual caterer to have enough of everything.
8. It is easier to pass on the costs of rental equipment than the costs of owned equipment to clients. There is no question in a client's mind that there will be a charge for the rented items, since the caterer cannot be expected to pay for them

from profit. Yet without an invoice in hand for an exact amount, some caterers charge less for use of their own equipment—or don't charge at all.

Now consider the advantages of owning equipment:

1. Off-premise caterers who own equipment have greater control over the time of delivery. They are not dependent on the rental company's schedule.
2. Rental companies can be short of certain items, or out of stock altogether, and unable to fill the order. Or, in the case of a rural community, there may be no rental equipment available in the area.
3. Rented equipment may not be maintained up to the caterer's standards.
4. Rental companies are not always accurate when counting returned equipment back into inventory. They have been known to miscount in their own favor, then charge the caterer to replace "missing" items.
5. When rental companies invoice clients for lost or damaged equipment, they bill at "replacement cost," which is often higher than the actual cost. Their reason for this is that it takes their time to reorder, and while the item is not in service, it cannot be rented, thus resulting in lost revenue.
6. In a competitive bidding situation you can discount the cost of your own equipment, or even not charge for it, in order to underbid the competition. This certainly is not a good business practice on a routine basis, but there may be particular situations in which it is appropriate.
7. You may be able to rent your own equipment to other caterers, or to clients who need only the equipment, but not the food.
8. Off-premise caterers who own equipment can create a distinctive signature or identity with the style of equipment they choose.

In a case study prepared by Teri Woodard Polster for off-premise catering seminars conducted by the National Restaurant Association, certain assumptions were made in order to compare the cost of owning versus renting equipment. In this study, it was assumed that a caterer would purchase or rent sufficient equipment to serve two dinners and two cocktail receptions per week for 100 guests. In addition to the actual cost of the equipment, she computed theoretical costs for:

- Renting warehouse space
- Utilities
- Truck lease
- Rental warehouse manager
- Truck driver
- Utility person
- Necessary packing container
- Repair and maintenance
- Shipping containers
- Replacement of broken and missing equipment
- Cleaning supplies
- Laundry equipment
- Insurance
- Payroll benefits

✗ Advertising
✗ Bad debt expense
✗ Security
✗ Depreciation
✗ Any other miscellaneous expenses

In this example, the rental expense for the year was double the cost to purchase and maintain the equipment. This example in no way will directly apply to every off-premise caterer, but it does identify the indirect costs of owning, as well as the high costs of renting.

Of course, you have to determine the best solution for your own circumstances. There is no single "right way." One Washington, D.C., caterer began as a rental company and now owns a huge equipment inventory that contributes greatly to the firm's bottom line. Another caterer rents all equipment for the front-of-the-house and charges the client a price slightly higher than list. For this particular business, income from rental equipment adds at least 5 percent more profit to the bottom line.

It really does boil down to profit—and that, for a brand new business, is difficult to pin down. But over time, it is smart to examine your income statements and determine what percentage of profit you generate from (1) equipment or items that you own and rent out and (2) equipment or items that you rent from others, passing on the charges to clients.

✗ Dealing with Rental Companies

The relationships between rental equipment dealers and off-premise caterers can be "win-win" for both parties or a constant source of mistrust, tension, and aggravation. The key to working with a rental dealer is to understand dealers' terms. The following terms, obtained from a prominent South Florida firm, are typical:

1. List prices are for one day's use only, and they apply to all rented equipment even if some is not used. If equipment is returned late, there is an additional charge; however, there are special rates for rentals in excess of one day. For example:

One day	Pay one-day rate
Two days	Pay for one and one-half days
Three days	Pay for two days
Four to seven days	Pay for three days

2. Most rental dealers provide special containers for china, glassware, flatware, and other equipment to ensure that all equipment is received sterilized, undamaged, and table-ready.

It is imperative that all rented equipment by counted and inspected upon receipt. Shortages and any item that came in damaged should be reported to the rental company immediately. If this is not done, the caterer will more than likely be billed for replacement costs for equipment not received, or for that which was damaged upon receipt. Rental companies also charge for missing shipping containers and other items, such as hangers for table linens.

3. Rental companies generally do not set up tables and chairs, and they expect them to be taken down and stacked upon conclusion of the event. Some companies will do the setup and breakdown, but at an additional charge. Care should be taken not to leave equipment where it may get wet by being exposed to lawn sprinklers or rain.
4. The caterer's staff is usually responsible for rinsing all china, glassware, and flatware free of food particles and packing these items back into the shipping containers. Some companies require that all equipment be washed; others, only the china, flatware, and stemware. Otherwise, they add a ware-washing charge to the invoice.
5. Table linens should be shaken out (no food residue is to be left on them) and dried to prevent staining and mildew. If linens are wet, it is best to spread them out to dry after the party ends.
6. Most rental companies charge additional fees for deliveries above the street level, for locations outside their normal delivery areas, and to any other unusual locations where extra labor or time is necessary.
7. The off-premise caterer takes full responsibility for rental equipment from the time of delivery to the time of return. The rental company's insurance does not cover equipment while it is out on rental. Off-premise caterers must ensure that rental equipment is secure and protected from the weather. The rented items should all be counted again at the end of an event, and an attempt should be made right then to look for missing items. Generally, a complete inspection of the party site will turn up missing items—don't wait until the next day to do this.
8. Rental companies generally do not require advance deposits from established off-premise caterers, and many extend credit and offer discounts. First-time renters can expect to pay "cash on delivery" (COD), plus a security deposit. In some cases, a rental company charges a cancellation fee to a caterer who orders equipment in advance and then cancels the order so close to the party date that the rental company is unable to re-rent the equipment. Most rental companies have minimum order amounts for delivery of equipment.

Loss Prevention

Off-premise caterers can purchase insurance that covers loss of major items while at a party site. One off-premise caterer was billed $900 for the replacement cost of a 400-pound oven that was left overnight and stolen from a party site. Insurance is available to cover this type of substantial loss, but not for smaller losses like pieces of flatware or china.

Another way to limit losses is to ask that the rental firm pick up the equipment at the end of the party, instead of waiting until the next day. If the pickup occurs late at night, this usually results in an additional charge. Some off-premise caterers do not leave the highly pilferable items at a party site, but take them back to their commissaries for pickup there by the rental company. These types of items include silver pieces, flatware, samovars, and linens.

Off-premise caterers should always train their staff to handle equipment properly. For example: Use caution when handling candles so as not to drip the hot wax on the linens. Provide plenty of ashtrays for smokers. When staff members are working in very windy conditions, stemware should be cleared into bus bins and transported to the kitchen area.

An organized and efficiently operated dish return area can greatly contribute to a reduction in losses. Everyone in the foodservice business has seen the chaotic dish room where dishes are stacked from floor to ceiling and breakage is inevitable. It's much smarter to set up tables for the efficient return and handling of the soiled dishes. There should be sufficient space for trays and bus boxes, and soiled dishes should be immediately rinsed—or washed, depending on the rental company's rules—and packed for return.

The relationship between off-premise caterers and rental dealers can be excellent, as long as there is mutual respect. Caterers should follow rental companies' rules, and they should ask their rental dealers how they can make their relationship work better. In turn, rental companies should recognize that off-premise caterers work under extreme pressure; that rental merchandise must be delivered on time, all the time; and that the equipment must be usable, with no shortages.

✗ Effective Purchasing

After carefully considering the pros and cons of purchasing equipment, caterers who choose to buy all (or some) of it must consider various factors that impact the purchase decision. No matter what the item, the areas to be researched are:

Purchase price
Cost to operate
Cost to install
Cost to maintain
Cost of insurance
Depreciation
Obsolescence (Is it already outdated, or will it soon be?)
Safety (Underwriters Laboratory approval for electrical appliances; American
    Gas Association for gas appliances)
Design (Is it easy to use? Does it do what it was designed to do?)
Proper size for operation
Stock or custom (Stock is often better and less expensive.)

Leasing equipment is generally very expensive, but some dealers will finance 40 or 50 percent of the purchase price.

As a general rule, it is best to buy what is needed to meet the current business demands, rather than buying more equipment than necessary to meet projected demands in future years. All one has to do is survey the large restaurants that have gone bankrupt, in comparison with the small ones (40 or so seats) that continue to thrive. The same concept should apply to off-premise caterers—less equipment in a smaller space is most often better than more equipment in a larger space.

When purchasing china, flatware, glassware, and other tabletop items, off-premise caterers should be able to negotiate with the seller to arrive at a price somewhere between 50 and 100 percent of the list price. Remember that 50 percent of "list" is generally the dealer's costs before shipping. You can also get some good deals by purchasing slightly damaged linens. On a buffet table, it's easy to hide the flaws by using them as accent cloths. When considering quantities, off-premise caterers should plan on having a sufficient supply to handle most events, but should have the flexibility to buy additional items that are available on short notice for a particular event, or rent a similar pattern or style from a rental dealer.

Used equipment is readily available in most areas for significantly less money than new equipment. When shopping for used equipment, review the local newspaper's classified advertisements, visit the used equipment districts in larger cities, and even contact new equipment dealers who may have used equipment taken in as trade-ins.

Larry Levy, owner of Biddle Street Catering and Events in Baltimore, Maryland, says that before you spend time driving someplace to check out used equipment, call first to obtain the following information:

- Name of the equipment, model, voltage, amps, and energy source.
- Length of ownership, and whether the equipment was purchased new or used.
- The reason the equipment is for sale.
- Has it ever been repaired? By whom, and when?
- Is the seller reasonably flexible on the price?[3]

Levy also advises that when considering equipment for sale at an auction, you can obtain a list of the items to be sold, then pre-inspect the equipment and narrow the list to only those items that may be worthy of a bid. Conduct further research by checking service labels, learning the original cost when purchased new, and determining the installation cost. Finally, decide what your own maximum bid will be—*and do not exceed it.* For equipment that is sold in lots, you might organize a group of buyers to purchase the complete lot, or you may buy the desired item(s) from the successful bidder of the complete lot.

✗ *Equipment Trends*

Here, in no particular order, are a few of the interesting equipment innovations we've seen lately in our own off-premise catering business, along with website addresses for their manufacturers if you'd like to know more. No matter what the trend, remember to consult your staff members for their input about its usefulness to your business.

One of our most handy discoveries has been the black ice chests made by Igloo (www.igloocoolers.com). They are black on the outside and metallic gray on the inside. These look classy and don't show dirt, inside or out, like the white coolers. We know one caterer who has affixed plywood pieces to the bottoms of his black ice chests to prevent them from wearing out as quickly. Busy catering employees have a tendency to drag full, heavy coolers on the ground, and this helps protect them.

Tired of using the same ho-hum style of chafing dish, we've invested in polished aluminum and copper serving pieces. They're nice looking and inexpensive, and the service from their manufacturer, CHEFfield (www.cheffield.com), has been prompt and courteous.

The Versailles chair is a high-end alternative to the Chiavari that has become increasingly popular. High-end disposables are also hugely popular, including flatware by Christofle (www.christofle.com) and stemware by Mikasa (www.mikasa.com). In addition to contacting the manufacturers, we always check with Regal International (www.regalinternational.com) before we buy. Regal is the nation's largest rental equipment dealer, and it sells some equipment too. Regal's size allows individual caterers to take advantage of its enormous bulk purchasing power when stocking up on everything from folding chairs to triangular serving trays to ceramic bowls.

Afterglow stations (to serve after-dinner desserts and coffee drinks) have become very popular. Many caterers are now investing in their own equipment to make specialty coffee drinks like espresso, cappuccino, iced mochas, and more. There is big money in little drinks, and having your own equipment should pay off handsomely in this area.

In terms of smallware, one of the most useful tools we take with us everywhere is the cordless, rechargeable hand blender from Cuisinart. It's lightweight and durable.

And finally, we suggest that today's caterer be as computerized as possible. Check the options on www.hospitality101.com for computer programs, some of which even allow frequent customers to place their own orders with your company, online.

A closing thought: Make your equipment purchases on credit cards that offer airline mileage or other premiums. Why not give yourself a perk as you build your inventory?

✕ Conclusion

Before you can buy equipment, remember—you must figure out where you're going to install or store it. A professional foodservice planner can help with an efficient layout for your commissary, but it's up to you to make the appliance choices. Because you'll be working off-premise at most events, a critical part of your inventory should be food holding equipment to keep prepared foods at their optimum, safe temperatures.

There are hundreds of items to consider—from vehicles, to salt and pepper shakers, to tables, chairs, linens, and elaborate tents for outdoor events—and there are advantages and disadvantages to either renting or owning these items. Your up-front expenditures will be considerable if you set out to buy all your own supplies. It is smarter to buy some, rent some, and add to your own permanent inventory as your budget allows.

Notes

1. Lois Bloom and Patricia Boyer, in *Food Arts* magazine, September 1993.
2. Tara Rosier, in the newsletter of the International Special Events Society, Chicago, Illinois, May/June 1992. (www.ises.com)
3. Larry Levy, owner, Biddle Street Catering and Events, Baltimore, Maryland. (www.biddlest.com)

✖ Chapter 6

Logistics of Off-Premise Catering

This chapter deals with the planning and execution of the off-premise catered event. Off-premise catering creates unique challenges, as compared with catering performed in the caterer's own facility. This chapter covers the sometimes complex arrangements that are necessary when working away from your "home turf," including the following tasks:

- Discovering unique, exciting party locations and event sites
- Inspecting the site
- Planning and designing the off-site event
- Determining the party "packing list" and how to assemble, pack, and load what goes with you to an off-site event
- Delivering and unloading food, supplies, and equipment
- Presenting "The Show!" (the party itself)
- Reloading, returning, and reviewing the event

In her book *Entertaining for Business*,[1] Nancy Kahan provides a list of "Secrets for a Great Party." Some of her ideas apply to off-premise catering and are excerpted here:

"Plan ahead." The great locations and the best orchestras are booked years in advance.

"Aim to delight, aim to please; do not aim to impress." The "most expensive" is not always the right choice. The purpose of a party is to please the guests, not to impress them with the importance or wealth of the host or hostess. For example, a troupe of waiters who suddenly break into a dance routine between courses might be delightful—and certainly would be far less expensive—than a professional dance group that would cost thousands of dollars more!

"Don't settle for the ordinary—find an undiscovered place." The choices are almost limitless. An event under a bridge, or on the unoccupied top floor of an office building? Anything is possible!

"Don't be afraid to take calculated risks." Schedule a summer dinner under the stars, with an alternate plan in case of rain. Try a "progressive dinner," at which guests enjoy different courses of a meal at various locations within a neighborhood or area.

"Never assume anything." All details must be checked and double-checked. Astute off-premise caterers will review every detail with the client, including all other arrangements that the client has made with any other service providers: decorators, musicians, photographers, entertainers, valet parking services, and so on. For example, at some locations, electricity is limited. If power is to be shared between catering needs and the musicians, videographer, and lighting technician, a disaster could occur when fuses and circuit breakers blow. Prevent such disasters by taking precautions before they happen.

"Know your clients' entertaining goals." Caterers need to understand both the entertaining goals and entertaining style of the client. When a party fails to meet the entertainment objective, it is considered a failure. For instance, if the purpose of a corporate event is for employees to relax and have fun—but the menu is formal and the senior executives give long, boring speeches—ultimately, the event will not meet its goal.

✕ Scouting Unique Party Locations

Astute off-premise caterers have developed lists of unique and exciting party locations. They are as much location scouts as a filmmaker, going beyond the obvious locations—private homes, museums, places of business—to uncover and negotiate for the use of more unusual spots. Don't think of this kind of sleuthing as wasted time. Often, you will get a booking simply by suggesting the most interesting venue for a particular event.

Go online and see what you can find in your area. Look for theaters, museums, historical sites, and movie houses. Contact your local convention and visitors' bureau, and area chambers of commerce. Read local magazines as well as social event and society columns. Speak to real estate agents about private estates and homes that may be available for parties. Network with other caterers, rental firms, and suppliers. Local colleges and high schools often have facilities available; state and city film commissions know of numerous interesting spots that may be suitable for catered parties, wedding, or other events.

Clearly, many of these venues will offer unusual challenges, which must be addressed prior to your event. A thorough site inspection is mandatory weeks ahead of time, with these critical details in mind:

- Any cost(s) associated with use of the facility.
- Weather, and alternate plans in case it doesn't cooperate.
- Parking and valet availability, if needed.
- Utilities: water, power, waste removal, backup power in case of emergency.

- Rules about deliveries.
- Existing kitchen facilities or equipment that may be used.
- Ability to obtain a permit for the particular use or event. Does the use meet the basic requirements, such as fire and safety codes, for the number of people expected?
- Rules about (or a prohibition of) alcohol service on the premises.
- Neighbors and noise ordinances.
- Sufficient space for the planned activities (seating, risers, portable dance floor, etc.).
- Insects and pest control options (if outdoors).
- Security and emergency requirements.
- Adequate number of restrooms for the crowd.
- Sufficient lighting, interior and exterior (parking lot, etc.).
- Insurance and other contingencies.

In fact, if a client comes to you with a site already in mind that you aren't familiar with (or is not normally used for events of this type), don't promise that you can "make it happen" until you discuss each of the items on the checklist with the property owner or manager, as well as the city or county department(s) that may be involved in issuing permits.

Each venue poses unique issues regarding layout and design. Probably the most frequent problem you'll run across is a lack of adequate area for guest seating. Will a tent be required, or can you provide additional seating areas by covering a swimming pool with a portable floor? Make sure to consider door sizes. Every caterer at one time or another has had the unhappy experience of trying to wedge a much-needed rented oven through a door or gate that was too small.

✕ *Site Inspections*

All the reasons just mentioned make it mandatory for the caterer to visit the site personally, rather than rely on a client's enthusiastic description of the location. A dose of realism is necessary, and a firsthand look is the only way to get it. In addition to permitting you to assess the items on our checklist, a visit allows you to meet the key people at the site who may be able to assist you. Most off-premise caterers bring all or some of these things to a site inspection:

- Sample menus, brochures, business cards (if you like the site, you'll bring them more business!)
- Notes or contracts from prior discussions with clients
- Paper, pen or pencil, and clipboard
- A small camera to photograph the party site and its features
- An oven thermometer (if using an existing oven onsite)
- Your preprinted Site Inspection Checklist

What exactly are you looking for, other than the perfect ambience for the upcoming event? A detailed discussion of each element of the site inspection follows.

✳ *Electricity.* It would be unusual to find an off-premise caterer who has not blown a fuse with a basic electric coffeemaker. Every caterer quickly learns that two coffeemakers cannot be plugged into the same 20-amp circuit, because each appliance requires about 16 amps. Because fire marshals are becoming more concerned with the safe use of propane, butane, and Sterno, off-premise caterers should understand some of the technical aspects of the electricity they'll be using. There are a few basic measurements of electricity with which you should be familiar:

An *ampere* (or "amp") is a term used in indicating how much electric current flows through a circuit. The larger the diameter of an electrical wire, the more amperes it can safely carry.

A *volt* is the driving force that sends the ampere through the electrical wire. (One volt is the force it takes to push 1 amp of electricity for 1 second.) Common voltage needs for appliances are 110–120 and 208–240.

A *watt* represents the actual consumption of the electric energy. (One watt equals the flow of 1 amp of electricity, at a pressure of 1 volt.) Electrical appliances are often rated in terms of both watts and volts.

So, to determine the total amount of electricity needed, it is necessary to compute how many watts will be needed to run all the electric appliances—everything from the lighting and musical amplifiers, to the kitchen equipment, plug-in video gear, and anything else. To determine the watts required, multiply the number of volts needed by the number of amperes needed (volts × amps = watts).

Here are some examples of power needs in off-premise catering situations:

Kitchen lighting = 1 watt per square foot
Tent lighting where guests will be = 2.5 watts per square foot (not counting "extra" stage lighting or electricity for musicians)

Luckily, wattage requirements aren't too tough to determine. On most commercial equipment, the watts are listed on the UL (Underwriters Laboratory) or other safety approval label; you can ask musicians, lighting personnel, and others for their needs.

Once the total wattage is determined, divide it by 100 to determine the total amps required. (Technically, the voltage is actually 120, but multiplying by 100 provides an extra safety factor.) For example, if 28,000 watts are needed, when this amount is divided by 100, it will reveal that 280 amps are needed—which means fourteen 20-amp circuits. To provide the necessary power, be sure to order a generator with a minimum capacity of 280 amps. And don't forget the "little details"—you can't plug too much into a single circuit. Only *one* coffeemaker at a time, or you'll blow a fuse!

Most buildings actually use a little more than half of their available electrical power, and there is a way to access the rest when you need it. A licensed electrician can use what is called a "gray box," a circuit panel board, to tap directly into the power surplus for a particular event. If the event is in (or even near) an existing building, this may be less expensive and more efficient than renting an electric generator. In the event of a power outage, you do need to be prepared with a backup power source. The smallest generators usually produce 50 amps of electricity.[2]

✗ *Water.* We've already discussed the idea of bringing bottled water to party sites for mixing drinks. However, much more of this vital substance is needed for cooking and cleaning, as well as filling ice water glasses at tables. During the site inspection, identify the water sources, check the potability of their water, and note whether a hose or carrying containers are required. Obviously, if there is no water available—at a ceremony at a building newly under construction, for instance—then it will be necessary to bring enough water. Many caterers fill their own 5-gallon containers of bottled water and haul them to the site.

Trash. When the event ends and everyone goes away smiling, who cleans up and what happens to the trash? In some areas, where there is no scheduled trash pickup, off-premise caterers must take all garbage with them. At other locations, there are trash cans available, and even staff to remove them. (But are there *enough*?) If there will be deep-frying at the party site, you must check to see if there is a container for used cooking oil. Otherwise, it will be necessary to bring your own. You must never dispose of oil or food on the ground, or down a drain, at a party site.

Off-Premise Kitchen and Staging Area. This is where the caterer will complete on-site preparation and arrange everything for the service of the event. Some locations—churches, synagogues, community centers, and the like—are equipped with commercial kitchens. This generally makes the job much easier; however, during the site inspection it is still necessary to check the facility's exhaust systems, trash containers, drainage, hot and cold running water, doorway size leading into and out of the kitchen, refrigeration, freezers, ice machines, and fire extinguishers.

All too often you'll be setting up in a place where there is no commercial kitchen, making it necessary to evaluate various locations in (and around) the party site for a suitable kitchen/staging area. Think about whether the area is:

- Covered, in case of inclement weather
- Out of the guests' view
- Well lit
- Close to where the guests will be
- Close to the loading or receiving area
- Easy and safe for service staff to enter and exit

Let's examine some typical locations used by off-premise caterers for cooking and staging catered events, to check out their possible advantages and disadvantages.

Existing home kitchens. These are fine for small parties, but for larger events they pose many obstacles—ovens that are too small for full sheet pans and steam table pans, little storage space, inadequate refrigeration, and poor layout. When it is the only alternative, then caterers must remember to bring smaller baking pans, check the oven for accurate temperature controls, store as much as possible in a back room or garage during the party to avoid cluttering the kitchen, bring adequate cold food holding equipment, and be sure there is adequate ventilation to remove cooking odors and heat from the home.

Garages and carports. These are excellent in warmer climates, because the off-premise caterer has more open space and is able to lay out the kitchen based on the needs for the specific party. Six- and eight-foot banquet tables can be placed strategically around the area for use as work tables. In most areas it is fine to cook inside garages with butane, electricity, or Sterno, but if propane gas is to be used for cooking, both the propane and the cooking equipment must not be located inside the garage. It can be placed close to the garage, but always outside, for safety reasons.

⚔ **Cook tents.** In areas where there is no suitable, covered space for a kitchen, off-premise caterers will frequently rent or provide cook tents. They are available in various sizes, the smallest being 10-feet square. They frequently are used in parking lots or outside commercial or public buildings with no interior cooking facilities. Cook tents may or may not need side panels and lighting, depending on the weather and the time of day they'll be used. If all sides are closed, ventilation is limited, so it is best to close only the sides that may be affected by inclement weather.

✝ **Other cooking and staging areas.** The options are endless, but most experienced off-premise caterers have at one time or another worked on loading docks, alleyways covered by overhangs, empty rooms or offices, or vacant storefronts. Adaptability is key! Where there is a will to have a party, the ingenious off-premise caterer will find a place to prepare the food under safe conditions.

✗ **Kitchens on wheels.** Buses, semi-trailers, trucks, vans, trailers, and motor homes are all candidates for conversion to mobile kitchens. Film industry caterers, for instance, are fully equipped to prepare a gourmet meal in custom-designed kitchens, no matter where the film crew is working. These units require a major investment of time and money, but if you'll really use them, you should investigate the options and talk with caterers who use such mobile facilities.

✗ *Rain Plan.* A "must do" at any site inspection is an agreement between caterer and client on a plan of action in case of inclement weather. Mother Nature can smile on, or ruin, a fabulous outdoor event. Sometimes tents will provide the solution; at other times it may be necessary to move the party indoors. The important thing is that this solution *should be agreed upon in advance* of the event, and the client and caterer also should agree upon *what time the decision will be made.* The time may be the morning of the event, so that there is enough time to call for a prearranged, last-minute tent installation or to move the party to another location. We had one outdoor wedding at which a group of the bride's friends had a copy of the guest list, complete with phone numbers. Each member of the group was given a portion of the list so he or she could call and confirm a location change with all the guests when it began to pour that morning.

✗ *Insurance.* As a business owner, you should have:

✗ **General Liability coverage**—This protects your business in cases of personal injury, bodily injury, or property damage. A minimum coverage amount of $1 million is suggested.

✗ **Professional Liability coverage**—This protects your business from claims that you did not render the professional services usually associated with your business. It's sometimes called "Errors and Omissions" insurance.

✗ **Liquor Liability coverage**—As its name implies, this protects your business against claims that you, or your staff members, served liquor illegally or irresponsibly.

Many off-premise venues now require proof of insurance (and minimum amounts of coverage) for General Liability and Liquor Liability, as well as proof of Workers' Compensation. Many sites demand naming the location as an additional insured. Some sites also require that the client (your customer) provide proof of insurance. Some companies offer a "Wedding Insurance" package that covers everything from wedding photos to nonrefundable deposits to damage on rented property. It's smart to know a little about the coverage, or to have a couple of insurance agents' names, to share with brides and grooms.

More specific policies for individual catered events include "Event Assurance" insurance (sometimes called "Adverse Weather Coverage"), which is highly recommended. This type of insurance policy is very specific, detailing the date, hours of coverage, locations, and weather conditions (amount of precipitation, wind speed, temperature, etc.) under which an event will be canceled. For more information, visit www.goodweather.net.

There are other types of insurance that may cover cancellation of events due to incidents beyond your control. There is "Cancellation or Abandonment" insurance, which covers vendors' advance deposit fees in case an event (from a wedding to a rock concert) is canceled. Sometimes "Non-Appearance" is combined with "Cancellation/ Abandonment" in one policy, which provides indemnity for the planners or promoters of an event if specific persons (named in the contract) don't show up as a result of accident, illness, or death. There's even a clause for "Disgrace," meaning that if a celebrity does something that is publicly offensive before an event, his or her presence may no longer be desired there—again, leaving planners and contractors in the lurch, having already paid deposits, rented equipment, and made arrangements. The type of coverage, and who should pay for it, depends on the type of event and your role in it.

❴ *Existing Equipment.* Many locations already have some features necessary for the catered event—perhaps a bar, some tables and chairs, an outdoor barbecue grill. As long as you're allowed to use them and they're in good working order, they can reduce the amount of equipment you'll need to bring along. Experienced caterers note these features and discuss them with clients to decide whether they will be used at the party. Part of the agreement should detail who is responsible if something is broken or damaged during the event.

❴*Delivery and Pickup of Food, Equipment, and Supplies.* Where will you, and any rental equipment companies, unload at the site? This can be very complicated, particularly in high-rise buildings where there are crowded loading docks and a couple of different sets of elevators to reach the party site. While inspecting the site, caterers should decide where to unload equipment, food, and supplies, and where the rental companies should do the same, because it often happens that the rental company makes its delivery long before the off-premise caterer arrives on-site.

There must be a place for secure storage of this equipment, as well as someone to receive and sign for it, and a place to store it after the event until is retrieved by the rental company. If there is no secure place, then the rental company may need to pick up at a specific time (and usually at an extra cost) immediately upon conclusion of the event; or, as the caterer, you will need to keep an eye on it or take it with you when you pack up.

✗ *Proposed Party Layout.* At this time, the off-premise caterer (usually with the client) will begin to discuss where everything will take place during the event. Some public locations have floor plans drawn to scale; most private residences do not. Techniques for laying out and designing catered events are discussed later in this chapter. But during the site inspection, you should at least prepare a "rough" diagram of the event, noting those significant features that will affect the layout.

✗ *Permit Requirements.* Zoning, fire, and other permits can be surprisingly problematic. Rental companies can often help in this arena. Some caterers insist it is less expensive to hire off-duty firefighters than to meet the flame-retardant codes for tenting. If guests are traveling by motor coach to a private mansion in a private neighborhood, neighbors may complain about the noise from the motor coaches. Noise restrictions in some neighborhoods can ruin a perfectly outstanding party when the police arrive to shut down the event. Ask about every possible type of permit, and its availability at *this* location for *this* type of event, before you or your clients commit to a site.

✗ *Meeting the VIPs.* At many public party sites there are those "behind-the-scenes" people who are familiar with the venue and know how to get things done, and they can be of supreme assistance to the caterer. Experience teaches off-premise caterers to find these people during the site inspection and advise them of the requirements for the event. These helpful folks include loading dock personnel (who can make deliveries and pickups more efficient), building engineers (who know the locations of utilities, circuit breakers, etc.), and the security staff (who can assist with securing equipment, parking rules, etc.). For home parties, many clients employ cleaning and maintenance workers, who will know where things are and can help solve minor problems before and during the event. Be nice to these people!

✗ *Other Site Inspection Details.* There are a number of miscellaneous, but important, details to be considered: rental fees for the space (and cleaning fees afterward), rules and regulations, policies regarding liquor service, security, and parking for guests. All of these must be confirmed at the site inspection. Many off-premise caterers have been surprised by rule changes at a facility they thought they were familiar with. For example, a caterer prepares to set up a bar in a particular spot and is informed that this cannot be done because the rules were just changed—but no one told the caterer. Some off-premise caterers require that someone from the facility sign a written copy of the rules to avoid these last-minute hassles or frustrations.

Site inspections should include a check of restroom facilities, as well as accessibility for persons with disabilities. Problems in these areas should be resolved in advance, not during the event.

Timing. The timing for party setup and tear-down is critical. Many museums and historic sites are open until late in the day, leaving off-premise caterers a limited amount of time to set up for private after-hours functions; others book back-to-back functions and let the caterers and rental companies figure out how to juggle them. At the end of an evening, most of these facilities require removal of all party equipment. Some have special fees for loading in and out, some require use of union labor, and many have restrictions on rolling tables over expensive flooring.

If there are elevators, know how they work and where they go. Be sure that the clients have arranged for their use. Off-premise caterers should allow additional time for setting up and tearing down parties that are not on a ground floor. We've discovered a major problem in high-rise office buildings the hard way—that cleaning personnel often have exclusive use of some or all of the elevators, making it impossible for caterers to enter and exit. If this is the case, it is imperative that the clients or building management make the necessary arrangements.

Alerting Your Staff. Advance planning for the staff members who will work the party should include providing them with an exact address and directions to the party site, finding out where the staff will park, and determining where the staff will change into their uniforms after setup but prior to the event. There should also be an emergency phone number at the site that will be answered after hours. This can be a problem in an office, where the receptionist goes home as the party begins. It is imperative to know the name and phone number of the person in charge of the facility during the party. The prevalence of cellular phones should make this fairly easy.

Caterers should be aware that some restrictive rules are actually subject to negotiation, particularly if they will prohibit a party from being held at a facility. Such things as early setup can be discussed with the facility manager and can sometimes be resolved by paying an additional fee. Off-premise caterers who frequently work at unique, public off-premise locations have learned to advise the client that there may be additional costs involved in catering the event due to unforeseen circumstances, and a contingency clause should be included in the catering contract. An example: If the site is not made available to the caterer on time, and the caterer needs to hire extra last-minute staffers to have the party set up on time, this would be a situation in which the caterer would be able to charge for the extra staff.

✗ Planning and Designing the Catered Event

The results of the site inspection, coupled with the menu and other information, are the input for the party layout. For simple parties, the layout can be roughly sketched during the site inspection; but for large, involved, complicated events, the rough diagrams and notes from the site inspection should be incorporated into a scale diagram of the event. This diagram should include:

- Registration tables and check-in areas
- For weddings: gift, cake, and place card tables

- Bars, buffets, and food stations
- Seating for guests during cocktails and dinner
- Service stations for staff
- Dance floors, stages, and space for entertainers
- Off-premise catering kitchen and staging area

The diagram should be to scale to ensure that things will fit where planned. Disasters have occurred when off-premise caterers "assumed" that a certain number of tables would fit into a specific room and they did not.

Caterers used to make such diagrams with a sharp pencil and graph paper, and perhaps some still do, but others have purchased computer software programs to assist with layout and design at off-premise venues. These programs take the guesswork out of design, and they present an extremely professional image to clients.

Find out more about various catering software packages at www.leadingcaterers.com/cateringsoftwarelist.asp.

Layout and Design Criteria

Front of the House (Guest Spaces)

Unlike hotel ballrooms and catering halls, off-premise locations used for catering have specific primary uses unrelated to foodservice, thus creating unique challenges. The size, shape, and flow of the location influence the layout and design. Questions to ask while determining an overall layout include:

- How many guests will be attending?
- Where will they be arriving?
- What are the menu and beverage arrangements?
- Are there other planned activities—dancing, speeches, etc.?
- Are there existing features, such as bars and seating?
- Where is the off-premise kitchen in relation to the party?
- What is the theme of the party?

Prior to considering each element of the layout, it is important that readers understand some generally accepted square footage requirements.

TYPE OF PARTY OR REQUIREMENTS	SQUARE FEET PER PERSON
Stand-up cocktail party	5 to 6
Cocktail party—some seating	8
Dinner—rectangular tables	8
Dinner—60 in. rounds for 10	10
Dinner—48 in. rounds for 6	12
60 in. rounds for 8	12
72 in. rounds for 10	12
Theater-style seating (weddings)	6
Dance floor	2 to 4
Speaker's platform	10

For bands, allow 10 square feet per musician, 20 square feet for the drummer, 30 square feet for a spinet piano/keyboard, and 100 square feet for a grand piano. If the musicians are on risers or platforms, steps and railings should be provided for safety.

For theater-style seating, allow 3 feet from the front of one chair to the back of the next one. Suggested spacing is 5 feet between guest tables at seated events. For large events with hundreds of guests, the seating area should be divided into "groups" of tables, with 6-foot-wide main aisles between sections. For example, a party with 40 tables could be divided into four groups of 10 tables each, with a 6-foot aisle in between. Head tables at which guests are seated on only one side are usually impractical at off-premise events where space is at a premium, because they require twice as much space as regular guest seating at round tables.

Coat checks and registration tables should be placed near the entrance for security and convenience of the guests. Off-premise caterers should advise clients to provide adequate registration personnel to prevent long lines, which may extend outside the party site. Bars, buffets, and food stations should be strategically placed around the room—never clustered all in one area. Bars should be set up so guests may see them upon arrival, but not so close to the entrance as to block the flow of guests into the party. Bars generally require 100–150 square feet of space. One bar with one or two bartenders is generally adequate for efficient guest service, depending on the type of drinks offered and the skill of the bartenders.

Displaying the Food. Dramatic buffets and food stations create excitement, interest, and intrigue. They should act as magnets, drawing guests into the room and reflecting the theme (and sometimes, even the budget) of the event. A buffet is simply a style of service that permits the guests to portion and plate their own food. Buffets save on labor costs, but they can actually increase your profit margin because not everyone "loads up" at a buffet. Ironically, the more attractive the display, the less people eat, because they do not want to ruin its appearance!

Straight, long tables are boring for these types of displays; Exhibit 6.1 depicts more creative designs. There are some basic rules for buffet setup:

- Never place a buffet (or a bar) adjacent to the dance floor or music.
- Allow plenty of space between stations for guests to circulate.
- Allow adequate surfaces on which empty drink glasses may be placed.
- Attempt to locate the food as close as possible to the kitchen, to minimize the distance traveled for initial setup and replenishment.
- Place lowest-cost items first on the "line."
- Expensive items (caviar, beef tenderloin) should be portioned by servers and carvers.
- Preportion appropriate items into smaller portions, because people may prefer small amounts of certain things.
- Remember that guests tend to take less food from small containers.

If all guests are eating at the same time, 50 to 75 people can be promptly served by each line. Because two-sided self-service lines take less space, 100–150 guests can be served from one double-line table instead of two singles. A carver or server can

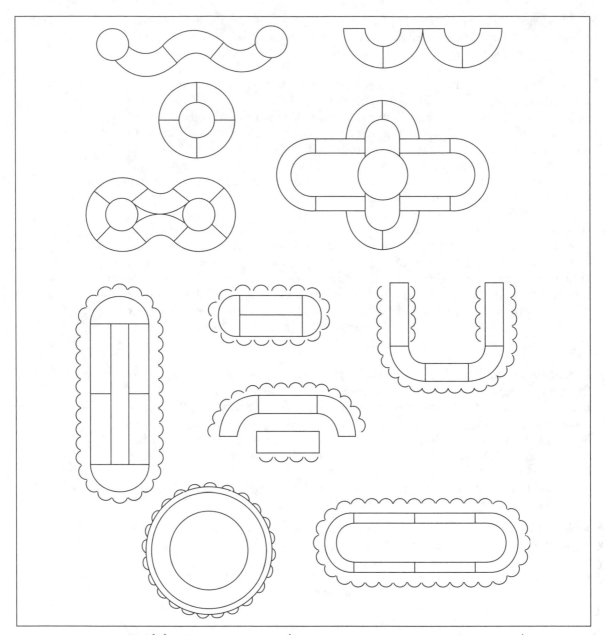

Exhibit 6.1 Buffet Layouts (Courtesy of American Rental Association)

stand at the end of each line, portioning or carving one or two expensive items. Exhibit 6.2 diagrams a simple buffet with food servers and one carver.

Buffets longer than 16 feet should be the width of two tables, or 60 inches. A wider buffet seems in better proportion, more like a lovely, generous display and less like a cafeteria line.

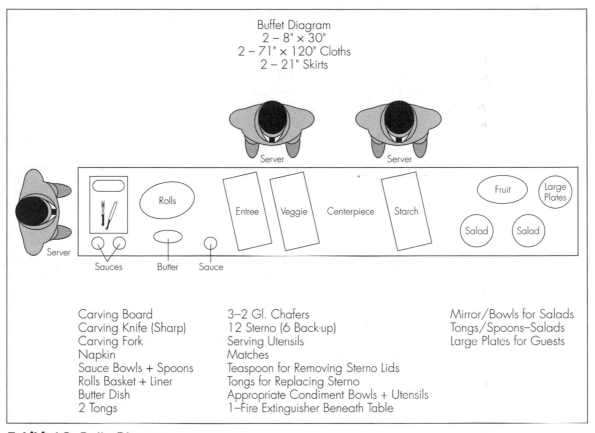

Exhibit 6.2 *Buffet Diagram*

The "props" you'll use to decorate the buffet lines must be organized and transported to the event site like everything else. Centerpieces and even some buffet dishes can be elevated for visual effect with the use of sturdy, empty crates or boxes covered with attractively "bunched" linens. (You can purchase damaged linens from rental companies for this purpose.) Mirrors can be used beneath cold foods or flower arrangements; marble slabs, acrylic trays, and tiered cake stands add interesting looks and dimensions to the display. Portable spotlights, floodlights, and lamp stands will also come in handy, as a little extra lighting will showcase a beautiful buffet. But you've got to remember to bring all of these items along when you leave the commissary!

Back of the House (Kitchen and Staging Areas)

For smaller events in homes and offices, off-premise caterers generally use the existing facilities, making the best of some very difficult situations. Of course, the menu must be compatible with the facility. The answers to the following questions will help an inexperienced caterer organize an off-premise kitchen within the confines of an existing one:

- Where can backup supplies be stored?
- Where will items be cooked and kept warm?
- Where can cold foods be prepared and kept cold?
- Where will the hot and cold food dish-up take place?
- Where will the food servers pick up food and return dirty dishes?
- Where can coffee be brewed?

For larger events where hundreds are to be served, cooking tents are generally erected if there is no existing (or adequate) kitchen facility. Exhibit 6.3 depicts one way to lay out and design a large, off-premise catering kitchen. The following design criteria should be considered:

- Design the kitchen so that servers can easily pick up food (and return soiled dishes) without going through the kitchen. It is good overall safety policy to keep everyone who is not part of the kitchen staff out of the cooking area.
- The busing area for dirty dishes should contain trash receptacles, water for rinsing dishes, and room for empty dish and glass crates. This area ideally is distanced from the cooking area, especially at larger events.
- Four-, six-, and eight-foot banquet tables are excellent for use as kitchen worktables. Caterers should be sure to allow enough worktables for the type of foodservice to be provided.
- The coffee and dessert should be kept at the rear of the tent until ready to be served, and adequate space must be determined for all items pertaining to coffee and/or dessert service.
- For each course, the necessary equipment and supplies should be gathered together and kept in a common spot, to be used and then set aside as attention shifts to the next course.
- There should always be arrangements made to warm plates for hot food courses.
- Tables are necessary next to the ovens to provide space for the cooks to set down hot foods from the oven.
- The same area used to assemble ("plate up") salads can be used to plate up desserts.
- Place portable liquid-fuel warming ovens at the edge of the tent for ventilation. A large sign on an easel for the event's menu, which also lists ingredients of each item, should be placed near the food pickup area.
- Proper placement of grill equipment is essential for safety. Barbecues fueled by gas or charcoal require good ventilation and should be placed where smoke doesn't drift over staff members or guests.

Experience is probably the best teacher in learning to utilize space for catered events. The guidelines presented here are only suggestions. Readers should remember that a well-designed party will go a long way toward satisfying the client's needs and can make everyone's job more efficient—and more enjoyable—during the event.

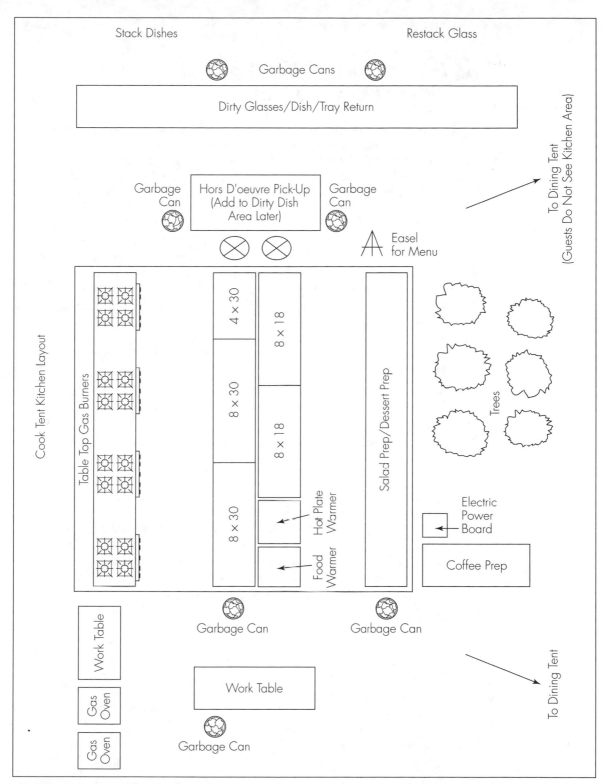

Exhibit 6.3 Cook Tent Kitchen Layout

⚔ *Rental Order Forms and Party Packing Lists*

Once the layout and design are complete for the catered event, the party packing list (also called a *pull sheet*) and the final rental order form can be prepared. Most off-premise caterers have forms that make these tasks easier and reduce the likelihood of errors. You'll see samples of each form in this section.

The idea behind these lists and forms is to ensure that all food, supplies, and equipment necessary for the party are delivered on time to the site. Items that are provided from the off-premise catering commissary are included on the pull sheet; items to be rented are included on the rental equipment order form. An exception to this rule occurs when an off-premise caterer obtains a small equipment order directly from a rental company. In this case, the rental equipment should be included on the packing list, which reminds the caterer's staff to bring it to the event.

Some caterers just use copies of the rental order form supplied by the rental firm, but this may cause confusion if you deal with more than one rental company, because the forms are not consistent in style. It's probably easier for everyone on your staff to develop and use your own form, such as the one in Exhibit 6.4. A rental order form can be developed by listing these major categories:

Chairs	Flatware
Tables	Serving pieces and equipment
Tenting and accessories	Glassware
Kitchen equipment	Other (generators, gazebos, one-time items not
Linens	commonly rented)
China	

The rental equipment list should detail the size, type, and color of each item. It is a good idea to leave space on the form for caterer's notes. For instance, there may be four 8-by-30 tables needed for the buffets, eight 8-by-30 tables needed for the kitchen staff, one 8-by-30 for the gift table, and two 8-by-30 tables for bar service. A total of fifteen 8-by-30 tables need to be rented, and it helps when completing this order form to have room to "place one's thoughts," which saves time in the long run.

The top of the form or a cover page should indicate:

- Name of client
- Date of event
- Delivery address
- Delivery date
- Time of delivery
- Date of pickup
- Rental company name
- Name of salesperson who took order
- Date the order is placed

The objective of developing a rental order form is to list everything needed for the event that is *not being provided by you*, the off-premise caterer. The caterer's current

⊠ Exhibit 6.4 *Rental Equipment Order Form*

NAME OF CLIENT _____

DELIVERY ADDRESS _____

DELIVERY DATE _____   TIME TO DELIVER _____

DATE TO PICK UP _____   ORDER PLACED WITH _____ (NAME)

DATE ORDER PLACED _____

QTY ORD	QTY REC'D	QTY RET'D	ITEM AND DESCRIPTION	PRICE
			CHAIRS	
___	___	___	SAMSONITE	___
___	___	___	WHITE WOOD WITH PADDED SEAT	___
___	___	___	BALLROOM	___
___	___	___	OTHER _____	___
			TABLES	
___	___	___	8 FOOT BY 30" BANQUET TABLES	___
___	___	___	8 FOOT BY 18" BANQUET TABLES	___
___	___	___	6 FOOT BY 30" BANQUET TABLES	___
___	___	___	6 FOOT BY 18" BANQUET TABLES	___
___	___	___	4 FOOT BY 30" BANQUET TABLES	___
___	___	___	72" ROUND TABLES	___
___	___	___	60" ROUND TABLES	___
___	___	___	48" ROUND TABLES	___
___	___	___	36" ROUND TABLES	___
___	___	___	30" ROUND TABLES	___
___	___	___	QUARTER ROUND TABLES	___
___	___	___	QUARTER ROUND PIE TABLES	___
___	___	___	HALF ROUND TABLES	___
___	___	___	OTHER SPECIAL TABLES _____	___
___	___	___	UMBRELLA TABLES AND CHAIR SETS	___
			TENTING AND ACCESSORIES	
___	___	___	DINING TENT SIZE ____ WITH SIDES? _____	___
___	___	___	COOKS TENT SIZE ____ WITH SIDES? _____	___
___	___	___	CEILING FANS _____	___
___	___	___	TENT LINER _____	___
___	___	___	POLE COVERS _____	___
___	___	___	ASTROTURF _____	___
___	___	___	FLOORING _____	___
			OVENS, RANGES, AND FOOD-WARMING CABINETS	
___	___	___	SIX-BURNER RANGE WITH OVEN	___
___	___	___	FOUR-BURNER RANGE WITH OVEN	___
___	___	___	SIX-BURNER RANGE ONLY	___
___	___	___	OVEN ONLY	___
___	___	___	FOOD-WARMING CABINETS	___

⊠ Exhibit 6.4 (continued)

LINENS, CHAIR COVERS, AND TABLE SKIRTING
132" ROUND CLOTH COLOR
120" ROUND CLOTH COLOR _____
108" ROUND CLOTH COLOR _____
90" ROUND CLOTH COLOR _____
NAPKINS TYPE _____ COLOR _____
60" BY 120" BANQUET CLOTH COLOR _____
90" BY 90" BANQUET CLOTH COLOR _____
62" BY 62" CLOTH COLOR _____
CHAIR COVERS COLOR _____
CHAIR COVER SASHES COLOR ____
SKIRTING COLOR ____ SIZE ____
SKIRTING COLOR ____ SIZE ____

CHINA—SELECT PATTERN AND COLOR _____
SERVICE PLATE (SHOW PLATE)
DINNER PLATE
DESSERT/SALAD PLATE
BREAD AND BUTTER PLATE
SOUP CUP UNDERLINER
SOUP CUP
COFFEE CUP AND SAUCER
DEMITASSE CUP AND SAUCER
CREAMERS
SUGARS
GRAVY BOATS
SALT AND PEPPER SETS
OTHER _____

FLATWARE—SELECT TYPE _____
DINNER KNIFE
BUTTER SPREADER
FISH KNIFE
TEA KNIFE
DINNER FORK
SALAD/CAKE FORK
COCKTAIL FORK
TEASPOON
SOUP SPOON
DESSERT SPOON
ICED TEASPOON
DEMITASSE SPOON
PASTA SPOON

SERVING PIECES AND EQUIPMENT
LARGE SERVING SPOON
SMALL SERVING SPOON
SERVING FORK
LADLE
CAKE/PIE SERVER
CAKE KNIFE

____   ____   ____   ONE GALLON ROUND CHAFER   ____
____   ____   ____   TWO GALLON OBLONG CHAFER   ____
____   ____   ____   EXTRA PANS HALF _____ FULL _____   ____
____   ____   ____   50 CUP SAMOVAR   ____
____   ____   ____   100 CUP SAMOVAR   ____
____   ____   ____   COFFEE POURER   ____
____   ____   ____   WATER PITCHERS   ____
____   ____   ____   OVAL TRAYS   ____
____   ____   ____   ROUND TRAYS   ____
____   ____   ____   GLOW ICE DISPLAY   ____

____   ____   ____   GLASSWARE   ____
____   ____   ____   TULIP CHAMPAGNE   ____
____   ____   ____   BUBBLE WINE GLASS 12 OZ   ____
____   ____   ____   BUBBLE WINE GLASS 9 OZ   ____
____   ____   ____   IRISH COFFEE MUGS   ____
____   ____   ____   CRYSTAL CHAMPAGNE FLUTE   ____
____   ____   ____   CRYSTAL WINE GOBLET   ____
____   ____   ____   CRYSTAL WATER GOBLET   ____
____   ____   ____   BRANDY SNIFTER   ____
____   ____   ____   CORDIAL GLASS   ____

____   ____   ____   OTHER RENTAL EQUIPMENT   ____
____   ____   ____   GENERATOR   ____
____   ____   ____   PLATFORMS FOR MUSIC AND SPEAKERS SIZE ____   ____
____   ____   ____   STEPS FOR PLATFORMS   ____
____   ____   ____   RAILING FOR PLATFORMS   ____
____   ____   ____   SKIRTING FOR PLATFORM COLOR ____ SIZE____   ____
____   ____   ____   DANCE FLOOR SIZE _____ TYPE ____   ____
____   ____   ____   CHAMPAGNE FOUNTAIN   ____
____   ____   ____   BRIDAL KNEELING BENCH   ____
____   ____   ____   BRIDAL ARCH   ____
____   ____   ____   GUEST BOOK STAND   ____
____   ____   ____   FLOWER BASKET STAND   ____
____   ____   ____   WHITE LATTICE GAZEBO   ____
____   ____   ____   WHITE LATTICE CHUPPAH   ____

____   ____   ____   OTHER MISCELLANEOUS EQUIPMENT   ____
____   ____   ____   _____   ____
____   ____   ____   _____   ____
____   ____   ____   _____   ____

____   ____   ____   SUBTOTAL OF ORDER   ____
                               EXTRA FEE FOR NIGHT PICKUP
                               ABOVEGROUND DELIVERY FEE
                               TOTAL PRICE OF ORDER

                       NOTES FROM RENTAL CHECK-IN, I.E., DAMAGED
                       OR MISSING EQUIPMENT, OTHER PROBLEMS
____   ____   ____   CREDIT DUE FOR THE ABOVE   ____

____   ____   ____   BALANCE DUE RENTAL COMPANY   ____ equipment inventory and the proposal or contract will determine which items must be rented. When completing this form, check the menu, necessary kitchen equipment, and other services that will be provided. Ask questions like:

- Is there another event taking place at the same time for which the caterer's own equipment will already be needed—grills, trays, china, glassware, etc.?
- How will each menu item be presented? Think about the plate sizes and necessary utensils and whether you have enough of them on hand. Include serving pieces, not just flatware needed by the guests.
- Does the contract specify providing platforms, dance floors, audiovisual equipment, special lighting, etc.?
- Table size impacts service items: Will 60-inch or 72-inch rounds be used for dining? If using 72s at an upscale event, three creamers and three sets of salt and pepper shakers per table are necessary.
- What other services are being contracted? The minister may need a sound system. The bride and groom may request kneeling benches. The harpist may ask for a small platform. The musicians may need chairs.

The list goes on and on! When developing a rental order form, consider having it printed in multiple copies so that the same form can be used to check the order in before the event and to perform an inventory after the event. Anything that arrives damaged on delivery should be noted on the form and replaced right away if possible. An inventory after the event will verify to the caterer any losses charged by the rental company.

It is important to read the contract thoroughly and to know your own inventory very well, so you'll be able to order what you need in advance—and not those items you can provide from your own inventory. A Sunday afternoon, hours away from the big bridal reception, is not the time to contact a rental company because something wasn't ordered. And remember, a few additional chairs, napkins, and place settings never hurt, in the event unexpected party guests arrive.

A party packing list can be developed by listing these main categories of event supplies:

- All foods, both uncooked and prepared
- China, glassware, flatware
- Tables and chairs
- Ovens and other types of cooking equipment
- Pots, pans, kitchen utensils
- Coffeemakers and samovars
- Sodas, juices, ice, and bar supplies
- Coolers (with ice)
- Buffet and food station equipment and décor

There are also essentials used at every event; you might as well count on bringing them along:

- Aluminum foil, plastic wrap
- Napkins
- Tool kit
- Broom, dust pan, and mop
- Fire extinguishers
- First aid kit

No two caterers will have the same party packing list, although they will include the same basic items. There are two characteristics that all lists should share: One is that they should be very specific, including everything the caterer may bring to the event. For example, "pots or pans" is not specific enough. The details are mandatory: What size? How many of each type?

Second, the order of the list should coincide with the various storage areas within the caterer's operation and, if possible, be arranged in the same order as the shelving. If, for instance, an off-premise caterer has a front storeroom and a back storeroom, items for the front storeroom should be listed together on one section of the packing list, with those for the back storeroom listed in a separate section.

These pull sheets (indicating what to "pull" from inventory and take along) should include a front, or cover page, that states the following:

- Name, day, and date of the event
- Client's name and contact information
- Exact address of the event, including directions
- Deadline for having catering vehicle(s) fully loaded
- Specific vehicle(s) to be loaded
- Departure time for your crew to leave for the event site
- Names of those responsible for packing and loading

The objective of developing a party packing list (like the one in Exhibit 6.5) is to detail everything needed for the event that *you* will provide, as the off-premise caterer. And, to save time in the whole process, you must know that the items you have promised to provide are, indeed, in your inventory and available for use that day, at that event.

Filling out a party packing list can be daunting when you're a beginner. The best way to start is to refer to the party contract, which lists all foods, beverages, equipment, and services to be provided by the caterer, and compare that list to what's on the completed rental order form. Break things down to their individual ingredients or components:

- **Raw ingredients:** Exactly what will you need to produce the food item at the party site? A Caesar salad, for example, will require romaine lettuce, croutons, Parmesan cheese, and a Caesar dressing (if prepared in advance) or the components to toss one at tableside.
- **Preparation techniques:** How will this item be prepared? For the Caesar salad, the caterer will need a large mixing bowl, a grater for the Parmesan, a ladle for the dressing, and plastic gloves for mixing and dish-up personnel.
- **Service style:** How will this item be served? On a buffet, the Caesar salad may be served from a variety of bowls. If it's a seated meal, salad plates will be necessary. And do not forget salad forks or tongs, trays, and tray stands.
- **Preparation area requirements:** Where in the kitchen will the salad be mixed and plated? Plan for sufficient worktables. Fancier salads that are assembled on-site require more worktable space than those that are tossed, stored in big containers, and simply kept chilled until plating.

⊠ Exhibit 6.5 *Party Packing List*

NAME OF PARTY _____

DATE OF PARTY _____

LOADED BY _____

VEHICLE TO BE LOADED _____

DEPART BY _____

NAME AND PHONE NUMBER OF CLIENT _____

LIST ALL FOOD TO BE LOADED FOR THE PARTY:

Display Fruit

_____

Display Vegetables

_____

Cheese:
    Parmesan
    Cheddar
    Swiss
    Brie
    Blue
    Saga Blue
    Gruyere

_____

Half & Half
Whipped Cream
Indiv. Creamers

_____

Butter Solids—Unsalted
Butter Solids—Salted
Butter Molds

_____
_____
_____
_____
_____
_____
_____
_____
_____
_____
_____
_____
_____
_____
_____
_____
_____
_____

Leaf Lettuce
Romaine
Watercress
Hydroponic
Bibb Lettuce
Radicchio

_____

Fresh Basil
Fresh Dill
Fresh Tarragon

_____

Lemons
Limes

_____

Hearts of Palm
Hearts of Artichoke

_____

French Bread
Italian Bread
Specialty Bread
Hot Dog Buns
Hamburger Buns
Crackers
Nuts
Croutons

_____
_____
_____
_____
_____
_____
_____
_____
_____
_____
_____
_____
_____

✖ Exhibit 6.5 (continued)

Indicate quantities for all nonfood items and equipment:

Pantry Items

_____ Salt
_____ Pepper
_____ Spices
_____ Sugar packets
_____ No-cal sweetener
_____ Individual packets
_____ Individual packets
_____ Salt
_____ Pepper
_____ Mayo
_____ Ketchup
_____ Relish
_____ Mustard
_____ Pam
_____ Frying oil
_____ Vegetable oil
_____ Bread crumbs
_____ Flour
_____ Olives
_____ Onions
_____ Cherries

_____ Coffee
_____ Decaf
_____ Iced tea bags
_____ Regular tea bags
_____ Pastry shells
_____ Sherry
_____ Cooking wine

_____ Cola
_____ Diet cola
_____ Ginger ale
_____ Lemon-lime
_____ Tonic
_____ Club soda
_____ Flavored waters
_____ Bloody Mary mix
_____ Orange juice
_____ Cranberry juice
_____ Grapefruit juice

Linens
_____ Napkins (Color)
_____ 62 by 62 (Color)
_____   (Color)
_____   (Color)

_____ Banquets (Color)
_____   (Color)
_____   (Color)
_____ 132″ Round (Color)
_____   (Color)
_____   (Color)
_____ 120″ Round (Color)
_____   (Color)
_____   (Color)
_____ 108″ Round (Color)
_____   (Color)
_____   (Color)
_____ 90″ Round (Color)
_____   (Color)
_____   (Color)

_____ Towel mop
_____ Bib aprons
_____ 13-foot skirt
_____ Black waiter jackets
_____ White chef coats
_____ Logo T-shirts
_____ Theme uniforms

_____ _____
_____ _____
_____ _____
_____ _____

Pots and Pans
_____ Bus pans
_____ Bus pan lids
_____ Full sheet pans
_____ Half sheet pans
_____ Full food pans
_____ Half food pans
_____ Full deep pans
_____ Medium sauté pans
_____ Large sauté pans
_____ Omelette pans
_____ Fry pans
_____ Medium sauce pans
_____ Small sauce pans
_____ Large cast iron fry pan
_____ 32-quart stock pot
_____ 15-quart stock pot
_____ Braziers
_____ Fry baskets
_____ Large colanders
_____ Medium colanders
_____ Skimmers

_____ Strainers
_____ Large steel funnel
_____ Extra large stainless steel bowls
_____ Medium stainless steel bowls
_____ Utility bowls
_____ 2-quart measuring container
_____ 1-quart plastic containers
_____ 2-gallon chafing dishes
_____ Plate covers
_____ Full shallow aluminum food pans
_____ Full deep aluminum food pans
_____ Half shallow aluminum food pans
_____ Half deep aluminum food pans
_____ Oval waiter trays
_____ Round cocktail trays

_____ _____
_____ _____
_____ _____
_____ _____

China, Glassware, Flatware, and Tabletop Items
_____ Dinner knives
_____ Dinner forks
_____ Salad forks
_____ Teaspoons
_____ Bouillon spoons
_____ Cocktail forks
_____ Salt and pepper shakers
_____ Ashtrays
_____ Water pitchers
_____ Coffee pourers
_____ Large rectangular silver trays
_____ Medium round silver trays
_____ Small oval silver trays
_____ Silver bread baskets
_____ 12-inch silver bowls
_____ 7-inch silver bowls
_____ 5-inch silver bowls
_____ Large rectangular aluminum trays
_____ Medium round aluminum trays
_____ 4-inch Acoroc bowls
_____ 5-inch Acoroc bowls
_____ 7-inch Acoroc bowls
_____ 12-inch glass bowls
_____ Special bowls _____

_____ _____
_____ _____

_____ Black lacquer trays
_____ Oval mirrors
_____ Round mirrors
_____ Glass carafes
_____ Large punch bowls
_____ 12-ounce bubble wine glasses

_____ Tulip Champagne glasses
_____ Brandy snifters
_____ Cordial glasses
_____ Martini glasses
_____ Coffee mugs
_____ 9 1/2-inch plates
_____ 7 1/2-inch plates
_____ 6-inch plates
_____ Coffee cups
_____ Saucers
_____ Creamers
_____ Sugars
_____ Votive candle holders

Plasticware and Paper Goods
_____ 8-ounce styro cups
_____ 6-ounce styro cups
_____ 10-ounce hard plastic glasses
_____ Plastic forks
_____ Plastic spoons
_____ 10-inch plastic divided plates
_____ 10-inch plastic plates
_____ 7-inch plastic plates
_____ 6-inch plastic plates
_____ Plastic Champagne flutes
_____ 7-inch plastic bowls
_____ 12-inch plastic bowls
_____ Plastic gloves
_____ Cocktail napkins
_____ Dinner napkins
_____ Large doilies
_____ Small doilies
_____ Mini baking cups
_____ Swordpicks
_____ Wet-naps
_____ Wood stir sticks
_____ Sip straws
_____ Toothpicks
_____ Plastic storage bags
_____ Duct tape
_____ Film wrap
_____ Aluminum foil
_____ Bar kits
_____ Pourer spouts

Buffet and Food Station Décor
_____ Shells
_____ Glass pebbles
_____ Vases: type _____
_____ Hurricane lamps
_____ Glass blocks
_____ Fans
_____ Stapler gun and staples

☒ Exhibit 6.5 (continued)

_____ Ribbon: colors _____
_____ Scissors
_____ Floral wire
_____ Floral tape
_____ Large carving boards
_____ Oval carving boards
_____ Small baskets: color _____ For _____
_____ Medium baskets: color _____ For _____
_____ Large baskets: color _____ For _____
_____ Extra large baskets: color _____ For _____
_____ Stick candles
_____ Votive candles
_____ Candelabras
_____ Wooden crates
_____ Plastic crates
_____ Fresh flowers and ferns

_____
_____
_____
_____
_____

Heavy and Bulky Equipment

_____ Convection ovens
_____ Gas grill
_____ Hibachi
_____ Tabletop gas burners
_____ Empty coolers
_____ Coolers with ice
_____ Charcoal
_____ Garden hose and nozzle
_____ 5-gallon insulating containers
_____ Plastic tarp
_____ 100-cup coffee makers
_____ 50-cup coffee makers
_____ Garbage cans
_____ 6-foot tables
_____ Handtrucks
_____ Dollies
_____ Tall warming cabinets
_____ Short warming cabinets
_____ Rolling racks with covers
_____ Wire frame chafers
_____ Dust pan
_____ Broom
_____ Butane fuel
_____ Propane fuel
_____ Large Sterno
_____ Small Sterno
_____ Fire extinguishers
_____ Matches (place with utensils)

_____ Liquid smoke
_____ Lighter fluid
_____ Ant spray
_____ Insect repellant
_____ Extension cords
_____ Spotlights
_____ First aid kits (check supplies inside)
_____ Tray stands
_____ Table cassette au feu stoves
_____ Lava rock
_____ Rented equipment delivered to commissary

Utensils

_____ Plain cook's spoons
_____ Slotted cook's spoons
_____ 2-ounce ladles
_____ 4-ounce ladles
_____ 6-ounce ladles
_____ 8-ounce ladles
_____ Extra-large ladles
_____ Wire whips
_____ Piping bags and tips
_____ Pastry brushes
_____ Plastic ice scoops
_____ Can openers
_____ Bottle openers
_____ Plastic funnels
_____ 9 1/2-inch utility tongs
_____ 6-inch tongs
_____ Silver serving tongs
_____ BBQ tongs
_____ BBQ knives
_____ BBQ forks
_____ Ice cream dishers
_____ Size _____
_____ Size _____
_____ Wooden spoons
_____ Aluminum serving spoons
_____ Sauce spoons
_____ Carving knives
_____ Carving forks
_____ Kitchen forks
_____ Cook's spatula
_____ Rubber spatula
_____ Hamburger spatula
_____ Pie server
_____ Pie cutter
_____ Cake knife
_____ Cake server
_____ Sharpening steel

- **Decorative requirements:** This category includes whatever it takes to make the food presentation stunning: buffet décor pieces, tables, skirting, garnishes, boxes or baskets used to "tier" the foods at different levels on the table.
- **Other services:** What other services have been promised by contract? For instance, before a company picnic, if some of the guests are having a softball game, they'll want sodas, bottled water, and ice handy. The term "other services" truly covers it all!

The larger the catered event, the more involved and complex this process is. Again, experience is the best teacher, and almost everyone has a memorable tale to tell about the time he or she forgot an important item and had to improvise—sometimes with hilarious results!

It requires some real "quality time" to prepare pull sheets and rental order forms. This type of work requires total concentration, so find a time and place where you can work uninterrupted. For some, this is early in the morning; for others, later in the evening. These lists should be prepared long before the party dates to determine whether you, and your rental suppliers, will have the necessary items available at that time. If not, this builds in ample time to order additional equipment and supplies.

✖ *Food Production Sheets*

Yes, more lists! Food production sheets are detailed lists of all the food items necessary for a particular party, wedding, or event. In the aforementioned Caesar salad example, the production list would indicate the following:

- Wash and trim 24 heads of romaine lettuce.
- Prepare one gallon of Caesar dressing.
- Cut, season, and toast two loaves of Italian bread for croutons.

Production sheets also assist with ordering ingredients, because they include the quantities of food required, and they help the catering team decide the order of preparation. For example, some hors d'oeuvres can be prepared in advance and frozen. Cold sauces and salsas can be prepared a few days in advance. Meats can be marinated the day before the party. Some vegetables can be cut late in the day before the party.

As each item is completed, a check is marked on the sheet next to the name of the item, indicating that it has been completed. Another checkmark is made when it is loaded.

✖ *Getting the Goods to the Party*

These are critical steps in the execution of the event. A sufficient amount of time should be allocated so that everything arrives on time at the party site. For smaller events that are close to the commissary, these steps take little time, but for larger, more detailed events, "pulling," assembling, packing, and loading can be accomplished one or more days in advance.

↳ *Pulling and Packing*

Before "pulling the party," review the packing list and ensure that all goods on the list are actually in stock. In most off-premise catering facilities, party items are not all in one location, but spread throughout the commissary or in storage. Carts, dollies, hand trucks, and even supermarket-style shopping carts will help move the items to the vehicle, or to a central assembly location, prior to loading. Teamwork by your staff makes for a much smoother operation.

As the items are located, the larger, bulkier ones should be taken to the delivery vehicle. Smaller, loose items should be assembled in a particular area and packed in containers, like plastic packing crates with handles for carrying. Fragile items should be wrapped in bubble wrap, linens, or wadded-up paper to prevent breakage. Bowls will not stick together if paper or bubble wrap is placed between them. Remember, all equipment should be checked again when pulled to see that it is in working order and/or is not broken, cracked, or chipped. A few suggested packing tips follow:

- Old briefcases can be used for carrying knives and serving utensils.
- Plastic crates can be used for plates (plates should be wrapped in film after drying).
- Use wrapped racks for cups, glasses, creamers, and sugar bowls.
- Custom-made plywood boxes can be used for coffeemakers, samovars, and chafing dishes.
- Flatware, film-wrapped in groups, can be packed in plastic crates.
- Most discount and larger drug stores carry an assortment of plastic packing crates.
- Empty ice chests (to be used later at the party site for beverages) can be loaded with small unbreakable equipment or utensils.
- Whenever possible, pack food in the same container in which it will be cooked at the party site; for example, stuffed mushroom caps on half sheet pans, covered with film wrap and placed atop packed ice chests.
- Used plastic containers (like 5-pound honey drums) are handy for packing bar utensils such as pourers, stir sticks, wine and bottle openers, sword picks, and ice picks.
- Plywood boxes with sliding tops can be custom-made to store doilies and linens.
- "Slim Jim"-type garbage cans are excellent for packing tray stands.
- Empty bus boxes with lids can be used for packing small utensils.
- Cold foods can be stored in assorted sizes of plasticware (with lids) and should be delivered in a refrigerated truck or on ice in ice chests, depending on local health department regulations.
- Hot foods are best shipped in insulated plastic containers, warming cabinets, or insulated thermal bags.

This list is not intended to include all packing techniques, but should at least stimulate creativity when it comes to the myriad ways to pack for off-premise catering events. Readers should note that parties that are packed neatly and carefully will not only be delivered intact, but will also make a positive impression on clients, who will compare this well-organized operation with the performance of caterers who arrive at a party site with food and equipment virtually spilling out of their vans in beat-up, old cardboard boxes, rattling loose with no packing at all.

Equipment and supplies designated for certain areas at the party site should be packed together and labeled for a smoother unloading and distribution process at the site. In fact, this procedure is critical for larger parties, where food stations, buffets, bars, and off-premise kitchens are spread out over a large area, or on a number of floors, as in an office building or department store. Some caterers even color-code items so their staffers know exactly where to take them as they are unloaded.

Loading the Vehicle

The loading process should not be taken lightly. It is physically demanding, and improperly packed items may break, spill, crack, or chip. Rare is the off-premise caterer who has never arrived at a party site with food spilled inside a vehicle, so here are some suggestions to minimize this risk:

- Everything should be packed together tightly. Whenever possible, crates and racks should be nestled together to avoid shifting in transit.
- Large, heavy square or rectangular items should be loaded first and kept in the bottom portion of the load. This category includes such things as ice chests, glass and china racks, soft drinks in cases, and square or rectangular plastic or plywood containers.
- Lightweight and unusually shaped items should be loaded last and inserted in areas where they will fit snugly to help keep the load from shifting in transit.
- Cold foods should be transported in accordance with local health department regulations, which may require a refrigerated truck, or sealed and packed in ice chests.
- Hot foods should be kept at a safe temperature (above 140 degrees Fahrenheit) in insulated carrying containers, thermal bags, or hot food holding cabinets.
- Loading staff must be trained in proper lifting techniques to avoid injury. This subject is addressed in Chapter 12.
- Hooks, eyelets, and bungee cords can help secure items in the truck. Items can also be kept from slipping by placing them on nonslip surfaces, old rugs, towels, linens, cardboard, or crumpled paper.

As each item is packed in the vehicle, it should be checked off on the pull sheet. Once the pull sheet is complete, it is advisable to double-check (and sometimes even triple-check!) that all items are loaded. The checking process should be thorough for all parties, but for those that will take place far from the commissary, off-premise caterers cannot afford to forget even one item, because there is no time to return. Some caterers leave a staff person at the commissary for the specific purpose of rounding up and bringing forgotten items to the party site.

Delivery

The delivery process involves physically moving the food, supplies, and equipment from the catering commissary to the party site. The types of delivery vehicles are discussed in Chapter 5. In this section, we discuss delivery procedures and standards.

Catering vehicles should always be free from dents and scrapes, as well as immaculately clean and waxed. The delivery vehicle is an important marketing tool and should reflect the caterer's business image. United Parcel Service (UPS) is known throughout the world for its perfectly clean and well-maintained vehicles. They set the standard in this arena. Most caterers display the company name, address, and phone number on their vehicles. This is good marketing, because it boosts name recognition to have your vans seen all over town. Off-premise caterers from around the country report receiving business from people who have simply seen their trucks and jotted down the phone numbers.

The drivers of these "rolling billboards" should also be immaculately attired, uniformed, impeccably groomed, and courteous. Drivers represent your company image and are often the "first impression" when they arrive at an event site.

When it comes to improving the quality and timing of deliveries, learn from experience:

1. First, allow enough time to reach the destination. Many caterers allow twice the amount of time necessary or even make practice runs when traveling to unfamiliar areas. Pay attention to weather reports, check road conditions, and allow extra time if bad weather or heavy traffic is expected. It's always better to arrive early than late.

2. Institute a preventive maintenance program for all vehicles. Pinpoint potential problems before they occur, rather than repairing when something breaks. (Nothing *ever* breaks when you're not swamped!) Drivers should not be permitted to make their own repairs, but should make daily "pre-trip" inspections, just like a professional truck driver, checking brakes, tires, lights, horns, wipers, steering, unusual noises, batteries, oil and wiper fluid levels. Trucks with propane ovens should also be routinely checked for gas leaks.

3. Drivers should be provided with petty cash, a road map, written directions, a highway emergency kit, a first aid kit, rain gear, an umbrella, and a beeper, radio, or cellular phone.

4. On hot, sunny days catering vehicles must always be parked in the shade.

5. For large events, many suppliers will deliver certain prepared products—such as desserts or specialty ethnic items—directly to the party site. For mega-events with thousands of attendees, your suppliers will often provide their own trucks, filled with their products, at the event site. Moreover, when circumstances dictate, caterers should consider alternative methods of delivery: taxis, UPS, or a courier service. Building relationships with these folks, just as with any other vendor, can serve you well.

⅄ *Unloading at the Party Site*

Off-premise caterers should have policies for unloading catering vehicles at event sites—and we don't mean simply instructions about dropping off platters, but written procedures for larger, more complex events.

The most critical unloading rule is to separate items based on where they will be used. In some instances, things can be taken directly to their final destination: the buffet, bar, food station, or kitchen. In other instances, where access is restricted, items may be stored together and moved later. This procedure does not work well, however, when delivering quantities for large parties into high-rise buildings. In these instances, sorting cannot occur until the goods reach the proper floor.

Unloading is best accomplished with only a few staff members, not the complete party crew. It is easier to keep things organized when fewer workers are present and their job is specifically to unload. Under ideal conditions, everything for each food station, buffet, bar, and off-premise kitchen should be delivered to the spot where it will be needed—so that the set-up crew arrives to find everything positioned correctly. Off-premise caterers simply provide a diagram with an item list of the setup to the people responsible for the setup. This procedure alone will prevent major confusion, frustration, and wasted time by eliminating staffers' frantic searches for supplies and equipment.

Hand trucks, dollies, and carts save time and energy. Men should never lift items weighing more than 50 pounds; women, not more than 25 pounds. You should also strive to minimize the number of times things are moved, creating a flow pattern to send materials along the shortest and straightest routes possible to their final destinations. Equipment, food, and supplies to be used on buffets, food stations, and bars should be stored as close as possible to their eventual points of use. This means that at a pasta station, the extra pasta, sauces, and ingredients are kept as close as possible to the station to minimize the steps required for replenishment. Furthermore, some tools, utensils, and equipment should be stored at every event in the same area, so staff members will always know where to go in a hurry. For example, scissors are always kept in a crate, under a worktable in the off-premise kitchen; backup soft drinks are always kept outside the cooks' tent, and so forth. Setting up systems gives your employees more confidence about successfully handling their parts of the event.

Once the necessary equipment is on-site, the setup and party execution begins. This subject is discussed in detail in Chapter 8, "The Show." For now, just assume the party is over, and it's time to reload the vehicle and return to the catering commissary.

⅄ *Reloading and Returning*

Most caterers can complete cleaning, packing, and reloading within one hour of the conclusion of their responsibilities, inasmuch as some of the cleaning and repacking should be accomplished as the party progresses. Once the catering responsibilities are complete, the caterer can leave the party site. It is best to wait to reload the vehicle until most things are packed and ready for loading, rather than load things randomly. It is just as important to pack and load the vehicle wisely on the trip home as it was when you first packed it, once again reducing the chances of spills and breakage.

Back at the commissary, most off-premise caterers require that vehicles be completely unloaded and cleaned and everything returned to its original place. This often makes for a long day—but a productive one! And it's better to clean up at that moment than to have to face these chores the next day.

Post-Party Review

A post-party review should be conducted after every catered event to pinpoint specific problems that require attention and discuss better ways to do things in the future. The largest room in the world is the room for improvement! Try to look at the event from this perspective: If you were given an opportunity to cater it again, what would you do differently? Some caterers sit down with staff members immediately after the event; others wait until the next day to assess it. Some require their staffers to complete a report, and others request written comments from clients. Whatever the procedures, it's smart to get the comments in writing, and things requiring improvement should be acted upon immediately. Topics such as these may be addressed:

- Was there ample time for setup?
- Quality and quantity of staff.
- Quality and quantity of food and service.
- Quality and quantity of equipment and supplies.
- Adequacy and appropriateness of music, flowers, décor, parking, security, etc.
- Any particular problems to be addressed or suggestions from staffers.

In addition to the post-party review, procedures should be in place for:

- Submission of payroll hours to bookkeeping
- Reporting discrepancies to rental equipment company
- Ensuring all invoices for the party are submitted to bookkeeping
- Invoicing client for any remaining balances
- Writing and mailing a thank-you letter to the client
- Establishing a follow-up date for contacting the client about future events

Exhibit 6.6 shows one off-premise caterer's system for keeping track of the logistical details discussed in this chapter. Called an "Event File Routing Schedule," it leaves spaces for dates and the initials of the person who performed the task.

 Conclusion

Although we know you are *always* creative and well-organized, this part of the catering business is where your creativity and organizational skills are most evident to the client. However, the client won't know even a fraction of what is being done behind the scenes to ensure his or her successful event. Being able to offer unusual,

Exhibit 6.6 *The Perfect Route—Routing Schedule (Reprinted with permission of the author, Ginger Kramer, and the CommuniCATER, official publication of the International Caterers Association.)*

by Ginger Kramer
COAST—A Special Events & Catering Company
Santa Clara, CA

EVENT FILE ROUTING SCHEDULE

	By:	Date:
Sales & Front Office:		
Verbal Quote Only		
Written Proposal Faxed & Mailed	___	___
Event File:		
File Label & Folder	___	___
Return to Sales (Tentative Status)	___	___
Acceptance Sheet Received from Client	___	___
Post to Board (Definite Status) & Master Book	___	___
Deposit Received from Client	___	___
Coordinating:		
Event Report Initiated		
Pre-Schedule Staff	___	___
Send Event File to Purchasing	___	___
Purchasing:		
Food Sheet to: Chef/Kitchen Production/Inventory Control		
Beverage Order (copy to Inventory Control) (Order Placed)	___	___
Regular Linen Order	___	___
Custom Linen Order	___	___
Floral Order (_____)	___	___
Decor Order	___	___
Guest Equipment Order (_____)	___	___
Site Rental Agreement (_____)	___	___
Ice Delivery	___	___
Entertainment Order (_____)	___	___
Serviceware Order (_____)	___	___
Special:_____ (_____)	___	___
All check requests issued	___	___
Coordinating:		
Complete Event Report:		
Load Sheet	___	
Attach map to location	___	
Make copies for Event File	___	
Reconfirm Staff	___	
Buffet Design Completed:	___	
Final Guest Count: (#pp ___ by ___)		
File Completion: (Sales & Front Office)		
Client Contacted for Verbal Review		
Invoice: Copies to Acct./Event File/Invoice File	___	___
Verbal Review forwarded to General Manager	___	___
Critique Letter	___	___
Thank-You Card	___	___
Lost Business Report forwarded to General Manager	___	___
Add to Mail List	___	___

FOOD FOR THOUGHT: CATERING COMMISSARY TIPS

According to Mike Roman, catering consultant and president of CaterSource, here are the main things to observe when evaluating a catering commissary operation. How does yours stack up?

How are the kitchen leaders [chefs, team leaders] seated? Is anyone facing the back door? Is anyone sitting close to the back door, to watch what comes in and out of the kitchen?

Do chefs kick oven doors closed, and handle kitchen equipment roughly?

Does the staff eat freely from the foods that are being prepared? Do they eat while working?

Is there evidence of smoking in the kitchen? Do chefs carry cigarettes?

Does the hand sink really work, and does it have soap and paper towels?

Is the walk-in cooler well organized?

Are all food packages emptied completely?

Are foods being sent out in the proper quantities?

Does there seem to be a fear of asking questions?

Are there proper inventory controls?

Does the staff report for work on time?

Are food orders properly packed, and do they leave on time?

Is the chef or kitchen leader cooperative with the entire culinary, sales, and management team?

Source: CaterSource, LLC, Chicago, Illinois (www.catersource.com)

interesting sites—and to make sure they actually work well for the event itself—is a big part of the logistics puzzle. The layout of the event, and the equipment needs that it dictates, are the dull but absolutely necessary details that follow. Conscientious staff members who are clear on their responsibilities are the other keys to your success in making logistics plans that work beautifully for every event.

Notes

1. *Entertaining for Business*, by Nancy Kahan with Eleanor Berman, Clarkson Potter, 1990, New York.
2. Chris Coe of Event Technical Services, Los Angeles, California, in *Special Events* magazine, May 1991. (www.specialevents.com)

Chapter 7

Human Resources

This chapter discusses all aspects of off-premise catering personnel management, including the federal laws relating to employers. We'll touch on recruiting, hiring, training, paying, evaluating, motivating, disciplining, and terminating catering staff, as well as guidelines for:

- Managing turnover
- Staff uniforms
- Preparing an employee handbook
- Maintaining personnel records

Excellent personnel management begins with selecting people with whom the caterer will enjoy working—and those who enjoy working in off-premise catering. This means creating job requirements and finding people who meet them, then training these people to meet your company's standards and setting rules for what happens when they don't. It also means providing a healthy working environment where managers:

- Listen to and involve staff members in operations
- Deal with employees fairly and consistently
- Discipline fairly and promptly
- Are well organized and decisive
- "Catch" the staff doing things right and tell them
- Create an enthusiastic, upbeat, and positive environment
- Are on the floor, actively managing the staff, rather than "hiding in the office"

Off-premise caterers know that happy workers are productive workers. They realize that work is *not* the most important thing in many Americans' lives, and that a good employee has a number of other employment choices rather than put up with an untenable situation.

According to Fern Canter, longtime director of Human Resources Development for Turnberry Isle Resort & Club in Aventura, Florida, "Trust and understanding are the foundation of a long-lasting relationship." She's created a list of "employment vows" (surprisingly similar to marriage vows!) for improved employer–employee relationships:

Employer to Employee

I will make sure that you understand the requirements of the job before I hire you.
I will listen more than I speak during our employment interview.
I will ensure that you are given sufficient training.
I will not be afraid to admit when I've made a mistake.
I will praise you publicly, but criticize you in private.
I will not hide behind my office door.
I will discuss your performance with you on a regular basis.
I will try to set a good example.
I will be supportive.
I will treat you with respect.

Employee to Employer

I will arrive on time.
I will ask questions when I don't know, and never assume.
I understand that servicing our clients is our number one priority.
I will work safely to prevent accidents.
I will not leave telephone inquiries on hold until they expire.
I will thank every customer and client.
I will not talk unfavorably about the company.
I will learn from my mistakes.
I will treat everyone with respect.[1]

These vows, when followed in an off-premise catering firm, would certainly help create an outstanding working environment. Posting copies of them around the workplace, and at off-premise party sites, would provide an excellent reminder of the mutual responsibilities of staff and management.

✗ *Federal Laws*

Off-premise caterers are directly affected by many federal laws regarding personnel. The major ones are:

Enforced by the U.S. Department of Labor

- Fair Labor Standards Act of 1938, Amended (FLSA)
- Immigration Reform and Control Act
- Family and Medical Leave Act
- National Labor Relations Act (Wagner Act; Taft-Hartley Act)
- Employee Polygraph Protection Act
- Occupational Safety and Health Act (OSHA)

Enforced by the Equal Employment Opportunity Commission (EEOC)

- Americans with Disabilities Act
- Civil Rights Act, Title VII

- Age Discrimination in Employment Act
- Equal Pay Act of 1963

Enforced by Individual States

- Workers' Compensation insurance laws

It is important to understand the basic requirements of each law to determine its applicability. For example, the Fair Labor Standards Act affects all off-premise caterers, whereas the Family and Medical Leave Act generally exempts businesses with fewer than 50 employees. Here we review the major aspects of each of these laws; off-premise caterers should consult legal counsel regarding specific questions.

✕ *Department of Labor–Enforced Laws*

The Fair Labor Standards Act of 1938

Learn more about this law at the U.S. Department of Labor website, www.dol.gov. The basics are presented in the following paragraphs.

Minimum Wage. This law created the minimum wage, and it applies to any business that grosses $500,000 a year. Currently, the minimum is $5.15 per hour. Employees who receive tips as part of their compensation may be paid as little as $2.13, as long as the wages paid by their employer and their tips equal at least the minimum wage amount. Employees must report tips earned to their employers so that appropriate amounts for federal income tax and Social Security tax may be withheld from their paychecks. Employers must also pay their portion of Social Security tax on the tips reported by their employees.

There's an alternative minimum wage, called a *subminimum wage*, for teenage workers. At this writing, it is $4.25 an hour, but it applies only to the first 90 days on the job. After 90 days or when the teen turns 20 (whichever comes first), the pay must be raised to $5.15 per hour.

Overtime Pay. Pay at the rate of no less than time and one-half the regular hourly rate must be paid for hours worked in excess of 40 within the workweek. Each workweek stands alone, and the averaging of hours from a series of weeks is not permitted. In addition, the workweek itself must be established in advance and must not be changed from week to week to avoid paying overtime. For example, a workweek can begin at 12:01 A.M. on Monday and end Sunday at midnight.

Child Labor Laws. This law affects those who employ young people to bus and wash dishes, set tables, and perform other tasks. Highlights of its impact on those who employ 14- and 15-year-olds follow:

- They may not work more than 3 hours on school days, and no more than 18 hours in school weeks.
- They may not work more than 8 hours on non-school days, and no more than 40 hours during non-school weeks.

- They cannot maintain or repair machines or equipment, cook (except in an area not separated by partition and in customers' view), bake, operate power-driven food slicers, grinders, choppers, cutters, and bakery-type mixers.
- They cannot work in freezers or meat coolers or perform any tasks in preparation of meals for sale *except* wrapping, sealing, labeling, weighing, pricing, and stocking.
- They cannot load or unload trucks or engage in occupations in warehouses except clerical or office work.
- They cannot work hours prior to 7:00 A.M., and after 7:00 P.M., except between June 1 and Labor Day, when they can work until 9:00 P.M.

There are also restrictions for older teens (ages 16 and 17), but they're a little less stringent. There are no hours or time restrictions on these workers, but they still can't operate, clean, or repair power-driven meat-processing machines, including slicers; nor can they operate, clean, or repair most power-driven bakery equipment, including dough mixers, roll dividers, and rounders. Pizza dough rollers with a number of safety features are an exception.

Periodically, fast-food chains come under close scrutiny regarding the hours worked by 14- and 15-year-olds. Many are now reluctant to hire these workers because of the penalties that can be incurred for violations. For example, a 14-year-old scheduled to work until 7:00 P.M. during the school year can't be asked to stay an extra half-hour, even if the place is extremely busy and the teen wants to stay. It's still a violation, punishable by law.

How severe is the punishment? Fines can range from to $400 for that 14- or 15-year-old who works extra or during prohibited times, to $10,000 for illegally employing a minor who suffers a fatal injury.

Some off-premise caterers reduce their payroll expenses by employing young people to perform simple tasks like setting tables, which can save money, and using more experienced and better-paid personnel elsewhere. Just be aware of the federal laws whenever you hire minors.

Record Keeping. This requires that all payroll records—including journals, time sheets, wage and rate sheets, and individual earnings records—be kept for a minimum of three years and that they be made available for inspection by authorized individuals.

Off-premise caterers must maintain accurate records. Some employers have allowed workers to arrive for work early or stay late, but because this was the workers' idea, not the employers', they did not pay overtime. These employers asked the workers to punch the time clock to show an eight-hour day. This is falsification of records, and it can cost employers hundred of thousands of dollars in overtime, back pay, and penalties.

Overtime Exemptions. This section of the law establishes criteria for those bona fide executives, administrative staff, certain managerial employees, and outside salespeople who are exempt from receiving overtime pay. This is a very technical area, and readers are advised to contact an attorney before excluding someone from overtime payment. For executives to be exempt from overtime, they must meet all of the following criteria:

- Their primary duty must be management of the enterprise.
- They must customarily and regularly direct the work of at least two or more other employees.
- They must have the authority to hire and fire, or make hiring and termination recommendations.
- They must customarily and regularly exercise discretionary powers.
- They must devote no more than 20 percent (40 percent in retail or service establishments) of their hours worked to activities not directly and closely related to managerial duties. (These percentage tests for nonexempt work would not apply to an employee who is in sole charge of an independent establishment, or a physically separated branch of an establishment, or who owns at least a 20 percent interest in the enterprise.)

There are also exemption rules for those employed in outside sales, which may apply to catering companies large enough to have their own sales specialists. The criteria include:

- Persons employed for the purpose of selling, who customarily and regularly work away from the employer's place of business
- Those who sell "tangible and intangible items"—goods or services.
- Those whose hours worked in activities other than selling are less than 20 percent of their total weekly hours worked

There's a lot more to overtime exemptions, but these are the basics. Do you see now how technical this topic is, and why you'll probably need legal advice to help you decide the specifics for your company?

Immigration Reform and Control Act of 1986

The Immigration and Control Act restricts the hiring of illegal entrants into the United States, and it's been controversial ever since its passage by Congress. This is the Act that requires employers to obtain a completed Form I-9 from each employee on the first day of work, by close of business. Employers are required to obtain written proof of a worker's identity and employment eligibility, and to record the information on the I-9 form within three days of the worker's first day on the job. Acceptable proof of identity and employment eligibility documents have changed with the nation's heightened awareness of terrorism, but they are usually listed in the Form I-9 instructions. We've included the most current list on page 190.

> Having a "U.S. citizen only" hiring policy, unless required by law, or having a "green card only" policy is illegal. Refusing to hire a qualified applicant who can perform the job tasks because of an accent or desire to only have employees speak English on the job is strictly forbidden.[2]

U.S. Department of Justice
Immigration and Naturalization Service

OMB No. 1115-0136
Employment Eligibility Verification

Please read instructions carefully before completing this form. The instructions must be available during completion of this form. **ANTI-DISCRIMINATION NOTICE.** It is illegal to discriminate against work eligible individuals. Employers **CANNOT** specify which document(s) they will accept from an employee. The refusal to hire an individual because of a future expiration date may also constitute illegal discrimination.

Section 1. Employee Information and Verification. To be completed and signed by employee at the time employment begins

Print Name: Last	First	Middle Initial	Maiden Name

Address *(Street Name and Number)*		Apt. #	Date of Birth *(month/day/year)*

City	State	Zip Code	Social Security #

I am aware that federal law provides for imprisonment and/or fines for false statements or use of false documents in connection with the completion of this form.	I attest, under penalty of perjury, that I am (check one of the following): A citizen or national of the United States A Lawful Permanent Resident (Alien # A_____) An alien authorized to work until___/___/___ (Alien # or Admission #_____)

Employee's Signature	Date *(month/day/year)*

Preparer and/or Translator Certification. *(To be completed and signed if Section 1 is prepared by a person other than the employee.) I attest, under penalty of perjury, that I have assisted in the completion of this form and that to the best of my knowledge the information is true and correct.*

Preparer's/Translator's Signature	Print Name

Address *(Street Name and Number, City, State, Zip Code)*	Date *(month/day/year)*

Section 2. Employer Review and Verification. To be completed and signed by employer. **Examine one document from List A OR examine one document from List B and one from List C** as listed on the reverse of this form and record the title, number and expiration date, if any, of the document(s)

	List A	OR	List B	AND	List C
Document title:	_____		_____		_____
Issuing authority:	_____		_____		_____
Document #:	_____		_____		_____
Expiration Date *(if any):*	__/__/__		__/__/__		__/__/__
Document #:	_____				
Expiration Date *(if any):*	__/__/__				

CERTIFICATION - I attest, under penalty of perjury, that I have examined the document(s) presented by the above-named employee, that the above-listed document(s) appear to be genuine and to relate to the employee named, that the employee began employment on *(month/day/year)* ___/___/___ and that to the best of my knowledge the employee is eligible to work in the United States. (State employment agencies may omit the date the employee began employment).

Signature of Employer or Authorized Representative	Print Name	Title

Business or Organization Name	Address *(Street Name and Number, City, State, Zip Code)*	Date *(month/day/year)*

Section 3. Updating and Reverification. To be completed and signed by employer

A. New Name *(if applicable)*	B. Date of rehire *(month/day/year) (if applicable)*

C. If employee's previous grant of work authorization has expired, provide the information below for the document that establishes current employment eligibility.

Document Title:_____Document #:_____Expiration Date (if any):__/__/__

I attest, under penalty of perjury, that to the best of my knowledge, this employee is eligible to work in the United States, and if the employee presented document(s), the document(s) I have examined appear to be genuine and to relate to the individual.

Signature of Employer or Authorized Representative	Date *(month/day/year)*

Exhibit 7.1 *Form I-9*

INSTRUCTIONS
PLEASE READ ALL INSTRUCTIONS CAREFULLY BEFORE COMPLETING THIS FORM.

Anti-Discrimination Notice. It is illegal to discriminate against any individual (other than an alien not authorized to work in the U.S.) in hiring, discharging, or recruiting or referring for a fee because of that individual's national origin or citizenship status. It is illegal to discriminate against work eligible individuals. Employers **CANNOT** specify which document(s) they will accept from an employee. The refusal to hire an individual because of a future expiration date may also constitute illegal discrimination.

Section 1 - Employee. All employees, citizens noncitizens, hired after November 6, 1986, must complete Section 1 of this form at the time of hire, which is the actual beginning of employment. **The employer is responsible for ensuring that Section 1 is timely and properly completed.**

Preparer/Translator Certification. The Preparer/Translator Certification must be completed if Section 1 is prepared by a person other than the employee. A preparer/translator may be used only when the employee is unable to complete Section 1 on his/her own. However, the employee must still sign Section 1 personally.

Section 2 - Employer. For the purpose of completing this form, the term "employer" includes those recruiters and referrers for a fee who are agricultural associations, agricultural employers, or farm labor contractors.

Employers must complete Section 2 by examining evidence of identity and employment eligibility within three (3) business days of the date employment begins. If employees are authorized to work, but are unable to present the required document(s) within three business days, they must present a receipt for the application of the document(s) within three business days and the actual document(s) within ninety (90) days. However, if employers hire individuals for a duration of less than three business days, Section 2 must be completed at the time employment begins. **Employers must record: 1)** document title; **2)** issuing authority; **3)** document number, **4)** expiration date, if any; and **5)** the date employment begins. Employers must sign and date the certification. Employees must present original documents. Employers may, but are not required to, photocopy the document(s) presented. These photocopies may only be used for the verification process and must be retained with the I-9. **However, employers are still responsible for completing the I-9.**

Section 3 - Updating and Reverification. Employers must complete Section 3 when updating and/or reverifying the I-9. Employers must reverify employment eligibility of their employees on or before the expiration date recorded in Section 1. Employers **CANNOT** specify which document(s) they will accept from an employee.

- If an employee's name has changed at the time this form is being updated/ reverified, complete Block A.

- If an employee is rehired within three (3) years of the date this form was originally completed and the employee is still eligible to be employed on the same basis as previously indicated on this form (updating), complete Block B and the signature block.

- If an employee is rehired within three (3) years of the date this form was originally completed and the employee's work authorization has expired **or** if a current employee's work authorization is about to expire (reverification), complete Block B and:
  - examine any document that reflects that the employee is authorized to work in the U.S. (see List A **or** C),
  - record the document title, document number and expiration date (if any) in Block C, and
  - complete the signature block.

Photocopying and Retaining Form I-9. A blank I-9 may be reproduced provided both sides are copied. The Instructions must be available to all employees completing this form. Employers must retain completed I-9s for three (3) years after the date of hire **or** one (1) year after the date employment ends, whichever is later.

For more detailed information, you may refer to the INS Handbook for Employers, (Form M-274). You may obtain the handbook at your local INS office.

Privacy Act Notice. The authority for collecting this information is the Immigration Reform and Control Act of 1986, Pub. L. 99-603 (8 U.S.C. 1324a).

This information is for employers to verify the eligibility of individuals for employment to preclude the unlawful hiring, or recruiting or referring for a fee, of aliens who are not authorized to work in the United States.

This information will be used by employers as a record of their basis for determining eligibility of an employee to work in the United States. The form will be kept by the employer and made available for inspection by officials of the U.S. Immigration and Naturalization Service, the Department of Labor, and the Office of Special Counsel for Immigration Related Unfair Employment Practices.

Submission of the information required in this form is voluntary. However, an individual may not begin employment unless this form is completed since employers are subject to civil or criminal penalties if they do not comply with the Immigration Reform and Control Act of 1986.

Reporting Burden. We try to create forms and instructions that are accurate, can be easily understood, and which impose the least possible burden on you to provide us with information. Often this is difficult because some immigration laws are very complex. Accordingly, the reporting burden for this collection of information is computed as follows: **1)** learning about this form, 5 minutes; **2)** completing the form, 5 minutes; and **3)** assembling and filing (recordkeeping) the form, 5 minutes, for an average of 15 minutes per response. If you have comments regarding the accuracy of this burden estimate, or suggestions for making this form simpler, you can write to both the Immigration and Naturalization Service, 425 I Street, N.W., Room 5304, Washington, D. C. 20536; and the Office of Management and Budget, Paperwork Reduction Project, OMB No. 1115-0136, Washington, D.C. 20503.

EMPLOYERS MUST RETAIN COMPLETED I-9
PLEASE DO NOT MAIL COMPLETED I-9 TO INS

Exhibit 7.1 (continued)

LISTS OF ACCEPTABLE DOCUMENTS

LIST A		LIST B		LIST C
Documents that Establish Both Identity and Employment Eligibility	**OR**	**Documents that Establish Identity**	**AND**	**Documents that Establish Employment Eligibility**

LIST A — Documents that Establish Both Identity and Employment Eligibility

1. U.S. Passport (unexpired or expired)

2. Unexpired foreign passport, with *I-551 stamp or* attached *INS Form I-94* indicating unexpired employment authorization

3. Alien Registration Receipt Card with photograph *(INS Form I-551)*

4. Unexpired Temporary Resident Card *(INS Form I-688)*

5. Unexpired Employment Authorization Card *(INS Form I-688A)*

6. Unexpired Employment Authorization Document issued by the INS which contains a photograph *(INS Form I-688B or I-766)*

OR

LIST B — Documents that Establish Identity

1. Driver's license or ID card issued by a state or outlying possession of the United States provided it contains a photograph or information such as name, date of birth, sex, height, eye color, and address

2. ID card issued by federal, state, or local government agencies or entities provided it contains a photograph or information such as name, date of birth, sex, height, eye color, and address

3. School ID card with a photograph

4. Voter's registration card

5. U.S. Military card or draft record

6. Military dependent's ID card

7. U.S. Coast Guard Merchant Mariner Card

8. Native American tribal document

9. Driver's license issued by a Canadian government authority

For persons under age 18 who are unable to present a document listed above:

10. School record or report card

11. Clinic, doctor, or hospital record

12. Day-care or nursery school record

AND

LIST C — Documents that Establish Employment Eligibility

1. U.S. social security card issued by the Social Security Administration *(other than a card stating it is not valid for employment)*

2. Certification of Birth Abroad issued by the Department of State *(Form FS-545 or Form DS-1350)*

3. Original or certified copy of a birth certificate issued by a state, county, municipal authority or outlying possession of the United States bearing an official seal

4. Native American tribal document

5. U.S. Citizen ID Card *(INS Form I-197)*

6. ID Card for use of Resident Citizen in the United States *(INS Form I-179)*

7. Unexpired employment authorization document issued by the INS *(other than those listed under List A)*

Illustrations of many of these documents appear in Part 8 of the U.S. Justice Department's Handbook for Employers (M-274).

Penalties for violating these antidiscrimination provisions and for hiring illegal aliens are severe and can range from $250 to $10,000. According to federal law, there are criminal penalties for those who engage in a "pattern or practice of knowingly hiring or continuing to employ unauthorized aliens, or engage in frauds or false statements, or otherwise misuse visas, immigration permits, and identity documents."

Do not confuse the I-9 form with the W-9 form, which new workers must also sometimes fill out. W-9s are for getting the Social Security or Taxpayer Identification numbers of part-time workers, such as freelancers or contractors—those you will be paying, but not withholding any taxes from their paychecks because they pay their own.

The Immigration Reform and Control Act applies to any company with more than four workers. Employers must retain an I-9 form for three years after termination of an employee and may be fined for not retaining it. And when an employee's employment eligibility document expires, caterers must verify the new document for the person's employment file.

Family and Medical Leave Act

The purpose of the Family and Medical Leave Act is to protect the jobs of those who must take off work for family or medical reasons. Effective since August 1993, this law states that employees may take up to 12 weeks of unpaid leave every year for the following reasons:

- Birth of an employee's child
- Placement of a child with the employee for purposes of adoption or foster care
- Caregiving for a spouse, child, or parent who is seriously ill
- An employee's own serious health condition that makes him or her unable to perform the functions of the position

The Act does not require that the company pay the worker's salary during the leave, but that the company must hold the worker's job for that worker and maintain his or her insurance benefits while that person is on leave. There are also some important exemptions to this Act:

- An employee who has less than one year of employment
- A part-time employee, who works less than 1,250 hours per year
- Companies with fewer than 50 employees

The 50-employee requirement, and the exemption of part-time staff, means that this law affects only the largest off-premise caterers.

The National Labor Relations Act

The National Labor Relations Act is union-related. It prohibits an employer from restraining employees in any way as they exercise their collective bargaining rights. It means a company can't discriminate against a worker for joining a labor union; can't interfere with the operation of a union; can't donate to the union to sway its members or officers; can't refuse to participate in collective bargaining on behalf of union members, and so forth. The law also prohibits unions from engaging in the same types of behavior, including not discriminating against a worker who chooses not to join a union. A division of the U.S. Department of Labor, the National Labor Relations Board (NLRB), enforces this Act.

✎ *The Employee Polygraph Protection Act*

A federal labor law, the Employee Polygraph Protection Act, restricts the use of lie detector (polygraph) tests, except in certain specific cases. For instance, it is acceptable to test an employee when a company is investigating a theft or material loss and to test prospective security guards or job applicants who would have access to controlled substances. In most cases, the catering business doesn't include these types of situations.

✎ *The Occupational Safety and Health Act*

The Occupational Safety and Health Act is enforced by its own special branch of the U.S. Department of Labor. The Occupational Safety and Health Administration (OSHA) is concerned with workplace safety. It requires most employers to keep records about on-the-job safety, illnesses, and injuries. It also prevents companies from retaliating against workers who make health- or safety-related claims against them. Because OSHA is concerned primarily with firms that "engage in interstate commerce," its rules may or may not apply to the off-premise caterer, depending on your business area.

✎ ✗ *EEOC-Enforced Laws*

The Americans with Disabilities Act (ADA)

The ADA prohibits discrimination against a qualified person with a disability, who, with or without reasonable accommodation, can perform essential functions of a job. Discrimination applies to hiring, firing, paying, promoting, and other terms and conditions of employment.

Employers must "reasonably accommodate" the disabilities of qualified applicants or employees unless doing so would result in an undue hardship. An accommodation poses an undue hardship if it is unduly costly or would fundamentally alter the nature or operation of the business. An "undue hardship" is one that requires significant difficulty or expense, accounting for such factors as cost and company resources.

Employers may not use employment tests to screen out people with disabilities unless they can show that the tests are job related and consistent with business necessity. Employers also have the right to reject applicants or fire employees who pose a significant risk to the health or safety of other individuals in the workplace.

The ADA also states that employers may not discriminate against employees who are infected with the HIV virus, whether or not it has manifested itself as AIDS, as well as those who "are perceived to have" this disability. An important side note: A caterer cannot make an HIV test a requirement for hiring or continued employment unless that caterer can justify or prove that the test is a "bona fide" occupational qualification for a particular job. Persons with AIDS can certainly perform catering functions, because the virus can be contracted only by intimate sexual contact, exchange of blood products, or mother-to-infant contact during pregnancy or delivery.

All employers with 15 or more employees must comply with this law. Employers with 15 or fewer employees are exempt.

For handling ADA issues, the best practices for off-premise caterers are reflected in the following guidelines from the Florida Restaurant Association:

- ■ Compile accurate written job descriptions before advertising or interviewing. Carefully list the essential functions of each job.
- ■ Limit questions on the application form to those that concern the applicant's ability to do the job.
- ■ Don't ask job interview questions about disabilities, past health problems, use of prescription drugs, hospitalization history, or Worker's Compensation claims.
- ■ Review the way you conduct interviews to be certain you focus on an applicant's ability to do a specific job.
- ■ Conduct all job interviews at locations that are accessible to people with physical disabilities.

It is interesting to note that half of all workers with disabilities can be reasonably accommodated at a cost to the employer of less than $50. Think about how to accommodate workers by restructuring jobs, modifying work schedules, and allowing for part-time positions.

The Civil Rights Act of 1964 (Title VII)

Title VII of the Civil Rights Act prohibits discrimination on the basis of a person's gender, national origin, skin color, or race. It also forbids sexual harassment in the workplace. It was amended in 1972 and again in 1991, so be sure you are working with the current version of the law. Workers who successfully prove they've been harassed or discriminated against on the job can recover back and future wages, lost employment benefits, attorneys' fees, and court costs, as well as compensatory damages—for the pain, suffering, and embarrassment caused by the harassment—and punitive damages, to punish the company for its actions (or lack thereof). The law applies not only to managers, but also to employees. Their supervisors can get in just as much trouble if the employees are participating in discriminatory or harassing behaviors and nothing is done to stop them.

Interestingly, in bar or restaurant businesses, sexual harassment can also be claimed when servers are hassled by guests. Anything that is considered "intimidating, hostile, or offensive" can be cause for a harassment claim.

From the University of Houston's Conrad N. Hilton College of Hotel and Restaurant Management, Stephen C. Barth offers suggestions for avoiding these types of problems:[3]

- Adopt clearly defined anti-sexual harassment policies.
- Establish a method to report sexual harassment, and inform everyone of this method.
- Train and inform employees about what is and is not appropriate.
- Ensure that reported incidents are taken seriously.
- Take immediate corrective action.

Before investigating this type of claim, a caterer must get the claimant's permission in writing. Then, the investigation itself should be thorough, well documented, and done with discretion. When it is complete, the employer must take immediate corrective action (as warranted) that effectively ends the harassment without penalizing the claimant. Exhibit 7.2 includes three sample forms that may be used in a sexual harassment claim: an "Intake" (or initial report) form, a Resolution of Complaint form, and a Request for No Further Action form.

X **Exhibit 7.2** *Sample Forms in a Sexual Harassment Claim*

INTAKE FORM

I. Name: _____

II. Position and Title: _____

III. Facts of Situation: (attach as many pages as necessary)

_____
_____
_____
_____
_____
_____

IV. I hereby request that the company investigate the facts set forth above. I also authorize the company to disclose as much of the facts set forth above as necessary to pursue the investigation. I also understand and acknowledge that the company shall use due diligence in keeping this matter as confidential as possible. I recognize, however, that in the course of the investigation the information may need to become public to do a thorough investigation.

Signature _____ Date_____
                        Employee

RESOLUTION OF COMPLAINT

I. Name: _____

II. Position and Title: _____

III. On the _____ day of _____, 199__, I previously completed an in-take form which alleged facts regarding the environment in the workplace, a copy of which is attached to this document. I have been made aware of the results of the investigation by the company, as well as its proposed resolution of this matter which I understand to be as follows:

(i) The alleged harasser shall undergo sensitivity training;

(ii) The alleged harasser shall be suspended without pay for five (5) days beginning on the _____ day of _____ and ending on the _____ day of _____, 1999__;

(iii) It is agreed by both parties that the alleged harasser shall return to work at the time stated above, but only after having undergone the sensitivity training.

I am satisfied with the resolution set forth above, and understand fully that in the event the matter is not completely resolved by the foregoing actions, I have been encouraged to bring my concerns to the company for immediate attention.

Signature _____ Date_____
                Employee

REQUEST FOR NO FURTHER ACTION

I. Name: _____

II. Position and Title: _____

III. On the _____ day of _____, 199__, I previously completed an in-take form which, among other things, requested that the company investigate certain facts stated by me, a copy of which is attached to this document. I have now decided that it would not be in my best interest to pursue this matter, and am very comfortable with my environment in the workplace, as it presently exists. I have been made aware that in the event that I become uncomfortable, I can seek the assistance and support of the company at any time, and have been encouraged to do so. At this time, however, I am requesting that at least for my benefit, no further action be taken in this regard, and I fully understand that an investigation for my benefit shall not take place. I do understand, however, that the company, after having been made aware of these circumstances may elect to pursue an investigation on its own behalf and for the benefit of other employees.

Signature _____ Date_____
                Employee

Age Discrimination in Employment Act

We've discussed younger workers, but what about older ones? The Age Discrimination in Employment Act states that companies that employ more than 20 persons can't discriminate against those job applicants or workers who are over age 40.

Equal Pay Act of 1963

The Equal Pay Act requires equal wages to be paid for jobs that are "substantially equal in skill, effort and responsibility" in the same workplace. In short, it was written to prevent sex discrimination by paying men and women differently for performing the same tasks. It applies to all employers, both private and government.

State-Enforced Laws

Worker's Compensation

Each state has its own insurance fund that covers bodily injury or death while a person is on the job. Employers pay into the fund quarterly, based on the number of employees they have and the type of business they have (which indicates the amount of risk or exposure to injury that workers in this field generally have), and you can get into a world of trouble for not paying this bill on time or for understating your number of workers to try to save money. Any employee who is injured on the job or becomes ill as a result of his or her work has the right to file a Worker's Compensation claim.

As you can see by reading this section, it is incredibly important to fully comprehend the aforementioned employment laws. They must be followed in order to avoid severe penalties, which may contribute to business failure. Any smart caterer will also have an attorney in mind with whom to consult when making major personnel decisions.

Determining Staffing Levels

Start-up caterers usually find themselves performing most job functions themselves—sales and marketing, food preparation, and staff scheduling. As the business grows, staff members should be added to your operation based on two key factors: business volume, and your own business strengths and weaknesses. Some caterers prefer to cook, and hire other people to handle sales and administration; whereas others prefer to do their own sales and marketing, and hire a chef. As the business grows, additional cooks are hired, as well as off-site event mangers and an operations manager—and so it goes. Some of America's largest catering firms employ sales staffs of 20 or more, with scores of cooks and off-site event managers and lists of on-call staffing personnel well into the hundreds.

Another key to staffing for off-premise caterers is to have the proper balance between regular staff who handle the day-to-day operations and those part-timers who are on call to work off-premise events as necessary. As a general rule, payroll costs as a percentage of sales should be between 20 and 30 percent. Smaller caterers may employ only one or two regular staff members and schedule the remaining staff as needed, when there are parties.

When computing payroll costs it is very important to consider, in addition to the hourly wages paid, the cost for other benefits such as:

Employer's share of Social Security benefits
Federal and state unemployment insurance
Worker's Compensation insurance
Holiday, vacation, and sick pay
Employee meals
Bonuses and other compensation
Health insurance paid by the employer

These costs can add 15 to 20 percent or more to payroll cost, over and above the regular hourly wages paid. Astute caterers realize that for every $1,000 they pay in wages, the true cost is actually $1,150, $1,200, or more.

Much has been written about staffing levels for various events. It is dangerous to state exactly the number of staff required for a particular event, because there are many tangible and intangible elements involved in making this determination, such as:

Number of guests expected
Level of service expected by the client
Price charged for staff
Type of menu
Competency of the staff
Arrival of guests (all at once or staggered)

Elegant dinners with multiple courses require as many as one server for every 5 guests, and one kitchen staff person for every 20 guests. However, an informal barbecue using plastic, with self-service, can be staffed with a skeleton crew of one or two staff members for each 100 guests. Obviously, the price paid for the elegant dinner will be far greater than the price for the barbecue.

Off-premise caterers are continually perfecting the art and science of properly staffing an event. For many events, the staff size scheduled is purely an estimate based on the caterer's experience. As more experience is gained, caterers learn better and more efficient ways to schedule.

When determining the size of the regular staff, it is always better to err on the low side. For most caterers, it is easier to bring in additional staff during busier times than to keep a larger staff in anticipation of busy periods, and paying them, when business does not warrant their presence.

✗ 🍴 *Recruiting Workers*

How do off-premise caterers build a staff of qualified and highly motivated people? This process begins with recruitment through a variety of sources. There are thousands of people who would love off-premise catering work. The hours can be flexible, the work is interesting, the pay is good, and there is definitely a change of routine and scenery from one party to the next.

One of the best recruitment sources is referral from existing employees. Most will recommend only those who they believe will work out. The employees who recommend others feel that their own reputations are on the line, and they also want to work with others with whom they are compatible. However, off-premise caterers should use caution in hiring too many staff members who are close to one another or who are friendly away from work. A problem with one of them could result in a problem with all of them. It is always best to recruit from a variety of people with different backgrounds and interests. Sources of potential staff include:

- Local high schools
- Culinary schools
- Colleges and universities
- Homemakers
- Senior citizens
- Off-duty firefighters
- Private industry councils
- Employment agencies
- Government job-training agencies
- Day labor companies
- Local restaurant employees
- Off-duty flight attendants
- Actors, actresses, and models
- Firms that specialize in providing catering staffers

An innovative way to recruit new staffers is to hold an "Opportunity Meeting" for potential workers. Devote the first hour to the rigors and challenges of catering. Then, after a scheduled break, resume the meeting. Those who have stayed are more likely willing to work hard and adapt to off-premise work. Some caterers offer bonuses to staff members for bringing in other workers who stay for a minimum number of weeks. Others offer "buddy" job guarantees so that two friends or neighbors can work the same shifts. Another recruiting tactic is to ask new employees about good workers at their former jobs.

Be sure you inform your vendors of job openings—they can often put out the word for you. Placing ads in local and neighborhood newspapers can also be effective. Many caterers advertise on bulletin boards in their locale. A great sample advertisement appeared in the *National Off-Premise Caterers' Roundtable Newsletter,* and we reprint it courtesy of Wayne Lavis, of Lavis Catering, Bloomsburg Pennsylvania.[4] See Exhibit 7.3.

⊠ *Exhibit 7.3* *Sample Advertisement (Courtesy of Wayne Lavis of Lavis Catering, Bloomsburg, Pennsylvania)*

WANTED!
PART-TIME HELP

Do you like people and wish to help make them happy?

THEN JOIN OUR TEAM!
LAVIS CATERING TEACHES:

That work can be fun	Communication skills
That we work in a clean and healthy environment	Interpersonal skills
Responsibility	What it is like to serve others
Care and concern for others	Self-esteem
The personal and social joy of working	Flexibility
The skills which open opportunities within the industry	

CONTACT OUR PERSONNEL OFFICE FOR AN INTERVIEW!!

Other ads can simply state the need for part-time staff who are energetic, hard-working men and women who wish to work once, twice, or more a week. Applicants need not be experienced, but they must be willing to learn.

Ads should reflect no bias against individuals because of their race, color, religion, sex, national origin, or disabilities. Smaller companies are not immune from charges of hiring discrimination, even if they consist of only a few employees. In fact, it's smart to ask an attorney to review employment ads before you use them.

What are the qualities necessary for success as an off-premise catering staff member? These include:

- Shows initiative (looks for things to do, is a self-starter)
- Is enthusiastic
- Has a high energy level
- Is well organized, detail oriented
- Is assertive, yet tactful
- Is a team player
- Is flexible (can do or learn different jobs)
- Has a sense of showmanship
- Is an extrovert
- Is good under pressure
- Enjoys serving others
- Is not afraid of "getting hands dirty"

Some of these traits can be determined in advance through testing and checking references, but the best way to see if people will be successful in off-premise catering is to schedule them for a larger party, where there is a need for many staff persons. By observing the people at work, astute off-premise caterers can determine whether they have the necessary traits to become regular staff members.

Interviewing and Hiring Staff

For many off-premise caterers, hiring is basically a guessing game. They have little or no idea of what to look for, or they are so desperate for staff that they will hire virtually anyone who seems vaguely interested in the work. Caterers who understand the hiring process realize that the interview is the key factor in making the hiring decision. Prior to the interview, they have screened out those who do not seem to possess the needed communication skills, enough experience, or the necessary work attitude.

Exhibits 7.4 and 7.5 show an employment application, in English and Spanish, that meets today's legal requirements. The two versions were prepared by the Florida Restaurant Association. Exhibit 7.6 is a Personnel Record form that is very useful when doing staff scheduling. Off-premise caterers may ask applicants to complete this form along with the application.

SEVEN DEADLY HIRING MISTAKES[5]

- *Hiring Too Quickly*—Warm bodies mean lukewarm business.
- *Hiring by "Gut Feeling"*—All caterers have been disappointed when hiring this way.
- *Hiring Because of Impeccable References*—Candidates are smart enough to provide references that will assure them of a glowing critique.
- *Hiring Because Former Employers Had No Criticism*—Because of the potential for lawsuits, employers today are reluctant to reveal negative information about an ex-employee. Many, too, harbor unresolved guilt about firing someone, so they refrain from being negative.
- *Hiring Because the Applicant "Aced" the Interview*—Applicants today are groomed for the interview, and know exactly what to say.
- *Hiring Because of an Impressive Resume*—Today's resume writing firms have a talent for transforming the most meager of job histories into the Great American Novel.
- *Hiring Because They Come Highly Recommended*—This usually is just as bad as hiring on gut feelings.

Gregory Lousig-Nont, *Restaurant Hospitality*, October 2002.

The Employment Interview

Fern Canter, of Human Resources Development, offers these tips every off-premise caterer should follow regarding interviews:[6]

Before: Establish the philosophy or personality of your organization. Is it a bureaucracy, or a flexible structure under which competence can flourish? Write this down and communicate it to every applicant, . . . [then] seek out the individuals with the appropriate characteristics. Prepare a job description prior to the interview.

During: Establish a cordial relationship. Even if the interview is squeezed into 10 minutes of a hectic day, try to avoid interruptions. Ask only job-related questions.

Maintain control. If the candidate is saying something you do not need to hear, bring the interview back on track. Let the applicant do the talking . . . lead the interview, but don't overwhelm it. Concentrate. Evaluate the answer to a question before you jump to another.

After: Close the interview with an explanation of the status of the person's application. Evaluate (the applicant) against the job. Remember we all tend to be trapped by "mirror-imaging," hiring those who most resemble ourselves.

Liking the person is not enough; make sure he or she fills the requirements of the job. Keep written records of your contact with each person interviewed. Do not lose sight of good applicants because you cannot remember who they were or what they said.

Another foodservice expert—Jim Sullivan, president of Pencom Inc. and owner of five high-volume theme restaurants and bars in Denver—offers more suggestions for interviewing[7]

- Treat the applicant like a guest. Smile, acknowledge the person right away, and do not keep [him or her] waiting.
- Offer a beverage.
- Keep your application forms clean and up-to-date.
- Vary your application times. Operators tend to make interview times convenient for management rather than for the potential employees.
- Hire the smile! Inject some humor into the interview, and judge whether the person has a quick, charming and genuine smile.
- Ask yourself, "How would I feel if this person worked for the competition?" If your response is, "I don't care," the interview is over.

Ask Job-Related and Legal Questions.

Federal law prohibits discrimination on the basis of race, age, color, religion, sex, national origin, and disability. State laws may be even more stringent concerning preemployment questions. Based on guidelines issued by the Equal Employment Opportunity Commission (EEOC), the following are topics to be avoided:

- Age or date of birth, unless needed to show that a minor is of legal age to serve or dispense alcohol
- Country of origin, place of birth, or citizenship
- Maiden name
- Relatives' names (unless the applicant is a minor)
- Past residences
- Religious affiliation
- Memberships in organizations (other than professional)
- Marital status
- Pregnancy status or future childbearing plans
- Age and number of children, or child care arrangements for them
- Diseases or major illnesses
- Credit rating
- Whether a person owns or rents his or her home
- Arrests that did not involve convictions
- Native language

Employers also may not photograph an applicant until the person is actually hired. Okay, so what *can* you ask? The following questions are appropriate:

- Can you meet specified work schedules? Do you have other activities, commitments, or responsibilities that may hinder this ability?
- Are you of legal age to perform jobs such as bartending, and can you provide proof of this?

APPLICATION FOR EMPLOYMENT

*AN EQUAL OPPORTUNITY/
AFFIRMATIVE ACTION EMPLOYER*

Instructions: PRINT IN BLACK INK OR TYPE. Fill out the application form completely: if questions are not applicable, enter "N/A". Do not leave questions blank. Resumes will be accepted as additional information but not in place of a completed application. Be sure to sign the application when it is completed.

EQUAL OPPORTUNITY EMPLOYER: It is our policy to abide by all Federal and State laws prohibiting employment discrimination solely on the basis of a person's race, color, creed, national origin, religion, age, sex, marital status, or physical handicap, except where a reasonable, bona fide occupational qualification exists.

NAME _____   Social Security No. _____ - _____ - _____
　　　　　　　(Last)　　　　　　　　　(First)　　　　　　　　(Middle)

ADDRESS　(Current) _____   Work _____
　　　　　　　(Street)　　　　(City)　　　　(State)　　　(Zip)　　　Home _____ (Phone)

　　　　(Permanent) _____   Work _____
　　　　　　　(Street)　　　　(City)　　　　(State)　　　(Zip)　　　Home _____ (Phone)

Type of position desired _____

Salary Expected $ _____   Full-Time ☐   Part-Time ☐   Date available for work _____

CAN YOU *AFTER EMPLOYMENT*, SUBMIT PROOF OF U.S. CITIZENSHIP OR VERIFICATION DOCUMENTS OF YOUR LEGAL RIGHT TO WORK IN THE UNITED STATES?   Yes ☐   No ☐

WERE YOU PREVIOUSLY EMPLOYED BY THIS ORGANIZATION?   No ☐   Yes ☐   If yes, date(s) _____

HAVE YOU EVER BEEN CONVICTED OF A FELONY, OR PLEADED NO CONTEST IN A FELONY, OR BEEN CONVICTED OF A MISDEMEANOR RESULTING IN IMPRISONMENT OR A FINE OVER $500 IN THE LAST TWO YEARS (Conviction will not necessarily disqualify an applicant)?   Yes ☐   No ☐

　　　If yes, explain _____

IS THERE ANY REASON YOU CANNOT PERFORM THE ESSENTIAL FUNCTIONS OF THE POSITION/POSITIONS FOR WHICH YOU ARE APPLYING? _____

　　　If yes, explain _____

EDUCATION:

(NOTE: TRANSCRIPTS MAY BE REQUIRED FOR VERIFICATION OF EDUCATION)

MILITARY: Active Duty Dates From _____ To _____

Branch Served _____
　　　　　　　　　　(Rank, Rate or Specialty)

Type of School	Name and Location of School	Number of Semester Hours Completed	Graduated?		Type of Diploma or Degree	Major Field of Study
			Yes	No		
HIGH SCHOOL OR G.E.D.						
COLLEGE, UNIVERSITY, TECHNICAL OR VOCATIONAL						

Current licenses/registrations (Indicate types and dates received): _____

Fill out only if applying for a position which requires a driver's license.

　　　Driver's License: No._____   State_____

　　　LIST ANY MOVING VIOLATIONS IN THE PAST FIVE YEARS: _____

If applicable, are you of legal age to serve alcohol (18 yrs. or older)?   Yes ☐   No ☐
Special Skills/Qualifications: List all special skills you possess and machines or office equipment you can use:_____

OTHER LANGUAGES (INCLUDE SIGN LANGUAGE)

	SPEAK			READ			WRITE			SIGN		
	Fair	Good	Excellent	Fair	Good	Excellent	Fair	Good	Excellent	Fair	Good	Excellent
_____	☐	☐	☐	☐	☐	☐	☐	☐	☐	☐	☐	☐
	Fair	Good	Excellent	Fair	Good	Excellent	Fair	Good	Excellent	Fair	Good	Excellent
_____	☐	☐	☐	☐	☐	☐	☐	☐	☐	☐	☐	☐

EMPLOYMENT RECORD: Please indicate previous employment. Start with present or most recent position, including military service. Use additional sheets if necessary.

Employer: Mailing Address: City and State:				Type of Business		Full Time ☐ Part Time ☐ Seasonal ☐
				Business Phone No.		
Starting Date		Leaving Date		Starting Base Salary	Ending Base Salary	Starting Position Title	Present or Last Title
Mo.	Yr.	Mo.	Yr.				
Immediate Supervisor's Name:				Briefly describe your duties and responsibilities:		

Explain reason for leaving:

Employer: Mailing Address: City and State:				Type of Business		Full Time ☐ Part Time ☐ Seasonal ☐
				Business Phone No.		
Starting Date		Leaving Date		Starting Base Salary	Ending Base Salary	Starting Position Title	Present or Last Title
Mo.	Yr.	Mo.	Yr.				
Immediate Supervisor's Name:				Briefly describe your duties and responsibilities:		

Explain reason for leaving:

Employer: Mailing Address: City and State:				Type of Business		Full Time ☐ Part Time ☐ Seasonal ☐
				Business Phone No.		
Starting Date		Leaving Date		Starting Base Salary	Ending Base Salary	Starting Position Title	Present or Last Title
Mo.	Yr.	Mo.	Yr.				
Immediate Supervisor's Name:				Briefly describe your duties and responsibilities:		

Explain reason for leaving:

Employer: Mailing Address: City and State:				Type of Business		Full Time ☐ Part Time ☐ Seasonal ☐
				Business Phone No.		
Starting Date		Leaving Date		Starting Base Salary	Ending Base Salary	Starting Position Title	Present or Last Title
Mo.	Yr.	Mo.	Yr.				
Immediate Supervisor's Name:				Briefly describe your duties and responsibilities:		

Explain reason for leaving:

Do you have any relatives working for our company?   No ☐   Yes ☐   If yes, list names, relationships, and place employed _____

Who were you referred by?_____

Please read carefully before signing. If you have any questions regarding the following statements, please ask for assistance.

I hereby certify that the following statements, as well as those on any attachment(s) to this form, to the best of my knowledge are true and correct and that they are all given of my own free will. I agree that any misstatement(s) or omission(s) as to material facts will constitute grounds for unfavorable consideration or dismissal from employment.

I authorize you to communicate with all my former employers, schools, officials, and persons named as references. I hereby release all employers, schools and individuals from any liability for any damage whatsoever resulting from giving such information.

I understand that, as this organization deems necessary, I may be required to work overtime hours or hours outside a normally defined work day or work week. If employed, I understand and agree that such employment may be terminated at any time and without any liability to me for continuation of salary, wages, or employment related benefits.

YOU MAY CONTACT:

Present Employer   Yes ☐   No ☐
Former Employer   Yes ☐   No ☐

_____
Applicant's Signature   Date

SOLICITUD DE EMPLEO

*Empleador afirmativo de
oportunidades iguales para todos*

Instrucciones: En letra de molde o en máquina de escribir. Llene la solicitud por completo; si la pregunta no applica, indique "N/A". No deje las preguntas en blanco. Los resumenes serán aceptados como información adicional pero no como substituto a la solicitud. Asegúrese firmar la solicitud cuando la complete.

Empleador de oportunidades iguales para todos: Es la norma de esta compañia de cumplir con las leyes Federales y estatales que prohiben la discriminación de empleo basado solamente en la raza, color, credo, origen nacional, religión, edad (mayor de 40), sexo, estado civil, o desabilidad física, amenos que exista una razionable cualificación del puesto.

NOMBRE _____ No. de Seguro Social. _____ - _____ - _____

(apellido)   (nombre de pila)   (segundo nombre)

DOMICILIO (Actual) _____

(calle)   (ciudad)   (estado)   (zona postal)

Teléfono _____

(trabajo)   (casa)

(Permanente) _____

(calle)   (ciudad)   (estado)   (zona postal)

Teléfono _____

(trabajo)   (casa)

Clase de posición deseada _____

Sueldo esperado $ _____ tiempo completo ☐   tempo parcial ☐   Fecha disponible para trabajar _____

¿ Puede Ud., después de empleado, someter prueba de ciudadanía de verificación de su derecho a trabajar permanentemente en los Estados Unidos Norteamericanos?

Si ☐   No ☐

¿ Ha sido empleado previamente por esta organización?   Si ☐   No ☐   Si, de fecha _____

¿ Ha sido Ud., en cualquier ocasión, convicto de un delito mayor, o ha declarado no contesto en un delito mayor, o ha sido convicto de un delito menor que resultó en su encarcelación o en multa de más de $500.00, durante los últimos 2 años (Convicción no necesariamente descalificará al solicitante)   ¿Si ☐   No ☐

Si la respuesta es afirmativa, explique _____

¿ Hay algún motivo por el cual no pueda desempeñar las funciones esenciales de la posición/posiciones por las cuales está solicitando? _____

Si la respuesta es afirmativa, explique _____

EDUCACIÓN:

(NOTA: Documentos de educación podrán ser requeridos para su verificación)

Servicio militar: Fechas de servicio de _____ Hasta _____

Ramo de Servicio _____ Especialidad _____

(Titulo-Categoria o Especialidad)

Clase de escuela	Nombre y localidad	No. de horas creditors cumplidos	Graduación		Clase de titulo/ grado	Campo de especial- ización
			Si	No		
Escuela Secundaria o equivalente						
Universidad, Colegio o escuela técnicia/vocacional						

Licencias/registraciones actuales (indique clases y fechas recibidas) _____

Complete solamente si solicita una posición la cual requiere licencia de conducir _____

Licencia de conducir automóvil: (número) _____ (estado) _____

Enumere infracciones de tránsito durante los últimos 5 años _____

¿ Es Ud. de edad legal para servir alcohol (18 años o mayor)? _____

Cualificaciones: Enumere todas sus habilidades y maquinarias y equipo de oficina que puede operar: _____

Idiomas que habla (incluya lenguaje de señas para los sordos)

	Hablar			Leer			Escribir			Seña		
	regular;	bien;	excelente	regular;	bien;	excelente	regular;	bien;	excelente	regular;	bien;	excelente
_____	☐	☐	☐	☐	☐	☐	☐	☐	☐	☐	☐	☐
_____	☐	☐	☐	☐	☐	☐	☐	☐	☐	☐	☐	☐

Forma 2
Junio 1993

Enumero todo empleo pasado, empesando con el presente; incluya servicio militar.
Si es necessario, use páginas adicionales.

Empleador Domicilio Ciudad y estado				Tipo de negocio	Tiempo completo ☐
					Tiempo parcial ☐
				No. de teléfono	Temporal ☐

Fecha al comenzar		Fecha al terminar		Sueldo al comenzar	Sueldo al terminar	Puesto al comenzar	Titulo actual
Mes	Año	Mes	Año				

Nombre del Supervisor	Brevemente describa sus obligaciones y responsabilidades

Explique el motivo por el cual dejó el trabajo:

Empleador Domicilio Ciudad y estado				Tipo de negocio	Tiempo completo ☐
					Tiempo parcial ☐
				No. de teléfono	Temporal ☐

Fecha al comenzar		Fecha al terminar		Sueldo al comenzar	Sueldo al terminar	Puesto al comenzar	Titulo actual
Mes	Año	Mes	Año				

Nombre del Supervisor	Brevemente describa sus obligaciones y responsabilidades

Explique el motivo por el cual dejó el trabajo:

Empleador Domicilio Ciudad y estado				Tipo de negocio	Tiempo completo ☐
					Tiempo parcial ☐
				No. de teléfono	Temporal ☐

Fecha al comenzar		Fecha al terminar		Sueldo al comenzar	Sueldo al terminar	Puesto al comenzar	Titulo actual
Mes	Año	Mes	Año				

Nombre del Supervisor	Brevemente describa sus obligaciones y responsabilidades

Explique el motivo por el cual dejó el trabajo:

Empleador Domicilio Ciudad y estado				Tipo de negocio	Tiempo completo ☐
					Tiempo parcial ☐
				No. de teléfono	Temporal ☐

Fecha al comenzar		Fecha al terminar		Sueldo al comenzar	Sueldo al terminar	Puesto al comenzar	Titulo actual
Mes	Año	Mes	Año				

Nombre del Supervisor	Brevemente describa sus obligaciones y responsabilidades

Explique el motivo por el cual dejó el trabajo:

¿ Tiene familiares empleados por nuestra compañia?   Si ☐ No ☐   Si respuesta es afirmativa, de los nombres, relaciones y lugar de empleo. _____

¿ Quien to recomendó? _____

Favor de leer cuidadosamente antes de firmar. Si teiene preguntas sobre las siguientes declaraciones, favor de pedir asistencia.

Yo certifico que las siguientes declaraciones, junto con los anexos, son fieles, correctas y exactas dentro de lo mejor de mi conocimiento y que todos están redactados a mi voluntad. Estoy de acuerdo que cualquier misinformaciones o omiciones de hechos constituyen motivo para consideración no favorable o despedida de trabajo.

Autorizo que se pongan en comunicación con patrones anteriores, escuelas, oficiales y personas cuyos nombres se dieron de referencia. También descargo de toda culpa a todos empleadores, escuetas e individuos de cualquier responsabilidad-obligación por cualquier daño que resulte por facilitar dicha información.

Comprendo que, como sea necessario por esta organización, tal vez se me requiera que trabaje más de las horas normales o mas de la definición de un dia o una semana de trabajo. Si empleado, comprendo y estoy de acuerdo de que tal empleo puede ser terminado en cualquier instante y sin ninguna responsabilidad a mi por la continuación de salario, pago, o beneficios relacionados con el trabajo.

Ud. puede comunicarse con:
Empleador presente: Si ☐   No ☐
Empleador pasado: Si ☐   No ☐

_____   _____
Firma del solicitante   Fecha

⊠ ***Exhibit 7.6*** *Staff Personnel Record*

NAME_____

ADDRESS _____

SOCIAL SECURITY NUMBER _____

LIST ALL PHONE NUMBERS _____

PHONE NUMBER WHERE THERE IS AN ANSWERING MACHINE _____

BEST TIMES TO CALL_____

DAYS AND TIMES AVAILABLE TO WORK_____

ARE YOU OF LEGAL AGE TO SERVE ALCOHOLIC BEVERAGES? _____

UNIFORM SIZE _____

IN CASE OF EMERGENCY, NOTIFY (NAME, ADDRESS, AND PHONE NUMBER)

_____

_____

SKILLS (CHECK THOSE THAT APPLY)

_____ BARTENDING	_____ BAR RUNNER	
_____ AMERICAN SERVICE	_____ KITCHEN	
_____ RUSSIAN SERVICE	_____ PASTA STATION COOKERY	
_____ CARVING STATION	_____ (OTHER)	

OTHER INFORMATION _____

_____

_____

Employers may ask about education and experience in military service as it relates to a particular job, but not about the type of discharge from the military service. They may also ask these questions:

- What is the name and address of a person to be notified in case of an emergency?
- To what professional organizations do you belong?
- Who referred you? Whom may we contact for character references?
- What do you like most about off-premise catering?
- What did you like most about your last job?
- Where would you like to be in five years? If you could do anything in the world, what would that be?
- What do you feel are your strengths and weaknesses? If you could change anything about yourself, what would that be?

Always take notes during the interview. It's unfortunate, but you should have them in case you are challenged with a discrimination claim. It is also a good idea to send a letter to applicants who are not chosen, stating something like, "We have examined your qualifications and we have other applicants who are more qualified for the job."

In addition, it is never acceptable to ask for photos with job applications. If an applicant does attach a picture to a resume, or includes "inappropriate" information (age, race, marital status, volunteer information at church, etc.), these should never be used in the decision-making process.

Bill Marvin's "Foolproof Foodservice Selection System"[8] is an excellent method by which to screen prospective staff members. His questions help separate applicants who are more likely to succeed, and the list is based on his actual experience when he needed to create an organization of 150 people to feed athletes at the U.S. Olympic Training Center. These people would be needed for two weeks of intensive work and then dismissed. Marvin needed a fast way to find the right people. Extroversion, pride, responsibility, and energy were measured by asking a quick series of questions. The test works best when questions are asked without lengthy conversation. Those who scored the highest were hired, and those who were the most successful on the job had scored in the top one-third of the screening interview. This process could certainly be adapted to off-premise catering firms. Take a look at Marvin's questions and answers, adapted to off-premise catering. Notice that the "negative" responses aren't bad—they just don't show much enthusiasm or spark as the "positive" ones did.

The Foolproof Foodservice Selection System has been published in book form by John Wiley & Sons (1993) and is also available for sale on the website www.restaurantdoctor.com.

Gregory Lousig-Nont gives further advice:

> For optimal hiring, it is recommended that caterers use a reliable and scientifically valid honesty and integrity test. Honesty tests are written psychological instruments that claim to identify people who have a tendency towards dishonesty or irresponsibility in the workplace. A top-notch test not only can assess a job applicant's honesty, but other positive attributes, such as work ethic, as well.[9]

For more on honesty testing, visit www.plotkingroup.com/testing/integrity.

There are also hiring tests that match the applicants' strengths to the needs of the position. For example, a person who is quiet and reserved will not necessarily make the best server, but the same applicant might make an excellent bookkeeper or accountant. Hire Success is one of many firms offering these types of tests; learn more at its website, www.hiresuccess.com.

Checking References

Is it necessary for an off-premise caterer to check all references for every prospective staff member? The answer to this question lies in the types of positions to be filled. It would be irresponsible not to thoroughly check the references of someone applying for a general manager position, but this probably would not be necessary for applicants hired to fill a last-minute requirement to add two more staff to a large

FOOLPROOF FOODSERVICE SELECTION SYSTEM

1. As a member of the catering staff, how would you help develop repeat business?
   Positive replies: Show personal action or interactions, such as learn customers' names, ask questions, make suggestions, see that the food always looks and tastes good.
   Negative replies: Be friendly, give good service.

2. If I asked your best friend to describe you, what would he or she say?
   Positive replies: People-oriented answers, like outgoing, lots of fun, friendly, positive.
   Negative replies: Nice person, good worker.

3. If you saw someone you thought you recognized, but weren't quite sure, what would you do?
   Positive replies: Go up and ask, make an effort to talk to the person.
   Negative replies: Just keep walking, wait until I'm sure.

4. What qualities do you need to be a great staff member for an off-premise caterer?
   Positive replies: Like people, work hard, do more than expected; smiling, flexible, patient, lots of stamina, good work habits, attention to detail, good communicator.
   Negative reply: Be nice.

5. Is it difficult for you to carry on "small talk" with people?
   Positive reply: No, not at all.
   Negative replies: Sometimes, depends on the situation.

6. What recent accomplishments do you take pride in?
   Positive replies: Specific advancement toward a goal, completed courses, finished a difficult project, job advancement, family success.
   Negative reply: Can't think of one, don't have any specific goals.

7. What are some reasons for your successes?
   Positive replies: My personality, my optimism, desire to succeed, positive self-image.
   Negative replies: Just lucky, don't know.

8. What would your previous employers say about your work?
   Positive replies: Hard worker, dependable, ideal employee, valuable, would rehire.
   Negative reply: Did a good job.

9. What would you do to make a negative situation positive?
   Positive reply: Find out the problem and fix it.
   Negative reply: Get a manager and stay calm.

10. What kinds of people irritate you?
    Positive replies: Lazy, negative, complainers.
    Negative reply: I like everyone.

11. What do you do with your time off?
    Positive replies: Make lists, get organized, get right at things.
    Negative replies: Not much, don't do it very well, go with the flow.

12. What activities have you been involved in during the past two years?
    Positive replies: Participatory activities, aerobics, sports, volunteer or charitable work.
    Negative replies: Not many, I just work.

13. What motivates you to get your job done?
    Positive replies: Money, recognition, pride in my work.
    Negative replies: Making people happy, giving good service.

14. How do you feel about doing more than one activity at a time?
    Positive reply: It is a challenge.
    Negative replies: Can only do one thing at a time, it doesn't bother me.

When grading the exam, allow two points for positive answers, no points for negative answers, and one point if it's a "maybe," or "too close to call" type of response. The highest possible score is 28. Scores over 22 represent prime candidates; scores of 18 to 22 indicate marginal candidates.

catered event. As a general rule, the more responsible the position, the more thorough the reference-checking process.

In regard to gathering other information about an applicant, state laws vary. Off-premise caterers should speak with their attorneys before conducting reference checks.

What kinds of records might be checked?

Criminal Records. More than 90 percent of the nation's counties will release criminal records by telephone or mail. However, a number of states will not release records of arrests that did not result in convictions. Attorney Tim Owens of Columbus, Ohio, says, "Employers are on thin ice when they ask about criminal records. If you're going to ask, it's better to ask about convictions than about arrests. There must be some logical business justification in order for you to exclude an applicant based solely on conviction records. Consider, at the very least, the nature and gravity of the offense, the time that's passed, and the nature of the job being filled.

"If you are going to hire someone as a Controller and discover that 10 years ago, he or she was convicted of embezzlement, that is a clear job-relatedness you can act upon," Owens continues. "This is a challenging area, because catering employers also have a duty to screen out individuals who may harm other employees or customers. Lawsuits for 'negligent hiring' often result when an employer neglects due diligence in screening new hires."[10]

Driving Records. For those positions that require employees to drive company vehicles, employers should check driving records.

Worker's Compensation Records. A number of states will provide information about whether a person has submitted a Worker's Compensation claim. In some cases, however, requests for this information are covered by the federal and some state consumer credit laws.

Federal and State Court Records. All federal judicial districts can provide information about civil, criminal, and bankruptcy cases. In most states, employers can find out whether a person is, or has been, either plaintiff or defendant in a lawsuit. In some states, you can actually review the court transcripts.

Educational Records. Virtually all colleges and universities will verify attendance and degrees for employers.

Credit Information. Private companies can provide credit histories for a fee. As with Worker's Compensation records, this type of information may be obtained only in accordance with certain consumer credit protection laws. It often requires the applicant to sign a release at the time of application.

Previous Employers. Many employers will simply verify dates of employment, whereas others will offer more information. A key question to ask is, "Would you rehire the person?"

Employment Agreements

Some caterers use an employment agreement—a document that spells out job duties, work hours, days off, pay rates, the length of any probationary period, and so on. It includes conditions or clauses called "nondisclosure" clauses (stating that if a worker quits or is fired, he or she will not divulge names of customers, procedures, or methods of operation to any of your competitors), and "noncompete" clauses (stating that the worker will not go to work, whether paid or unpaid, for one of your competitors in the same geographic area for a period of 12 months after leaving your employ).

Another clause that is becoming increasingly common is a mutual agreement to arbitrate. This basically says that all claims and disputes regarding employment and termination will be arbitrated by a mediator, rather than taken to court—covering everything from discrimination, to contract and compensation terms, to injury claims. This clause generally does not cover Worker's Compensation and unemployment claims, or employee benefits claims with a company plan, because each of these includes its own arbitration procedure.

An arbitration is conducted in accordance with the rules of the American Arbitration Association, with the arbitration fees and/or expenses split equally by the parties and prepaid. Each party usually pays the fees and expenses of its own attorneys, experts, and witnesses. It's ironic, but representative of the times we live in, that any arbitration agreement should be carefully drafted by an attorney to avoid lawsuits that challenge the agreement itself.

Paying Catering Staff

Regular Pay

When caterers gather, a sure topic of controversy is the issue of whether to pay catering staff as independent contractors, rather than employees. The advantage to employing those with independent contractor status is that the caterer need not pay the employer's share of Social Security taxes (FICA), federal unemployment taxes (FUTA), Worker's Compensation insurance, and other expenses directly related to payroll. The amount of savings can be sizable, as high as 20 percent of total payroll expenses for some caterers. Staff employed as independent contractors are pretty much self-employed—they're responsible for paying their own taxes and do not receive unemployment benefits when laid off or terminated.

The Internal Revenue Service (IRS) has developed a series of questions to be used in individual situations when trying to ascertain someone's status as an independent contractor. The following questions are asked of the employer. The more "yes" answers, the more likely the person is an employee, not an independent contractor.

1. Do you provide the worker with instructions on when, where, and how work is performed?
2. Did you train the worker?

3. Are the worker's services a vital part of your company's operations?
4. Is the person prevented from delegating work to others?
5. Is the worker prohibited from hiring, supervising, and paying assistants?
6. Does the worker perform services for you on a regular and continuous basis?
7. Do you set the hours of service for the worker?
8. Does the worker work full-time for your company?
9. Does the worker perform duties on your company's premises?
10. Do you control the order and sequence of the work performed?
11. Do you require the worker to submit oral and written reports?
12. Do you pay the worker by the hour, week, or month?
13. Do you pay the worker's business and travel expenses?
14. Do you furnish tools or equipment for the worker?
15. Does the worker lack a "significant investment" in tools, equipment, and facilities?
16. Is the worker insulated from suffering loss as a result of the activities performed for your company?
17. Does the worker perform duties solely for your firm?
18. Does the worker not make services available to the general public?
19. Do you have the right to discharge the worker at will?
20. Can the worker end the relationship without incurring any liability?

After reviewing these questions, it becomes quite apparent that more catering staffers are classified as employees and should be paid as employees. It is highly unlikely that a caterer would win an argument with the IRS about this issue, so in our estimation, it is best to pay staff members as employees. Even in those situations when they are paid directly by clients, if the caterer is actually supervising the client's event, the IRS can argue that the workers are working for the caterer, not the client. Why hassle with it? Pay them as employees, including all the necessary deductions and taxes.

To determine a fair hourly rate or salary, off-premise caterers should review the wage rates of competitors and other local employers, the cost of living in the area, the existing supply of qualified staff members, and the caterers' ability to pay. As a general rule, wage rates in rural areas are lower than in metropolitan areas. In our experience, you get what you pay for in terms of employees—those who pay at least average, or above-average, wages for their geographical area are more likely to attract above-average staff. Paying less per hour, you'll be unlikely to attract the best job candidates.

Premium Pay

When employees need to travel long distances to party sites that are far from the catering commissary, compensation becomes an issue. Many off-premise caterers choose to pay staff members for those two or three hours they spend commuting to a party site—not for every commute, but for the really long ones. Others split the difference and pay for one-way travel to remote locations. Either way, it is wise to have a formula that is fair to both employer and employee, and stick to it. Policies on issues like travel time are made at the discretion of the caterer and are influenced by competitive factors, so find out what your competitors do—and do a little more, if possible.

✖ Overtime Pay

We've already discussed the federal wage and hour law that includes overtime pay, or paying one and one-half times a person's regular hourly rate for hours worked in excess of 40 per week. Some states have enacted different laws, requiring overtime pay for hours worked in excess of 8 per day, so check with your state labor department for the particulars.

Most employees understand the need for working overtime, especially in an industry like catering that requires intense planning and crazy hours. Many of them need and appreciate the extra money too. You may even have to require overtime work in order to meet certain production deadlines; however, overtime hours should be distributed as fairly as possible among your staff.

Whenever possible, overtime should be planned in advance. This way, workers can make the necessary arrangements at home to spend more time on the job, and as their employer, you can budget for the extra expense. Here's a tip from experience: It's important to have a policy stating that before anyone can work overtime, it must be approved in advance by management. Under no circumstances can employees decide on their own to work extra hours.

Sometimes, the hours of catered events extend beyond the planned stopping time. In this situation, most caterers pay their staffers extra hours of pay for those extra hours worked. This is not to be confused with overtime pay, which is for hours worked in excess of 40 per week. Do you see the difference?

✖ Recording Hours Worked

Recording employee hours worked at off-premise events can pose unique problems, because few off-premise caterers use time clocks at party sites. Actual hours worked should be recorded by the party supervisor. Staff members should not be permitted to start work prior to their scheduled starting time unless approved in advance by management. Staff members who are late should be paid for the actual hours they worked, not for their scheduled hours. Some off-premise caterers even send staffers home if they arrive noticeably late; others give written or verbal warnings. Exhibit 7.7 is a sample payroll recording form that can be adapted for use by off-premise caterers.

✖ Tipping Policies

Off-premise catering staffers may receive a portion of their compensation in the form of tips provided by clients. Catering staff members must report tips given directly to them by clients on IRS Form 4070 (Employees Report of Tips to Employer) if the amount exceeds $20 per month. Employers, in turn, must deduct federal income tax and Social Security tax from the employee's paycheck on these reported tips and, of course, pay the employer's share of the Social Security tax.

Many caterers add a "service charge" and distribute a portion of it to staff members for their work at an event. The service charge is generally paid in lieu of a gratuity, but some clients also opt to tip. The IRS refers to this "group gratuity" as

---

⊠ Exhibit 7.7 *Payroll Record*

NAME OF THE PARTY _____

DATE OF THE PARTY _____

NAME OF EMPLOYEE, FIRST AND LAST	SCHEDULED START TIME	ACTUAL START TIME	STOP TIME	HOURS WORKED

NAME AND SIGNATURE OF PERSON PREPARING THIS REPORT

NAME _____

SIGNATURE _____

"Allocated Tip Income." No matter what you call such amounts or who collects them, tips distributed to employees are still subject to all payroll taxes.

✕ *Employee Benefits*

This section covers various employee benefits that may be offered by off-premise caterers. It is important to note that, at this time, none of these benefits are required by federal law, but most caterers provide at least some of them:

- Employee meals and breaks
- Vacation pay
- Sick pay
- Holiday pay
- Employer-paid health insurance
- Pay for jury duty

Employee Meals and Breaks

For regular staff members, most caterers establish times for breaks and meals throughout the day. For staff working at off-premise events, the question of meals and breaks becomes more complex. Some caterers prefer to feed the staff prior to the start of the event, and they bring separate meals for staff members. Others feed workers after the guests have eaten, making use of the leftover food. Still others do not feed their staff members unless they are working a shift that is longer than five or six hours.

It is smart to offer brief breaks to staff members after the party is completely set up, but before the guests arrive. After the party begins, there is no time for breaks until after foodservice comes to a close. Most caterers allow those workers who arrived first to go on break first; those who came later take their breaks later. As long as guests are present, some staffers should always be on duty, no matter how late into the evening an event continues.

Vacation Pay

Who is entitled to vacation pay? Most caterers offer vacations to permanent, regular employees, but not to part-time staff members who work on-call. The amount of vacation pay is usually computed based on the average number of hours a person works per week, up to 40. For example, a person who averages 30 hours of work per week will be paid 30 hours for each week of vacation pay earned.

It is considered bad policy to pay employees their vacation wages and allow them to work through vacations for regular pay instead of taking the time off. Vacations are necessary for relaxation and rest. They should be scheduled at a time mutually convenient to both employer and employee, which, in catering, usually means during the slower seasons and never during the busiest times. It's an unfortunate reality that holidays like Christmas and New Year's Eve also tend to be the busiest times for a good off-premise caterer.

The majority of employers do not permit employees to take vacations until they have completed a minimum of one year on the job. Exceptions may be granted only with the employer's permission and the time off is generally unpaid. Common vacation polices are:

- One week of paid vacation after completing 1 year of service
- Two weeks of paid vacation after completing 2 to 5 years of service
- Three weeks of paid vacation after completing 5 to 15 years of service
- Four weeks of paid vacation after completing 15 years of service

At termination, employees are generally paid for any vacation time they have accrued but have not used, but caterers should not permit staff to build up large amounts of unused vacation time. Many caterers adopt the "use it or lose it" policy common in other industries—employees must use the vacation in the year in which they accrue it, or lose it when a new year begins. The "year" can be either a calendar year or based on the worker's employment anniversary date.

Sick Pay

Most companies allow employees to accrue five to ten sick days per year. However, such policies do tend to encourage a "use it or lose it" mentality—smart for vacation time, but not for sick leave. Others allow "sick days" to include time a parent must spend with a sick child, not just leave for the employee's own illness.

Interestingly, many progressive employers have no specific sick pay policy. They decide entitlement to sick pay on a case-by-case basis for their regular, permanent employees. In off-premise catering situations, an employee's calling in sick at the last minute cannot be tolerated. Some caterers even require that staff members who are unable to work find their own replacements.

Off-premise caterers who offer a written policy allowing a certain number of sick days per year and who feel that the policy is being abused by employees may consider such actions as:

- "Buying back" unused sick time when an employee leaves
- Disciplining staff members who abuse the benefit
- Paying bonuses for good attendance
- Paying only one-half the daily rate for days taken off due to illness

Holiday Pay

In the United States, major holidays that typically affect employers are:

New Year's Day	New Year's Eve
Martin Luther King Day	Labor Day
Presidents' Day	Columbus Day
Easter (and Good Friday)	Veterans Day
Memorial Day	Thanksgiving
Independence Day	Christmas

Of course, there are others, but the holidays listed here are those most likely to involve holiday pay, requests for days off, and so forth. Holidays pose some interesting dilemmas for off-premise caterers, inasmuch as they are generally among the busiest times. How do caterers pay staff who work—or do not work—on holidays? Policies vary from company to company. Some caterers choose not to work holidays. Those who cater on holidays may pay nothing extra, and others choose to pay double time and pass the costs on to the clients. For regular staff members who are given holidays off, most caterers pay their regular pay. Competitors' holiday pay practices should be noted—for instance, it is not unheard of in big cities to pay double the hourly wage, or even more, for staff members who work on New Year's Eve.

Health Insurance

Medical costs continue to skyrocket and, therefore, the cost of health insurance has done the same. More and more caterers are reevaluating their decisions to offer health insurance coverage to staff members. Some follow the lead of companies in other industries and split the costs with employees. Others obtain the group policy, but require anyone who wants coverage to pay the full amount. Ultimately, it is the competition for employees that will help you make the final decision.

Jury Duty

From time to time regular employees are required to perform jury duty. Most employers pay the employees the difference between their regular pay and the pay they receive for jury duty (usually a pittance, only a few dollars) as long as the employees present documentation stating that they were actually on jury duty for the time.

Summary

No matter what benefits you decide to offer to staff members, it is important to consider the true costs of each of them, and to be well aware of what your competitors are offering, in order to attract the best possible workers. Benefits must always be provided in a clear and consistent fashion, so that all workers understand what's being offered and feel that they are being treated fairly.

Orientation and Training

The first day on the job determines, to a great extent, how well things will go in the future. It should be no surprise that turnover is highest among new employees. All too often, this is the fault of the employer for not properly acclimating new people and making them feel welcome on the job.

Proper orientation is not "Go find Jim, and he'll show you what to do." For new employees, many caterers have found it works well to conduct orientation meetings at the beginning of each season. This allows part-time staff members, who work the parties but are not involved on a daily basis, a refresher course about the overall operation. For regular, daily employees, orientation should include such things as:

- A personal welcome for new employees.
- An introduction to co-workers.
- A look at how the new employees fit into the overall operation or a particular event.
- The purpose and history of the company.
- A brief tour of the event site or commissary operation, including where to store uniforms and personal belongings.
- A review of on-the-job rules and regulations, including any grounds for dismissal. Your policies may cover making and receiving personal phone calls during work hours, use of cellular phones during events, breakage, behavior both before and after hours while on-premise (commissary or party sites).
- A review of pay rates, overtime rules, taxes that will be deducted, and scheduling procedures.
- An explanation and/or demonstration of major job duties.

At the orientation, each new employee should be assigned to another employee to "job-shadow," or follow, and time should be scheduled periodically with a new worker to see how things are going.

Learning should include regular training sessions, usually conducted in groups, and individual on-the-job-training, which is an ongoing process. Some caterers have formal training programs for staff, and others conduct training more informally, choosing a topic or two for each employee meeting, for instance. The higher a company's employee turnover rate, the greater its need for more and better training. However, all caterers should offer continuous learning opportunities if they are to provide first-class service. The following are key points to consider when developing a training program:

- What specific things do my staff members need to know to be successful?
- Who can best help them learn these things?
- How can training results be evaluated?

Ideally, group training sessions should last no more than 30 minutes, focusing on one or two topics that relate to keeping the needs of guests and clients in mind. Staff involvement should be encouraged by allowing discussion during the sessions. Potential topics for off-premise caterers may include:

- Techniques for carrying trays and plates
- Cooking pasta at a pasta station
- Carving meats at a carving station
- Creating attractive displays
- Correct wine service
- Dealing with "problem" guests (drinking, loud, rude, etc.)
- Personal grooming standards and expectations on the job

Other sessions can be aimed at building enthusiasm and esprit de corps among the staff. Progressive caterers have long used generic videos, with supplemental materials to reinforce the video's important points. There are some excellent video series that deal with customer relations, responsible alcohol service, sales and marketing, and more. CD-ROM and DVD training has emerged as an even better alternative, because these formats offer interactivity. They present information, ask questions to determine comprehension, record responses, provide reinforcement, and subsequently report on performance to the trainee and his or her managers. All that is needed to take advantage of web-based training is a computer with high-speed Internet access and browser software.

No matter what the format, successful caterers and restaurateurs constantly work with their employees to further their development. They are never happy with the way things are, always striving to improve.

Motivating Workers

Motivating catering staff members to perform to the best of their individual abilities, and still work as a team to keep the client's needs at the forefront, is a never-ending challenge, no matter how experienced the caterer. Off-premise caterers develop their own styles of motivating people. Most understand that all employees need to be challenged by their work, and recognized for their good work; to feel they are an important part of the company, and to feel safe in the workplace. These underlying needs can be met in many ways:

- Offering wages that are commensurate with the work, as well as with the wages paid by the competition
- Offering adequate employee benefits
- Running a well-organized workplace
- Displaying firm and fair leadership
- Never treating a client better than a staff member
- Rewarding those who do things right
- Fairly disciplining (and even terminating) those who continually do things wrong or are troublemakers
- Empowering employees to solve customer service problems themselves
- Being flexible about scheduling whenever possible
- Scheduling the best performers for the most and best shifts
- Allowing the best staff members to grow into supervisory and managerial positions
- Scheduling employee breaks and meals as appropriate
- Providing hot and cold beverages for staff members at off-premise sites
- Holding briefings prior to each event about its purpose and importance, and management's expectations
- Conducting frequent performance appraisals
- Allowing opportunities to attend pertinent seminars and conferences
- Allowing job rotation between positions

✑ ■ Making the off-premise catering operation a truly hospitable place to work by projecting a lively image, conducting upbeat staff meetings, and including staff members in future planning

We believe the use of uniforms on the job is one way to promote teamwork as well as a positive, professional image—for individual workers and for the company. Off-premise caterers should require specific uniforms for all staff members, to be worn prior to and during an event. This policy should be extremely specific; "white shirt" is not specific enough if caterers require a wing-tipped collar tuxedo shirt with black studs. The policy should address accessories that may and may not be worn, the use of cosmetics, exactly how the uniform is to be worn, and who will purchase and clean the uniforms. Some employers provide the complete uniform, some pay for part of it, and others require the employee to pay for the complete uniform. (Caterers and staff should consult their accountants regarding deductibility of uniforms for income tax purposes.) It's logical that you require staff members to keep their uniforms clean and to wear name tags, especially at event sites. It's important to ask your employees' opinions when making uniform choices or changes. After all, it is the employees who will be wearing them. Consider the look, wearability, purchase price, and availability for reorders, as well as the ease and cost of cleaning the uniforms.

Baltimore caterer Jerry Edwards of Chef's Expressions, president of the National Association of Catering Executives, shared his philosophy about motivating staffers during busy periods in the *National Association of Catering Executives Newsletter*:

> When in the depths of overtime, work side-by-side with them, or at least make your presence known. If they see you working as hard as they, it lessens the chance they'll resent you for not doing the same.
>
> Do some dirty work! Not all of it, rather just enough to remind them that you can. It lets them know that you have done it and will continue to do so whenever necessary.
>
> Listen to their problems. While it's likely you can't solve them, it shows that you are there for them to talk to and that you care enough about them to listen.
>
> And never forget to give recognition to your staff for all their hard work, especially during stressful and overbooked periods. Help them understand the "big picture" by letting them know that it can't happen without them.[11]

There are plenty of ways, some of them offbeat, to prompt fun as well as loyalty among your employees. Reward the younger staff members with things that are meaningful to them—help with college tuition, give gift certificates for clothing or CDs, buy concert tickets. You can even exchange catering services with other local merchants to obtain the gift certificates to pass along to employees. Hold a lottery, with the prize being a round-trip commute from their home to work in a limo! Hire a masseuse to give chair massages during especially hectic times at the commissary. For a job well done, give bonuses or lottery tickets on employment anniversaries. Give employees their birthdays off—their own personal paid holidays! And, finally, there's nothing like a handwritten thank-you note to express your gratitude with meaning.

Employee Turnover

Staff turnover is a measurement of how long workers remain in the employ of a particular company. It can be computed by dividing the number of W–2 forms you issue at year's end by the number of staff members. For example, a caterer who issued 100 W–2 forms and has an average staff of 50 persons would have a 200 percent turnover.

For some caterers, turnover is practically nonexistent; for others, there's virtually a whole new staff every two years. The typical quick-service restaurant chain, for example, completely turns over its staff two or three times a year! In catering, with the complexity of work, this would be crazy.

Some percentage of employee turnover actually has advantages. It keeps workers from becoming too complacent in the performance of their duties. Yet catering an event with all new employees is not much fun either. Turnover created by people moving away, students who graduate, and other external reasons is unavoidable. Unfortunately, some caterers do not treat their staff members properly, and they soon

TOP 10 REASONS PEOPLE QUIT THEIR JOBS[12]

Gregory P. Smith, president, Chart Your Course International, a management consulting firm in Conyers, Georgia

1. Management demands that one person do the jobs of two or more people.
2. Management cuts back on administrative help, forcing professional workers to use their time doing mundane and routine tasks.
3. Management puts a freeze on raises and promotions, when an employee can easily find a job earning much more somewhere else.
4. Management doesn't allow the rank-and-file staff members to make decisions or allow them pride of ownership.
5. Management constantly reorganizes, shuffles people around and constantly changes direction.
6. Management does not have or take the time to clarify goals and decisions.
7. Management shows favoritism and gives some workers better offices, trips, and fringe benefits.
8. Management relocates the offices to another location, forcing employees to quit or double their commute.
9. Management promotes someone who lacks training and/or necessary experience to supervisor, alienating staff and driving away good employees.
10. Management creates a rigid structure and then allows departments to compete against each other while at the same time preaching teamwork and cooperation.

Gregory Smith notes, "Isn't it interesting that all ten factors begin with the word, *management?*" Learn more about Chart Your Course International and its work at www.chartcourse.com.

defect to other employers. This type of turnover should be avoided at all costs through excellent hiring, training, motivation, pay, and benefits.

✖ *Performance Reviews*

Employees require feedback about their performance, and professional managers see that they are given useful feedback on a timely basis. Performance reviews serve a dual purpose—as a basis for encouraging more effective work performance, and to provide dates for decision making about future job assignments and compensation.

Permanent employees should be evaluated at least once a year, except in the first year on the job, when evaluations should be performed no fewer than three times. It is advisable to establish probationary periods for all new employees, which can last from three to six months. During the probationary period, employees who are not meeting expectations may be terminated without warning. At the end of the probationary period, every employee should receive a performance review.

Progressive catering managers also take time to evaluate the performances of all staffers after each catered event, to identify problem areas and determine needs for further training. Many use these evaluations for future scheduling purposes. Excellent performers receive the best schedules and shifts; those whose work was mediocre will be scheduled less frequently. Those who performed poorly may not be rescheduled at all.

Exhibit 7.8 is a Staff Evaluation Form. It addresses performance areas such as quality and quantity of work, ability to follow directions, ability to interact with guests and fellow employees, and so on. This form can be used for either full- or part-timers.

Management and supervisory staff members should be evaluated with the use of additional criteria: their judgment, analytical and planning abilities, profit and cost sensibilities, effectiveness as a supervisor, and more. Above all else, the caterer should always use his or her own independent judgment and avoid the inevitable rumors that always seem to circulate in this type of close-knit work group. Also evaluate a staff member based on his or her "typical" behavior, eliminating both "good" and "bad" extremes. You might consider using peer group evaluations, in which fellow staff members (often anonymously) evaluate their co-workers.

✖ *Discipline and Termination*

To be effective, discipline must be consistent. It must be administered as a result of specific behavior problems, rather than personality conflicts. Discipline normally follows a particular series of steps:

1. Verbal warning
2. Written warning(s)
3. Suspension without pay
4. Termination

⊠ Exhibit 7.8 *Staff Evaluation Form*

NAME OF EMPLOYEE _____

EMPLOYEE'S POSITION _____

NAME OF PERSON(S) RATING _____

_____

DATE OF REVIEW _____

RATING SCALE OF 1 TO 5

1   UNSATISFACTORY

2   NEEDS IMPROVEMENT

3   SATISFACTORY

4   ABOVE AVERAGE

5   OUTSTANDING

<u>QUALITY OF WORK</u>   <u>QUANTITY OF WORK</u>

ACCURACY _____   AMOUNT COMPLETED _____

NEATNESS _____   COMPLETED ON TIME _____

ORGANIZATION _____   CONSISTENCY _____

ATTENTION TO DETAIL _____

<u>FOLLOWING DIRECTIONS</u>

COMPLY WITH INSTRUCTIONS _____

FOLLOWS RULES AND REGULATIONS _____

CARE AND USE OF EQUIPMENT _____

FOLLOWS SAFETY AND SANITATION RULES _____

<u>OTHER CRITERIA</u>

PUNCTUALITY AND ATTENDANCE _____

GETS ALONG WITH GUESTS _____

GETS ALONG WITH OTHER EMPLOYEES _____

PERSONAL APPEARANCE AND HYGIENE _____

OTHER BEHAVIOR _____

DATE REVIEWED WITH EMPLOYEE _____

EMPLOYEE'S COMMENTS AND REACTION _____

_____

_____

_____

MUTUALLY AGREED-UPON STEPS TO IMPROVE PERFORMANCE _____

_____

_____

_____

SIGNATURE OF EMPLOYEE _____

SIGNATURE OF PERSON REVIEWING PERFORMANCE WITH EMPLOYEE

_____

Employees who steal, who are insubordinate, or who use alcohol or drugs while working should be terminated immediately.

Documentation of unacceptable behavior is imperative. For staffers who are frequently late, it is not enough for a manager to warn them by saying, "You're always late!" Documentation of exact times and dates is essential. Some efficient managers keep track of such details by making verbal notes on cassette tape recorders. Verbal and written warnings should include clear statements of expectations: "You must be dressed and working at your workstation by 8:00 A.M. each day." Finally, warnings should include the consequences for not doing what is necessary. Can the violation result in suspension, transfer, demotion, termination?

The two forms of termination are voluntary and involuntary. A voluntary separation occurs when an employee resigns. Smart managers always identify the reasons why employees leave and obtain letters of resignation so that employees who quit cannot receive unemployment benefits—because claims of this type often directly contribute to an increase in the employer's unemployment rates.

Involuntary separation, or firing, should be considered a last resort after trying all else. Elio Bellucci, JD, professor of hospitality management at Florida International University, offers these procedures:

> Include in staff manuals that the relationship between the employer and employee will continue to be that of an employee at will and that the employer shall have the right to terminate the relationship without just cause, or any cause at all.
>
> Discharge employees for only legitimate, non-discriminatory reasons. Employees' race, color, age, sex, national origin or other protected characteristics must not play roles in decisions to dismiss.
>
> Establish certain procedural rights concerning rules and regulations, except for those infractions which provide for immediate termination such as stealing, destruction of property, fighting, etc.
>
> Document all personnel actions. Do not delay necessary actions, and when taking action, be specific and always tell employees the truth.
>
> Consult legal counsel before terminating employees.
>
> Insure that all procedures and policies as outlined in employee handbooks have been fully complied with before terminating employees.
>
> Conduct exit interviews with terminated employees.
>
> Treat all employees alike, and be sure that terminations are consistent with past practices.[13]

Additional termination guidelines, according to Paula Michal-Johnson, author of *Saying Good-Bye: A Manager's Guide to Employee Dismissal*, published by Scott, Foresman (1985, but still in print and available), include:

> Anticipate an employee's reaction and how it might affect you. Your goal is to remain calm no matter what the other person does.
>
> If you feel that the employee could endanger you or your company through reprisal, request security support. You also might want a third person present during the termination interview.
>
> Never express how badly you might feel, as this will be interpreted as hypocrisy. Treat the person who is losing the job with dignity.

Experts recommend dismissing an employee early in the week so he or she can begin looking for another job.

Don't try to make an example of the fired employee. Limiting the number of people who know the details of the firing will lessen the chance of the employee suing for defamation.[14]

Frankly, in our experience, many employees in the largest catering firms are below average and do not produce to the level expected of their counterparts in smaller companies. We know companies that routinely evaluate and weed out their lowest-performing employees, as frequently as every six months, to increase productivity and reduce costs. Other firms put the lowest performers on a performance improvement plan, with goals and time lines for results. This policy, although not foolproof, will definitely improve the morale of the worthy workers. Although it will produce some anxiety, the bottom line is that good employees want to work with other good employees.

✗ *The Employee Handbook*

All off-premise caterers, regardless of size, should have their employment rules, standards, and procedures in writing, in an employee handbook. This book will not replace personal contact and can't possibly answer every potential question, but it can at least inform staff about the most vital company policy information. Generally, the larger the company, the more information should be included. You can try writing the handbook yourself, with the assistance of a good local freelance writer and input from your attorney. Ask executives in other industries if you can look at their manuals for ideas. Or you can hire a human resources consulting firm to craft a manual for your company. Many companies now keep their employee handbooks online, on their own internal website, so they can be updated regularly and are available to anyone who has access to a computer. But it's also good to have printed copies available. Ask new employees to sign a short statement affirming that they have received a copy of the handbook, have read it and had an opportunity to ask questions, and have understood its contents.

Every employee handbook should begin with a basic "welcome" and a policy statement that summarizes the way business is done by the company. Here's an example of a policy statement:

ABC Catering is known throughout this area as a reputable, service-oriented firm that provides excellent food and service to its corporate and social clientele. Our goal is to astonish the guest by delivering more than promised on a consistent basis. This can be accomplished through teamwork within our company. All staff members are expected not only to perform their own jobs, but also to assist other staff members whenever needed.

At ABC Catering we put our staff first. We realize that an outstanding staff will deliver and produce the types of events that will exceed the guests' expectations, creating wonderful word of mouth that will generate future business.

Our staff is made up of friendly, caring, courteous, and concerned individuals who enjoy working for us. They smile; they keep their promises; they are always pleasant to our clients and guests. They listen attentively to guest requests and always exhibit a positive, "can-do" attitude. We try to empower our staff members to handle any special customer request quickly and courteously.

We produce special events and parties that are user-friendly for the guests, and hassle-free for the clients. We treat clients and guests the same way that we wish to be treated when we are out.

Our staff members have self-pride, pride in our food and service, and pride in our organization. We are pleased to welcome you to the ABC team!

Following the policy statement, include a checklist of wide-ranging topics— whatever fits best for your company.

✔ Employee Handbook Topics

Alcohol and drugs (policy to prohibit use)

Americans with Disabilities Act (company compliance)

Attendance policies

Automobiles (where to park, including a statement that the company is not responsible for personal vehicles or their contents)

Breaks (when and where)

"Carry in" bags

Compensation (payroll deductions, signing in and out, minimum shift lengths)

Courtesy (a statement regarding kind, professional treatment of others)

Equal opportunity employer ("ABC Catering reaffirms its policy of treating all employees and applicants equally, according to their individual qualifications, ability, experience, and other employment standards. There is to be no discrimination due to race, religion, color, national origin, sex, age, disability, or veteran status.")

Exit interviews (to be conducted for all terminated staff prior to leaving)

Family and Medical Leave Act (company compliance)

Gambling (on-the-job prohibition)

Grievance procedures

Grooming policies

Holidays (and related pay policy)

Hours of work (normal office hours, shift times, etc.)

On-the-job injuries (all of these, regardless of their nature or severity, must be reported immediately to the supervisor. All employees are insured through Worker's Compensation. Those employees who do not report injuries are subject to disciplinary action.)

Personal appearance (policy on excessive tattoos, body piercings, dreadlocks)

Personal phone calls, cell phone use, mail

Moonlighting (rules about working for other caterers, restaurants, etc.)

Overtime policy

Payroll discrepancies (pay dates; adjustments for errors, advances, lost paychecks; reimbursement for out-of-pocket expenses at an event, etc.)

Pension plan (if applicable)

Performance reviews (who conducts them, how often, where records are kept, how the results can be questioned or challenged)

Probationary periods

Promotions and transfers

Property (care of company property; not responsible for personal property)

Rules and regulations (miscellaneous)

Safety and sanitation rules

Security (policy for checking employees' bags and personal property, policy on employees taking home leftovers, etc.)

Sexual harassment (Potential problems must be reported to management, and management will investigate by interviewing the alleged offender and others, ask for legal advice in those situations that are unclear, and take appropriate disciplinary action if necessary)

Sick leave (sick pay policy)

Smoking (should be prohibited in all food production and service areas and on client event sites)

Suggestions (are encouraged; how to submit them)

Teamwork (importance of working together)

Telephone courtesy and incoming calls (policies and procedures for answering telephones, taking orders on proper forms, etc.)

Termination policies

Training programs

Uniforms (specifics, who pays for uniforms, use of name tags, etc.)

Vacation policy (how much, how it is accrued, how to ask for it)

 Conclusion

It is important to keep in mind that off-premise catering is a people-oriented and service-oriented business. Excellent food served by a poorly trained, indifferent, unkempt staff never tastes as good and sometimes is even ruined by the service. On the other hand, a well-trained, highly motivated staff can make even the best food taste better and can ensure the success of your catered events.

Notes

1. Fern Canter, director of Human Resources Development, Turnberry Isle Resort & Club, Aventura, Florida.
2. *Anti-Discrimination Law: Employer Responsibilities*, Florida Restaurant Association, Hollywood, Florida, 1993.
3. Stephen C. Barth, in *Club Management* magazine, August 2000.
4. Reprinted with permission of the author, Wayne Lavis of Bloomsburg, Pennsylvania, and the *CommuniCATER*, publication of the National Caterers Association, September 1989.
5. Greg Lousig-Nont, in *Restaurant Hospitality* magazine, October 2000.
6. Fern Canter, Turnberry Isle.
7. Jim Sullivan, in *Top Shelf* magazine, July/August 1992.

8. *The Foolproof Foodservice Selection System,* by Bill Marvin, John Wiley & Sons, Hoboken, New Jersey, 1993.

9. Greg Lousig-Nont in *Restaurant Hospitality* magazine, October 2000.

10. Tim Owens, attorney, in *Catering* magazine, May/June 1999.

11. Jerry Edwards, president, Chef's Expressions Catering, Baltimore, Maryland, and National Association of Catering Executives.

12. Gregory P. Smith, president, Chart Your Course International, Conyers, Georgia.

13. Elio Bellucci, professor of hospitality management, Florida International University, 1994.

14. *Saying Good-Bye: A Manager's Guide to Employee Dismissal,* by Paula Michal-Johnson, Scott, Foresman, 1985, Glenview, Illinois.

✕ Chapter 8

The Show

The Show is the term caterers use for the event itself. All the planning, purchasing, and preparation leads up to a single event, and it's your job to make it everything the clients expect. This chapter is about delivering what you promise. We discuss those elements that are key to the success of off-premise catered events, including:

- The importance of client service
- The role of the party supervisor
- Table-setting rules
- Buffets and food stations
- Proper service techniques
- The importance of the off-premise catering kitchen

"The Show" is by far the most important time for off-premise caterers. This is the time when the clients and their guests receive what was agreed on in the planning and contract-signing phases of the negotiations. There is only one opportunity to perform, so it must be right the first time.

Everyone who attends the event will evaluate the food, the service, and the off-premise catering company. Good reviews should bring future business, but bad reviews create negative word of mouth that can quickly spread, resulting in lost business.

Four out of five dissatisfied guests won't necessarily complain to the caterer or on-site staffers, but they'll tell others. For every 10 dissatisfied guests, 7 of them will tell 20 others! So the caterer must focus all of his or her attention on client satisfaction if that caterer wants to continue to be successful and profitable. A sad commentary is that the average American company will spend six times more to get new customers than in trying to retain old ones. Doesn't it make sense to go all-out in customer service to retain existing clients, rather than spend money advertising for new ones?

Customer service is a delicate, intangible product. It cannot be stored for future use; once given, it is lost. It is a direct function of the customers' expectations and perceptions. The perceived level of service equals how closely the guests' experiences match their expectations. And, ironically, when the service experience matches their expectations, it is often unnoticed or taken for granted. You might say the customer's impression is "neutral" when the service is "neutral." On either side of "neutral" is the memorable experience—which may be good or bad.

To make a positive memorable impression, what has to happen? The service must be efficient and attuned to the mood of the event as well as the cultural level of the guests. Staff members must be caring, courteous, concerned, and reliable. The people, and surroundings, must be clean, safe, and pleasant. Overall, the client must consider the outcome worth the investment.

Yet good service is often a matter of opinion or perception. It is not what is said, but what is seen and heard. Miscommunication is often at the heart of service problems. For example, suppose an off-premise caterer says roast beef will be served on the buffet. The customer is accustomed to eating beef tenderloin and assumes that beef tenderloin will be served. The caterer serves a steamship roast. The caterer never said *tenderloin*, but the client "heard" *beef tenderloin.* Some caterers will say, "Not my fault, and not my problem." But it is! We are dependent on clients for future business, so we must at least meet their expectations and, ideally, exceed them. In this case, the caterer should have been specific about what type of beef would be served. Of course, the client could have asked, but that is not the point. We are considered the experts, so we must take the ultimate responsibility for clarification.

The five most common service-related complaints are:

- Broken promises
- Rudeness
- Indifference
- Not listening
- Negative attitudes

What do they have in common? They are all, to a large extent, matters of opinion and personal perception. And they all occur when there is contact with clients and guests. These "moments of truth" occur thousands of times during an off-premise event—with the bartenders who serve the drinks, with meal servers, with the person at the door who says "good night." The goal for caterers should be to create the entire experience so that guests float through the party, barely noticing the servers, having their needs anticipated. The experience should be user-friendly and hassle-free. Long waits for food and beverages, unpleasant servers, poorly prepared food, and disorganized or unclean surroundings are examples of situations that antagonize guests and ruin any chances for future business.

Everyone in all catering organizations must be motivated to create a wonderful experience for clients and guests. Everyone from the chef to the busperson must aim for guest satisfaction. Progressive off-premise caterers empower their staff members to solve service problems on the spot without involving a supervisor, which may take too much time. This could mean anything from obtaining a special meal for a guest, to helping a person who may have difficulty walking to a buffet.

Complacency regarding customer service will quickly result in clients taking their business to the competition. In most markets, there are other catering firms waiting for a competitor to "blink"—by not delivering as promised.

Caterers who think that food quality is the most important aspect of their service are mistaken. Clients are equally concerned with such things as the caliber of the service staff, the table appointments and buffets, and even the accessory services such as the music. A band or deejay blaring loud music while guests are conversing and dining will ruin an event. The Disney organization perceives itself as providing a "fantasy experience" in its theme parks. It does not think of its facilities merely as amusement parks. In similar fashion, the successful off-premise caterer realizes that he or she provides a complete entertainment experience, not just food.

Great customer service has to feel sincere, warm, and, most important, spontaneous. There is nothing worse than robotic service that's delivered without enthusiasm. Great service makes everyone feel that he or she is truly special. "Bumping good service up" to extraordinary can be something as simple as reversing the place settings for left-handed guests. At Charlie Trotter's restaurant in Chicago you are greeted as you would be when going to a friend's home. At Signature Grand in Davie, Florida, guests are wowed with a surprise Irish coffee station at the end of the event.

Caterers should handle servers' accidental spills graciously, in a courteous and professional manner. If possible, get spilled-on clothes cleaned while the guest eats; if not, offer to pay the cleaning bill. Other examples of extraordinary service include escorting guests to the restroom, rather than simply pointing, and giving them tours of your commissary or off-premise catering kitchen before an event.

The bottom line here is that extraordinary service will bring extraordinary sales and profits and will ensure that you will have repeat business. Service sells! In the rest of this chapter, we discuss how you can establish service standards and follow through to see that they are met, and exceeded.

Supervising and Managing

Before discussing specific techniques for providing outstanding service, here we address the role and responsibilities of the event supervisor or manager. In Chapter 6 we detailed the delivery of food, equipment, and supplies to the party site. At this point, we are assuming the catering truck(s) have arrived, one of them perhaps being driven by the event supervisor, and it's time to start setting up.

The supervisor, with some assistance, first needs to oversee the unloading and organizing of the equipment so that the staff can find it. If there is rental equipment, this must also be organized, unwrapped, sorted, and counted. If there are problems with the equipment, the supervisor should call the rental company immediately to correct them.

The supervisor is also responsible for checking in staff and assigning them setup duties as they arrive. This includes giving the staffers written diagrams for the various bars, buffets, and stations and the off-premise kitchen. Many caterers prefer to stagger the arrival of staff members, scheduling a few workers early to help unload, organize the equipment, skirt buffet tables, and so on. Once things are organized, other staffers arrive to perform other functions, like setting tables, stocking the bars, arranging buffet decorations, and so forth. For those who will be setting the tables, the supervisor should set up a sample place setting.

As the crew sets up, the supervisor should meet with the client for a last-minute check: Are the various accessory service providers on schedule? How can the food service schedule be best coordinated with the program and the music? Pre-party setup can be hectic, but never ignore the client.

The event supervisor must also be aware of the kitchen setup in order to direct the service staff as to where food will be picked up and where soiled dishes will be placed. Normally, a separate person is in charge of the kitchen. The kitchen supervisor sees that the cooking facilities are set up as shown in the event diagram and operated in a manner that meets the client's needs. This person takes charge of these duties:

- Is the kitchen set up properly, neatly, and safely for the particular function?
- Are all the necessary utensils, food, and supplies—even down to plastic gloves for the food preparers—on hand in sufficient quantity?
- Has the scheduled staff checked in and been assigned duties?
- Are these people properly trained and briefed?
- Are the recipes on-site for preparing this menu?
- Are there any last-minute changes in the menu or service to be discussed?

If all is on schedule, the party site should be completely set up approximately one hour before the guests arrive. This will give the setup crew a chance to change and freshen up. At this time the supervisor should conduct a detailed meeting to discuss everyone's responsibilities during the party. For large events, a large poster or handouts can be very effective for informing the staff members of their responsibilities. This briefing should include some information about the purpose of the event, the clients, and the guests and any other information that will assist the staff in properly serving the event. It should also include:

- Complete discussion of menu and beverage arrangements
- The schedule of events
- Restroom locations for guests
- Review of all serving procedures (how to pass hors d'oeuvres, serve the meal, and bus dishes, etc.)

- Making sure that staffers each have a few business cards to hand to guests who ask about the catering

It's important to answer any of their questions and to give your team an up-beat send-off for a great party. Tell them how much you appreciate their hard work and courtesy to the guests. Once the briefing is complete, the staff members report to their assigned stations, and the supervisor should begin a last-minute check of all stations, bars, the kitchen, the accessory service providers, and other details. If the party is on target, the supervisor will have an opportunity to mingle a bit with guests and perhaps develop some contacts for future business. The supervisor should see that everything is kept on schedule and may help out at busy times—at the bar early in the party, in the kitchen when the main course is being plated, assisting with dirty dishes at the end of the event. In other words, a supervisor is expected to do what-ever is necessary to ensure the success of the event.

In addition, once the *food service* is complete, the supervisor should see that staffers receive short breaks, and a meal if appropriate. Although it is true that every event seems to have one last-minute crisis (small or large) to be dealt with, a good floor supervisor operates more like a mayor than a firefighter. He or she walks the floor, noticing every table, setting the pace for the staff, and assisting as necessary without getting stuck in one job. Great supervisors observe, anticipate, prioritize, and act. They must be capable of multitasking, keeping everything in perspective while never let-ting staff or guests "see them sweat."

Good supervisors and managers not only serve the guests, but must also serve their staff members. Sensitivity to the needs of the staff ranks first for outstanding leaders. Good leaders nourish the staff. They give energy, rather than deplete it!

Normally, by the time the staff has finished its break period, the guests are leav-ing. Breakdown can begin as soon as the guests leave. The main responsibilities for the supervisor at this point are:

- Count all equipment and see that it is returned to a safe place or loaded into the catering vehicle.
- Be sure all trash is bagged and put in the proper place.
- Deal with any leftovers in the manner decided by contract or by mutual agree-ment on-site with the client.
- Check out staff members and ensure they have left the party site.
- Collect any funds due from the client (if not already paid or arranged for).
- Safely return the catering vehicle to the commissary and unload it.

✖ Setting Up for Meal Service

Most off-premise caterers allow two to three hours of setup time prior to an event. The amount of time will vary, depending on the size of the event, the complexity and location of the setup, and other factors, but it's always better to allow too much time, rather than too little, in the event there are unforeseen problems during the setup. The setup crew can be a skeleton crew—maybe 25 to 50 percent of the total staff scheduled to serve the event. They should be attired in a setup uniform, designated by the caterer. It may something as simple as a T-shirt or golf shirt with the caterer's logo, matching slacks or shorts, and comfortable shoes. Most pre-party work involves heavy lifting, so don't make it fancy. A uniformed, efficient, and well-organized setup crew is a signal to the client that things are already going well and will continue to do so.

It is advisable to have all the tables set at least one hour prior to the start of the event. Why?

- The client is reassured that everything will go as planned and can also take a break before the event.
- It allows time for problem solving if something goes wrong.
- It gives staff time to freshen up and change into service uniforms.
- It leaves time for a staff meeting before the event.

Unlike hotels, where nonservice staffers set up the tables, many off-premise caterers rely on their service staff to perform this function. A diagram of the room layout will show where tables are to be placed. A supervisor should check that each table leg is locked in place for safety reasons and that there is at least 5 feet between the tables to allow room for chairs and walking space. When rolling round tables, staff members should keep the legs opposite their bodies and wear heavy work gloves to protect their hands from slivers and sharp metal edges. Tables must be carried, rather than rolled, over certain floors that may scratch, and over dirty or muddy surfaces.

The menu for a seated, served meal determines the place setting. Guided by the sample place setting completed by the supervisor, staffers may begin to set the tables once they are all in place. It is easier to set the tables without the chairs in place, because they get in the way as servers are moving around the tables. If this is the case, how do the staff members know where to place the flatware? They can use the creases on the linens as guidelines, as shown in Exhibit 8.1. Imagining that the table is the face of a clock, they place the knives at twelve and six o'clock, and then evenly place the remaining knives according to whether the table is to be set for 8, 10, or 12 guests. When placing the linens on the tables, servers should be trained not to drag clean linens on the floor or ground, to see that they hang evenly from all sides, to ensure that the hem sides are down and that the creases all run in the same direction for uniformity. Servers' hands must be clean before handling linens.

Although not always possible, it is advisable to place the centerpieces on the tables as soon as the linens are on, but prior to setting the tables. By doing this, the servers know how much room will be available for the place settings. When very large floral arrangements are placed on already-set tables, the glasses may be knocked over or the place settings may have to be compacted to make room. For a damp floral arrangement, a napkin should be folded and placed under it to protect the more expensive cloth. Wet cloths can mildew quickly if not handled properly after the event.

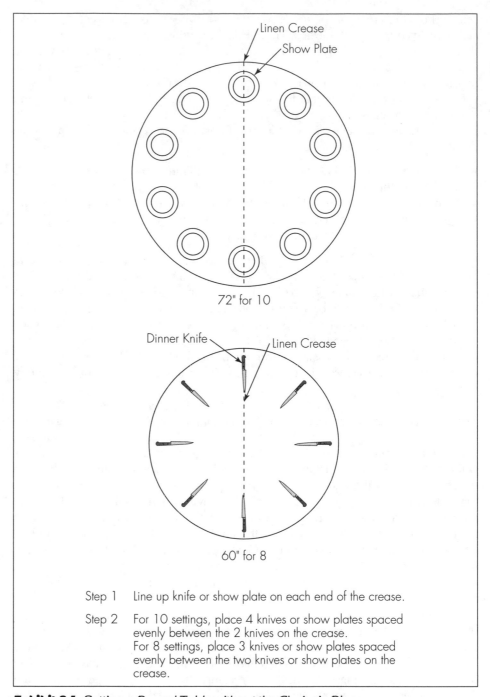

Exhibit 8.1 *Setting a Round Table without the Chairs in Place*

The basic pieces of a place setting, and their purposes, include:

Dinner knife	For main course
Butter knife	For butter
Salad knife	For salad course
Fish knife	For seafood dishes
Dinner fork	For main course
Salad fork	For salad course
Fish fork	For seafood dishes
Oyster fork	For shellfish
Soup spoon	For soups or pasta
Teaspoon	For desserts or sorbets
Iced tea spoon	For iced tea
Bread and butter plate	For bread and butter
Show plate (charger)	Under any courses served before the main course
Water goblet	For water
Wine glasses	For wines
Champagne glass	For Champagne
Coffee cup and saucer	For coffee or hot tea
Napkin	

Of course, you'll never put each and every one of these items in a single place setting all at once! A very efficient way to set a large number of tables is to assign one particular item per setup person. This eliminates presorting into sets of 8, 10, or 12 for each table and assigns responsibility for a particular item to one person: Jane sets the dinner knife, Joe sets the dinner fork, Sue sets the salad fork, and so on. When each is finished setting his or her assigned utensil, the person starts with a new one until the tables are all set. It is very easy to misplace items when everyone is handling all of them—one server has extra teaspoons, momentarily sets them down, and forgets where. Another server is short of teaspoons and can't find any more. Setting tables in a more organized fashion can save significant time, effort, and frustration. Once the place settings are on the tables, the chairs may be positioned at each place setting by just touching the front edge of the chair to the linen. The chairs should never be shoved under the table or pushed into the tablecloth, which makes the whole table look rumpled and unattractive.

Exhibit 8.2 is a sample place setting for a multiple-course dinner. Note that the utensils are placed in order of service from outside in. The bottom edges of the flatware and show plate should be one inch from the edge of the table. Please note that the coffee cup and saucer are not pre-set, which is standard for a meal of this caliber. In circumstances where speed is important, or for breakfasts and lunches, the coffee cup and saucer may be pre-set. Again, the saucer should be one inch from the edge of the table, and the cup handled should be angled at four o'clock. Because this place setting is very full, the dessert fork and coffee teaspoon can be placed prior to the coffee and dessert service.

In addition to the items depicted in Exhibit 8.2, tables will also require salt and pepper shakers, sugar bowls, creamers, and ashtrays (if smoking is allowed). The salt and pepper shakers are pre-set but removed when the main course is cleared. The

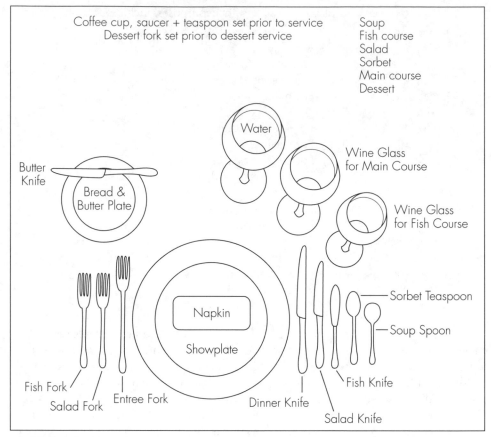

Coffee cup, saucer + teaspoon set prior to service
Dessert fork set prior to dessert service

Soup
Fish course
Salad
Sorbet
Main course
Dessert

Water

Wine Glass
for Main Course

Butter
Knife

Bread &
Butter Plate

Wine Glass
for Fish Course

Napkin

Showplate

Sorbet Teaspoon

Soup Spoon

Fish Fork

Salad Fork

Entree Fork

Dinner Knife

Fish Knife

Salad Knife

Exhibit 8.2 *Place Setting*

sugar and cream containers should be placed prior to the coffee service. Ashtrays are seldom seen on tables anymore, but if the client requests them, they must remain in place throughout the meal, and they must be kept clean.

Standards vary from caterer to caterer, but a general rule for numbers of these "ancillary items" per table is:

Tables of six	Two sets
Tables of eight	Two to three sets
Tables of ten/twelve	Three sets

Exhibit 8.3 shows a variety of napkin folds. In some parts of the country, placing a folded napkin in a glass is considered unsanitary. Off-premise caterers should also remember that if the first course is to be pre-set, the napkin cannot go in the center of the show plate. In this instance, it must go above the show plate, or perhaps in a simple, flat fold underneath the forks.

When setting tables with small candles, supervisors must check that the candles are placed so as not to ignite a centerpiece or napkin. At one event, a quick-thinking,

Tuxedo	Candle	Crown

Tuxedo

- Fold napkin in quarters,
- Roll the first layer of napkin toward you to the center.

- Fold the second layer toward you and under the first—DO NOT ROLL.
- Leave the same width of napkin as the rolled edge.
- Fold the next layer of napkin away from you and under the same width as other two folds,
- Fold under the right and left side edges to center back.

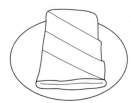

Candle

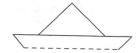

- Fold napkin in half diagonally, forming a triangle.
- Fold one fourth of the base edge of napkin up, forming a cuff.

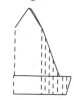

- Turn napkin over. Carefully roll left to right.
- Tuck the remaining corner inside the cuff to hold the Candle firm.

- Position the Candle with the highest point of the napkin facing you.

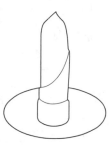

Crown

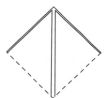

- Fold napkin in half diagonally, forming a triangle.
- Fold the left and right hand corners of the triangle to the top, forming a square.

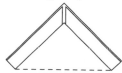

- Turn the napkin to form a diamond. Fold the bottom point two-thirds of the way to the top point and fold the bottom point back again to the base line.

- Turn napkin over and tuck the far corners into one another, forming a round base.
- Stand a napkin upright and flair out the two top corners to form a Crown.

Exhibit 8.3 *Napkin Folding Made Easy (Courtesy Artex International)*

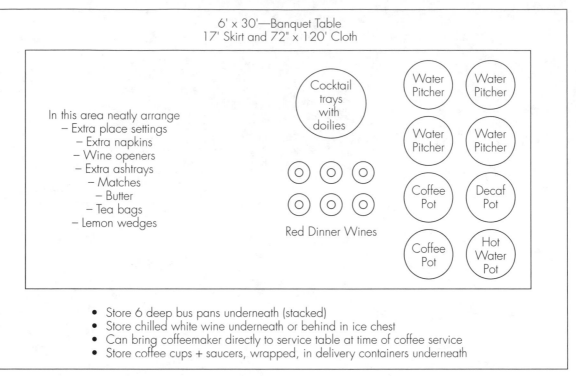

Exhibit 8.4 Service Table

observant waiter discovered that a centerpiece was on fire and simply doused the fire with the water from a water glass, which averted what could have been a major disaster. When removing candles with hot wax after the event, servers must be instructed to wait until the wax is hard to avoid dripping wax on the linens or on themselves.

Exhibit 8.4 depicts a sample setup for a service table to be used by the service staff for storing items required during the meal. One table is required for approximately every 100 guests. Most items are kept on top of the table, but some—such as chilled wines, bus boxes, dirty dishes, and racked wrapped cups and saucers—are kept underneath the service table. Service tables may be used in conjunction with served dinners, as well as with buffets and food station parties.

✕ Serving Procedures

Serving Butlered Hors D'Oeuvres

Frequently, prior to served meals, off-premise caterers serve hors d'oeuvres that are passed "butler-style." Although this is a relatively simple procedure to learn, there are a few rules that servers must follow to make this part of the evening most enjoyable for the guests:

- Know the name of the item and any accompanying sauce, along with the ingredients and method of preparation (fried, oven-baked, grilled, etc.).
- Warn guests if foods are very hot or spicy.
- Always smile and show courtesy toward the guests.
- Carry a supply of cocktail napkins in your free hand.
- Always return to the kitchen with dirty dishes and glassware.
- Keep the passing trays looking neat. If guests place dirty cocktail napkins or skewers on passing trays, remove them immediately and carry them in your hand underneath the tray until you can dispose of them.
- When passing hot food during times that are not busy, return to the kitchen after five to ten minutes, because the food will be cold.
- Once a tray of hors d'oeuvres is depleted to the point that it does not look appetizing, return to the kitchen for a fresh one.
- Always pass to different guests during each "trip" around the room by going different routes.

Serving the Meal

Your servers are responsible for serving food and beverages to guests. Many off-premise caterers have found that each member of the service staff can be designated as either a "server" or a "runner." The runners bring the food from the kitchen, assist in serving the guests if necessary, and return to the kitchen with soiled dishes. The servers stay with the guests at all times, serving and clearing. The ratio of servers to runners depends on the menu, the distance to the kitchen, and other unique factors. A ratio of one-to-one is a good place to start, and you may adjust this depending on the event and the skill of your staff members. The total number of people on the service staff will vary according to the level of service to be offered—anywhere from one staff member per 5 guests to one per 20 guests is standard.

There are a number of standard service procedures that never seem to go out of style, no matter in what geographic area you work, for instance:

- Serve food from the left, with your left hand, while moving forward in a counter-clockwise direction.
- Always serve the female guests at each table before serving male guests.
- Clear from the right, using your right hand, except for such items as bread and butter plates, side dishes, and unused silver that are on a guest's left. These should be cleared from the left, using your right hand.
- Serve beverages from the right with your right hand, moving clockwise around the table. Some caterers consider soup a beverage.
- Never reach across in front of guests, and if two guests are leaning toward each other talking, clear and serve from their outsides.
- Servers should not make unnecessary noise and should be as inconspicuous as possible.
- Service staff should never touch flatware that is on plates, nor put their fingers inside glasses when clearing a table.

- Water glasses should be replenished throughout the meal, and ashtrays should be emptied frequently by placing a clean ashtray over the top of the dirty one, removing both from the table, and setting the clean one on the table.
- Table numbers and unused place settings should be removed when all the guests are seated.
- Tables, chairs, buffets, and bars should not be broken down and removed until the guests have left the event.

The rules that relate to the actual serving of the food and clearing of the plates can be practiced in your weekly staff meetings, using some employees as "customers" and others as servers. Your service personnel should learn to make every move count, to avoid wasting motions by anticipating their next moves. In short, a good server remains vigilant, plans ahead, rarely stops, and is always accomplishing something.

During the staff meeting prior to a meal service event, the supervisor must instruct the service staff if there is an order in which certain tables will be served. (For instance, if there's a table of guests who will be speaking at an event, they are typically served first so they can complete their meals and get ready to give their speeches.) An acceptable way to do this is to divide the seating area into sections of five to ten tables, with a lead server in charge of each area. The lead server will not only serve, but will ensure that the tables within the section are served in the correct sequence. The lead server knows that each table must be completely served before starting at the next table. For smaller events, the supervisor can direct the order of service. Of course, the head table is always served first, then others in designated sequence.

Water, Roll, and Butter Service

Ice water should be poured 10 minutes prior to the guests being seated, and the glasses should be kept filled throughout the meal. Chilled bottled water is not served until after the guests are seated, since it is not served with ice to keep it chilled. Butter is placed on the bread and butter plate in a uniform fashion, also prior to guests being seated. Warm rolls or bread can be placed in baskets on the table just after the guests are seated or can be pre-set in baskets or on the bread and butter plates if not served hot. For smaller events, a warm roll may be placed on the plate after the guests are seated. Servers should make sure to replenish breads or rolls and butter frequently throughout the meal.

Seating the Guests and Starting Service

Servers may assist the guests with seating, seeing that they are comfortable, placing the napkins across their laps, and serving a last-minute drink from the bar. Next, hot rolls or bread should be served. If the first course was not pre-set, then the first course should be served. Some items (such as chilled soups) work well pre-set, but hot appetizers and mixed salads (like Caesars) must be served after guests are seated.

As a general rule, each course should take about 15 to 20 minutes to serve, consume, and clear. Most guests at parties prefer to dine at a moderate rate—that is, not rushed, but not having to wait 15 to 30 minutes between courses. Most meals can be served within 60 to 90 minutes, no matter how many guests attend.

As servers start serving a table, it is essential that the runners have supplied a sufficient number of orders to service all the guests at that table. Never should servers begin a table, serve only a few guests, and then have to wait for more meals. Be sure that everyone at a table is completely served before starting to serve the next table.

The key to excellent banquet service is the timing of the service of each course. Guests in the same area of the room should receive their food at approximately the same time. Aside from scheduling sufficient service staff, there must be sufficient kitchen staff, with an organized system for dishing up each course in the off-premise kitchen. Some cold courses may be pre-plated, which eliminates the pressure of dishing up to order. Hot food that is pre-plated and held in warmers is simply not as fresh or as good as hot food plated and served within a matter of minutes.

Off-premise caterers have developed their own systems for hot food dish-up, and some are better than others. Exhibit 8.5 is a proven dish-up system which, when properly staffed, will plate 200 hot meals in 15 minutes or less. Please note that this is a double-sided line, with plates being prepared on each side. This system involves the use of hot plates, hot food, efficient dish-up staff, and plate covers.

Another method is to serve the hot food from skirted buffets set up around the perimeter of the area where the guests are seated. For this type of setup, the kitchen staff must be impeccably attired, as they are in view of the guests. They stand behind the buffet lines and portion food onto plates carried by the servers. Each server carries one plate in each hand with a napkin, walks through the line just as a guest would (but at a much quicker pace). Then, when the plate is complete, the server walks toward the supervisor, who directs the server to the table that is to receive the meal. The servers continue to return to the line and walk through it again, until everyone is served.

When hot food is plated, all plates should look the same. A sample plate should be prepared and shown as an example of how all plated dishes are to look.

Clearing the Tables

When everyone at a table is finished with a course, the dishes and flatware for that course must be removed, including flatware designated for the course that guests did not happen to use. If one or two people at a table have not finished a course and they are way behind the others, it is permissible to ask them if the course may be set to the side so that the next course may be served. Clearing should be done from the right, with the right hand. A plate should be kept below eye level until it is clear of the guest and in the aisle space. Then it may be transferred to the left hand. Generally, clearing starts with a female guest's plate and continues clockwise around the table.

Glassware is also cleared from the right side, with the right hand. Stemware should be held by the stem or bottom of the glass. Glasses, plates, and flatware should be carried to the dirty dish area on large waiter trays or in bus boxes, which should always be kept out of sight behind the service table. Bus boxes are excellent when there are long distances to walk, when it is very windy, or when the service staff is unable to carry heavy trays. Broken glass should never be placed in a bus box, but should be deposited into the trash. Glasses, china, and flatware should be placed in separate bus boxes to minimize breakage and loss.

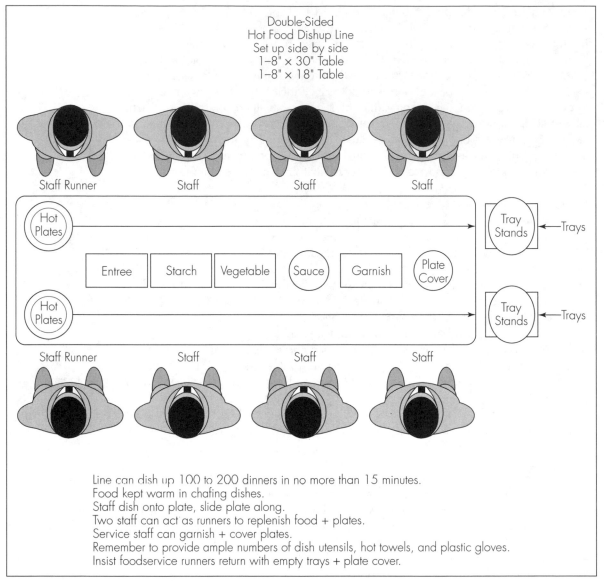

**Double-Sided
Hot Food Dishup Line
Set up side by side
1–8" × 30" Table
1–8" × 18" Table**

Staff Runner   Staff   Staff   Staff

Hot Plates

Tray Stands ← Trays

Entree | Starch | Vegetable | Sauce | Garnish | Plate Cover

Hot Plates

Tray Stands ← Trays

Staff Runner   Staff   Staff   Staff

Line can dish up 100 to 200 dinners in no more than 15 minutes.
Food kept warm in chafing dishes.
Staff dish onto plate, slide plate along.
Two staff can act as runners to replenish food + plates.
Service staff can garnish + cover plates.
Remember to provide ample numbers of dish utensils, hot towels, and plastic gloves.
Insist foodservice runners return with empty trays + plate cover.

Exhibit 8.5 *Double-Sided Hot Food Dish-up Line*

When clearing the main course, clear the bread and butter plate and knife, as well as the salt and pepper shakers. Good service also dictates that the tables should be cleared of crumbs, preferably with the use of a small metal rod, known as a *table crumber*, run gently and discreetly over the table linens.

Carrying fully loaded waiter trays can be dangerous. Million-dollar lawsuits have resulted from accidents involving dropped trays. Before lifting a tray, the staff member should see that it is properly loaded and balanced and that there are no items that may tip over. Before a tray is loaded with dishes and glasses, it should be clean and have either a nonskid surface or a damp napkin on its surface to keep items from sliding. Heavier items should be loaded in the center of the tray, and lighter items toward the exterior. Plate covers should be properly nested together. Servers should only carry trays that they can comfortably handle—there's no point in "showing off" how much you can carry.

You're looking out not only for the guests' safety, but for your own. Trays should always be lifted by squatting down. One hand should go under the tray, and the other should support the tray as you stand up using your thigh muscles. The tray should be carried above the shoulder and steadied with the free hand if necessary. If you have to go through a door, the tray should be carried with the hand that is farthest from the door hinges to ease entry and exit. It isn't always possible, but try to carry trays around, rather than through, crowds. The tray should be lowered, using the squatting technique, onto a service table, kitchen table, or tray stand, which should be opened up with the free hand before lowering the tray. When unloading trays, you should unload from the center out, or from opposite sides, so that the tray does not become unbalanced and tip over.

Tray stands should never be placed in the center of the room, other than just prior to serving or clearing. Otherwise, they should be kept around the perimeter of the room away from guests' sight lines, if not out of sight altogether.

Beverage Service

When serving cocktails and other drinks from the bar, servers should always carry the cocktail tray in the left hand, and serve beverages from the right with the right hand.

When pouring wines at the table, the glass should be filled one-third to one-half full, depending on the glass size. The wineglass should never be lifted from the table when it is being filled. Normally, a 4- to 5-ounce portion is sufficient. There are an increasing number of nondrinkers, so servers should consider their needs as well, and offer nonalcoholic beverage choices. When guests decline wine, their wineglass(es) should be removed from the place setting, indicating to the other servers not to offer wine.

Wines may be served at the tables by the foodservice staff or some of the bar staffers who are not busy during dinner. Specific assignments should be made as to who is responsible for wine service at each table.

Before serving coffee, there's a little extra work to do, and someone must also be appointed for this. Servers (or, often, their runners) must place creamers and sugar on each table, as well as the coffee cup, saucer, and spoon if they were not pre-set. The cups and saucers should be placed to the right of the place setting, with the edge of the saucer 1 inch from the table's edge and the handle of the coffee cup angled to about four o'clock. The cup should be seated in the center of the saucer. For some events, cognac, cordials, and after-dinner drinks are also served at this time, in addition to dessert.

A growing number of people are enjoying hot tea at the end of a meal. One way to make them feel really special—rather them make them wait until everyone else has been served coffee—is to offer tea first. The server at each table might ask, "Ladies and gentlemen, we are about to begin our coffee service; but first, who would prefer hot tea?" Then a tea box is presented, offering several tea choices. Hot water, in individual pots, soon follows.

Many guests prefer to have their coffee or tea with their dessert and cordials, and caterers should try to coordinate these activities so that guests receive desserts and beverages at about the same time. This can be accomplished by assigning different duties to different servers. For example, at a party for 50 guests with six servers, two can pour coffee for everyone, two can serve cordials, and two can be runners and serve dessert. Of course, all servers should start at the same table and serve tables in the same order.

Coffee should be poured from the right, with the right hand. Servers should not remove the cup and saucer from the table when pouring coffee. They should use a clean napkin, held in the left hand next to the left of the coffee cup, to ensure that coffee does not splash on the guests while they are pouring. Extreme caution should always be used when handling and serving hot beverages.

Decaffeinated coffee must be identified by some method, such as tying a ribbon around the handle. A nice little trick we learned at the Inn at Little Washington in Washington, Virginia, is to serve regular coffee in cups on patterned saucers, and decaf in cups on plain saucers. That way, the server isn't always having to interrupt guests to ask, "Regular or decaf?" And please make servers aware that people who ask for decaffeinated coffee actually deserve to get it. When you're busy, it is certainly easier to pour whatever's handy, but many have a specific health-related reason for wanting decaf. Don't serve them regular coffee just because it is convenient for you.

As coffee is served, servers should replenish cream and sugar as needed.

Russian Service

Russian service involves serving food from platters that are prearranged in the kitchen. The food servers transfer the food from the platters to the guests' plates with a spoon and fork. Skilled personnel are required for this type of service. It is not often used at off-premise events because it is more difficult than plated service and requires additional equipment and utensils. An excellent description of this service technique is contained in *Food and Beverage Service*, by Bruce H. Axler and Carol A. Litrides (John Wiley & Sons, 1990).

✕ Buffets and Food Stations

The service for buffets and food stations differs from served meals in that guests generally serve themselves. There are some exceptions to this—perhaps a pre-set first course, followed by guests going to buffets, or dessert and coffee being served at the table. Place settings may or may not be provided for buffets and, in most instances, food station menus are designed so that the foods can be eaten on small plates and require only forks instead of full table settings. There may not be seating for everyone, and guests may eat standing up. When there are no place settings or seats, the flatware and napkins must be provided on the buffets or food stations.

Setting up buffets and food stations can require additional time, because of the time-consuming process of designing and decorating the food display. If there is a theme for the event, there may be specific items to be included in the displays. If these items are provided by clients or decorators, off-premise caterers must be certain that they are delivered on time for the setup. Ice carvings are the exception, although the container for the carving may be pre-set.

Sketching a diagram to ensure correct placement of your buffets and stations is a critical step in achieving a smooth setup, so that staff may work without continually having to ask questions of the party supervisor. The diagram of the buffet or station should include:

- The name and location of each component or area
- The number and size of the tables, cloths, and skirts needed for each area
- A list of all equipment, china, flatware, and serving utensils needed at each area

When packing at the commissary, these items may be grouped together in containers, with removable labels on the containers. Food items may be grouped the same way, by station. Before starting the setup, everything necessary, as shown on the diagram of the buffet or station, should be placed next to the location for the buffet or food station. This makes the setup process much faster.

On-site, your staff should be instructed about how much overall "creativity" is allowed in designing the displays. Some clients prefer a clean, simple look, while others appreciate a profusion of colors and textures.

No matter how elaborate the décor, there are a few generic procedures regarding food stations and buffets:

For Planning
- The number of food stations and buffets may vary, but approximately one buffet or type of food station should be provided for every 50 to 75 guests.
- In general, each main dish will require 18 to 24 inches of space on the buffet table or station.
- The backs of buffets and food stations should be skirted if guests will see them.
- Bring extra bowls, display props, utensils, dishes, platters, cassette au feu stoves and fuel, chafing dishes and chafer fuel. These items will be essential if items are broken in transit, misplaced, or out of order.
- Determine replenishing methods for foods, and provide the necessary containers and utensils. Some backup food items may be stored beneath the station or buffet, as long as they are kept at proper temperatures and covered.

For Setup
- Cassette au feu stoves and heating appliances should be tested to make sure they work properly as they are placed, long before the guests arrive. Extra fuel should be stored beneath the station.
- Staff members who use cassette au feu stoves for tabletop cooking should be thoroughly instructed on their proper use, and how to replace fuel safely and properly.

- Chafing dishes should be filled with water as soon as they are put in place. Chafer fuel tops should be loosened, but not removed, and the fuel installed under the chafer water pans. Most chafers have fuel holders; for those that do not, fuel should never be placed directly on the table. A small plate or ashtray should be used. It is a good idea to leave a pack of matches near the chafing dishes and to store extra fuel beneath the table. The chafer food pans should be taken to the kitchen, where they will be filled later with hot food.
- Chafer fuel should be lit 30 to 45 minutes before the hot food is brought out.
- Fire extinguishers should be placed near buffets and food stations with open flames.
- Plates for the guests' use should never be stacked more than 9 inches high. Taller stacks detract from the appearance of the table.
- Votive candles should never be placed next to napkins or any other flammable item.
- Candelabras should be positioned so that hot wax will not drip onto food, napkins, or service ware.
- Food in chafing dishes must be kept hot, and this means it must be very hot before it is placed in the chafer. Chafers are not designed to warm food, but to keep it hot. Ways to keep food hot include:
  1. Place solid food items only one layer deep in the pans.
  2. Cook fried foods only as needed.
  3. Keep lids on the chafers until the guests arrive unless they contain fried foods, which will become soggy if covered.
  4. Avoid setting chafers in drafts or in the wind.
  5. Use custom-made plastic shields that stand up around the perimeter of the chafing dishes to protect the fuel from drafts.

For Serving

- Instruct the staff about proper portion sizes, particularly for high-cost items.
- Servers should know what they are serving and the ingredients of each item in case a guest wishes to know.
- Carvers should be instructed as to the number of orders they should be able to cut from each piece of meat.
- Servers who are cooking foods to order must be trained about ingredients and procedures.

For Replenishing Fuel and Food

- Staff should be instructed about how long "canned heat" fuel burns and trained in how to replace it safely. Extreme caution is required here. When replacing fuel, it should be recapped with its own lid or extinguished with the top of the chafing dish fuel holder. Used cans of fuel should never be touched barehanded, because they can be very hot and the flames are often tiny or invisible. Staff should be instructed to use tongs that will grasp the can tightly, and then place the can on a small china plate. Once this is accomplished, a new can of fuel can be properly placed beneath the chafing dish and lit.
- Chafing dishes full of food and water are very hot and heavy. When removing a pan of food from the chafer, extreme caution must be used to keep hands, arms, and faces away from the rising steam.

- Specific staff members must be assigned to bring food from the kitchen to the food stations and buffets. Bowls, hot food pans, or platters should not be removed from buffets or stations until their fresh replacements are ready to be set down; there's nothing more unsightly than a gaping "hole" on a buffet table where a full dish should be. In some cases, food may simply be added to the existing container. Once a container of food is half-depleted, it should be replenished.

For Break-Down

- Staff members should never break down food stations and buffets until specifically directed by the event supervisor. This is a sensitive area, and staff should not be permitted to make this decision. When most guests have eaten, some duplicate food stations may be discreetly disassembled, with foods consolidated at those that remain open. Where there is only one station or buffet, it is always best to leave it open until it is evident that everyone has eaten; even then, check with the client before beginning disassembly. Dessert and coffee stations are normally kept open until the very end of the event.
- After extinguishing all chafing dish fuel, the food pans should be removed from the chafing dishes and carried to the off-premise kitchen, along with other foods from the buffet. Extreme caution must be used when carrying chafing dishes containing hot water, so as not to splash hot water on anyone.
- The kitchen should be ready to receive the buffet items. Advise the kitchen supervisor in advance so space can be arranged for receiving chafers, bowls, baskets, and the like. This requires a lot of "landing space."
- Skirting and other linens should never be removed from buffet tables and food stations until absolutely all the guests have departed.

✕ *Handling Complaints*

When events are executed properly, complaints should be few. In those rare situations when complaints arise, there are some basic ways to handle them:

1. Allow the complainer to blow off steam. In other words, let the person say what is on his or her mind. Never interrupt unless the person needs to clarify a certain point or perhaps provide more details.
2. An excellent way to diffuse a guest's anger is to ask politely, "Have I done something *personally* to anger you?" This tactic, in most cases, will calm the person down, because most complaints are not of a personal nature, but are usually about some specific aspect of the food or service.
3. If you're not the supervisor, tactfully get the supervisor involved as soon as possible.
4. Try to identify the problem, and let the person know you understand the problem by repeating what you heard him or her say.
5. Offer a brief apology, let the person know the alternative solutions and resolutions, and tell the person what you intend to do.
6. Follow up if necessary, and always remember to be polite and courteous at all times, regardless of how you really feel.

7. No matter how minor the situation, jot a note about it. If your company has an Incident Report form (which it should), fill it out as soon as you get a chance. Even if there is no particular legal liability, the incident may be a learning experience for others on the staff.

✕ *Conclusion*

Properly supervised and executed, off-premise catered events are guaranteed to create positive word of mouth, which will generate future business. "The Show" is your time to shine! Nothing in the catering business is more important. There are no second chances to get it right.

Readers who would like to learn more about excellence in service techniques can visit www.usawaiter.com or see our other service-related book recommendations:

Knock Your Socks Off Service. This series of books is by Chip Bell and Ron Zemke and published by AMACOM, a Division of the American Management Association, 1992.

Lessons in Excellence from Charlie Trotter, by Paul Clark, published by Ten Speed Press, 1999.

Lessons in Service from Charlie Trotter, by Edmund Lawler and Charlie Trotter, Ten Speed Press, 2001.

Serve'Em Right: The Complete Guide to Hospitality Service, by Ed Solomon, Lorin Solomon, and Shelley Prueter, published by Oak Hill Press, 1997.

We found all of these books recently available on www.amazon.com, including bargain-priced used copies.

✗ Chapter 9

Marketing

Marketing off-premise catering requires that you develop an image and a marketing plan for your company and its unique services. The whole idea can seem rather mysterious until you break it down to its essence. Marketing means using various tools or methods to:

- Produce prospective shoppers and buyers
- Qualify these shoppers and buyers
- Sell to the qualified buyers

The end results of these efforts should be profit and satisfied clients. Customers are becoming more demanding and selective when shopping for catering services, and it certainly takes more than the ability to cook and serve excellent food to be successful in the catering profession. If clients do not know about you, they cannot buy from you.

Competition for off-premise business is increasing, as more and more caterers are entering the field. Supermarket delis, national foodservice management chains, hotels, restaurants, private clubs, and others look to off-premise catering as a way to increase sales.

Smart caterers cannot accept excuses for poor sales performance. They must find ways to increase sales through better marketing, showing prospective clients how their companies are different from competitors, and how clients can benefit from doing business with their firms.

In this chapter, we examine ways to develop a marketing plan and how to use marketing tools to build business.

✗ Catering Markets

The two major off-premise catering markets are the corporate market and the social market. Let's look at each of them.

Corporate Catering

The corporate market involves catering for business events such as grand openings; groundbreakings; retirement parties; holiday parties; employee parties; receptions to promote business, give awards, unveil new products, and so on; as well as catering business meals for meetings and seminars.

Corporate catering is generally more profitable than social catering, although caterers of high-dollar society weddings may disagree. However, for the most part, corporate event planners generally have predetermined, larger budgets than planners of social events, with leeway for add-ons. They are also more experienced in planning these events, knowing exactly what they need. Many have limited time and prefer to work with off-premise caterers whom they can trust to handle all the details. Most are willing to pay a premium price for this service.

Bill Hansen, coauthor of this book, surveyed 625 corporate meeting and event planners to better determine how caterers can best meet corporate entertaining needs. Major findings include:

- Although food is important, service is even more important.
- Corporate planners need proposals on time—often the same day.
- Caterers need to listen to the planner's needs before offering ideas.
- Planners look for the caterer to be creative.
- Planners do not like talking to answering machines or slow responses to e-mail requests.
- When selecting a caterer, planners rely mostly on recommendations from others.
- When comparing two similar corporate catering proposals, planners choose the caterer whose personality is most compatible, whose energy level is higher, and who is easy to communicate with.

In the same survey, things that stood out as negatives to corporate planners were:

Inexperienced staff	Unfriendly staff
Improper food temperatures	Rushed setups
Small food portions	Poor equipment
Dirty uniforms	Staff wore too much jewelry
Unkempt hair	Poor breads and desserts
Food description did not match the food	Over-budget costs
Poor busing of plates, glasses, etc.	

Corporate planners want to work with caterers who'll do whatever it takes to produce a successful party. They must be easy to work with, punctual, and able to work within a budget. They should also be able to give little extras at no charge and to go the "extra mile" for their clients.

Social Catering

The social market includes personal parties at home, fund-raisers, wedding receptions and anniversaries, reunions, bar and bat mitzvahs, baptisms, graduations, proms, birthday parties, and holiday or other theme parties.

Of course, many of the same qualities that would attract the corporate event planner will also impress the social client—punctuality, creativity, ability to work within a budget. Social catering can be very rewarding, but it is often quite labor-intensive. It means dealing one-on-one with clients or charitable committees who require more of the caterer's time. These groups also tend to watch the pennies more closely and want to become involved "hands on" in every aspect of the event. It takes a lot of patience to handle this graciously.

Within each of these markets, there are levels of catering: budget, midscale, and upscale.

- A budget event for a corporation could entail dropping off luncheon platters, and one for a social client may be a child's birthday party. Budget parties are low-priced and therefore usually involve little service.
- Midscale events are those that involve more service and are more expensive than budget events, but not as expensive as upscale events. A midscale event may be a retirement dinner for a middle manager or a modest wedding reception held at a community center.
- Upscale events are the most expensive, involve the most intensive service, and are typically the most profitable. An upscale corporate event might be a grand opening for a fine jewelry store. For a social client, it could be a bar mitzvah with seven food courses, three bands, the finest crystal and linens, and one server for every five guests.

It is important to note that there will be times when off-premise caterers are not marketing directly to actual clients, but to "intermediaries." These intermediaries include:

- Independent meeting planners, who are hired by small and medium-size companies and government agencies
- Special event producers, who specialize in events for large gatherings
- Independent party planners or wedding consultants, who work with noncorporate clients.
- Ground transportation companies and/or destination management companies that handle arrangements for convention groups and/or hotel guests
- Travel agents and representatives of convention and visitors' bureaus

As you can see, it's not enough to market to the "end user." These types of service providers must also be seen as prospective clients, who generally represent major pieces of business. They may also expect a commission or fee from you for providing referrals. By directing your marketing to these intermediaries, you can realize some excellent revenue and build a different kind of customer loyalty.

Some people in the catering business subscribe to what's known as the "80/20 Rule": 20 percent of a caterer's business comes from 80 percent of catering clients, and 80 percent of the business comes from 20 percent of the clients! It makes a sound case for gearing the greater part of your marketing plan (and budget) toward capturing the more lucrative 20 percent.

✗ Developing a Marketing Plan

Off-premise caterers frequently overlook the need for a marketing plan. They simply respond to clients' demands, and as long as there is a satisfactory profit, everything is fine. But effective marketing plans begin with a financial goal. A business without a financial goal is like a ship without a destination—it leaves its home port and sails around, with no particular place to go or reason to get there. Successful off-premise caterers develop clearly defined financial goals. They determine their financial needs and aspirations and then create a plan to achieve these goals. Moreover, start-up caterers who need financing from a financial institution will be expected to develop a marketing plan for inclusion with their loan request.

For example, some start-up off-premise caterers wish to earn an annual profit of $100,000 per year after five years in business. This is certainly a lofty goal, but it can be reached in increments. First-year profits could be $20,000; $40,000 the second year; $60,000 the third year, and so on. (We discuss budgeting in Chapter 14.) The point is that these caterers realize that if they earn 20 percent profit on their sales, they can make projections like these:

YEAR	PROJECTED SALES	PROJECTED PROFIT	PERCENT PROFIT
1	$100,000	$ 20,000	20
2	$200,000	$ 40,000	20
3	$300,000	$ 60,000	20
4	$400,000	$ 80,000	20
5	$500,000	$100,000	20

The first step for the beginning caterer is to conduct a market survey to determine a variety of things such as the size and population of their target market, the *demographics* and income levels of the area, and the potential demand for their services—how many competitors are there? This type of information can be gleaned from:

County population, density, and distribution figures
Maps of major trading areas
Articles on area businesses in local newspapers and magazines
Telephone books (for competitors)
Local chambers of commerce
The state's Department of Commerce
Internet website searches

Even your school or university may have a marketing department with students willing to assist you in compiling data. Just as important as demographics are the *psychographics*, meaning the habits and preferences of your target customers. This kind of information may be harder to obtain, but with it, you can more accurately decide what types of food and services to provide, and how much money to charge for them.

As you glean this information, be on the lookout for the signs of positive growth in an area. Are stores and restaurants opening regularly—and thriving? Is the Chamber of Commerce an active, progressive organization? Who's moving into the area, and why? Are there good schools, good public transportation systems, good public services?

Another key task is to evaluate the competition for catering dollars. This can be done by talking to rental dealers, surveying local companies who use caterers, attending catered events and asking questions, and even posing as a potential customer to analyze the competitors' advertisements, menus, contracts, and sales pitches. If you're planning your own party, why not hire one and see what it does? Armed with this knowledge, successful off-premise caterers can position themselves in the market to fit an interesting niche that others have failed to see or take advantage of.

It's important that the market you choose to enter fits well with your image as a caterer. A new caterer who makes fabulous barbecue could market to both social and corporate clients for budget or midscale events, but may not be successful in marketing itself as an upscale caterer to the same clientele. In short, you can't be everything to everyone. A caterer's image reflects its reputation, style, and personality, and these are the elements that, together, can be used to create a vision for the company. Knowing who you are, and whom you wish to reach, will greatly assist you in selecting the best tools to create a marketing plan.

✕ *The Marketing Budget*

The next step is to establish a marketing budget. How much do off-premise caterers spend in marketing their businesses? Some spend very little, while others may spend up to 5 percent of their gross sales. Start-up caterers should ask themselves:

- Is there available cash to spend on advertising?
- How quickly do we want business?
- Are we ready to handle the business?
- How much business can we handle?

Most learn by trial and error which marketing tools produce the best results. As they gain experience, they hone their marketing strategies to be more effective, and they always think in terms of the bottom line when evaluating their marketing plans. If one form of marketing does not bring the desired results, they discard it and look for better alternatives.

A written marketing plan should show prospective clients how one firm differs from its competition and how this firm provides specific benefits to clients, such as:

- We are professional and easy to work with.
- Our parties are hassle-free and user-friendly.
- There are never long lines, and there is always plenty of food.
- We guarantee you will be satisfied with our services, or your money back.
- We will assist you with other areas of your event such as music, flowers, photography, rental equipment, and valet service.
- You will receive the best in service from our caring, courteous, and friendly staff, who are empowered to meet all your catering needs.
- You can be a guest at your own party!

An underlying theme of all marketing plans is the smart use of time and money to bring the greatest return on investment. For example, five visits to a major corporation prior to obtaining a contract for a large catered event will bring more bottom-line profits than five visits to a social client, planning one house party for 30 guests.

An examination of the myriad marketing tools should lead both beginning and experienced caterers to a better understanding of the best ways to develop, implement, and budget for marketing endeavors.

✕ *Marketing Tools*

Exactly what's in a marketing toolbox? In this section, we examine the various forms of advertising, publicity, promotions, and other actions that off-premise caterers may use as part of their marketing plans.

Company Names and Logos

Some business owners believe that, if at all possible, it is best to begin the name of a catering firm with the letter *A* in order to be listed first in telephone directories, as well as on lists of approved caterers at various off-premise catering sites—historical places, museums, and other facilities. "A Michael Smith Culinary Production," for instance, is far superior to "Mike's Catering."

No matter what the first letter, a caterer should choose a business name carefully, because this is what becomes the "brand name" of the firm. In our example, clients will expect a higher level of catering from "A Michael Smith Culinary Production" than from "Mike's Catering." And, of course, with the classier name, Michael can achieve higher price points for his products and services, particularly if he is located in a metropolitan area. In a small rural area, the fancier name may be detrimental to business, as folks might assume the prices are too high for them.

You'd do well to narrow a list down to three or four names and consult an advertising or design professional for advice on the final choice. The name should lend itself to a simple but eye-catching logo that is not too complicated or expensive to reproduce on signs, vehicles, uniforms, cocktail napkins, and so on.

Positive Word of Mouth

Word of mouth is the simplest but by far the best form of marketing, and many caterers' complete marketing plans are based on the good words of satisfied clients and guests. They realize that one successful party leads to another, and another. They also realize they're only as good as their last party; therefore, they dedicate all of their energies to making each catering assignment the best it can be.

The problem for start-up firms is that it's tough to generate this positive word-of-mouth without a track record. It's kind of like job hunting as a teenager with no work experience. Some new firms agree to cater parties or events for charitable groups at cost, or even at a loss, in order to generate goodwill and grow their business reputation.

When you receive compliments or letters after an event, always remember that they may be used to generate more business. Ask those who send letters if you can quote them—perhaps on your website or in a brochure—or simply keep copies of the nice letters you receive in a notebook to show prospective customers.

Quotes from people who like what you do are called "testimonials," and they offer a proven way to market to new clients. Potential customers love to read and/or hear what others have said about a caterer. You can use testimonials in many ways: in brochures, on websites, in direct mail pieces and newsletters. One South Florida catering firm includes verbal testimonials from actual customers in its "on-hold" telephone message!

Just remember to always get written permission to use the remarks from the persons who made them, and keep these written permissions on file. (Lest you think we're being too cautious, we've seen instances in which people wanted to be paid for using what had been their genuine compliments, freely given.)

Networking

Networking, in this sense, means meeting and talking with people. It could be talking with other local business owners, a woman in the supermarket produce section, a person you meet at church or strike up a conversation with on a flight home.

The idea is that, sooner or later, any of these people may need catering services. The more folks you know—who know what you do for a living—the greater the number of people likely to call you when they have catering needs. However, it is not enough to meet these people. It is also necessary to keep in touch with them.

A popular way to hone your networking skills with those who are potential buyers of off-premise catering is to join and be active in such groups as:

Chambers of commerce
Civic clubs (Rotary, Kiwanis, Eagles, Lions, Elks, etc.)
Church or synagogue groups
Special-interest groups (like "Leads Clubs" for salespeople of all types)
National Association of Catering Executives (NACE)
Meeting Planners International
The International Special Events Society
Convention and visitors' bureaus
The Society of Incentive Travel Executives
Memberships at local museums or other arts groups

A main advantage of networking is that it focuses on establishing relationships with people first. You're not going directly to these people and asking them, after the initial handshake, to buy your catering services. Instead, you get to know them and keep in touch with them casually. When they are ready to buy, they will contact those they know. Good networking concentrates on building long-term relationships, with long-term benefits. It is one of the best ways to do business—with people you know.

Websites and E-mail

It is irresponsible for business owners nowadays not to have an Internet website for their companies. A website is convenient for both you and prospective customers. You can use it to give people far more detail about your catering services than you ever could in a networking setting, or even in a brochure. And customers can access it whenever they want, stay as long as they like, and e-mail any questions they have back to you.

The primary costs of Internet marketing are:

- Designing the website (writing copy, physically programming the site, putting photos and other graphics on it, and so on). This may seem expensive at first, depending on how fancy and interactive you want the site to be. You will also want to maintain a relationship with your site designer so the site can be updated regularly, which can be done at a more nominal cost.
- Registering a domain name (the "_____.com" that people type in to access your site) that hasn't already been taken by someone else.
- Placing your website on search engines (Google, Yahoo!, AOL, and others) so that people who are looking for catering services can find it even if they don't know the company or domain name.
- Buying "links" on other websites (your city's Chamber of Commerce, web-based business directories, etc.) so that people who are searching on those sites will find you.

There are computer specialists who excel at getting top search engine placement for their clients. Leading Caterers of America (www.leadingcaterers.com) is a leader in Internet marketing for caterers and has long enjoyed top search engine placement under the keyword search "caterers." It is also important to see that your catering firm is listed under "catering," as well as the name of your city or state, such as, for example, "Boston caterers" or "Idaho caterers."

Be sure that your website is linked to as many other websites as possible. The more links, the closer to the top of their lists when search engines place the site.

Give clients a reason to visit your site and leave their e-mail addresses. On the Leading Caterers of America site, for example, there is a "Buyer's Guide" for those interested in learning more about how to buy catering services. This prompts people to leave their e-mail address by offering something free that will be e-mailed back to them. It may be recipes, interesting articles, or handy hints, such as "Ten Secrets for a Successful Party, Wedding, or Event."

Remember to include the basics on your site: your company's physical address, phone and fax numbers, and e-mail address. We've noticed a number of catering websites do not include an e-mail address, and/or force the visitor to complete a lengthy form in order to contact them by e-mail.

Your website should contain news about the company, menus, recipes, trends, and professional photos of food, staff, weddings, and events. It should be constructed so that it can be easily updated and expanded (at least seasonally) and very easily navigated. Keep in mind that the attention span of a potential client is very short. If a site does not capture his or her attention in a few seconds, the person will move on—probably to a competitor's site.

Publicity

Publicity is free media exposure, which directly and indirectly produces revenue. In most cases publicity is an editorial recommendation, an unbiased opinion that says an off-premise caterer is good. Publicity can help establish off-premise caterers as leaders in their field.

The basic way to generate publicity is to write and submit a news release (sometimes called a "press release") to your local newspaper, radio, and/or television stations. If you hire a person or company to do this, the task of getting publicity is known as *public relations*.

According to David F. Ramacitti, author of *Do-It-Yourself Publicity*, "Virtually any small business could legitimately send out a minimum of six press releases per year, and many could easily double that number. . . . In today's increasingly competitive marketplace, you should be taking advantage of every opportunity available to receive positive public exposure, especially if it doesn't cost anything."[1]

Some events that are worthy of news releases for off-premise caterers are:

- Your business's Grand Opening or anniversary
- An exciting party or unusual challenge (You know—the underwater wedding? The skydivers' wedding? Catering for a unique themed event? Teaching grade-school kids about nutrition?)
- An expansion or renovation
- A hiring (new chef, etc.) or staff change within the company
- The appointment of a person in your company as an officer in an affiliated group (National Association of Catering Executives, etc.)
- Catering for a celebrity or charitable cause
- Winning an award for business or culinary skills

The thing about news releases is that they truly are a crapshoot—a reporter may call, or not. Your recent award, or the hiring of an excellent new chef, may merit a single paragraph in the Business section of the newspaper, a front-page feature article in the local Food section, or both—or nothing at all. This should not deter you from writing and sending news releases.

Great Performances, a New York City–based catering firm, has received coverage from *People* magazine and numerous other publications. But to obtain this type of publicity, caterers must have a unique story to tell. Great Performances's story was that it conducted training to teach their staff—mainly composed of actors, actresses, writers, and musicians—service techniques for serving the Passover seder dinner. This caught the eye of local and national press and contributed to the rapid rise of Great Performances as one of the nation's top catering firms.

Caterers need to develop what reporters call a "hook," something that will attract the media's attention. This is the difficult part. Simply catering an event for charity is not enough—but making the world's largest pizza or paella? Now that would generate interest! Helping to improve the cafeteria food at your local elementary school, and teaching the kids how to properly set a table, would be a terrific feature story—or catering for an exclusive group aboard a privately chartered jet that entertains corporate clients who fly from Los Angeles to Paris and back.

A final thought on publicity: Although the definition is "free media exposure," it really isn't free, because there are costs involved in producing the news release and following up. Caterers should also consider investing some money in a public relations firm to help them "mine" these publicity opportunities. Virtually every famous chef in the country does this, as do many restaurants. Caterers on a limited budget should consider going to a local university and finding students in a marketing curriculum who could help.

Brochures

Many off-premise caterers rely heavily on brochures. A caterer in Canada identified the major businesses in his area that employed more than 200, called each firm and obtained the names of the catering decision makers, then produced a sales brochure that he mailed to 900 companies. This generated more than $100,000 in sales.

Successful brochures must not look like typical pieces of "junk mail." A first-class brochure should include colorful, high-quality photos and interesting text. When it comes to the format of the brochure, there are a couple of options:

■ The trifold, which is produced on a standard $8\frac{1}{2}$- by 11-inch paper that is folded in thirds and easily sealed for mailing.
■ The "press kit" style is a pocket folder that can be "stuffed" with different types of information, depending on the recipient. It includes a slot for a business card and/or Rolodex card and pockets in which to place news releases, proposals, menus, price lists, and so on. These cost more to mail than trifolds, of course, because they are full-sized ($8\frac{1}{2}$ by 11 inches).

Here are some tips for brochure contents:

1. Establish credibility by telling readers about your number of years in business, prominent clients, awards, memberships, and other significant facts.
2. Brag a little! Tell readers how they will benefit from doing business with your firm.
3. Guarantee your work. Inform readers that you will not overlook any detail and that their events will be perfect.
4. Deliver your message in as few words as possible, and make sure they are descriptive—not unduly flowery or verbose. Brochures should be easy to read and interesting, but not too "busy."
5. Brochures and other pieces of direct mail should be addressed to a specific person. Personalized, handwritten envelopes are opened more frequently than those with computerized labels addressed to "Occupant" or "President." Interestingly, items with unusual or colorful postage stamps also attract more attention than those stamped by a postage meter.

Newsletters

Sending newsletters has proven to be one of the best ways for caterers to maintain and reinforce awareness of their services and to generate repeat business as well as gain new clients. Newsletters can be sent via regular mail or as e-mail, the latter being the most economical. In fact, it's smart to offer both and ask clients which way they would rather receive their newsletters. Publishing a newsletter is a major task and should not be taken lightly. Larger caterers may wish to outsource this project to a professional writer—a local freelance "foodie" can handle most of the legwork (and brainwork) for a reasonable price, as long as you provide the ideas and tone for each issue. Smaller caterers with limited budgets will need to produce them internally in order to keep costs low.

Either way, the first step in newsletter production is to determine its tone and content. The best newsletters for this type of service are warm and friendly, presented as a way to get to know the caterer and his or her services. Often, they contain several regular columns by the same author—the owner, the chef, or a wine expert—or a feature on a local food grower or producer whose wares the caterer uses and recommends.

Of course, anything newsworthy that's coming up for the company should be mentioned, whether it's a guest appearance on a local TV station by the owner, or a charitable or unusual event at which you'll be serving. At the start of a particular season or holiday, feature a roundup of seasonal recipes. Include information about food and menu trends, interesting new ways to use catering services, tidbits about celebrities who've hired you, food trivia and humor. Do a short profile of a different member of your kitchen or serving staff in each issue. Quote some of your customers who just loved what you did for them. You might include a coupon or promotion in the newsletter, which will also help you track its usefulness as you see how many people respond to it. And always include contact information (e-mail, phone, physical address, website address) as well as a small form new readers can send to you to sign up for the mailing list or to update their address information.

There are as many newsletter topic ideas as there are off-premise catering companies, and a good writer will suggest even more. But no matter who writes it, your newsletter should be written with the reader in mind and should be published on a specific timetable. A newsletter is a commitment to those who read and look forward to it. Monthly newsletters require quite a bit of work and often become a real pain for busy businesses, but three or four times a year is doable. In the rush to "fill the space," always keep the end results in mind: increased awareness of your business and services.

Letterhead and Business Cards

Letterhead and business cards are necessities for all off-premise caterers, and in today's computerized world, they include "e-stationery" as well as printed materials. They should reflect the caterer's image and should make good use of the logo you've already designed. A caterer who markets budget events does not need to go to great expense; no multicolored or gold-lettered business cards are necessary. A simpler approach will be less costly and just as effective.

Some experts recommend against using unusually shaped business cards, or those that fold over, as they are not easily stored in standard business card cases; yet some businesses use "gimmicky" cards with great success. All catering staff should be given cards to hand out, not only while working, but also to people they meet outside work. At catered events, cards should be given out only if requested by guests.

Men should carry business cards in their shirt or jacket pockets for quick retrieval. It is very awkward to wait while a person rifles through a wallet. There are some good card carrying cases available, and some caterers give a nice case and a supply of cards to each of their staff members.

Remember that "letterhead" includes more than just stationery for correspondence. Use your logo on contracts and proposals and any other type of printed or e-mailed form you have created for regular use, whether it is the clients or the vendors who see it.

And what do you put on that letterhead? An excellent selling tool, although admittedly time-consuming, is a personal note written to a potential client or a handwritten thank-you to clients after a party, wedding, or event. Handwritten notes show a personal touch, and those that are signed by a number of key catering staff members are even more effective. The best ones are written as if the writer is talking, not writing. They evoke gratitude and surprise from the reader, because so few people take the time to handwrite things, and this will be remembered when catering services are needed again.

Photos, Awards, and Plaques

Photos, awards, and plaques are excellent marketing tools for establishing credibility with clients. They show the client some of the caterer's past successes. Many off-premise firms display these items in the lobbies leading to their offices, or in their offices. Nicely made copies of photos and awards can be put into albums that customers can look through, or reproduced in your newsletters, brochures, and direct mail pieces.

It is important to get copies made while the award or photo is new, clean, and unwrinkled (this also goes for letters of praise or recommendation). Keep the copies filed in a safe place. One of those "Murphy's Laws" is that when you really, really want to show an item to someone, that's when you can't seem to locate it anywhere.

Direct Mail

Direct mail is the term for information mailed "directly" to prospective clients. This information may be a menu, brochure, newsletter, coupon, or any other type of promotional literature. All direct mail pieces should attract attention, arouse interest, and stimulate enough desire that the reader "takes action." All successful direct mail pieces are written with the readers' interests in mind.

The best mailing list is one that you develop yourself, a combination of existing and prospective clients. Mailing lists can also be purchased, but it is important to get what you pay for. This means ascertaining the freshness of the list and obtaining references from others who have used it. For information on mailing lists, visit one of the Internet search engines and type in the term "mailing lists."

A list of 35 ways to improve direct mail efforts appeared in *Celebrate*, a publication for caterers by Korbel Champagne Cellars.[2] They're reproduced here:

1. Make time for file maintenance. For every 1,000 people in your database (mailing list), you can figure that your file will need one update per day.
2. A database has a half-life of about three years—in other words, if it's unattended, only half the names and addresses will still be valid three years from now.
3. Your own customer list will generate two to ten times the response you'd get to a rented mailing list.
4. Don't retain what you can't maintain. Never include information in your database that your company cannot or will not maintain. It will eventually undermine the integrity of the entire system.
5. On a business database, always store both job titles (for addressing) and job function codes (for selecting).
6. A customer list used several times a year with no routine "cleaning" procedure will have approximately 5 percent inaccurate zip codes.
7. Unlimited one-year use of a mailing list is usually only double the cost of one-time use.
8. For better response rates, have the reply form go back to a specific individual, not just to the company or department.
9. Use first-class postcard mailing as a low-cost way to clean your in-house customer and prospect database.
10. Knowing something about your customers is just as important as knowing everything about your product.
11. It takes an average of ten days to deliver a piece of third-class mail.
12. Six months after receiving an advertising specialty in the mail, almost 40 percent of the recipients could recall the name of the advertiser.
13. You should plan to mail something to all names in your database at least four times a year.
14. Ninety percent of all mail responses will be returned within the first two weeks after they're mailed.
15. Carefully consider the size of your direct mail piece. Overly large or small sizes often cost more for preparation as well as postage.
16. Fulfillment of requests should be mailed out within 48 hours of receipt. This applies to requests for most catering proposals and basic menu-related inquiries.
17. Get full value for your postage by including additional enclosures. You can mail up to 3.4948 ounces under bulk rate at no additional cost.
18. A well-timed follow-up will often yield response equal to or greater than the initial mailing.
19. For faster processing and delivery, drop your mail at a General Mail Facility (GMF) rather than at a branch post office.
20. To increase your sales without increasing your budget, mail to one-half of your list, but mail two separate mailings to this half.

21. Personalized response forms make responding easy and increase results.

22. The most important parts of a direct mail letter are the first sentence and the postscript ("P.S."). Why? They are the most frequently read.

23. More than 50 percent of your future business will come from current customers. It costs five times as much to get a new customer as it does to maintain current ones.

24. Multiple mailings are more effective than single mailings on a cost-per-lead basis.

25. Ask for referrals—"Do you know of anyone else who would be interested in this product or service?"—on all response forms.

26. Offer prospects several ways to respond or request more information: conventional mail or e-mail, facsimile, or toll-free telephone number.

27. To save money on oversized mailings, use booklet envelopes (that open on the long side) rather than end flap openings, so they can be machine-inserted.

28. Reply devices should always restate the entire offer.

29. Write the reply device first, then the rest of the copy to match it.

30. Rely on a full-service direct mail firm for your next project. Experience counts more than it costs.

31. Self-mailers (trifolds) will not generate as high a response as a letter with a typed envelope and separate business reply card.

32. In presenting your offer, use the word 'you' and 'your' often in a direct mail pitch. These words are personal and powerful communicators and will increase your response.

33. Include a reply-paid response card with a reward. Your fulfillment package should always have a business reply card, questionnaire or telephone "hotline" number to further qualify leads.

34. A separate reply device generates a better response than one that needs to be detached.

35. Use only white, ivory, ecru, or light gray paper for personalized direct mail letter packages. Using colored stock for reply cards, however, will usually yield a higher response.

Here are a few additional interesting statistics about direct mail, from Judd Goldfedder of The Customer Connection in Escondido, California:[3]

- 80% of direct mail returns come from existing customers.
- 61% of third-class bulk mail is read when the recipient knows the sender and/or is a customer.
- 58% of third-class postcards are read.
- There is no difference in response rates between first- and third-class mailings.

Telephone Directory Advertising

Most off-premise caterers advertise in at least one local phone book, whether it's the venerable Yellow Pages or one of the competitor directories that have sprung up over the years.

A study conducted by Statistical Research, Inc., of Westfield, New Jersey, revealed that nearly one-third of all customers consult a telephone directory before obtaining a service. One way to gauge your own ad's effectiveness is to track the source of your incoming business. Some caterers have a special number they publish only in phone directories; other ask callers, "How did you hear about us?"

A drawback is that directory ads can be quite costly. For example, a caterer who invests $20,000 in an annual phone directory ad, and whose profit margin on catered events is 40 percent, needs to generate $50,000 in additional sales just to break even on the ad costs! (See Chapter 14 for accounting details.)

In many metropolitan markets, upscale caterers with established clienteles either skip this type of advertising altogether or take a low-key approach with a small ad, leaving the half-page and full-page ads to caterers that appeal to more budget-conscious clients who are more likely to shop around.

According to catering industry consultant Mike Roman, president of Chicago's CaterSource (www.catersource.com), excellent directory ads should differ from the rest. He suggests caterers consider putting the owner's picture in the ad; use words like "casual," "corporate," and "social"; and mention that "prices will be gladly discussed by phone." With an owner's photo, the text might read: "I'm Joe Doe, president of ABC Catering. Let me invite you to discuss your catering needs. I know my team of friendly professionals will be able to please you and your guests! And I promise you that our service is 100% satisfaction guaranteed."

Look through your local phone directories, paying special attention to the advertising—not just for caterers, but for a number of business types. The best ads are uncluttered, but full of useful information. They have strong headlines and contain complete descriptions of the products or services. They include the business's addresses (physical, website, e-mail), phone and fax numbers, and business hours.

Photographs and graphics are fine—but only as long as they reproduce clearly. Timing is also critical in placing an ad, because missing a deadline can result in one full year with no exposure in that particular directory.

An advantage of phone directory ads is that, like websites, they are available anytime, day or night. They are there when the client is ready to buy.

Preprinted Menus

A complete listing of menu choices is an excellent sales tool that can be mailed and given to prospective clients. These preprinted menus may or may not include prices. According to Nancy Loman Scanlon in her book *Catering Menu Management*, "The presentation of catering menus in an effective marketing format can lead customers to purchase the most profitable menus and services."[4]

A popular size for menus is 9 by 12 inches, a standard size in the printing industry and one that fits easily into business mailing envelopes. The quality of the paper should match the quality of the catering company—that is, budget caterers should use less expensive paper, and upscale caterers could choose textured 24-weight bond paper, usually in a pastel color with a contrasting print color. Most professional printers can provide advice as to typeface and styles, illustrations and artwork. Better yet, with today's technology, a good computer program and a laser printer, a talented employee can turn out a good-looking menu template. Just make sure it's easy to read, not too "busy," and has all words correctly spelled. Your menu can (and should) also be used on your website.

Some descriptive copy about menu items is helpful to readers and helps to sell offbeat or ethnic items. In today's nutrition-oriented environment, everyone wants to know about ingredients and preparation techniques. If something is a "heart-healthy" dish, or if you can adapt foods to certain groups (low-calorie, diabetic, "fun foods" for kids), add a line about that.

Cold-Calling

Cold-calling means contacting someone, without being invited, and asking that person if he or she has use for your services. It can be done in person or over the telephone. New off-premise caterers should definitely cold-call prospective clients within their market area, and there's a great reason to do it—to introduce yourself and your services, "conveniently located" right in their area. This is also the way you learn the names and titles of people at these other businesses who are responsible for planning catered events for them. If the person is not in when you call or drop by, you can leave or mail some information and plan to make a follow-up call at a later time.

Established off-premise caterers who resort to cold-calling need to be aware of the negative effects it may have. Clients may perceive it as annoying or indicative of business problems: "Why else would it be necessary for them to call door-to-door?" they may think. So approach it carefully, and with class.

Jeffrey Gitomer is president of BuyGitomer, Inc., a Charlotte, North Carolina, company that trains and motivates salespeople. Gitomer says one way to view cold-calling is not as a way to make a sale but as a way to learn to sell. In the process of this "learning," occasionally you'll make a sale anyway. With this approach you can learn, and rejection will just be part of the learning process, not a personal failure. Some of the objectives of cold-calling, according to Gitomer, should be to:

- Develop a fast opening that grabs attention
- Build instant rapport
- Gain acceptance
- Find and/or qualify the decision maker
- Develop powerful questions
- Gain a prospect's interest
- Learn to persuade quickly
- Learn persistence
- Learn to "think on your feet"
- Learn creativity in your sales presentation
- Learn the "Joy of Rejection" (yes, that's what he calls it!)

"Add a dose of humor to rejection," Gitomer counsels. "For example: Thank people for telling you 'no.' Tell them they're helping you get one step closer to 'yes!' Tell the prospect that only one in four people buy. Ask them if they know anyone else who might *not* be interested, because you still need three more 'no' responses before someone says 'yes.' It'll blow them away—and make them laugh. Make me laugh, and you can make me buy."[5]

Learn more about Jeffrey Gitomer's sales style and advice on his website, www. gitomer.com.

For caterers who prefer not to make their own sales calls, there are telemarketing firms that will do this. For a fee, they'll call businesses in any part of the country, find the person who makes the catering decisions, and set up an appointment for the caterer to make a personal contact or sales presentation. One such firm that we have used with success is Access Direct Marketing (www.accessdirect.cc).

Truthfully, it is a rare individual who likes to make cold calls and can do so successfully. The most you can hope for is to learn some patience, refine your sales skills, and hope for that elusive "yes!"

Signage and Billboards

We've already discussed choosing a name and designing a logo for your catering business—items that can set the tone, attract attention, and help create the caterer's image in the public eye. Now let's talk about what to do with them.

You'll need several types of signage, depending on your business. Be prepared to pay for signs and logos that are large enough to be easily seen and very professional-looking. This is not an area where you can cut corners; you're trying to impress clients. For some ideas about custom signage, take a look at the website of Classic Design Studio in Boise, Idaho (www.classicdesignstudios.com), known for its custom sign work for everything from guitar shops to upscale restaurants to housing developments.

Signs can be used on your office/commissary site and on vehicles. You'll also want to have smaller, portable signs for use at food tastings, booths, fairs, and other events at which you may advertise your business. In Wisconsin, Miles Theurich of Theurich Catering has found that silk-screened signs purchased in quantity for present and future trucks are far more economical than hand-painting the vehicles. He also suggests magnetic signs for sales vehicles and vans, because they do not destroy the value of the vehicles for resale or trade-in.

Billboards are not commonly used by caterers to advertise, primarily because they are expensive. However, you might be able to barter a portion of the cost in exchange for catering services for a billboard company. Prime billboards located on major thoroughfares certainly can bring off-premise caterers significant name recognition.

Your logo may be stitched or printed onto staff members' uniforms or name tags, or printed on disposables like cocktail napkins, plastic cups, and matchbooks.

Paid Advertising

There are all types of places to advertise, ranging in price from a very low cost to the almost astronomical. The most common options include:

■ **Event programs and newsletters.** These range from the local opera or theater productions' programs handed out at performances, to the newsletters of civic and church groups. The audience is small, and, generally, so is the price for advertising. Your decision to advertise here should be based on whether the printed piece actually gets into the hands of your target customers, because, after all, they won't consult a theater program the next time they're looking for a caterer. So, for the most part, advertising in these venues is done more to build goodwill than to actually get business. Some caterers advertise only in the programs of events for which they are actually catering, like charitable fund-raisers.

■ **Magazines.** Many areas have city or regional magazines with relatively small circulations but high-end readers. In our experience, these have been good advertising vehicles for caterers because, in addition to the ads, your involvement with the magazine staff often generates some form of editorial mention. It builds a relationship, so you may be contacted for an occasional story idea or quote in feature articles about food or entertaining. The glossy ads within the magazine pages may be pricey, but they also look classy and are good for building high-end business. Many magazines also offer "back-page" advertising, which looks more like classified ads. The back-page space is smaller and therefore more reasonable.

Massachusetts caterer Russell Morin, of Fine Catering by Russell Morin, reports success by advertising his company's wedding reception services in top-tier wedding magazines such as *Grace Ormond Wedding Style* and *Southern New England Weddings*. He invested $18,000 in these publications, but his elegant mansion weddings grew from 20 to 30 a year, to 120 to 130 a year! He's also added 15 to 20 more galas and corporate events from the resulting word-of-mouth publicity. Morin notes that this type of advertising needs to be backed up by very high levels of service.[6]

Morin's advertising budget runs one-half to three-quarters of 1 percent of his gross sales (the industry standard is 1 percent of gross sales). The magazines he works with help him to do the overall ad design, but he does his own food styling and, interestingly, uses commercial photographers who specialize in advertising, rather than wedding photographers.

■ **Newspapers.** Caterers in small to medium-sized communities may find that newspaper advertising generates substantial revenue. No matter where you live or work, we think you'll find newspaper ad rates rather shocking at first.

Prices are charged by the column inch, with the larger ads having lower per-inch rates. You will want to specify which sections and days of the paper your ad should appear in, depending on the type of reader you're trying to reach. Sunday is the universally "biggest readership" day for any newspaper, so it will cost more to advertise on that day.

In larger markets, some papers have special advertising sections for smaller firms and special sections and editions. The rates for these sections are often discounted, and you should take advantage of them. Newspapers have sales staff members who can guide you through the process, and the paper can also create the ad for you if you don't have one "camera-ready," as the papers call it.

■ **Radio and television.** These mediums are available, but they are generally expensive and require that the advertisement(s) be written, produced, edited, narrated, and duplicated, then placed on certain stations to attract your target clients at the "right" times of day when they might be listening. All this is a bit more complicated than you might imagine, which is why larger catering companies usually leave this work to advertising agencies.

The cost of running an ad depends on how often, and at what times of day, it airs. Some stations will produce an ad for you at no additional cost if you commit to buying a certain amount of airtime. One "sin" we've seen committed a few times is a business owner's insistence on being the star of his or her own advertisements, even when that person doesn't have the, shall we say, "star quality" to really do a good job of it. Our feeling is that this type of advertising is for large, well-financed catering companies. Smaller ones can best spend their limited marketing dollars elsewhere.

According to many advertising experts, it is far better to place smaller ads, on a regular basis, in publications that produce results, rather than larger ads in a helter-skelter fashion in a number of publications. Consistency is the key to effective advertising.

Advertising Specialties

Advertising specialties are useful items that bear the name, address, logo, web page, phone number, and/or message or slogan of the advertiser. They include items such as key chains, calendars, pens, wine openers, and coasters. There are some 15,000 articles of merchandise classified as "specialties" and numerous catalogs full of them from companies willing to personalize them for you.

If these are going to be part of your marketing tool kit, they should be handy and of good quality. They can be handed out as little niceties with catering proposals, at tastings and other events, as "thank yous" to customers with the final invoices, or as a conversation starter with a potential new customer. They're not necessities, and their use will not make or break your overall marketing plan. But if you can afford them, advertising specialties are small courtesies that can be used in variety of ways.

Food Tastings

Whenever off-premise caterers gather to discuss common needs and problems, the topic of food tastings is one that generates much discussion. Some caterers allow their prospective clients to taste the foods they've chosen for the menu prior to the party, but others strictly refuse to do so, claiming their reputation speaks for itself. Some caterers report that they will do food tastings only for major events or for those clients who have requested an unusual item or recipe that the caterer has never prepared before.

In our experience, today's clients expect to be able to taste food in advance, based on all that they read in bridal publications and on websites. Tastings are a cost of doing business. One Miami-based caterer has built three tasting rooms into her facility. Another charges a nominal fee to have a tasting, then credits the bill if the client books the event.

It is true that these private tastings are expensive and take time. The advantage is that when caterers actually sit down with prospective clients and spend time discussing the menu and the clients' needs, they significantly increase their chances of gaining the business.

When conducting food tastings, here are a few rules to follow:

1. The chef needs to be present for the tasting, and to directly receive feedback from the clients.

2. Tastings should be limited to no more than three "tasters." More people than that create a food happening, not a decision-making meeting.

3. The dishes should be presented exactly the way they will look for the event. Pictures should be taken of the presentation, as a reference.

4. Listen to the tasters. Some may have a great knowledge of foods and will give very candid (and valuable) opinions. Others will not, or may simply say (about a particular dish), "It just . . . needs something . . . " If the latter is the case, the off-premise caterer should be prepared to offer suggestions.

Another type of food tasting is designed to generate new business. Off-premise caterers may simply invite current and prospective clients to their commissaries, once or twice a year, to sample a new seasonal menu and ask questions. John Berryhill of Berryhill & Company did this for years in a small space he rented in a trendy shopping area of downtown Boise, Idaho. The walls were lined with nicely framed photos of his catered events, and his business license allowed him to sample wines with customers as well as food. Business was so brisk, and the location was so good, that Berryhill decided to make the place into a small (ten-table) restaurant in addition to his booming catering business.

A third option is to couple your food tasting site with another business trying to gain marketing exposure—an office building wishing to lease space, or an automobile dealership—or to commit to participating in two or three charitable food-related events per year that require you to offer tastes or tidbits, not entire meals. No matter where you host them, tastings can be very effective marketing tools if targeted at a large number of guests. They are part of almost every caterer's marketing arsenal.

Customer Referrals

Asking your existing customers to refer you to their friends and business colleagues is a powerful way to expand the borders of your customer base. It's not a good idea to ask them for a referral list, since that's putting the workload on them. Instead, just ask, "Do you know of anyone who could use our catering services? Would you mind if I use your name as a reference when I speak to them?" This is a terrific way to obtain good prospects.

Barter

Barter is an excellent way to conserve cash flow and increase business. Caterers can barter catering for needed services—dry cleaning, printing, plumbing, and more. Have your signs made by a local sign company and, in exchange, cater the grand opening of its new location. All kinds of "trades" like this are possible. You can also barter for employee incentives, like movie tickets and clothing.

The best time for barter transactions is during slower periods for catering. And it is best to not barter for the total bill, just for the projected gross margin. For example, if a party's "retail price" is $2,000, let's say the caterer has direct operating costs of $1,000. In this instance, the client pays the caterer $1,000, then offers products or services to the caterer that are worth the remaining amount of $1,000, at no cost to the caterer.

There are numerous barter exchange groups across the nation. These can be found through the International Reciprocal Trade Association at www.irta.net. It imperative to remember that barter sales too are taxable income. You will invariably run into vendors who use bartering as a sales tax dodge, and you should avoid doing business with them.

The Telephone

We are not talking about telemarketing here, but about telephone answering. Thousands of catering sales are lost every day by caterers (or their employees) who:

- Don't answer the phone promptly—or don't answer it at all
- Have an inaudible or otherwise unprofessional-sounding recorded message
- Have phones answered rudely or matter-of-factly by poorly trained staff members
- Just say, "Hello" (Are they working illegally, from home?)

Whatever happened to telephone manners? One of our "prime beefs" with caterers we've called from coast to coast is how unprofessionally the telephones are answered.

Caterers who answer their phones politely and in person are sure to increase their revenues—simply by being there. Caterers who do not use a cellular phone are operating in the Dark Ages, because business phones can be programmed to roll over to the cell phone when you're out of the office. Nothing pleases a potential customer more than talking to a real person who is polite, helpful, and courteous.

Phones should be answered in no more than three rings, and clients should not be placed on hold for long periods of time. Another thing caterers should not do is ask a client to call back if a specific person is not in. This leaves the callback to chance—a sure way to kill a sale. Instead, the caterer's staff member should take a message and make sure the person who left it is called back within 24 hours. All calls should be returned on the same day or first thing the following morning.

Making follow-up phone calls is another important aspect of catering etiquette, and yet it is frequently overlooked. For example:

"Hello, this is Larry from ABC Catering. We spoke briefly yesterday about pricing, and our availability for catering your wedding next September. I'm following up to see if you have any questions. I'm glad you're considering ABC, and wanted to let you know I've put some information in the mail (or sent it by e-mail) for you to take a look at. Please feel free to call anytime. You may also reach me directly on my *private line* at (your phone number here)."

There are other excellent opportunities for follow-up calls. Making one after an event will not only bring you prompt feedback (both raves and rants), but can also lead to future sales. We've found that clients don't always tell us the truth during the event—they're busy, stressed, preoccupied—but a few days later, after talking to others and thinking about the event, they may have constructive criticism to share. It's not only useful as a learning experience, but also as an opportunity to give a discount on a future party. If they say something nice, be sure to ask if you can use them as a reference.

Follow-up calls are smart when you simply have not heard from a client in a while, just to keep in touch. And they can be used as an up-selling opportunity for events that are already booked. In short, pick up the phone! It's one of the most overlooked, yet least expensive tools to market your catering business.

Catering for Charity

Caterers are besieged with calls each month to cater charitable events, either for free or at significantly reduced prices. The caller usually mentions the importance of the cause itself, that a lot of important guests will be at the event, and that the caterer will generate significant future business from the exposure. Perhaps this is all true, but many caterers find that the more "nonprofit" catering they do, the more charitable requests they receive.

These types of events are important for exposure and for the goodwill gained by assisting in a good cause. But you're a business, not a religious order. So here are some tips to help you decide how to handle charitable requests:

- Be sure to get the request in writing, on letterhead. This weeds out the scam artists.
- Keep track of how much you give to each charity each year, to avoid having a charity return the next year to challenge that figure and request more.
- Donate wisely by taking care of your best customers who are affiliated with particular charities.
- Create a buffer by appointing someone (a secretary, for example) who is familiar with your guidelines and limits and can handle and track the requests.
- Create a Charitable Donation Request form that addresses the key issues and needs of the event.
- Select a particular charity, or group of charities, and limit giving to these.
- Put the onus on the charity to bring you paying business first.
- Poll your major clients, and give to the charities they select.
- Ask staff members for their input.
- Avoid charitable events during busy times of the year.
- Consider staff members' schedules too. If you have to bring them in on a day they're scheduled to be off, this results in overtime pay for them—an additional (and unreimbursed) cost for you.
- Be sure the food reflects your corporate image. Do it right, or don't do it!
- Contribute to events that draw major corporate executives.
- Contribute to groups to whom you wish to cater. For example, for a barbecue caterer, a blue-collar crowd is perfect.
- Make the most of on-site marketing when catering these events. Use your portable signs. Distribute brochures and other marketing materials at the event.

■ Ask your suppliers for discounts and donations for these events, because they will also benefit from any increased business. If a supplier consistently refuses to give you items at cost or to donate anything, look for a new supplier.

Perhaps the most important step is to establish a budget each year for charitable events, and stick to it. You can always say, "We've already used our charitable budget for this year, but please contact us earlier next year." Be polite about it. Other answers are:[7]

"It's beyond our financial resources."
"We've sponsored too many non-profits this month."
"This isn't an acceptable non-profit for us."
"I'm booked."
And, on rare occasions, "There's absolutely no benefit to my company in this."

Up-Selling

Up-selling catered events can generate thousands of dollars in additional revenue once a party, wedding, or other event is booked. *Up-selling* is the sales technique of offering customers a little more than they thought they were looking for—more upscale, grander, or more lavish service. Examples include:

More expensive food choices
Upgraded liquor, wines, and Champagnes
Martini bars
Additional staff members
Higher-quality china, flatware, stemware, chairs, or linens
Ice carvings for seafood and other displays
"After-Glow Stations" with cappuccino, espresso, international coffees, cordials, cognacs, and after-dinner liqueurs
High-end floral services, such as lit topiaries
Ancillary services: music, valet parking, wedding cakes, lighting, cooling and heating, photography, etc.

In most instances, it's recommended to up-sell once the event is booked, rather than try it before closing the sale. It's best to have a deposit in hand, rather than confuse the client with too many options. In order to make the up-sell items more appealing from a cost standpoint, the caterer may wish to sell these products and services at reduced markups, because the caterer will already generate his or her major profit from the initial package. Profits from these sales are "icing on the cake" and worth going after.

Other Marketing Tools

Before you do any type of marketing, ask yourself two questions: Will it be an effective way to reach my target customers? And will it be profitable, as compared with the overall expense involved? To conclude this section on marketing tools, here's a quick roundup of some other effective ideas. You might:

- Make public appearances, speaking to groups about food-related topics.
- Create a PowerPoint presentation to make sales pitches using your laptop.
- If you've got the skill, try your hand at writing a food column for a local newspaper or magazine.
- Be the regular "Guest Chef" on radio or television.
- Offer special promotions and discounts during slow periods.
- Invite a well-known culinary author to your town; have an event at your commissary, or cater one at the local bookstore where the guest can autograph copies of his or her book(s).
- Hire a freelance camera crew to help you produce a video that shows party styles and locations. (Often, local news people will "moonlight" these on their days off.)
- Use customer comment cards to generate feedback and mailing list information.
- Offer free seminars for those who plan special events such as fund-raisers, employee picnics, and corporate client entertaining.

✕ The Marketing Plan

Now that you've got a working knowledge of your "tools," you can use them to create a marketing plan. This plan should be based on your knowledge of:

- The local catering market
- Your competition
- Your budget for marketing-related expenses

There is no universally accepted marketing plan or formula. But any marketing plan must be based on a realistic budget and should not exceed that budget. For example, if start-up off-premise caterers plan to spend 5 percent of projected first-year annual sales of $100,000, that means there is $5,000—and *only* $5,000—to spend on first-year marketing efforts. Prioritize your needs, and you might come up with this basic list:

Name and logo
Business cards and stationery
Preprinted menus
One food tasting (at your facility) for prospective clients
A quarterly newsletter
A small ad in one local phone directory
Signs for your building and truck
Do-it-yourself cold-calling of five new potential clients per week
A direct mail piece to send to those who have been cold-called

Plans for forthcoming years will be based on the successes and failures of each of these marketing tools. Half of great marketing is making the plan and deciding what to spend, but the other half is keeping good track of how effective each item on the list is *for you*, once you actually do it.

Ideally, the less that is spent on marketing, while still achieving desired sales results, the better off the caterer will be. The art to effective marketing is balancing marketing expenditures with actual revenues.

✕ Selling to Shoppers and Buyers

Up to this point, we have addressed those marketing efforts that will produce shoppers and buyers for off-premise catering services. We are now at the stage where we have some interested prospects, who are ready to discuss catering and specific parties with a knowledgeable person. Enter the catering salesperson—someone who can put him- or herself in the shoes of the shopper. A successful salesperson is one who's willing to serve before trying to collect, who always remembers that the client's message is: "Can you help me? Can you fix it? Am I important?"

Successful catering salespeople:

- Always put the client first. They know that if they satisfy the needs, wants, and desires of the prospective client, they will ultimately gain the client's business.
- Stay in touch with their clients and show appreciation for their support on a regular basis.
- Keep things in perspective, remembering that there will be good days and bad days. They look at things over the long term, rather than just day to day. They take their business seriously, but they also have fun and never take themselves too seriously.
- Take a sincere interest in their clients. They do their homework before meeting with clients, ensuring that they understand all there is to understand about a particular event. They know that when prospective clients interrupt, they mean that the point under discussion is a key point in the decision-making process.

To paraphrase Mike Roman, president of CaterSource, a Chicago-based catering consulting firm, catering can be very difficult to sell, because it is not tangible; it cannot be taken from the shelf and examined. A catering contract is nothing but a piece of paper that contains a series of promises. In fact, most buyers of off-premise catering have never bought catering services before, and these services are not required on a regular basis but only on occasion. The occasions are important enough, however, to enlist the caterer's expert assistance.

Smart salespeople are quite aware of these disadvantages and know how to turn them into advantages by:

- Showing pictures, laptop computer presentations, or videos of previous parties
- Guaranteeing their work will be executed to perfection
- Providing numerous reference letters to skeptical clients
- Giving explicit details in all catering proposals

The Catering Salesperson

How in the world do you find great salespeople? In many off-premise firms, it is the owner or manager who sells the majority of events and, frankly, many prospective clients prefer to deal with the person in charge. Off-premise caterers who do the selling themselves feel this maximizes their chances of gaining the business, which is the driving force behind the company. With no sales, there is no business! They also know that the business they book will meet their standards. And, of course, they need not worry about turnover in their sales staff if they just do it themselves.

Before hiring a person specifically to sell catering services, determine if perhaps hiring someone to answer the phone would be sufficient. Some owners and managers truly enjoy the selling process and, if that's true in your case, you should never give that responsibility to others. But other owners who don't feel that selling is their strength may wish to hire someone on a part-time basis or involve a family member in the business to handle sales. Hiring someone for a full-time position is a major step that must not be taken lightly. During busy periods there is great need for help, but at slower times the need diminishes.

It is tough to hire and train an effective salesperson. Those that come highly trained demand commensurate salaries and may not be especially loyal. Those with no experience require intensive training in food preparation and presentation, etiquette, local traditions, entertaining locations and trends, staff relations, client relations, organizational skills, food and beverage service, and numerous other details. The training is most often done personally by the catering company owner or manager, as this job is too important to delegate. Training is, and should be, the main investment you make in a new person.

The brand new salesperson can't be expected to create new sales immediately, but can start by responding to existing requests. An excellent beginning is to allow him or her to answer phones and obtain basic customer information and event details—time, date, location, number of expected guests, and tentative budget figure. Next, make sure the new salesperson sits in on meetings between off-premise caterers and clients. He or she can then begin to arrange small, simple parties in accordance with the company procedures.

The coauthor of this book has achieved moderate success in his catering business by engaging the services of independent contract salespeople who work on a straight commission, with no "pay draws" or advances. It is, indeed, difficult to find folks like this, but it can be an excellent way to grow a catering business without an up-front financial commitment. A good way to start a program like this is to provide these types of salespeople with "warm leads"—former clients with whom the caterer has not worked recently. The best candidates for commissioned sales positions should also have their own network of clients.

How much business should a catering salesperson sell, and how much should a catering salesperson be paid? This depends on the size of the catering firm and the prices the firm charges. Some catering salespeople sell in excess of $1,000,000 per year; others, much less. In sales, employees are paid by various methods, each with its advantages and disadvantages:

- **Flat salary**—Easy to administer, but offers no incentive for the person to produce or increase sales.
- **Hourly rate**—Little incentive to produce sales, with a tendency to "expand" hours in order to receive overtime pay.
- **Partial commission**—A combination of base salary with a commission for some types of sales offers a level of income security for the salesperson, as well as some incentive to increase sales.
- **Strict commission**—Little security for the salesperson; this system is also complicated to administer, but it does create the ultimate incentive for the salesperson: "You don't sell, you don't eat."

There is no perfect answer to the question about payment, and off-premise caterers must make such decisions based on their individual circumstances. Much will be determined by the payment practices of other caterers within the market and the sheer supply of (and demand for) talented salespeople in the area. Any pay plan must be in accordance with all federal and state laws, as you learned in Chapter 7 of this book.

Qualifying Shoppers and Buyers

An effective marketing plan will produce numerous catering inquiries each day. Some callers are interested in planning a specific event, whereas others are shopping for general information. Experienced caterers will all attest to the countless hours that can be wasted if prospective callers are not properly screened. Some caterers have driven miles to meet with a client, spent half a day meeting with the client, only to learn that the event is unworkable for the caterer because of the size of the party, the budget, the date, or the location.

Most callers do not truly understand the costs of off-premise catering. They are not concerned about budgets—until they hear the cost figure! They are nervous about the event and feel that their reputation hinges on having a great party. Some callers know exactly what they want, but others have not a clue.

Astute off-premise caterers all have learned the secret of qualifying callers to determine if they are truly prospective clients. They know how to separate the "time wasters" from the revenue producers. There are four key points to qualifying clients, and we'll discuss them one by one.

Date of the Event. This will almost immediately determine an off-premise caterer's availability, as well as whether the caller is inquiring about a specific party or just shopping. The date also reveals the caller's sense of urgency. Is the party next week or next year? Acting quickly on a party for the following week will more than likely gain the contract. The date also may be on a holiday, when prices may be higher or the caterer has chosen not to work.

Number of Expected Guests. The answer to "How many guests are you expecting?" will reveal whether the party is either too small, or perhaps too large, to undertake. If the caller has no idea, this could mean that the person is either not a serious shopper or is in the very early planning stages of the event.

Location and Type of Event. This information will help establish the caller's budget. A cocktail party at an exclusive private villa will most likely require a bigger budget than a barbecue at a city park. If the party is at a private home, the address may reveal the caller's lifestyle and income level, which often (but not always!) gives you an idea of the budget; the same holds true for some business addresses. An exclusive downtown law firm planning a grand opening of new offices, for instance, will have a larger party budget than an inner-city manufacturing plant planning a retirement dinner.

Approximate Budget. Getting the answers you'll need to prepare a budget for clients can be a real challenge. First, many people honestly do not have a clue early in the event-planning process about how much they want to spend. Others do, but do not wish to reveal this information, feeling it gives them some type of advantage over their vendors.

Ask the question anyway, listen to the answer for clues, and ask pertinent follow-up questions or make suggestions. You may hear things like: "I really don't know, but I want it to be perfect." "Last year we spent $___." "I want it all to look elegant, but I don't want to spend too much." When you think about it, each of these responses provides a bit of budget information.

Charlotte Williams, president of The Events Organization, Ltd., in Columbia, Maryland, uses what she refers to as the "Ouch Test." She explains:

> At my company, we will not start to prepare a preliminary event plan without a budget guideline from a client. Of course, many are hesitant to give a figure, especially if they are not the final decision maker. So I ask the following, "Somewhere in your company there is someone with decision-making authority who will say 'Ouch!' when they see a certain number. Tell me what you think that number is, and our plan will not exceed it." If they still are hesitant, I will float some number to select from. Using this approach, I always have gotten a number to start from.[8]

Similarly, you can find out a budget for a party, wedding, or event by suggesting various prices to clients and getting their reactions. Tell them, for example, "Well, a party like a party you're describing will cost somewhere between $8,000 and $11,000." If the client chokes (or has another equally uncomfortable reaction), then a lower price range is in order. Or perhaps this client is not one you can help.

Mary Tribble, CSEP, president of Tribble Creative Group in Charlotte, North Carolina, says the important thing is "to make the conversation a dialogue—one with an outcome that benefits your client, not you. This way, they will understand that your motivation is not to help spend their money, but to help them invest it wisely."[9]

The Next Step

Obtaining answers to the basic questions can be done in a matter of minutes. At this point, it is up to the off-premise caterer to decide on a next step, which could be any of the following:

- Continue the dialogue by scheduling an appointment with the caller.
- Offer to submit a written proposal that includes a budget.
- Offer to send the caller some general written information.
- Thank the person for calling, but explain that you'll be unable to cater the event (because the date, time, type, budget, etc., don't work for you).
- Establish a time for a follow-up call if the caller needs to round up more information.

The key point to remember here is that time is money. Caterers must use their limited time marketing and selling their services to the most qualified shoppers.

There are times, too, when caterers should refuse a party, such as when they are already too busy or when the party will not generate an adequate profit. There are also times when the prospective client is too difficult, indecisive, or overdemanding. It is usually best to gracefully decline working with such people, because the resulting frustrations and hassles are not worth the effort.

The Sales Interview

After qualifying clients, the next step is an in-person meeting to discuss the specific elements of the event in order to prepare a written proposal. During this meeting, off-premise caterers must establish their credibility with prospective clients by discussing prior events, showing photos and letters and providing references. (This is where your event scrapbook, video, PowerPoint presentation, and nice brochures do the selling.) During this meeting, a client is often nervous about the forthcoming event, and the professional caterer must dispel that nervousness. You do this by reassuring the client that you will do an outstanding job, as well as guarantee your work.

Clients also want to see suggested menus. Some will ask to see actual parties, and others ask about food tastings. Smart clients will ask off-premise caterers about their licenses and their insurance, so bring these documents (or a summary of them) along. Most will ask, in so many words, exactly what other arrangements you can handle in addition to food and beverages—rental equipment, flowers, music, and décor. Others wish to know which manager will supervise their party, and how many parties you commit to at one time.

Interestingly, we've found one of the most often-stated client fears is running out of food. Off-premise caterers can never stress enough that there will be more than adequate food for the guests. Smart salespeople will ask questions like:

"What type of party do you imagine?"
"What message do you wish to give your guests?"
"What is the overall goal of the event?"
"Who will be making the food and beverage decisions?"
"Is there a theme?"
"Was there a similar event last year? If so, what did you like (and dislike) about the outcome?"

Another key to a good sales meeting is to listen to what the clients have to say—really *listen*! Let them finish their sentences. Learn to focus on what they are telling you. Make good eye contact without staring, and refrain from fidgeting with things as they talk.

Part of even the most preliminary meeting includes negotiation, and this involves prioritizing the clients' needs and wants. What will they be willing to pay for and, if they balk at something, where can you afford to scrimp?

When clients say they want to "think it over," zero in on exactly what it is they wish to think *about*—the food, the service, the rental equipment, the overall cost?

Meet price objections by stressing quality, and negotiate by reducing menu choices, beverage choices, or rental equipment choices, in exchange for a cheaper price. The key to this process is: Never arbitrarily reduce the price without reducing or eliminating something from the event.

Choose your words carefully. Here are some ideas of terms to use:

- *Paperwork* rather than *contract*
- *Investment* rather than *price*
- *Approval* rather than *sign*
- *Opportunity* rather than *deal*
- *Visit* rather than *appointment*
- *Areas of concern* rather than *objections*

Exhibit 9.1 includes most topics that will come up during a sales interview. Using it as a guideline for these in-person meetings will keep you on task and keep the

---

✖ *Exhibit 9.1* Special Event Information

(This form can be referred to during sales interviews to ensure that all of the necessary details are addressed prior to preparing a catering proposal.)

Name and address of client(s): _____

_____

_____

Phone numbers: _____

Fax number(s): _____

Exact location of the event: _____

Day and date of the event: _____

Minimum number of expected guests:_____

Starting and ending times: _____

Proposed menu: _____

_____

_____

_____

_____

_____

_____

_____

_____

_____

_____

_____

_____

Type of beverages to be served (liquor, wine, beer, Champagne, cordials): _____

Number and location of bars: _____

_____

Equipment

  Tables for guests (number and size): _____

  Type of chairs and chair covers: _____

  Napkins and linens (color, sizes, number): _____

  Banquet cloths and skirting: _____

  China color and pattern: _____

  Type of glassware: _____

  Number of service tables: _____

  Size and location of cook's tent: _____

  Tenting for guests (size, location, lighting, plants, floor covering): _____

  Size and location of dance floor: _____

  Size and location of platforms and staging (skirting, railings and steps): _____

  Audiovisual equipment required: _____

Other Services

  Staffing to set up, serve, and clean up the event: _____

  _____

  Music and entertainment: _____

  Floral requirements (for guest tables, buffets and foot stations, passing trays and other areas): _____

  _____

  Photographer and videographer: _____

  _____

  Wedding or other specialty occasion cake: _____

  _____

  Valet parking: _____

  _____

  Security: _____

  _____

  Uniforms for staff: _____

  _____

Location Layout and Planning

  For weddings and receptions

    Ceremony: _____

    Receiving line: _____

    Gift table: _____

    Guest book table: _____

    Escort table (for place cards): _____

    Wedding cake table: _____

  Location of cocktail reception _____

  _____

  Locations of buffets and food stations _____

  _____

  Location of seating for guests _____

  _____

  Rain plan _____

client from chatting too much. Once the questions regarding these items have been answered, salespeople have sufficient information to produce a written proposal for the event.

The Written Proposal

As soon as possible after the personal meeting, the catering salesperson should prepare the written proposal. Many in sales are creative procrastinators, usually a result of their fear of rejection. Just remember, your company will not be able to cater everyone's party, and all you can do is the best possible job of convincing clients that they should hire you. The ultimate client turn-off is to delay providing the proposal, or not to submit it on the date it was promised. It is also much easier to prepare a proposal when all of the details are fresh in your mind. So sit down and get it done!

Catering proposals are basically unsigned contracts. Some off-premise caterers prepare them in a business letter format, and others have preprinted forms that are simply filled in. Proposals can be powerful sales producers. All proposals should include those elements discussed in the "Catering Contracts" section of Chapter 2 such as date, time, and number of guests; menu, beverage service, service staff, equipment, and other services; methods of payment and other legal details as appropriate.

Mike Roman of CaterSource suggests that proposals be very descriptive:

> Words such as "fresh" and "imported" are excellent if they are accurate. Clients should be informed of portion sizes, product origins, grades and cuts of meat and method of preparation and service. All words should be completely spelled out with correct spelling. Pricing should be accurate, with no surprises at a later time. In order to separate themselves from the competition, off-premise caterers make their proposals unique by:
> - Personally delivering them
> - Delivering promptly, by overnight or courier service
> - Using attractive stamps, rather than a postage meter
> - Putting the proposal in an elegant binder
> - Creating a sense of urgency by giving the proposal an expiration date for approval by the client.[10]

Catering proposals, as well as sales presentations, should sell benefits to clients. They should address how the clients and their guests will benefit from the services that are offered. Use statements such as:

> "Your guests will love the food, and we guarantee there will be plenty of it."
> "Your guests will not wait in long lines for food."
> "You can be a guest at your own party."
> "All you need to do is just attend."
> "We will handle the worries for you."
> "Your guests will rave about the party for months."

Exhibit 9.2 is a sample proposal template that can be stored on computer and customized with the specifics for each catered event.

(ON YOUR COMPANY LETTERHEAD)

Date of proposal

Client Name
Address
City, State, Zip

Dear (name of client):

Thank you for the opportunity to provide you this proposal for your forthcoming (name of event). I enjoyed meeting with you (include here the names of others at the meeting and any other specific things about the meeting such as time, location, and any other things that will make the proposal more personal). The specific details as I understand them are as follows:

> DAY AND DATE OF EVENT: (Fill in)
> MINIMUM NUMBER OF GUESTS: (Fill in)
> EXACT LOCATION OF THE EVENT: (Fill in)
> STARTING AND ENDING TIME OF THE EVENT: (Fill in)
> PURPOSE OF THE EVENT: (Fill in)

You can be assured that we will do an outstanding job for you and your guests. We rely on satisfied clients and guests for our future business! Unlike other caterers, you will find that at least one owner of our firm will oversee each detail of your event from setup to break-down. We guarantee perfection in the execution of each and every detail.

We proudly submit the following proposal that has been created exclusively for your event:

MENU (Include all menu items to be served.)

BEVERAGE SERVICE (Include details of beverages to be served, number of bartenders, and nonalcoholic items to be provided by caterer.)

EQUIPMENT PROVIDED (Include a listing of all items such as tables, chairs, linens, china, flatware, glassware, and other equipment.)

SERVICES (Include details regarding music, photographers, and other services to be provided by the off premise caterer.)

[Note: It is also advisable to include, in the equipment and services section of proposals, details of equipment and services that clients intend to provide themselves.]

PRICING Pricing for the food, equipment, and services is as follows: (Include all pricing details, including policies regarding gratuities, service charges, other charges, and sales taxes.)

Other pertinent information regarding our policies is included on the attached page.

Please feel free to call me with any questions, comments, or changes. We are in the service business, and we wish to provide you with the best of service and food.

Sincerely,

(Name and title of off-premise caterer)

✕ Exhibit 9.3 *Catering Policies*

1. Advance deposits are not refundable in case of cancellation.
2. Your price per person is based on a minimum guaranteed number of guests. If your final guarantee is less than the minimum guarantee, we reserve the right to increase the per-person price.
3. We do not serve alcoholic beverages to minors or to guests who appear to be intoxicated.
4. Clients are required to provide a final guaranteed number of guests no less than four working days prior to the party. This guarantee cannot be reduced.
5. We prepare for the number of guests that are guaranteed, and you will be billed for the guaranteed number, unless more than the guaranteed number attend the event.
6. Clients need to note the start and stop times of their event. Service that is provided prior to or after these times is subject to an additional charge.
7. Increases in guarantees 48 hours or less prior to the event may be subject to a surcharge.

✕ Closing the Sale

Once the proposal is delivered, clients usually wish to review it before making a final go-ahead decision. Often, others are involved in the decision-making process, such as committees, bosses, future spouses, family members, and so on. Some caterers give their clients a certain number of days to reply. They do this by guaranteeing the price. If clients go past the deadline, the price may increase. Going over a few basic rules, including the price guarantee (as seen in Exhibit 9.3), is important.

Most catering sales "closings" occur automatically, without the salesperson having to ask directly for a decision. The clients realize that the benefits offered by a particular caterer meet their wishes at a price they can live with. They may ask a few additional questions, or for some clarification. Then, they just sign the proposal and return it.

Training in this area never hurts, and there are a number of powerful video and audiocassette sales tapes available to teach proper sales and closing techniques. Off-premise caterers should develop a habit of listening to them and providing them to sales staffers. They are an outstanding marketing investment.

A particularly good program is one presented by Joel Weldon, a nationally known motivational speaker. His cassette programs address all areas of management, but the selling program is one from which any caterer could benefit. Weldon describes the sales process as "building blocks":

- **The Foundation** is one of honesty, client interest, knowledge, positive attitude, and preparation on the part of the salesperson.
- **Building Block One** is the "Pre-Approach," consisting mostly of the marketing tools that were presented in this chapter.
- **Building Block Two** is the "Approach." Weldon claims a salesperson has only seven to fifteen seconds to make a first impression, so it had better be good! The person should exude a positive attitude, confidence, sincerity, and a high level of expectancy. The salesperson's appearance should be professional; he or she should be well prepared for the meeting and should, of course, arrive at the meeting on time.
- **Building Block Three** is "Attention." To capture a client's attention, Weldon suggests that you may want to:
  Tell about a benefit.
  Make a promise.

Pay a compliment.
Arouse curiosity.
Exhibit something dramatic.
Ask a question.
Offer to be of service.
Use a startling statement.
Mention a referral.

- **Building Block Four** is "Qualifying," or finding out the prospect's needs. At this stage off-premise caterers should decide whether they are the best caterers to serve the client. Pursue the business if the answer is "yes," or walk away politely and quickly if the answer is "no."

- **Building Block Five** is "Interest," or selling the benefits that will meet this particular client's needs based on the qualifying questions. Excellent salespeople tell and show how clients will benefit from using these catering services. They sell *benefits* rather than *features*. What's the difference? Well, a feature of a caterer might be good food; but a benefit is, "Your guests will rave to you about the food if you choose our catering service!"

- **Building Block Six** is "Conviction." This is gained as salespeople ask questions and prompt the client either to agree or disagree with the question or statement. For example, after the previous statement—"Your guests will rave to you about the food"—a professional salesperson might add, "Won't that be great?" Most clients will respond favorably to this statement, creating a "unit" of conviction.

- **Building Block Seven** is "Desire," which is created by involving prospects in the presentation, showing them the potential benefits, and gaining units of conviction. Once enough units of conviction are earned, the sale can be closed.

- **Building Block Eight** is "Resolve to Buy Now." This is achieved by creating a sense of urgency to act quickly—"Others do want our services on this date, but we will hold it for you for two days while you decide." Another example is, "We're about to institute a price increase, but we'll guarantee you the lower price for one more week."

- **Building Block Nine** is the "Close." Weldon suggests the use of positive and expectant physical actions—writing things down, handing a proposal to a client for signature, and assuming the sale has been made with a statement: "We'll be at your house next Friday night at 5:00 P.M. with the food. It'll be great!"

- **Building Block Ten** is the "Sale." This occurs when your prospect "wins" and becomes a customer. At this point, a successful salesperson asks the client for referrals and why the client chose this caterer. It is also smart selling to give the buyer something extra after the sale is made. Tell the bride and groom you'll make sure a special picnic basket of food is made up for them to take to their hotel room after the wedding reception. Mention that you'll have one of the photographer's best shots at a corporate event framed for the client after the groundbreaking. Use your advertising specialties then and there.[11]

Listening to cassettes while in the car, while you're exercising, or at other times when your mind is free is an outstanding way to learn. Smart caterers realize that an investment in knowledge always pays dividends. Those who take advantage of motivational programs to improve their selling skills report increased sales, as well as increased job satisfaction.

No matter how good you are at selling, the very nature of sales involves some percentage of failure and rejection. Nobody lands every client, every time. Part of what a good sales training course will teach you is to handle discouragement by seeing the failures as learning experiences and as opportunities to develop a sense of humor. And, yes, in retrospect, some of your sales negotiations will be truly hilarious!

✗ Conclusion

Marketing is one of the major keys to success in off-premise catering, and good caterers are always marketing their businesses. Marketing becomes second nature to them, as they look for better ways to sell their services and to increase their share of the catering market in their area. For the successful caterer, marketing is a never-ending pursuit of excellence.

Notes

1. David F. Ramacitti, *Do-It-Yourself Publicity*, American Management Association, New York, 1990.
2. Bob Brace, "Improving Your Direct Mail Efforts," in *Celebrate*, Volume 1, No. 3, December 1992, a publication of Korbel Champagne Cellars.
3. Excerpted with permission of *Restaurants & Institutions* magazine, February 1, 1994. Copyright 1994 by Cahners Publishing Company.
4. Nancy Loman Scanlon, *Catering Menu Management*, John Wiley & Sons, New York, 1992.
5. Jeffrey Gitomer, president of BuyGitomer, Inc., in *South Florida Business Journal*, May 16–22, 2003.
6. Russell Morin, owner, Fine Catering by Russell Morin, in the *ICA Communicater* newsletter, May–June 2003.
7. Excerpted from *Catering* magazine, September–October 2000.
8. Excerpted from *Event Solutions* magazine, July 2001.
9. Excerpted from *Event Solutions* magazine, May 2002.
10. Interview with Mike Roman, president of CaterSource, Chicago, Illinois.
11. Joel Weldon, *Sell It with the Million Dollar Attitude*, Joel H. Weldon & Associates, Inc. 1993, Scottsdale, Arizona.

Chapter 10

Pricing Off-Premise Catered Events

Pricing off-premise catered events means accurately estimating the actual costs to produce the event and knowing how much (the amounts) to mark up these costs in order to produce satisfactory profits. The computation of the actual costs is the "science" of pricing, and the amount of markup is often referred to as the "art" of pricing. Astute caterers not only accurately compute costs, they also know how much they can charge for their services.

How much can they charge? The amounts vary, depending on such factors as the supply of caterers within a market area and the demand for their services. A greater supply of caterers when demand is constant can result in lower prices. Of course, those caterers who are in a market where there is little competition may be able to charge more for their services.

Supply and demand can be further identified by the types of caterers within the market as compared with the demand for various levels of service. For example, the few upscale caterers within a market where all other caterers provide midscale or budget service will have greater freedom in pricing events than those who have many competitors.

Caterers should carefully analyze clients and their needs. For example, a corporate client who, on a moment's notice, requires a very specialized service will not be very price sensitive—but a bride on a limited budget whose wedding is two years away has a year to shop. The bride's situation is much less urgent than that of the corporate client, so most brides tend to shop for the best price.

Many caterers effectively use pricing as a sales tool, because properly priced parties will create sales. These prices are fair from both the caterers' and the clients' perspectives. Effective pricing creates a win-win situation: Clients achieve their budget objectives, and caterers make satisfactory profits. Pricing policies should take a long-term view. A greedy off-premise caterer who overcharges a desperate client for a last-minute event will more than likely never again cater for this client, and this client may tell many others that the caterer charges too much. Fair prices, making winners of caterers and clients alike, will produce long-term profits and satisfied clients. Let's learn how to achieve this important balance.

✖ Pricing for Profit

The main goal of all pricing strategies is to maximize the bottom line. The art of pricing is learning the amounts to charge that will produce sales. Caterers whose prices are extremely high will earn large profits on those parties they cater, but the number of parties catered may not be enough to generate sufficient income to cover overhead expenses and required profits. Underpriced caterers may successfully sell virtually every client, but earn insufficient profits on each event to produce sufficient revenues to cover overhead expenses and profits. Either way, it's the caterer who loses—financially.

The art of pricing is to charge enough to earn an overall profit, but not so much that most proposals are lost. The middle ground is where most off-premise caterers are found. As a rule, somewhere between 50 and 75 percent of all your catering proposals should result in contracts. If they do not, the problem is frequently pricing.

Of course, clients often ask caterers to reduce quoted prices. Let's say, for example, that a caterer quotes a price for an event that will generate a $1,000 profit. The client says he will work with the caterer "if the price can be lowered by $250," which actually means $250 less profit for the caterer. Should the caterer take the party? This depends on the caterer's philosophy. Some believe that 75 percent of the pie is better than no pie at all. Others say, "Clients either do business on my terms or we do not do business." A good philosophy is not to reduce a price without reducing something in the party. In this example, the caterer might agree to the reduced price, but serve top sirloin instead of beef tenderloin. Another might compromise by catering the party for $125 less, making one or two minor reductions in the menu.

What should off-premise caterers expect to earn for their efforts, and what are the common percentages? These figures vary dramatically from caterer to caterer, depending on pricing structure, local market conditions, and other factors; however, some common ranges follow:

Food cost percentage	20 to 40% of gross sales
Payroll and benefits	15 to 30%
All other expenses	10 to 30%
Net profit percentage before federal income tax	10 to 40%

Prime cost is a term used widely within the foodservice industry. It is the total of the company's food costs and direct labor costs. Some operations may have low food costs but high labor costs, or vice versa. For example, caterers serving steaks will more than likely have higher food costs but lower labor costs, inasmuch as little labor is needed to cut, season, and broil steaks. Conversely, caterers serving upscale menu items that require significant labor to produce will have higher labor costs and lower food costs. For caterers, prime cost will normally be less than 60 percent of sales. Therefore, caterers with high food costs (say, 40 percent of sales), should have labor costs of no more than 20 percent of sales to stay within the range. Those with lower food costs will normally have higher labor costs.

"How Much Will It Cost?"

All too often, the first question asked by a nervous bride or her parents is, "How much will it cost for a wedding?" As we've discussed in previous chapters, a lot of folks just don't have much experience using caterers, so there are numerous potential clients whose main concern is cost. Smart caterers do not directly *answer* cost-related questions until they ask their own qualifying questions (as discussed in Chapter 9) regarding the date, number of guests, location, and entertainment goals and other questions that reveal the client's true perception of the event. Prices should not be given until these questions are answered to the satisfaction of the caterer and the pre-cost of the party has been computed. It is extremely poor policy to quote erroneous prices, only to later advise clients that there are additional charges "not originally estimated." It's tough news for you to deliver, and it creates an atmosphere of distrust in the entire negotiation. Clients will then question your credibility, and some may even refuse to pay, leaving you with the decision of whether to absorb (or "eat") the difference or decline the party.

✗ Pre-Costing Catered Events

Pre-costing parties involves accurately estimating all expenses that will be incurred in order to produce the event. These include:

Food costs
Commissary labor cost to produce the food
All costs to deliver, set up, serve, and clean up
Equipment costs (rental and owned)
Other costs (flowers, décor, music, miscellaneous)

Computing Food Costs

The first step is to accurately estimate the actual cost of the food necessary to produce the event. Off-premise caterers should maintain accurate, up-to-date cost records for most menu items. Costs for major items like meat and seafood are volatile and can change dramatically in a matter of days. Beef prices always increase prior to and during the Christmas holidays, and seafood prices change depending on weather and fishing conditions.

Standard recipe cards must be maintained and updated frequently. Costs must be computed for each recipe ingredient. Exhibit 10.1 shows this procedure. Costs are obtained from recent invoices and supplier price quotes.

⚔ *Exhibit 10.1* Costing a Recipe

Item: Baked Rice

Ingredient	Recipe Quantity	Price	Total Amount
Rice, long grain	8 lb.	$0.70/lb.	$5.60
Butter	1 1/2 lb.	2.00/lb.	3.00
Onions	2 1/2 lb.	0.40/lb.	1.00
Chicken stock	8 qt.	0.25/qt.	2.00
Salt	1/8 lb.	0.20	.03
	Total cost		$11.63
	Number of portions		110
	Cost per portion		0.11

In the following example, the cost for each item on the menu was computed on the basis of the standard recipe card, and the total food cost was computed by adding the costs of all menu items, as follows:

MENU ITEM	FOOD COST
Shrimp raw bar	$4.00
Caesar salad	.55
Beef tenderloin	6.00
Baked rice	.11
Stir-fry vegetables	.75
Garnish and sauce	.50
Rolls and butter	.50
Coffee, decaffeinated, cream, sugar	.50
Chocolate pecan torte	1.50
Total dinner price	$14.41

This total food cost per person is multiplied by the number of expected guests, plus a planned overage, which, is generally a percentage of the total number of guests. The larger the number of guests, the smaller the percentage, and vice versa. In Chapter 3, 10 percent is used as a planned overage for a dinner party for 100 guests. Using this as a guideline, the total cost for this meal for 100 guests is:

$14.41 per person × 110 guests (100 plus 10 percent extra) = $1,585.10

Many caterers prefer to round up to an even number, which in this case would be $1,590 for the food cost.

Computing Labor Costs

It's easy to overlook the cost of the commissary labor to prepare a party. In the preceding example, many preparation tasks will be completed in the commissary—things like cooking and cleaning the shrimp, cleaning the salad greens, trimming meat, peeling vegetables, and so forth. The labor required to perform these functions must be accounted for and included in the cost of producing the party. The ideal way to compute the labor costs is to actually time each process. For example, if it takes one cook (who is paid $10 per hour including payroll benefits) six hours to cook and clean the shrimp for the raw bar, this would equal $60. Labor costs should be computed for all items and totaled. In this case, let us assume the commissary labor costs to produce the rest of the menu are $240; the total is now $300.

After computing food and commissary labor costs, the next step is to compute the other labor costs necessary to produce the party; for instance:

- Cost to pull, pack, deliver, return, clean, and store
- Cost of commissary labor at the party site
- Cost of service and beverage staff at the party site

Most caterers use estimated figures based on past parties to estimate the cost of pulling, packing, delivering, returning, cleaning, and storing. Smart caterers know not to underestimate these costs. These costs are very real and can amount to hundreds of dollars for each party. In our example, let's assume that it takes 20 hours to perform these functions, and that the staff members are paid $9.00 per hour, including payroll benefits. Twenty hours times $9.00 per hour equals $180.

Commissary labor at the party site is computed by estimating the actual hours necessary. In this case, for example, labor is performed by six staff members for seven hours at $10.00 per hour, including payroll benefits.

$$6 \text{ staffers} \times 7 \text{ hours each} \times \$10.00 \text{ per hour} = \$420$$

Finally, the cost for service and bar staff must be computed. This is done, again, by simply multiplying the number of staff members times their hourly rate, times the number of hours worked. Assume that there will be ten servers and two bartenders for this event, each earning $15 per hour, including payroll benefits. Six staffers will work seven hours, and six will work five hours. The cost is computed as follows;

$$6 \text{ workers} \times 7 \text{ hours} \times \$15 \text{ per hour} = \$ \ 630$$
$$6 \text{ workers} \times 5 \text{ hours} \times \$15 \text{ per hour} = \$ \ \underline{450}$$
$$\text{Total service and bar staff} = \$1,080$$

Now we know the total labor cost to produce this event:

Commissary labor to prepare the food	$ 300
Labor to pull, pack, deliver, etc.	$ 180
On-site commissary labor	$ 420
Service and bar labor	$1,080
Total labor	$1,980

Computing Equipment Costs

Off-premise caterers frequently provide equipment such as china, glassware, flatware, tables, chairs, linens, and the like. In some cases these items are rented from party-rental companies, in others they are owned by caterers, and sometimes there is a combination of the caterer's equipment and rented items. So how do caterers charge clients for equipment?

Rental Equipment. Most off-premise caterers add markups to their costs for rental equipment. In addition, most rental companies offer discounts from list prices to caterers. This means that off-premise caterers produce profits from rental equipment. To compute the cost of the rental equipment, caterers simply add the costs of all rental items. Once the rental orders are placed, these costs may be verified with the rental companies.

For example, assume that the list price of all equipment necessary to produce this party is $2,000, and the rental dealer offers caterers a 10 percent discount. Therefore, the cost to the caterer of the rental equipment is $1,800.

How much is an acceptable markup for rental equipment? This varies from one caterer to another. All caterers must invest time to order, receive, handle, rinse or wash, and repack this equipment. For most large parties, there's also some loss to figure in, due to breakage, burns, and theft by guests. You can certainly add in a small allowance, automatically, for losses—but, politically, it's probably smarter to absorb these costs in the overall markups. Passing them on to clients directly can result in disputes ("Prove that three of those were stolen!" "If they were broken, I want to see them!") Then again, major losses that are due to a client's negligence must be charged directly to the client after the event, with or without a separate loss allowance in the contract.

Among the items in our sample $2,000 rental order, there will more than likely be minor losses, even with the most professional staff. Novice caterers have been known to sacrifice all of their profits from a party because of equipment losses. Off-premise caterers often mark up equipment from rental equipment dealers—some may charge their discounted price plus a small allowance for losses, while others may apply liberal increases to the prices charged by the dealers.

Owned Equipment. Off-premise caterers also own equipment that they provide to clients for their events. Some do not directly charge for it, and others charge just as if it were equipment rented from a dealer. Often, the charge varies, based on the situation. For a small home party, the caterer may charge the full local retail price (because, indeed, the client is "renting" the equipment from the caterer), but when bidding on a large event, the caterer may chose to charge little or nothing for the equipment, content with profits from the food and other features of their service.

Using the $2,000 rental equipment example, note the financial impact of various pricing strategies:

EQUIPMENT LIST PRICE	DISCOUNTED PRICE	SELLING PRICE	MARGIN
$2,000	$1,800	$1,800	0
$2,000	$1,800	$2,000	$ 200
$2,000	$1,800	$2,200	$ 400
$2,000	$1,800	$2,400	$ 600
$2,000	$1,800	$2,600	$ 800
$2,000	$1,800	$2,800	$1,000

Please note that in these examples, the margins are prior to any losses due to missing items or damaged merchandise.

Pricing Accessory Services

Many off-premise caterers assist clients by arranging for so-called *accessory services*—everything from music or entertainment, to floral design, valet parking, security, photography, and wedding and special-occasion cakes not made in-house. Some caterers include these services in a package plan, some price them separately, some ask clients to pay the vendors directly, and some charge a markup on some or all of these services. They reason that, as the professional who recommends these other services, the caterer shares some of the responsibility for the results. In addition, they spend time arranging for these services (and supervising or overseeing them on-site), and they feel that their expertise in knowing whom to recommend is worth something. Therefore, they add a markup when billing clients for these services.

How much markup is proper? This, like the markup for rental equipment, varies from caterer to caterer, but it is invariably less than markups applied to food costs. Markups in the range of 10 to 25 percent are fairly common. Sometimes, in an extremely competitive situation, caterers may simply provide these services at cost in order to gain a pricing edge.

Where the clients deal directly with the accessory service providers, is it ethical for off-premise caterers to receive commissions from the suppliers they recommend? This is a touchy subject that will spark debates from coast to coast. The main point is that commissions received from accessory service suppliers must be reported as income.

Pricing Beverage Services

Off-premise caterers frequently provide beverage mixers, ice, and other bar supplies and certainly must pass these costs on to clients. Again, the amount varies from one caterer to the next, with an average between $1 and $2 per guest. For this example, we will estimate that the costs of mixers and ice are $100.

For this event, we have estimated the following beverage-related costs:

Food costs	$1,590
Labor costs	1,980
Equipment rental costs	1,800
Beverage mixers and ice	100
Total cost	$5,470

✗ Pricing Food

With the estimated pre-costs computed, the next step is to determine the various markups and food cost percentages. There are various formulas that will give the same results. With a goal of a food cost in the range of 20 to 50 percent, let's examine two ways to obtain this for our sample menu with a $1,590 food cost. The first way is to divide the food cost by the desired food cost percentage. For example:

FOOD COST	DIVIDE BY FOOD COST PERCENTAGE	SELLING PRICE	MARGIN
$1,590	25%	$6,360	$4,770
$1,590	30%	$5,300	$3,710
$1,590	35%	$4,343	$2,753
$1,590	40%	$3,975	$2,385
$1,590	45%	$3,533	$1,943
$1,590	50%	$3,180	$1,590

By subtracting the actual food cost from the selling price, you can determine the amount of gross margin produced from the food sales. For instance, in the 25 percent food cost example, the gross margin from the food sale is $4,770 ($6,360 less 15 percent).

Another way to price food is to multiply the food cost by a *markup factor*:

- A markup factor of 5 will produce a 20 percent food cost.
- A markup factor of 4 will produce a 25 percent food cost.
- A markup factor of 3 will produce a 33⅓ percent food cost.
- A markup factor of 2.5 will produce a 40 percent food cost.
- A markup factor of 2 will produce a 50 percent food cost.

For example:

FOOD COST	MARKUP FACTOR	SELLING PRICE	MARGIN
$1,590	4	$6,360	$4,770
$1,590	3	$4,770	$3,180
$1,590	2.5	$3,975	$2,385
$1,590	2	$3,180	$1,590

Again, the gross margin is computed by simply subtracting the estimated food cost from the selling price.

✕ Pricing Labor

Some off-premise caterers add the labor cost to the food cost, and then apply a markup factor. In our example, the combined food and labor cost, or prime cost, is $3,570 ($1,590 + $1,980).

FOOD AND LABOR COST	MARKUP FACTOR	SELLING PRICE	MARGIN
$3,570	1.5	$5,355	$1,785
$3,570	2	$7,140	$3,570
$3,570	2.5	$8,925	$5,355

Notice in this example that the markup factors produce greater margins because we are not only marking up food cost, but also labor cost.

Some caterers mark up the food and labor; others simply mark up the food and charge for the labor at cost, or slightly above cost.

Determining the Markup

So far, we have discussed the math involved in pricing, but not the "art" of determining the amounts of markup. There are no easy equations for this purpose. Most caterers learn pricing by trial and error within their markets—they quote a price too high and don't get the job; or they quote too low, get the job, but lose money on it. Those who survive the learning process learn the art of pricing for profit.

Several factors influence pricing within various catering markets. We refer to them as *market factors*:

■ What are the competitors' prices for similar events?
■ What are the previous prices charged to clients?
■ How many guests are expected?
■ How badly is the business needed?
■ Is this a bidding situation, or not?
■ Who else is bidding on the event?
■ What is the customer's perceived value of the party?
■ Once it is quoted, do clients expect to negotiate the price?
■ Once it is quoted, do clients expect a discount?

Before you submit your proposal, you should always ask if the client is getting other bids. In some cases the answer is no, but if the client is asking other caterers for bids, it is fair to ask against whom you are bidding. Often, the client will tell you, and you then learn where you stand in the competitive arena and are better able to decide whether you want to bid or not. If the other bids are coming from low-end caterers and you're strictly upscale, you can't compete on price alone, so you may choose to emphasize other factors, such as quality or service.

If the client selects another caterer, it's good practice to look at the lost bid as a learning experience. Try to find out why another caterer was selected. The deciding factor may not have been price, but other factors that may be important to know. This information may also help you to further develop key marketing strategies to capture new clients or replace business you have either lost or failed to win.

Common Pricing Techniques

Mark Up More for Smaller Parties. For example, a markup factor of 2 for a chicken dinner that costs $5 each for 20 guests will produce a margin of only $100 ($5 × 20 × 2 = $200, less $100 cost). Is this sufficient profit? It is certainly not for a full-service caterer who is cooking at the party site. In this instance, a larger markup factor would be appropriate.

Mark Up More for Lower-Food-Cost Parties. In the preceding example, the food cost for chicken is low, as compared with the food cost of a lobster dinner, which may be $15. A markup of 2 on the chicken produces a $5 margin, whereas a markup of 2 on the lobster produces a $15 margin ($15 × 2 less $15 = $15).

Number of Expected Guests. With more guests, smaller markup factors may be sufficient. The $5 food margin on the chicken dinner for a group of 1,000 will produce a food margin of $5,000. Many caterers charge less per person for larger events.

Number of Previous or Expected Bookings for a Particular Day or Night. Special holidays and other major events, such as New Year's Eve, the last Saturday before Christmas, or the Super Bowl, are generally busy days for off-premise caterers. There is a large demand for work. Astute caterers realize that they can charge more on these days than during slow periods, such as a Tuesday night in July in Arizona. Moreover, because these days and nights are generally busy, when pricing, off-premise caterers should remember that there may be additional, unexpected expenses, such as renting extra vehicles and paying premium pay to staff on New Year's Eve.

Probability of the Need to Negotiate or Discount. In some instances it is better to price a party higher, realizing that you will later need to reduce the price or offer other concessions to truly please a particular client. As we've mentioned, it is not advisable to reduce the price without deleting something from the party or receiving a concession from the client. For example, a $2-per-person price reduction will result in the elimination of some food, or perhaps an agreement from the client to pay for the complete party one month in advance.

Some caterers offer discounts for parties held during slow seasons, or for those held at certain times of day. Others offer discounts for clients who sign contracts months or years in advance or who agree to engage them for all their parties.

Inexpensive Parties Breed More Inexpensive Parties. When pricing parties, every off-premise caterer has learned not to give a low price to clients who say that there will be many people at their events who will buy in the future. There may be—but these folks will inevitably expect the same bargain prices. Beware!

Value of Time. Off-premise caterers reach a point in their careers when they ask themselves, "What is my time worth?" It's not a rhetorical question! Situations crop up that will prompt you to make this kind of decision: "Do I sacrifice a long-awaited day off to earn a meager profit?" For a regular client, the answer may be "yes." In other situations, perhaps by quoting a higher price, you can earn a sufficient profit to make the sacrifice worthwhile.

Looking beyond the Price. There are clients who are looking beyond the price to things such as elegance, the "look and image," and other factors, both tangible and intangible. Some clients take pride in saying that "so-and-so is the caterer." Some, rare as they may be, enjoy telling others how much they paid for an elegant party.

✖ Pricing a Party

With the combined knowledge of pre-costing techniques and various pricing philoso-phies, off-premise caterers are now prepared to price parties. Using the particulars of the preceding example, *one way* to price this party would be as follows (please note that this is not policy, but only one example):

CHARGES TO CLIENT

$1,600 food cost times factor of 2.5	$4,000
Labor at cost	$1,980
Equipment	$2,200
Beverage mixers, ice, etc.. at $2 per person	$ 200
Total price	$8,380

TOTAL COSTS (FOR THE SAME EVENT)

Food	$1,600
Labor	$1,980
Equipment	$1,800
Mixers, etc.	$ 100
Total cost	$5,450
Total projected profit	$2,900

✖ Service Charges, Gratuities, and Sales Taxes

Each state has specific laws regarding gratuities (tips), service charges, and sales taxes, and it is incumbent upon caterers in every state to learn and comply with them. Penalties for violations are often severe. In most states, service charges are subject to sales tax, since they are not voluntary. But tips, which are voluntary, are not gener-ally taxed.

Service charges are basically specified percentages added to all or a portion of the price. Caterers use different techniques, depending on their circumstances. In the previous example, if there was a 15 percent service charge on all invoice items, this would be computed on the cost to the client ($8,380). Some caterers prefer to charge for service on food and labor only.

Reports from around the nation indicate that 50 percent of off-premise caterers do not charge a service charge, 25 percent do, and 25 percent sometimes do, de-pending on the situation. When considering whether to charge a service charge, off-premise caterers should review competitors' practices and develop an acceptable strat-egy. One strategy, in a market where all other caterers impose a service charge, may be to not impose one.

According to Mike Roman, catering industry consultant and president of Cater-Source in Chicago, "The successful caterers of the next five years will be those who discover how to charge both an hourly wage for workers and, in addition, a service charge percentage." Roman further states, "A buyer of catering would rather spend his or her money on anything else other than a service charge! A buyer getting a chance to purchase two identical menu packages from two different caterers will always buy the one with more value. Look at this scenario: One caterer is charging $24 per guest plus an 18 percent service charge, while another caterer is charging $27 per guest with a 14.5 percent service charge. Which do you think they buy?"

Roman thinks caterers should become more inventive with their service charges. Some thoughts are:

- Charge a 20 percent service charge instead of 15 percent or 18 percent.
- Change the name—call it a "support fee."
- Change the percentage—the higher the menu price and/or the larger the group, the smaller the service charge percentage.
- Charge a smaller service charge on slower days.

Catering for Charitable Events

Most charities or nonprofit groups are able to negotiate very low prices because there is always a novice caterer who is willing to work for nothing in order to obtain exposure. For newcomers to this field, these events can be great launching pads. However, most experienced caterers have learned that they must charge a realistic price that will not only result in a profit, but also ensure a sufficient budget to produce excellent food and provide excellent service. In catering charitable events, you cannot afford to reduce quality or quantity, regardless of the input received from the event planners, because the chief goal of catering these events, for you, is exposure to prospective new clientele. A charity's main goal, however, is to earn as much as possible. As noble as it is, this does not often work to the caterer's advantage.

Many states provide sales tax exemptions for sales made to charitable organizations, churches, synagogues, and not-for-profit organizations for their fundraising events. Off-premise caterers must obtain sales tax exemption certificates from these organizations, with the group's federal tax-exempt number, in order to avoid penalties.

Some states have laws regarding charging sales tax on labor. A California floral designer was led to believe that labor at a party site was not taxable, and for 18 months did not charge sales tax on this labor. He was audited, at which time he was told that labor was, in fact, taxable and that he owed the state $58,000 in back taxes.

Delivery and Overtime Charges

Some off-premise caterers charge delivery charges to cover the costs of delivering the food to the party. This is generally the case where there is no on-site preparation and the caterer is simply preparing the food and delivering it to the party. Some clients pay the delivery charge without hesitation, but others refuse to buy from those caterers who charge it. To avoid the latter situation, many off-premise caterers simply add the cost of delivery into the food cost, not showing it as a separate charge.

And what happens when a party continues beyond the specified stop time? How should caterers charge for this type of overtime? Normally, overtime charges are specified in the catering contract so that there are no surprises if the party goes longer than planned. These charges are usually based on the hourly rate paid to staff, the number of staff members, extra food and beverages served, and some form of markup to these costs. Most overtime costs are usually for labor because, by the end of the event, most guests have had their fill of food and drink. In those circumstances where off-premise caterers are providing accessory services such as music or valet parking, overtime fees must be added to the final bill.

For example, assume that a party goes one hour overtime and there are three staff members working the event who will stay. They are each paid $12 per hour, including payroll benefits. No extra food or beverages are expected to be consumed. Three staff members at $12 per hour equals $36 in extra payroll expenses. The caterer may wish to mark up the labor two or three times, to $72 or $108, to the client, thus generating an additional profit of $36 or $72.

An important note: If overtime is caused by caterers not fulfilling their responsibilities on schedule, it is considered unreasonable to charge clients the additional costs.

Other Pricing Methods

Off-premise caterers do not use one universal pricing method. Caterers have various methods for pricing that fit their style and needs. However, all successful caterers have one thing in common. They charge prices that not only produce sufficient profits but also generate repeat business. What are some other pricing techniques?

Budget Pricing Method. With the budget pricing method, the client sets the price by giving the caterer an overall budget for the event. It may be just for food, staff, and equipment, or it may also include accessory services like music and décor. For example, a client tells a caterer that the budget for a forthcoming event is $5,000 for 100 guests, and only for food, staff, and equipment. Astute caterers first determine their desired profit for the event, and then budget for the expenses as follows.

Assume that the off-premise caterer wants to earn a profit of $1,500 from this event. When deducted from the total budget of $5,000, this leaves $3,500 for all expenses, including food cost, labor, and equipment. At this point, the caterer simply computes the menu, staff, and equipment needs at costs that will result in expenses of $3,500. Please note that these are computed at cost, not at retail, because profit was budgeted first.

Cost-Plus Method. From time to time, off-premise caterers may be requested to cater a special event where the client wishes to provide some or all of the food. An example is the grand opening of a supermarket, for which the supermarket provides the food, but requires the off-premise caterer's expertise in executing the event. In this case, the caterer may charge a flat fee for time, expertise, and profit. The amount should be at least what the caterer would normally earn on an event of similar magnitude. Above the flat fee, the caterer would simply charge the client cost for labor, equipment, miscellaneous food expenses, and other specific costs for the event.

Range Pricing Method. This method is used when off-premise caterers are quoting prices for an event in the distant future, when costs may be uncertain. For example, when quoting a price for a Florida stone crab dinner or a Maine lobster dinner two years in advance, there is no sure way of knowing the cost of these fresh seafood items two years out. In such instances off-premise caterers may wish to simply quote a price range, which would include both best-case and worst-case scenarios.

Package Price. A package price includes all components necessary to produce an event, including food, beverage setups, staffing, equipment, music, flowers, and so on. Package prices should be designed for a minimum number of guests, because the price is determined per person. If there are fewer people than the minimum, there will be insufficient revenue to cover costs and produce profits.

Here's an example of a package price for 100 guests:

100 dinners at $15 per person	$1,500
100 beverage mixers and ice at $2 per person	200
Staffing	750
Equipment	1,000
Band	750
Flowers	300
Total (before tax and other charges)	$4,500

Here, the caterer may wish to price this package at $44.95 per person, for a minimum of 100 guests.

✕ Conclusion

The first subhead in this chapter says it all: "Pricing for Profit." Now you've seen a number of ways to cost and price parties. Successful and profitable off-premise caterers develop pricing strategies that work within their markets, and they are constantly aware of changes within their marketplaces that affect their price strategies. Their pricing, in turn, must reflect these changes. They must also know how to purchase intelligently to minimize food costs and maximize profit. We'll talk more about purchasing in Chapter 11.

✖ Chapter 11

Purchasing, Receiving, and Storing Foods

This chapter addresses techniques for purchasing, receiving, and storing foods. Poor execution in these areas can mean the difference between financial success and failure. Thousands of dollars a year can easily be lost by purchasing mistakes, as well as by failure to properly receive and store the merchandise you've purchased. This chapter will provide readers with the knowledge necessary for competence in these areas.

✖ Purchasing

Those who purchase foods for off-premise catered events need to know how to compute yields. For instance, how many Caesar salads can be produced from one case of romaine lettuce? How many heads of romaine are there in a case? Without knowledge in this area, how can a caterer purchase a sufficient quantity of romaine for a dinner party of 50 guests who will be served Caesar salad as a first course?

Product specifications, such as Prime and Choice beef, define the various qualities and forms of products. For example, when preparing shrimp salad, purchasing shrimp pieces or broken shrimp will be less expensive than buying whole shrimp. For beef stew, stew meat is more practical and less expensive than top sirloin butt.

Learning to correctly time your purchases is another important element of the purchasing function. Purchasers should know the shelf lives of products and understand how these products will be used by the culinary staff. A whole frozen turkey received on the day of the party for which it will be cooked will create turmoil in the kitchen. More lead time is needed so that the turkey may first be thawed properly and safely. Fresh strawberries to be used with a saboyan sauce, however, should not be received until the day of the party.

Off-premise caterers should realize that the goals of purchasing should be:

- To order the proper product
- In the correct quality and quantity
- At the best possible price
- To be delivered at the right time
- From a reputable supplier

Ethics in Purchasing

Many off-premise caterers purchase food and other products themselves, since they realize the importance of savings in this area. Others concentrate on other areas of their businesses and delegate this function to a staff member. In the latter case, the caterer should insist upon ethical purchasing practices. These include:

- Purchasers should be prohibited from accepting personal gifts of more than a specific dollar value. For example, during the holidays, a purchaser may accept a gift valued at no more than $50 from a supplier.
- Purchasers should show no one supplier favoritism and should buy from the best-qualified suppliers.
- Purchasers should not make personal purchases from suppliers for themselves or other catering company employees.
- In a bidding situation, the order should be awarded to the lowest bidder who meets the company specifications for the product.

Determining Purchasing Needs

Purchasing for off-premise catered events differs from purchasing for restaurants because caterers know the number of guests that are expected and their menus. Purchasing needs are determined by reviewing the catering menus for a certain period of time. Many off-premise caterers work on a week-to-week basis for major meat, poultry, seafood, and dry-store items, and daily for breads, produce, fresh fish, and other perishables. For example, each Monday morning, a purchasing agent may review the needs for the forthcoming week, starting with the following Wednesday, through the weekend, and for parties on Monday and Tuesday of the following week. All major needs for various parties are consolidated, and bids are received for these items. Produce and other perishable items should be ordered and received as close as possible to the time of use.

A typical purchasing mistake is the failure to check the amounts of products on hand in inventory before ordering. Frequently, purchasers order items that are not truly needed. It takes only a few minutes to check current inventories. Another mistake is ordering in too large a quantity. If the party requires only six heads of romaine, why order a whole case (24 heads)? If you only use three dozen eggs for a two-week period, why order a 30-dozen case from a wholesaler? It is normally better to pay a few cents a dozen more at a supermarket than to pay a bit less per dozen but have 27 dozen extra eggs taking up refrigeration space and tying up money.

In these and other cases, off-premise caterers are often better off going to a local supermarket or wholesale club and picking up these products, rather than ordering from suppliers who deliver only in larger-than-needed quantities.

Savvy off-premise caterers maintain very low inventory levels. They buy only the products they need. They realize that unneeded foods in inventory represent money that could be utilized elsewhere. They also realize that the more foods on hand, the more likely it is for theft to occur. It is simply much easier to control and inventory smaller supplies of foods.

Some large-volume caterers buy certain foods in bulk, but only when savings are significant, when they have available cash to pay for these items, and when they have sufficient, secure storage for these products. No matter how good the deal may appear to be, set limits for yourself—buy in bulk only when you are able to save 20 percent or more on the regular price, and only if you plan to use the items within a three-month period.

Purchasing Specifications

Purchasing specifications, like those shown in Exhibit 11.1, must be developed in writing for each menu item. Although this is time-consuming, the results can save off-premise caterers thousands of dollars annually. Purchase specifications for products should include:

- The intended use of the product
- Both general and detailed descriptions of the product to be purchased
    The exact product name
    The brand or manufacturer's name
    The U.S. product grade (or equivalent)
    The size of the product (container size, number of items in a carton, or weight of the package)
    For produce, the color, degree of ripeness, and type of trim
- Any other exact specifications
    The way you want the product packaged ("16-ounce resealable containers," "moisture-proof fiberboard containers," "packed in ice in reusable plastic bins," etc.)
    Storage requirements ("unrefrigerated," "frozen," etc.)

The key point to remember when developing purchasing specifications is to buy sufficient quality to meet the menu needs—no more, or less. For example, caterers who specialize in Prime beef must buy USDA Prime beef, whereas other caterers who specialize in deli platters will not need to order Prime beef. Caterers who specialize in pasta will produce their own rather than buy prepared pasta products.

Selecting Suppliers

When selecting suppliers, caterers generally have a large number from which to choose. To select the proper suppliers, learn whatever you can about their honesty and business reputation, product knowledge, inventory lists (will they have what you want, or can they get it quickly enough?), and pricing policies.

❌ **Exhibit 11.1** *Sample Product Specs (Source: Andrew Hale Feinstein and John M. Stefanelli, Purchasing: Selection and Procurement for the Hospitality Industry, Sixth Edition. ©2004. This material is used by permission of John Wiley & Sons, Inc.)*

Note how the specifications vary slightly, depending on the type of product being requested.

Red Delicious apples	Cauliflower, white
Used for fruit plate item	Used for side dish for all entrées
U.S. Fancy	U.S. No. 1 (high)
Washington State	12 count
30- to 42-lb. crate	18- to 25-lb. carton
Moisture-proof fiberboard	Moisture-proof fiberboard
Layered arrangement, cell carton	Loose pack or slab pack
Whole apples	Pretrimmed heads
Fresh, refrigerated	Fresh, refrigerated
Fully ripened	Fully ripened

Examples of fresh produce product specifications.

Fresh shell eggs	Broiler/fryer, raw
Used for fried, poached, scrambled eggs	Used for fried chicken lunch entrée
U.S. Grade A (high)	U.S. Grade A
Large size	Quarter chicken parts, cut from whole
30 dozen (full case)	birds weighing between $2\frac{1}{2}$ and
Moisture-proof carton	$3\frac{1}{4}$ lb. dressed weight
12 flats per case, $2\frac{1}{2}$ dozen per flat	No variety meats
White shell	Ice packed in reusable plastic tubs
Refrigerated	Approximately 30 lb. per tub

Examples of egg and poultry product specifications.

Australian lobster tails	New York strip steak
Used for dinner entrée	Used for dinner entrée
U.S. Grade A (or equivalent)	IMPS Number 1180
16/20 count	USDA Choice (High Choice)
25-lb. moisture-proof, vapor-proof	Cut from USDA Yield Grade 2 carcass
container	Dry-aged 14 to 21 days
Layered pack	12-oz. portion cut
Frozen	Individually wrapped in plastic film
	Layered pack
	10- to 12-lb. case
	Refrigerated

Examples of seafood and meat product specifications.

Off-premise caterers should choose suppliers who are known to sell clean, fresh, uncontaminated food products. Suppliers to the catering professional must be "user-friendly," providing extra service when unusual situations arise—and they certainly do. When clients add extra guests at the last minute, you need suppliers who can respond quickly. Reliable delivery is crucial to off-premise caterers, who are always working with deadlines, and this includes convenient delivery times. A meat delivery promised and expected at 9:00 A.M. will do no good if it arrives at 2:00 P.M. Excuses about traffic and mechanical problems cannot normally be tolerated. Timing is everything!

Many successful off-premise caterers think of their suppliers as partners. The relationships between such partners should be honest and up-front. Each should share and respect the policies of the other. When requesting quotations, off-premise caterers should give reasonable purchase estimates. For example, a caterer who expects to spend $20,000 per year for dry goods should give this estimate to the supplier, rather than overestimate to receive a potentially lower price. Suppliers and their drivers should be treated with respect and courtesy. They are indeed partners in an off-premise caterer's success.

How many suppliers are enough? The answer to this question will vary from one caterer to the next. Some choose to deal with only a few suppliers, but most buy from hundreds of sources every year, which gives them greater flexibility and control over pricing and quality. Recently, a few major suppliers who originally sold dry goods, supplies, and frozen foods have added meat, fish, and fresh produce to their product lists, offering essentially one-stop shopping for off-premise caterers and other foodservice companies.

The savings are extraordinary for caterers who shop at wholesale clubs, such as Costco, or at stores that sell exclusively to restaurants, such as Restaurant Depot. Savings of 20 percent or more are possible, as long as you're willing to devote the time necessary to search for these outlets, select the merchandise, and transport it to the commissary yourself. Large-volume caterers are also able to save money on purchasing by negotiating volume purchasing agreements with major foodservice suppliers. Smaller caterers do not have that kind of leverage, so they're better off buying from wholesale clubs. For meats, produce, fish, seafood, and dry goods, it is advisable to select two or three suppliers that meet your product standards (as outlined in your written specifications), and request bids for the majority of purchases. Food-product requirements for last-minute items, or for those in very small quantities, are normally picked up at a nearby supermarket or wholesale club.

Purchasing Meat

Off-premise caterers may purchase meat from three basic sources:

- Local retail markets are good for emergency purchases, but comparatively very expensive.
- A local butcher can buy meat by the case, break up the case lot, and cut the meat to satisfy a caterer's requirements. Such purveyors are responsive to caterers'

needs and are less expensive than local retail markets, but more expensive than meat distributors.

■ Meat distributors buy meat directly from the meat packer and then sell it to off-premise caterers by the case. They do not break up case lots.

It is recommended that each off-premise caterer obtain a copy of *The Meat Buyers Guide*, from the National Association of Meat Purveyors, Tucson, Arizona, 1991. By using this pictorial guide, caterers in all geographical areas of the United States are able to readily identify all cuts of beef, lamb, pork, and veal.

Purchasing Produce

Fresh fruits and vegetables are available from a variety of produce distributors, who buy directly from farming companies, produce packers, and local produce markets. These distributors deliver most orders that meet their minimum quantities, and they offer competitive prices. Most cities have at least one wholesale produce market where buyers may go and select fresh produce from a variety of wholesalers who display their products for viewing. Those who buy in this fashion can easily save 30 percent or more; however, the caterer must make time to shop and must have a vehicle in which to transport the produce. An alternative for the busy caterer is a "wagon-jobber," who buys directly from the produce market based on the orders received from clients and then delivers these orders to catering companies and other clients.

For more information on buying fruits and vegetables, visit this website: whatscookingamerica.net/BuyingGuide.htm.

Purchasing Fish and Seafood

Frozen fish and seafood are available from the major national wholesalers; fresh fish and seafood are sold by local firms who specialize almost exclusively in these products. Caterers located in cities that border oceans, gulfs, and rivers may buy fresh fish from local fishermen who sell their daily catches at the wharfs. It is always more desirable to use fresh rather than frozen fish when budgets permit, but it's hard to price—fish costs depend on the season, weather conditions, and overall demand. Some of the more popular fresh fish include salmon, swordfish, halibut, grouper, dolphin (the fish, not the mammal), haddock, snapper, trout (both freshwater and saltwater), bass (both freshwater and saltwater), tuna, and scrod (young cod). The popularity of fish varies from region to region, based on local preferences and availability.

Most off-premise caterers purchase at least some of their seafood in a frozen state—usually scallops, lobster tails, and shrimp. Whole Maine lobsters and stone crab claws are always purchased fresh. Sea scallops are sold by size, such as 20–30 count, which means there are 20 to 30 scallops, on average, per pound. Lobster tails are sold by size: 4- to 6-ounce tails, or 6- to 8-ounce tails.

For most off-premise caterers, shrimp is the most frequently used seafood. Like scallops, shrimp are sold by size, also called counts. For example, "16–20 count" means that there are 16 to 20 shrimp per pound. The range goes from "U-10," under 10 per pound, the largest shrimp, to 300–500, the smallest. The most common product form is green, headless shrimp, which is raw, with head off and shell on. Off-premise caterers with limited facilities should investigate cooked shrimp for use in cold shrimp cocktails and hors d'oeuvres. There are some excellent products on the market that taste as good as fresh-cooked, cost no more, save labor, and are always consistent. (Every off-premise caterer at one time or another has overcooked shrimp.) These shrimp are always cooked to perfection.

Using Purchase Orders

A *purchase order* (or PO) is a written order form used by off-premise caterers to document and verify orders placed for food and supplies. It is most highly recommended as a means of control for large-volume caterers. Smaller firms may also wish to use purchase orders to keep track of their orders and receipts. Most firms at least have an in-house form listing their purchasing needs by categories that can be used as an order form, but these forms do not replace purchase orders as a form of control.

How many copies of each purchase order are sufficient? This depends on the operational and bookkeeping needs, but some successful food operators report that a four-part form works well. Copy distribution works as follows:

- Original copy   Mailed or faxed to supplier
- Second copy   Sent to accounting for control
- Third copy   Sent to receiving department and kept until foods arrive. Upon receipt of goods, this copy is signed and forwarded to accounting with the invoice
- Fourth copy   Kept in purchasing

Purchase orders should always be numbered in advance to ensure control over the number of purchase orders issued by the company and to prevent employees from issuing unauthorized purchase orders. A PO should include the following information:

- Date the order was placed
- Payment terms
- The supplier's name, address, and fax number
- The off-premise caterer's name, address, and address for delivery
- Description, quantity, and quoted unit cost of each item ordered
- Blank column for the person receiving the merchandise to document the quantity of each item received
- Quoted prices; these should be extended and totaled on the purchase order after the merchandise has been received, and compared with the invoice; discrepancies should be reconciled with the supplier immediately.
- Signature of the purchaser and that of the person receiving the merchandise

Exhibit 11.2 is a sample purchase order form.

Any office supply store will have purchase order forms already made up, or you can easily create your own template on a computer. Another good source for information about purchase orders and other purchasing functions is *Purchasing: Selection and Procurement for the Hospitality Industry, 6th Edition*, by Andrew H. Feinstein and

❌ **Exhibit 11.2** *Sample Purchase Order Form*

PURCHASE ORDER NUMBER 0001

ORDERED BY:
ABC OFF-PREMISE CATERING FIRM
MAIN STREET
ANYWHERE, USA
FAX NUMBER

ORDERED FROM:
BEST SUPPLIER
MAIN STREET
ANYWHERE, USA
FAX NUMBER

ORDER DATE_____ DELIVERY DATE_____ PAYMENT TERMS_____

QUANTITY ORDERED	DESCRIPTION	QUANTITY RECEIVED	UNIT COST	TOTAL COST

GRAND TOTAL

SIGNATURE OF AUTHORIZED PURCHASER _____

RECEIVED AS NOTED ABOVE _____
(RECEIVING AGENT)

John M. Stefanelli, published by John Wiley & Sons, 2004, from which our sample product specs have been taken.

Tips for Effective Purchasing

Generally speaking, the purchaser wants to pay as little as possible, the seller wants to receive as much as possible, and the agreed-upon price is somewhere between these two extremes. *Market prices* for food items are based on the general supply and demand for any given product—as Christmas approaches, the demand for meats may increase while supplies either remain constant or decrease, resulting in higher meat prices.

There are a few good overall practices that should result in lower food purchasing costs:

Edible Portion Cost. A sharp caterer realizes that the lowest price is not always the least expensive. Think about it in terms of cost per serving, or *edible portion cost.*

For example, when purchasing meats, the least expensive cuts also contain more fat and bones and must be trimmed, which involves a labor expense to perform the additional butchering chores. Other inexpensive cuts may be too tough to eat or take too much time (and waste energy) in slow-cooking them to compensate. You may be wiser to buy cuts that are trimmed of fat and bone and are ready to cook, thus saving labor and energy expenses and resulting in a lower edible-portion cost.

The Make-or-Buy Decision. Off-premise caterers should carefully analyze their menus and determine which items to make in-house and which items to buy from suppliers. This question applies to things like pasta, breads, desserts, mayonnaise, dressings, and some sauces. For example, the cost of ingredients to make bread and pasta is a fraction of the price paid for prepared products; however, other factors enter into the make-or-buy decision:

- Is the necessary equipment available to make the product?
- If equipment is not available, what is the cost to purchase it?
- Is there skilled labor available? What is the cost?
- What are the quality considerations? Will a product made in-house be of superior quality to that which can be purchased?
- Is this product so unusual that the only alternative is to prepare it in-house since no supplier handles it?
- How does producing products in-house relate to the overall operation?
- What impact will it have on other commissary functions?

Competitive Bidding. It is critical to obtain competitive bids from at least three suppliers for most purchases, and to buy from the lowest bidder who meets your written specifications for a product. Exhibit 11.3 is a sample competitive bidding form for produce. Many caterers become comfortable dealing with certain suppliers, and soon they stop obtaining bids. Once preferred suppliers realize that there is no bidding for business, they are free to increase their prices. Competitive bids will help keep food costs under control.

Focus on Center-of-the-Plate Items. Because time is money, it makes sense to spend more time negotiating prices for the "major" items—seafood, meat, and poultry—than for salt or sugar (unless, of course, you're making potato chips by the ton, or candy by the truckload).

Can You Do Better? In a purchasing situation, it never hurts to ask certain suppliers if they can do better. This practice gives suppliers an opportunity to offer an extra incentive or give a discount. The worst case is that the supplier will say no, but it may be surprising how frequently suppliers will negotiate a better deal. Remember, your business and trust are valuable commodities to them.

Less Service for a Lower Price. Certain suppliers will offer lower prices as long as deliveries are limited to certain days. Some paper goods suppliers offer lower prices, but deliver only once or twice a month. Frequently, supermarkets and wholesale clubs offer better prices than those suppliers who deliver. An example is the

⊠ **Exhibit 11.3** *Quote Sheet*

PREPARED BY _____

DATE _____

PRICE QUOTES

ITEM / GRADE	UNIT OF PURCHASE	COMPANY A	COMPANY B	COMPANY C
APPLES, EXTRA FANCY, 88 COUNT	DOZEN/CASE			
AVOCADOS, HASS, 48 COUNT	DOZEN/CASE			
BANANAS (40# PER CASE)	POUND/CASE			
BROCCOLI, CALIFORNIA, 14 COUNT	POUND/CASE			
CABBAGE, RED, LARGE HEADS	POUND/50# BAG			
CABBAGE, WHITE, LARGE HEADS	POUND/50# BAG			
CARROTS, CALIFORNIA, JUMBO	POUND/50# BAG			
CAULIFLOWER, CALIFORNIA, 12 PER CASE	POUND/CASE			
CELERY, CALIFORNIA, 24 COUNT	STALK/CASE			
CUCUMBERS, SUPER SELECT	POUND/BUSHEL			
EGGPLANT, FANCY	POUND/BUSHEL			
GARLIC, JUMBO (30# PER CASE)	POUND/CASE			
GRAPEFRUIT, PINK, FLORIDA, 18 COUNT	DOZEN/CASE			
GRAPES, RED, CALIFORNIA, EXFANCY	POUND/CASE			
GRAPES, WHITE, CALIFORNIA, EXFANCY	POUND/CASE			
LETTUCE, LEAF, DOLE CALIFORNIA, FANCY	HEAD/CASE			
LETTUCE, ICEBERG, DOLE CALIFORNIA, FANCY	HEAD/CASE			
LETTUCE, ROMAINE, DOLE CALIFORNIA, FANCY	HEAD/CASE			
LEEKS, CALIFORNIA	BUNCH/CASE (24 BUNCHES/CASE)			
LEMONS, SUNKIST, US#1, 165/CASE	DOZEN/CASE			
LIMES, US#1, 150–160/CASE	DOZEN/CASE			
MELONS, CANTALOUPE, FANCY, 15/CASE	EACH/CASE			
MELONS, HONEYDEW, FANCY, 15/CASE	EACH/CASE			
MUSHROOMS, US#1, WASHED, 10# BASKET	POUND/BASKET			
ONIONS, JUMBO, SPANISH	POUND/50# BAG			
ORANGES, CALIFORNIA, 56/CASE	DOZEN/CASE			
PARSLEY, CALIFORNIA	BUNCH/DOZEN			
PEARS, ANJOU	POUND			
PEPPERS, GREEN BELL	POUND/CASE			
PEPPERS, RED	POUND/CASE			
PINEAPPLES, DOLE, 7/CASE	EACH/CASE			
POTATOES, IDAHO, 90/CASE	POUND/CASE			
POTATOES, BOILING	POUND/50# BAG			
RADISHES, POLY BAG	BAG/DOZEN			
SCALLIONS, BUNCH	BUNCH/DOZEN			
SHALLOTS	POUND/5# BAG			
SPINACH, CALIFORNIA, FLAT LEAF	POUND/10# CASE			
TOMATOES, VINE RIPENED, 5 × 6	POUND/18# BOX			
WATERCRESS	BUNCH/DOZEN			
WATERMELON, EXTRA LARGE, JUBILEE	EACH			

price of soft drinks, which are invariably less expensive at supermarkets and clubs. Off-premise caterers must determine if the savings are worth the time spent shopping for and transporting these bargain-priced items.

Less Expensive with No Adverse Effect on Quality. Basically, purchasers should buy the least-expensive product that will not reduce the quality of the end food product. Remember those broken shrimp pieces for dishes like shrimp salad? They're less expensive than whole shrimp and the end result is just as tasty. Random-packed boneless chicken breasts (which are not of uniform weight) can be used for many chicken dishes rather than breasts of uniform size, which are significantly more expensive. Ungraded tomatoes can be used for marinara sauce instead of paying extra for those that are graded.

Seasonality. Caterers should brush up on the seasonality of particular items. For example, there are times during the year when it is less expensive to use limes than lemons. In the late fall, fresh strawberries are expensive and generally not of good quality.

Pay with Cash. Certain suppliers offer discounts for cash purchases.

Price Trend Speculation. Some off-premise caterers who use large quantities of certain items become successful at speculating on prices. Let's say you expect to use 2,000 pounds of shrimp in the next three months. If you have the cash flow to do it, you can consider buying all 2,000 pounds now if you learn that the price is expected to increase.

Purchase in Larger Units. Larger units of purchase are usually less expensive than smaller units. Flour sold in 100-pound bags is less expensive per pound than in 10-pound bags. However, be careful not to overbuy. You can't afford spoilage and high inventory levels.

Special Promotions. Frequently, suppliers offer special promotions that can result in significant savings. Also ask your suppliers for value-added services, such as marketing and promotion ideas, recipe and presentation suggestions, and so on. This too is part of building a feeling of partnership that, in turn, builds business for both caterer and supplier.

Go to the Market. Significant savings are available to those who shop at wholesale clubs and local volume-purchase markets. Caterers who do this need time and transportation, but many report purchase savings of 50 percent or more.

Take Advantage of Rebate Programs. Many major brands offer rebate programs. These are available through distributors, as well as through outlets such as Restaurant Depot. Many caterers are not aware of these programs because sales reps are reluctant to take on the additional paperwork.

Buy Generic Products. Many generic products are produced by the same manufacturers who produce the brand names, but at a fraction of the cost.

Purchasing Tips from Caterers

Here are some tips from members of Leading Caterers of America (www.leadingcaterers. com):

- Bryan Young, of Catering Plus in St. Louis, buys shrimp by the case and saves 3 to 5 percent; he uses red leaf lettuce and kale for garnishes and underliners, enabling him to buy in case lots.
- Frank James, of Captain Wishbone Catering in Detroit, buys only what he needs and has it delivered the day it's need for prep.
- Elizabeth Silverman, of Lovables Catering in Miami, does her own shopping at Restaurant Depot, Sam's, and Jetro, rather than from Sysco/Henry Lee, where prices are higher. This way, she says, she buys only what she needs.
- Ben Bloom, of La Cuisine in Brandford, Connecticut, has negotiated a Master Distribution Agreement (MDA) with his primary supplier. In return for a commitment of 90 percent of his purchasing volume, he locks in a fixed percentage of cost from the distributor. For example, markups of 4 percent on meat and 8 percent on produce are written into the deal. He has the right to audit distributors' invoices as needed to verify that the cost of the product conforms to the agreement. Even when items are placed on special and the MDA price is higher, he's able to negotiate the price down. This system has worked well for him for more than five years, and the distributor has given him a laptop to order directly and to check pricing.
- Candace Voorhees, of Arizona Taste Catering in Phoenix, is able to buy in larger quantities to save money by using similar or the same menus on the same days for two or more events.
- Jeff Kerne, at FoodThoughts in northern New Jersey, shops at a farmers market that sells by the case and saves 20 to 30 percent. He also uses Restaurant Depot, goes to distributor shows for discounts on preorders and show specials, and uses miles on his credit cards for purchasing.
- Sam Sears, of South-Van Events in Central Kentucky, uses random chicken breast, and mixes in boneless thigh meat, for recipes that don't call for all white meat.
- Creig Balletine, of Creative Cooking in Phoenixville, Pennsylvania, asks his sales reps for suggestions on how he can lower his costs. He also suggests forming buying groups within certain geographical areas for more clout.
- Michel Malecot, of The French Gourmet in San Diego, uses a Costco Executive member American Express Card for his purchases and last January earned a rebate of nearly $3,000. He also uses beef shoulder clod (cut from the rib area) for his traditional beef station and beef sirloin tips for carving stations. He buys filet tails from a local meat company that cuts for portion control, and makes 4-ounce tenderloin medallions for about $5 per pound.
- Jani Janowick, of Big Ten Subs and Salads in Columbus, Ohio, buys salad items based on the seasons and ensures that his customers are familiar with this so that the menu changes on a regular basis.

- Caryn Hasslocher, of Fresh Horizons in San Antonio, Texas, analyzes all costs related to food and soft-goods items. She recently bought random sausage pieces for $1.52 per pound to accommodate a barbecue for 2,200 guests. Like Sam Sears, she combines thigh meat with random chicken breast meat for a cost-effective and flavorful mix at a 60/40 ratio. She has also just ordered a usage report from her main supplier to track pricing over the last year, and can use it as a negotiating tool for this coming year.
- Katherine Farrell, of Katherine's Catering in Ann Arbor, Michigan, outsources certain food items during busy times to save on staff overtime hours and prevent burnout. These include baked good, desserts, and prepackaged hors d'oeuvres. During the busy holiday season, she also limits her menu choices in order to buy specific things in larger quantities, as well as improve overall efficiency.

Learning how to negotiate prices, terms, and features will pay huge dividends in the long run, particularly when making major purchases, negotiating leases, or even with clients regarding their parties, weddings, and events. A good resource for this is www.e-learningcenter.com/negotiating.htms.

✂ Receiving

In regard to the purchasing function, *receiving* means accepting the shipments you have ordered for your business. The cardinal rule for this responsibility is that the person who orders merchandise should not be the one to receive it, unless he or she is the sole owner of the catering company. There are just too many opportunities for collusion between the purchaser and the supplier when the purchaser is also the receiver. A purchaser may indicate that certain goods were received when they were not, and then receive a kickback or other reward from the supplier; "extra" goods can "disappear" without being accounted for on purchase orders; and so on. It is essential to have at least two people involved in the all-important receiving function.

Many off-premise caterers make the mistake of not employing a qualified receiving employee—qualified, that is, to be sure the goods that were ordered are actually the goods that are now being delivered, with no scrimping on quantity or quality. The receiving person may have other duties (not purchasing), but should be thoroughly trained in product knowledge by the chef, catering company owner, or purchaser. When in doubt about the quality of a product, the receiver should consult with the chef, owner, or manager before signing for receipt of the merchandise, because it is always easier to reconcile problems with the supplier's delivery driver present. The driver can return the inferior or incorrect product, rather than leave it at the commissary where it must be stored or could even be used in error.

Those who receive food, supplies, and rental equipment should be extremely particular about checking and inspecting for quality and quantity. Successful caterers do not accept products that do not meet their standards. Even when receiving rental equipment, they check all items to make sure the correct quantity is being delivered. They open containers and inspect glassware and china for cleanliness, chips, and cracks, flatware for corrosion or tarnish, chairs for cleanliness and stability (any cracked wooden chair legs, missing screws, nuts, or bolts?), linens for snags and tears, portable dance floors and stages for missing pieces, rough edges, and other unsafe conditions.

There are two reasons for being so particular: First, you expect to get exactly what you ordered, and in good condition. Second, you don't want the supplier, after an event, to charge the catering company for causing the damage to damaged goods. So the receiver can never be too particular. For this reason, deliveries should always be scheduled during slow periods of business so that all products can be carefully examined, weighed when necessary, and quickly moved to their proper storage areas.

In many cases, correct receiving can only be accomplished with the right equipment. The commissary must have a designated receiving area, usually a loading dock that can accommodate delivery trucks. Receiving requirements include:

- Sturdy scales that are large enough to weigh items that arrive in bulk.
- Temperature probes to check temperatures of incoming fresh foods.
- Pallets (low, raised wooden platforms) on which cases or boxes can be stacked and stored. Pallets keep products off ground level and can be moved with a pallet jack or, in larger operations, a small forklift.
- Utility carts and hand trucks for moving small stacks of cases.
- Extra boxes and bags, in case questionable items must be stored and kept out of inventory until a supplier can be contacted.
- Shelves on which to organize and stack items.

The temperatures of foods received in refrigerated shipments should always be checked. Chilled products should be at least 45 degrees Fahrenheit, and frozen products below 0 degrees. Frozen seafood should be checked for excessive *glazing* (the ice encrusted on products like shrimp and lobster). Excessively glazed products should be returned, because your business does not include paying premium prices for frozen water, which increases the cost per pound of these already expensive commodities.

When receiving produce, inspect for ripeness, color, and cleanliness, as well as bruises, spoilage, and other adverse factors. Counts of produce items (like lemons and limes) are very important, and caterers should frequently count to ensure proper sizing. Items that do not meet or exceed standards are returned, and the receiver must insist that their supplier deliver the proper quality in time for the event. Of course, the best indication of produce quality is taste.

Off-premise caterers must first weigh all meat, fish, seafood, poultry, and any other product sold by weight. Often, short weights can result in direct losses on a catered event, or perhaps even running out of food. Packing ice should be removed before weighing poultry and fish (which are usually packed in ice). Short weights should be corrected by either a credit or delivery of additional product. After weighing, meats should be inspected to ensure they comply with specifications (your own written specs and those documented in *The Meat Buyers Guide*).

All meats should have been federally inspected, and their USDA stamp or verification can be confirmed in writing by the supplier. Meats that arrive in dirty, torn, damaged, or broken wrapping or boxes may be contaminated and should not be accepted. Any that smell sour or rancid should be rejected. Meat texture should be firm and elastic. Any meat that feels slimy, sticky, or dry should be rejected.

Fresh poultry should be kept below 45 degrees Fahrenheit and should be packed in crushed ice. Poultry that is purple or greenish in color should not be accepted, nor should any that smells bad, has darkened wing tips, or soft, flabby, sticky flesh.

Once fresh fish is weighed, it should be inspected for freshness, appearance, damaged flesh, and other signs. Fresh fish should always be packed in crushed ice and kept between 32 and 45 degrees Fahrenheit. Signs of freshness include clear eyes, bright skin, tight scales, bright red gills, firm, elastic flesh, and a fresh, not "fishy," odor.

Fresh and frozen seafood must be checked for quality and proper sizing. Often, the size on the label is not what happens to be in the container. For example, 5-pound boxes of raw frozen headless shrimp that are graded 16–20 count should contain between 80 and 100 shrimp per box, with an average of 90 per box. This number is obtained by multiplying 5 pounds (in the box) times the minimum, average, and maximum counts of shrimp per pound (16, 18, and 20, respectively). These counts are important, because they ultimately determine menu costs and selling prices for shrimp. If there are too few shrimp in the box, it may mean that the shrimp are larger than they should be, or that when they were frozen, too much water was frozen along with them. In this instance, the caterer's actual cost per shrimp will be more than specified. If the shrimp are too small, the costs will be lower per shrimp, but the client will not receive the size of shrimp promised by the caterer.

The standard pack for green headless shrimp is a 5-pound net weight block. With ice and packaging, the gross weight is generally 6 to 7 pounds. Two-kilo blocks are also sold, and off-premise caterers should be aware of paying for 5 pounds when they are receiving only 2 kilos (4.4 pounds). Cooked, individually quick-frozen (IQF) shrimp are packed in plastic bags weighing from 1 to 30 pounds, and they should also be checked for weight and proper sizing upon receipt.

Milk and dairy products should be checked for temperature, (40 degrees Fahrenheit), expiration dates, smell, and appearance. Cheese should be rejected if it is discolored, excessively moldy, or dried out. Cheese rinds should be undamaged.

Eggs are checked for cracks and excessive dirt. Eggs' temperature (40 degrees Fahrenheit) may be checked by breaking one and measuring the temperature of the yolk. Acceptable eggs will have firm yolks and no noticeable odor, and the whites will cling to the yolks.

Frozen foods should be checked for signs of thawing and refreezing—large ice crystals, ice at the bottom of a carton, and deformed containers. All frozen foods should be received at temperatures below 0 degrees Fahrenheit.

Canned foods should be checked for leakage, broken seals, dents along seams, rust, and missing labels—not only upon receipt, but again before using. Dry foods, such as sugar, cereal, flour, and dried beans, should be completely dry when received, and their packages must not have any broken seals or holes.

A common receiving discrepancy: There's a difference between the invoiced amount and the amount received. For instance, the invoice reports 70 pounds of Choice beef tenderloin, but upon weighing, there are only 68 pounds. This must be noted on the invoice, initialed by the receiving agent and the delivery driver, and immediately reported to the supplier for proper credit. The receiver must be absolutely sure to note all discrepancies on all invoices so that the bookkeeper can pay the proper amount. Carelessness in this area is very costly and cannot be tolerated. (Two pounds of tenderloin at $6 per pound is $12, so more than $600 per year would be saved by proper verification if this discrepancy occurred once a week.) There are lots of similar situations, and your receiving person must have a combination of people skills and professional knowledge to handle them without alienating the suppliers.

Receiving personnel should be required to submit all invoices daily to the book-keeping office, because discrepancies can be resolved more easily as they occur, or within a day or two. Trying to reconstruct what occurred on December 1, when it is January 10 of the following year, is virtually impossible.

✕ Storage

The following storage guidelines for foodservice operators are recommended by the National Assessment Institute. Off-premise caterers should comply with all of these standards in order to meet normal sanitation and food-handling standards.

Refrigerated Foods

Refrigerator temperatures should be kept below 45 degrees Fahrenheit. Place thermometers in several areas of the refrigerator where they can be easily read and checked often. Check the internal temperatures of refrigerated foods on a regular basis to make sure the foods are kept at 45 degrees Fahrenheit or less.

- Always refrigerate fresh meat, poultry, and fish.
- Cover stored foods to prevent contamination from other products or direct contact with refrigerator shelves.
- Fresh fish should be stored in crushed ice and kept well drained.
- If possible, provide separate refrigerators for different types of foods. If different foods must be stored in the same unit, store meats, fish, and dairy foods in the coldest part.
- To prevent cross contamination, be sure that prepared foods are stored above raw foods.
- Do not store packaged food and wrapped sandwiches where they can get wet.
- Do not overload the refrigerator. Packing too much food into it can raise the temperature of the entire unit.
- Do not store refrigerated foods on the floor of a walk-in refrigerator.
- Food packages should be stored so that cold air can circulate around all surfaces of the containers.

Frozen Foods

- Keep the temperature range for frozen foods between 0 and −10 degrees Fahrenheit.
- Never thaw and refreeze frozen foods.

- Do not thaw foods at room temperature.
- Keep frozen foods in moistureproof packaging.
- Use the "first in, first out" rule.
- Store frozen foods to allow for air circulation between packages.
- Do not freeze large quantities of unfrozen foods. This can raise the temperature of the entire unit and damage stored foods.
- Defrost freezers regularly.
- Be sure that foods do not thaw during the defrost cycle of self-defrosting freezers.

Dry Goods

- Apply the "first in, first out" rule.
- Keep foods in dry storage tightly covered and protected from contamination.
- Remember that cereals and pasta deteriorate rapidly, as do canned foods containing products that are high in acid, such as tomatoes.
- Keep these storage areas well ventilated and well lighted.
- Store foods at least 6 inches off the floor in a way that allows adequate air circulation.
- Store items on ventilated shelves.
- Install window coverings or frosted glass to reduce heat and exposure to light.
- Cover all interior surfaces with easy-to-clean, corrosion-resistant materials.
- Do not allow smoking, eating, or drinking in dry-storage areas. Check with the local health department for specific rules.
- Do not store garbage in dry-storage areas.
- Seal walls and baseboards to help keep out pests. Keeping the area clean and well maintained will discourage pests.[1]

✗ Payment Policies

Invoices for purchases should be paid when they are due. There is generally no advantage to those off-premise caterers who pay their bills early, unless a discount is offered by the supplier. Excess cash can, of course, be invested to earn interest. Caterers who regularly pay their bills past the due dates will be faced with higher prices and poorer-quality products, as well as late payment fees and interest charges. They'll also waste valuable time answering suppliers' phone calls regarding payments. Slow payers lose their negotiating edge, since suppliers offer their best prices to good customers who pay on time. A few companies offer 1 or 2 percent discounts for those who pay early. Obviously, these are attractive terms and should be utilized.

The unfortunate reality of this type of business is that most off-premise caterers will, at one time or another, be faced with a cash shortage and find themselves unable to pay certain invoices when due. Rather than ignore the problem and wait for suppliers to call, it is far better to meet with the suppliers, inform them of the problems, and develop a suitable payment plan. Honesty and a sincere effort to pay promptly will maintain good supplier relationships—and remedy that feeling of dread every time the phone rings!

Astute off-premise caterers know that when making large purchases for equipment and large food orders, it is advantageous to first negotiate the price and then negotiate the terms for payment. Most suppliers, eager to conclude a sale, will offer better terms once the price is agreed upon because they wish to ensure that the sale is made.

An interesting way to deal with suppliers is an arrangement by which a caterer opens an account with a new purveyor, and the purveyor is not paid for any merchandise for 30 days. After the 30 days are up, the caterer pays the supplier each week for any invoices more than 30 days old. Many suppliers like this arrangement, because they can expect a check each and every week.

Whenever possible, purchases should be paid for by check. Frequently, off-premise caterers need cash to pay for emergency purchases or to pay suppliers who accept only cash. Petty cash funds are the answer to such cash-payment situations. Whenever petty cash is handled by employees other than the owner, certain rules should apply:

- Only one person should have access to the petty cash fund, which is kept secure at all times. This individual signs a receipt for the money upon withdrawing it.
- The fund should be established for an amount commensurate with the off-premise caterer's cash needs. This amount usually ranges from $100 to $400 and is never more than $1,000.
- The fund must be available at all times for an audit or spot check, and it must contain cash and receipts equal to the designated amount of the fund. Shortages are the responsibility of the person in charge of the fund.
- The fund is replenished by turning in the receipts to the bookkeeping office for a check to replace the total amount of the receipts.

The advantage of this system is that it pinpoints control and responsibility for the money. Only one person is responsible and accountable.

✕ Conclusion

If, as the expression goes, "the devil is in the details," things like product specifications and checking each and every incoming order are proof of it! These parts of daily business may seem like so much busywork at times, but they are ultimately done to save you money and prevent problems. Luckily, most purchasing- and inventory-related hassles can be overcome with simple common sense and, as you gain experience in your business, with some practical knowledge of sufficient quantities to order, market conditions, and good business relationships with your suppliers.

Notes

1. National Assessment Institute, *Handbook of Safe Food Service Management*, Regents/Prentice-Hall, pp. 60, 61, 62. Englewood Cliffs, New Jersey, 1994.

✕ Chapter 12

Sanitation and Safety

Sanitation and safety procedures are of paramount importance to anyone selling or serving food products. The safety of customers and staff members must always come first. The examples and procedures in this chapter should assist off-premise caterers in making their businesses as safe as possible and preparing for the consequences when adverse incidents occur.

Food poisoning is every caterer's nightmare. It can ruin a business overnight, and it can strike even the finest foodservice establishment. Over the years many advances have been made in food safety, but it seems that every time an advance is made in the war on foodborne illness, new threats emerge that are more difficult to defeat. In recent years, news headlines about so-called mad cow disease have had consumers thinking twice about beef consumption. And remember the *E. coli* scare in a popular quick-service restaurant chain? The periodic health scares about eating oysters tainted with *Vibrio* bacteria? Improper storage or preserving of foods at incorrect temperatures can also prompt the growth of *Salmonella, Botulinum,* and other illness-causing bacteria.

Foodborne illness costs the U.S. economy between $5 billion and $22 billion each year in lost productivity, hospitalization, long-term disability, and even death. Half of all foodborne outbreaks reported to the Centers for Disease Control (CDC) have no identifiable cause. However, more than 200 known diseases can be transmitted through food, and most of the outbreaks are due to microorganisms in food.[1]

The average cost of a foodborne illness outbreak to a foodservice operation exceeds $100,000, including the cost of legal representation and financial settlements to victims, so caterers should not skimp in this important area. Before identifying procedures for preventing food poisoning, let us examine the various types of foodborne illnesses and how they occur.

Common Causes of Foodborne Illness

Some of the most distressing food-related news since the 1980s has been the discovery of what is commonly called "mad cow disease"—*bovine spongiform encephalopathy*, or BSE. The first case of suspect meat traced to a particular infected cow in the United States was reported in December 2003. At this writing, scientists do not know exactly how BSE is transmitted, so they can't pinpoint it as a virus or a bacterium. What they do know is that cattle are infected by eating feed that contains tissue from the spine or brain of another animal. The trouble is that BSE can be dormant for several years before symptoms appear, so it is difficult to trace the cattle's feed sources.

In humans, infection with the misshapen BSE protein molecules may result in a variant of Creutzfeldt-Jakob disease (CJD), a serious brain-wasting illness. In Britain, where BSE was first discovered in the 1980s, 143 people died of CJD. The incredible panic that followed has resulted in nations around the world rethinking the way animals are fed, as well as the inspection procedures for feedlots, slaughterhouses, and meat processing plants. However, CJD is still extremely rare and also has other causes, not food-related.

With assistance from the University of Florida Department of Food Science and Human Nutrition, we discuss some of the more common types of food-related problems:

Bacteria are the main causes of foodborne illnesses, and they are found in many foods—milk, milk products, eggs, meat, poultry, fish, shellfish, and edible crustaceans—that have not been handled, inspected, or prepared properly. Most bacteria grow best at temperatures between 45 and 140 degrees Fahrenheit.

- *Bacillus cereus* is the basic bacterium type that causes gastroenteritis—cramps, stomach ache, vomiting, and diarrhea. It lives in soil and shows up in foods that begin as agricultural crops: potatoes, rice, pasta products, and vegetables, as well as milk and cheese products. In 2000, the CDC's Foodborne Outbreak Response and Surveillance Unit reported seven *Bacillus cereus* outbreaks in the United States.
- *Campylobacter* is a type of bacterium that lives in the intestines of healthy birds and infects poultry. The most frequent cause of this infection is eating undercooked chicken or other foods contaminated by contact with raw chicken. In 2000, there were 15 campylobacteriosis outbreaks in the United States.
- *Clostridium* is a family of bacteria whose effects include the deadly illness *botulism*, usually associated with improperly canned foods. Food from cans with severe dents, cans or jars with bulging tops, and cans with ends that spring back when pushed in should not be used, even if the food inside appears normal. There were two such outbreaks in the United States in 2000, but the CDC reported 20 outbreaks caused by a related (and luckily, far less serious) bacterium called *Clostridium perfringens*, which causes at least 10 percent of all U.S. outbreaks of foodborne illness. Meats, poultry, sauces, and casseroles are the main sources when they have been cooked, then cooled and/or reheated improperly, giving the bacteria a chance to grow.
- *Escherichia coli* is commonly known as *E. coli*. Most strains of this bacterium are harmless, but one (*E. coli* O157:H7) produces a powerful toxin that can cause

severe illness, through contaminated meat or milk products that have not been pasteurized or cooked sufficiently. Hamburgers, roast beef, and unpasteurized milk are the primary sources of human infection. Symptoms, which occur 12 to 24 hours after ingestion, include severe diarrhea, cramping, and dehydration; in toddlers or frail elderly consumers, it may also kill red blood cells and cause kidney failure. Cooking beef to an internal temperature of 155 degrees Fahrenheit kills *E. coli* bacteria. The Centers for Disease control estimate that *E. coli* O157:H7 causes 73,000 foodborne illnesses and about 60 deaths annually in the United States. In 2000, the CDC reported 27 *E. coli* outbreaks; 18 of them were *E. coli* O157:H7.

- *Listeria monocytogenes* (L.m.) is found in both processed and uncooked vegetables, as well as meats and dairy products. It grows in the soil and is also found in animal manure (which is sometimes used as fertilizer). The illness, called *listeriosis*, causes stomach cramps, diarrhea, nausea, fever, and about 500 deaths per year in the United States. The L.m. bacterium was the culprit in only two U.S. outbreaks in 2000.

- *Salmonella* microorganisms live in the intestines of birds, reptiles, and mammals, and they are passed to humans in poultry, red meat, shellfish, and eggs, as well as in prepared foods such as chicken, egg, and ham salads. *Salmonellosis* is the name of the illness; symptoms start 12 to 26 hours after eating the contaminated foods and include nausea, vomiting, cramps, and fever, and, in young children and elderly persons, other potentially fatal infections like septicemia and typhoid. Poor personal hygiene by food workers and working with equipment and utensils that have not been properly sanitized may cause salmonellosis. There were 112 outbreaks in the United States in 2000, according to the CDC.

- *Shigella* bacteria can be acquired by drinking (or swimming in) contaminated water or eating contaminated food. A person infected with *shigellosis* will have fever, cramps, diarrhea, and bloody stools for about a week, but may be infectious for another two weeks after the symptoms end. This is one reason hand washing is extremely important to prevent the spread of infection. The CDC reported 10 shigellosis outbreaks in 2000.

- There are several strains of *Vibrio* bacteria found in seawater, which can infect those who eat raw or undercooked shellfish. One type (*Vibrio cholerae*) causes cholera. *Vibrio vulnificus* can infect the bloodstream, and the disease can be fatal if contracted by someone with an immune system or liver deficiency. *Vibrio parahaemolyticus* is less serious and causes typical food poisoning symptoms for about three days. The CDC identified three *Vibrio* outbreaks in 2000, all caused by *Vibrio parahaemolyticus.*

- The bacterium *Yersinia enterocolitica* is passed to humans through raw or undercooked pork, untreated water, or milk that has not been pasteurized. *Yersiniosis* causes fever, cramps, and diarrhea, and symptoms may take four to seven days to surface, lasting up to three weeks. No *Yersinia* outbreaks were reported in 2000 by the CDC.

Viruses are spread by food handlers who do not wash their hands after using the restroom, sneezing, coughing, and touching their mouths with their hands. Foods that are not heated after handling are those most likely to transmit viral illnesses.

- *Norovirus.* This is a whole family of viruses, also called "Norwalk" or "Norwalk-like" viruses, or *caliciviruses*. Each type of norovirus is named after the place where it was discovered, such as Taunton (in the United Kingdom), Sapporo (in Japan), and Snow Mountain (in the United States). As a group, they cause fairly mild food poisoning symptoms, often diagnosed by doctors as gastroenteritis. But they are prevalent enough to account for more than 180,000 infections in the United States each year. These viruses are not found in animals. They are passed strictly by human contact, usually via unwashed hands that come in contact with raw food.

- *Staphylococcus aureus.* "Staph" is a common foodborne illness, caused by toxins in protein foods (ham products, cold meats, mayonnaise-based salads) and dairy products (custards, milk-based products, cream-filled desserts). Unfortunately, staph germs resist drying and freezing, and they are not always killed by heating or cooling. Foods most likely to be contaminated by staphylococcus bacteria are the ones that require a lot of prep work, so proper hand washing and hygiene are critical. No one with a skin infection should be doing prep work, and sores or cuts must be bandaged, then the bandaged area must be covered with a finger cot or clean glove.

> Foods contaminated with staphylococcal microorganisms are usually those which require a lot of handling during preparation. Potentially hazardous food that is left too long in the danger zone is at risk because *once the food has been contaminated by the toxin, you cannot depend on heat or cold to destroy the toxin.*
>
> "A large percentage of healthy people have been shown to carry harmful staphylococci. *Staphylococcus aureus* is usually found on hands and in the nose and throat. Wounds, cuts, burns and infections in the nose or sinuses, and pimples are common places where staphylococcal microorganisms thrive; sneezing, coughing, or touching the skin can spread [the] bacteria. Food managers should watch for these problems in their employees. Employees with severe cuts, wounds, or burns must make certain their injuries are properly bandaged, and an effective barrier, such as a disposable glove, must be worn when handling food. Employees with infected cuts, burns, or boils should be excluded from food handling and warewashing (dishes, utensils, pans, etc.) duties.
>
> Symptoms of this illness appear quickly, usually within two to four hours, and include nausea, severe vomiting, diarrhea, cramps, chills, sweating, headache, and severe fatigue. The effects of staphylococcal food poisoning last for one or two days.[2]

Parasites live within animals and fish. The good news is that they are killed when food is heated to sufficiently high temperatures in the cooking process.

- *Ciguatoxins* cause a troublesome but rarely fatal poisoning called *ciguatera*. They are produced by microscopic sea plants that are eaten by small fish, which are then eaten by larger fish, and so on. Large predatory reef fish like barracuda, sea bass, snapper, grouper, amberjack, and mullet have been associated with ciguatera. The illness causes all the "usual" food poisoning symptoms, plus some others—weakness, itching, unusual taste sensations, and even hallucinations—that take one to four weeks to subside.

- *Cryptosporidium parvum* infects herd animals, both domestic (cows, goats, sheep) and wild (deer, elk). It lives in their intestines and is released in feces that can infect soil, water, and the produce grown in or irrigated with them. "Crypto" is tough to kill and chlorine-resistant, so it can live even in swimming pools and hot tubs. The illness it causes, called *cryptosporidiosis*, is very contagious. Symptoms include upset stomach, diarrhea, and a slight fever. They last about two weeks, but not everyone infected has these symptoms. Birds and mice also often have a type of *Cryptosporidium*, but it is not thought to be infectious to humans.

- Similar to *Cryptosporidium*, *Cyclospora cayetanensis* is spread by people who ingest food or water that has been contaminated with infected animal droppings. It affects the small intestine and usually causes diarrhea in humans.

- *Scombrotoxins* are not bacteria per se, but *scombroid fish poisoning* (also called *histamine fish poisoning*) is what happens when people eat fish that is spoiling—that is, when bacteria are breaking down the fish proteins. Symptoms, which can begin within a few minutes, include rash, diarrhea, headache, nausea, and sweating. The mouth may also swell or feel a burning sensation. These symptoms usually last only a few hours and may improve if the person takes an antihistamine. Between scombrotoxins and ciguatoxins, the CDC reports only about 30 cases a year, but adds that because most cases are mild, many probably go undiagnosed and/or unreported.

- *Trichinella* is a type of worm that sometimes infests pork products (like ham and sausage) and game meats. Nausea, chills, fever, and diarrhea are the first symptoms of *trichinellosis* (also called *trichinosis*), occurring within a day or two after infection, but other symptoms—headaches, joint and muscle pains, extreme fatigue and weakness—start from two to eight weeks after eating the infected meat and can last for months. The illness is not contagious between humans. Fewer than 40 cases a year are reported, usually by people who have eaten wild game. Precautions include cooking meat products to internal temperatures of 170 degrees Fahrenheit, freezing meat (in cuts less than 6 inches thick) for at least 20 days at a temperature of 5 degrees Fahrenheit, and cleaning meat grinders thoroughly between uses.

Chemical contamination is caused by certain food additives: sulfites; pesticides used to kill bugs, either by growers or in a foodservice operation; preservatives to lengthen freshness of produce; toxic metals such as copper, brass, cadmium, lead, and zinc (used in galvanized food containers) that come in contact with certain acidic foods; and cleaning products in accidental contact with foods. An example of the latter occurred in a New England restaurant, when a careless cleaning employee tossed detergent on raw lobster tails stored on shelves beneath the steam table.

Food Allergens

We should also mention a category of symptoms that are not infectious, but may also be life threatening because of food allergies. An *allergic reaction* happens when a person's body responds as if something he or she ingests is harmful, even when it's not. Some people break out in hives or a rash. The tongue or throat may swell, causing breathing problems. They may cough or sneeze, their blood pressure may drop, or they may feel a tingling sensation in the mouth when they eat a particular food. They may get cramps, feel nauseous, or have diarrhea. In the most severe cases, they can lose consciousness. According to the Food Allergen and Anaphylaxis Network (www.foodallergy.org), allergic reactions prompt 30,000 emergency room visits and cause as many as 200 deaths each year in the United States. More information can be obtained on the website of the Asthma and Allergy Foundation of America, at www.aafa.org.

There are two points of importance here. First, your catering staff should learn how to recognize an allergic reaction, and what to do about it, as part of ongoing emergency training. Second, there are "trigger" foods that cause up to 90 percent of all allergic reactions. You cannot possibly protect everyone, but if your recipes contain any of these items, they should always be very clearly labeled and identified—or not served at all, in some cases, rather than pose a health risk. Food scientists refer to these as the "Big Eight:"

- Eggs
- Fish
- Shellfish (clams, mussels, oysters, scallops)
- Milk
- Peanuts
- Tree nuts (almonds, Brazil nuts, cashews, filberts, hazelnuts, macadamia nuts, pecans, pine nuts, pistachios, walnuts)
- Soy
- Wheat (or barley, any form of gluten)

Clients should be asked if there are any known food allergies or sensitivities before the menu is planned, but don't expect them to be familiar with each and every guest's special needs. On-site, the caterer should always be prepared to accommodate allergic guests with something as simple as a fruit plate or an egg-free dessert, if requested.

In addition, we mentioned *sulfites* as a chemical contaminant. In fact, these sulfur-based preservatives are used in many cooked and processed foods. They also occur naturally in beer and wine as a result of the fermentation process. The U.S. Food and Drug Administration (FDA) estimates that about 1 in 100 people is sensitive to sulfites, and about 5 percent of asthma sufferers are also sulfite-sensitive. The FDA takes the issue seriously enough to require that the presence of sulfites be disclosed on food and beverage labels.

Employee Hygiene

Poor personal hygiene is a major cause of sanitation problems in the catering profession. Off-premise caterers should insist that health-related procedures be posted in catering commissaries and at off-premise sites and included in training programs and written training materials. These are absolutely critical to prevent the spread of foodborne illnesses. Employees who fail to follow them consistently should be disciplined and/or terminated. *These rules are not negotiable!* It takes only one careless person to ruin a successful catering company with a foodborne illness scare.

1. Workers should wash their hands before starting work and after:

Touching their hair, nose, or ears
Touching an open cut or sore

Sneezing or coughing (even if using a tissue or handkerchief)
Smoking
Visiting the restroom
Handling soiled or used tableware
Gloves become torn or soiled

Hand washing should be done with hot water and soap for at least 20 seconds, using a nail brush. The arms below the elbow should be washed, and single-service towels should be used for drying purposes. When turning off restroom faucets or opening restroom doors, staff members should use a clean paper towel, not their newly washed hands. Many caterers prefer hand washing to the use of gloves, inasmuch as many people don't use gloves properly.

2. If disposable gloves are used when handling foods, employees must be taught to use them correctly. This includes following the guidelines listed earlier, changing gloves whenever they change tasks (or every four hours even if they don't change tasks), and removing them properly (inside out) before throwing them away. If a worker's hands are not clean in the first place, he or she will contaminate the gloves. There are nonlatex gloves, for people with latex allergies, and cut-resistant gloves for kitchen work. Instructions for glove use should be printed *on* the glove dispenser.

3. Gloves should not be worn when working around open flames or other heat sources, however, because they can melt or catch fire. Cut-resistant gloves should not be used while operating electric slicers or using serrated knives, as these activities are more likely to pull at the internal fibers of the gloves and tear them.

4. Jewelry should not be worn when working on back-of-the house tasks, because items like rings can catch dirt and other types of jewelry can easily fall into the food. Front-of-the-house staff may wear minimal jewelry, but only if it is in keeping with the caterer's image.

5. For the same reasons, artificial nails are not permitted. Natural nails should be neatly trimmed and kept scrupulously clean, with the use of a nail brush when washing hands.

6. Any cut, burn, boil, or even a hangnail, must be kept clean and covered with a suitable bandage while working with food or food-contact surfaces—in addition to wearing gloves. There are also individual "finger cots," one-finger guards that can be worn over a bandage to keep it clean and dry.

7. Hats or hairnets should be worn in all food preparation areas. Hair that is long enough to be tied back, should be.

8. Kitchen garments should be light in color so as to reveal stains. An apron should be removed when the employee leaves the kitchen (to use the restroom, take out trash, etc.).

9. Clean shoes with closed toes and nonslip soles should be worn. Some caterers supply their employees with safety shoes or require that these be worn instead of tennis shoes, which can be slippery on wet surfaces. Steel-toed shoes are also a good idea for added protection from falling knives and heavy objects. Check this website for information on sturdy shoes: www.shoesforcrews.com.

10. Catering staff should never touch the "eating ends" of flatware or the rims of glasses, bowls, plates, and cups.

11. Smoking, gum chewing, and eating are never permitted in serving areas or in kitchens. That's what the smoking areas and employee break rooms are for. (Some city health codes do allow kitchen employees to sip from a closed container, with a straw, while working.)

12. Employees who say they are "fine" but come to work coughing and sneezing should be shifted, at least temporarily, to jobs other than food preparation. They can scrub floors, clean restrooms, remove trash, or perform other tasks.

13. Food left on plates, or that has dropped on the floor, should never be reserved.

14. All dropped flatware, napkins, and tableware must be replaced with clean items.

15. Food should not be touched with hands. Use disposable gloves.

16. The tops and bottoms of serving trays should be kept clean at all times.

17. Hard-working food handlers should be careful not to drip sweat onto equipment or into food products.

18. Staff must be trained regarding food allergies and know what to say if a guest inquires about whether a certain food contains a specific ingredient. (If you're unsure, it's best to tell the customer that you are not sure and will find out, if possible, before serving the item to him or her. Also be prepared to offer an alternative dish if the guest is allergic.)

✖ *Food Storage*

Safe storage is the first key to safely prepared foods. Upon arrival from purveyors, meats and poultry should be stored immediately at 41 degrees Fahrenheit or below. Frozen meat and poultry should be stored at a temperature that keeps it frozen, usually 0 degrees Fahrenheit. Raw meat and poultry should be wrapped and kept airtight, because it will turn brown when exposed to air. Meats that show signs of spoilage should be immediately discarded—and remember, you have every right to refuse products that come in from vendors looking less than perfect. Raw chicken that is received packed in ice can be stored in that ice; however, the ice bin must be self-draining and changed regularly with fresh ice.

Fresh fish should be stored at 41 degrees Fahrenheit or less and used within 48 hours. Fillets and steaks should be kept in their original packaging or kept tightly wrapped and free from moisture. Whole fish can be stored in flaked or crushed ice for up to three days. Again, ice beds must be self-draining, and the ice must be changed and the container sanitized regularly. Fish meant to be eaten raw must be delivered frozen, or must be frozen before serving, to kill any parasites.

Eggs must be stored at 41 degrees Fahrenheit (or less) and kept in their original containers. Produce should not be washed before storing. Most produce can be kept at 41 degrees or less, but whole citrus fruits, hard-rind squash, eggplant, and root vegetables (potatoes, sweet potatoes, rutabagas, and onions) may be stored in a cool, dry storage area at temperatures of 60 to 70 degrees Fahrenheit.

✖ *Preparing and Serving Food*

Bacterial growth in food occurs when food temperatures are in the "danger zone"— between 40 and 140 degrees Fahrenheit. Within this range, there's a heightened danger zone in which bacteria can grow more rapidly—that is, from 70 to 125 degrees Fahrenheit. Catering personnel must be trained to thoroughly understand that foods must be brought "through" this zone, either from cold to hot or from hot to cold, as quickly as possible. The longer foods stay in the danger zone, the faster bacteria will grow. The current understanding of food science experts is that foods must not stay in the danger zone for a total of more than four hours, including every moment from its arrival at your kitchen, to the time it is cooked or otherwise prepared, to the time it spends being held and/or reheated. Foods that exceed the four-hour rule should be discarded.

Frozen Foods. Frozen foods should never be thawed at room temperature, but as follows:

- Gradually, under refrigeration (at a temperature of 41 degrees Fahrenheit or lower)
- By cooking immediately after removal from the freezer
- In a microwave oven (but only if it will be cooked immediately after thawing)
- Submerged under potable running water for no more than two hours, with the water temperature at 70 degrees Fahrenheit or lower.

Cooked Foods. Foods must be cooked to the following minimum temperatures, with internal temperatures checked in more than one spot. When checking the temperature, it must be steady for at least 15 seconds, or it's "not quite done." These minimums are suggested in the *ServSafe* program of the National Restaurant Association's Educational Foundation.[3]

TYPE OF FOOD	DEGREES F
Poultry, stuffing, and stuffed meats	165
Steaks, roasts, and chops	145
Ground meats	155
Dishes that combine cooked and uncooked foods (like casseroles)	165
Cooked vegetables	140
Dishes containing eggs	165
Reheating foods	165

Cooked foods may be held before serving for only short periods of time, and at temperatures of no less than 140 degrees Fahrenheit. Holding equipment (like a chafing dish) is designed to keep already-hot food warm, but should never be used to heat food that is cold. It simply doesn't work fast enough to keep the food out of that danger zone. Foods should already be at safe temperatures of 140 degrees Fahrenheit or more when placed in holding equipment.

When cooked foods must be cooled, it's important to chill them as quickly as possible to 40 degrees Fahrenheit to get them out of the danger zone. This is *not* accomplished by plunging the hot food into a refrigerator or freezer, as these appliances are not designed for cooling. They are designed to keep cold foods cold and frozen foods frozen. This is critical, because hot foods stuck in the fridge can form a thin layer of ice on top. This "igloo effect" does exactly the wrong thing—it insulates the interior part of the food, keeping it at higher temperatures too long. It also endangers other cold foods by raising the temperature inside the refrigerator.

Instead, food should be divided into portions small enough to put into shallow containers (no more than 2 or 3 inches deep) and placed in a blast chiller, an appliance made specifically for quick-cooling foods. The shallowness of the containers prompts quicker chilling. As an alternative, you can place a shallow container in a larger container filled with ice and ice water, to pre-cool the food before putting it into a regular refrigerator. Either way, the quick-chilled food must be moved to normal refrigeration within three hours.

Cold (Uncooked) Foods. Because so many different raw food items are cut and diced in a kitchen, the risk of *cross contamination* is great. This occurs when a knife or other utensil or a cutting board is used for more than one food item without being properly sanitized between uses. Here's how you can prevent cross contamination:

- Clean and sanitize utensils, equipment, and work surfaces after each use.
- Use color-coded cutting boards for different types of foods (and make sure your employees understand what color board is used for what food). There are also color-coded containers, knives with color-coded handles, and color-coded kitchen towels for use in different prep areas.
- If a kitchen towel is used for wiping up spills in a particular area, use it only for that purpose. Store soiled towels in a sanitizing solution before washing. Or use disposable towels.
- Make sure employees know and use the proper hand-washing procedures.

Produce items, like salad greens, should be washed under running water, but there are also several brands of sanitizing additives that allow you to "dunk" fruits or vegetables in treated water for an extra bit of protection. (The prep sink, of course, must be properly cleaned and sanitized before using it for this purpose.) As salad ingredients are cleaned and chopped, they can sit in the prep area at room temperature as long as they are soon destined for refrigeration at a temperature of 34 to 38 degrees Fahrenheit. Store salads in shallow containers of no more than 10 pounds each to allow faster chilling. Cover them tightly with film or foil, making sure there's no layer of air between the cover and the salad itself.

Miscellaneous Additional Precautions. Caterers should use only pasteurized milk and milk products, stored at temperatures below 45 degrees Fahrenheit, and poured for use from their original containers. Ice cream must be served with a clean, dry scoop or one that is located in a *dipper well* with running (not standing) water.

Raw eggs should not be used in Caesar salads or other dishes that require little or no cooking. Only pasteurized eggs should be used in these dishes.

Ice used to cool stored food cannot be served to guests. Ice for human consumption should be dispensed only with clean ice scoops or tongs. Many people are under the mistaken impression that ice is cold enough to automatically be sanitary. Not true! Instead, the cold temperature essentially preserves whatever pathogens may have been in the water before it froze. Glasses, hands, or cups should never be used when the ice scoop is misplaced—have extras on hand!

Buffet-style service and self-service situations bring their own challenges. For buffets, "sneeze guards" or food shields are required by most health departments. Buffet foods should be labeled, not only for potential allergens, but so that customers don't feel the need to "sample" or return foods they have picked up. Food temperatures should be checked frequently by buffet attendants. The catering staff should offer a clean plate to those returning to food stations or buffet lines for "seconds," as this prevents guests' use of a "contaminated" plate near the buffet foods.

Supplying tongs, long-handled spoons, and ladles for every serving dish ensures that guests do not have to touch the food. Caters should never reuse ice, vegetable garnishes, or plants used to decorate the buffet if they have been touched by the buffet food.

Cold foods on buffets should be put out in small quantities, and replenishments should not be mixed with food that has already been sitting out on the buffet. It's better to use two small bowls—one on the buffet and one on ice in the prep area or refrigerated. When the bowl on the buffet runs low, it can be removed and the fresh, cold bowl replaces it.

For self-service condiments or coffee, off-premise caterers find it is more sanitary to use individually packaged items (sugar, ketchup, etc.) than bulk containers with spoons—not only for safety reasons, but for the overall appearance of the table.

The HACCP System

The standard on which most foodservice safety regulations are based is the HACCP system. (The initials stand for *Hazard Analysis Critical Control Points*.) HACCP has been used since the 1960s, and the system consists of seven basic steps:.

1. Identify hazards and assess their severity and risks.
2. Determine critical control points (CCPs) in food preparation.
3. Determine critical control limits (CCLs) for each CCP identified.
4. Monitor critical control points and record data.
5. Take corrective action whenever monitoring indicates a critical limit is exceeded.
6. Establish an effective record-keeping system to document the HACCP system.
7. Establish procedures to verify that the HACCP system is working.

From *Design and Equipment for Restaurants and Foodservice,* by Costas Katsigris and Chris Thomas (John Wiley & Sons, 1999), here is a brief explanation of each step.

Step One is to decide what hazards exist at each stage of a food's journey through your kitchen, and decide how serious each is in terms of your overall safety priorities. On your own checklist, this may include the following items, or others:

- Reviewing recipes, paying careful attention to times for thawing, cooking, cooling, reheating, and handling of leftovers.
- Giving employees thermometers and/or temperature probes and teaching them how to use them. Correctly calibrating these devices.
- Inspecting all fresh and frozen produce upon delivery.
- Requiring hand-washing at certain points in the food preparation process and showing employees the correct way to wash for maximum sanitation.
- Adding quick-chill capability to cool foods more quickly in amounts over 1 gallon or 4 pounds, etc.

The second step is to identify *critical control points (CCPs).* This means any point or procedure in your system where loss of control may result in a health risk. If workers use the same cutting boards to dice vegetables and debone chickens without washing them between uses, *that* is a CCP in need of improvement. Vendor delivery vehicles should be inspected for cleanliness; product temperatures must be kept within 5 degrees of optimum; expiration dates on food items must be clearly marked; utensils must be sanitized; and the list goes on and on.

The third step is to determine the standards and limits for what is acceptable and what is not, in each of the CCP areas, for your kitchen.

The fourth step in the HACCP system is to monitor all the steps you pinpointed in Step 2 for a specific period of time, to be sure each area of concern is taken care of correctly. Some CCPs may remain on the list indefinitely, for constant monitoring; others, once you get the procedure correct, may be removed from the list after several months. Still others may be added to the monitoring list as needed.

Step 5 kicks in whenever you see that one of your "critical limits" (sct in Step 3) has been exceeded, and corrective action must be taken.

Step 6 requires that you document this whole process. Without documentation, it is difficult at best to chart whatever progress your facility might be making. If there is a problem that impacts customer health or safety, having written records is also very important.

Finally, Step 7 requires that you establish a procedure to verify whether the HACCP system is working for you. This may mean a committee that meets regularly to discuss health and safety issues and to go over the documentation required in Step 6.[4]

With these steps in mind, health inspectors will periodically visit your commissary. In most places, they do not have to call first—they can show up unannounced. What will they be looking for? Our thanks to the University of Florida Department of Food Science and Human Nutrition for sharing this basic checklist:

- Food protection—whether containers are properly stored, sealed and labeled.
- Proper food temperatures during storage, preparation, holding and serving.

- Safe handling of food and ice; correct use and sanitation of utensils and food contact surfaces to prevent cross-contamination.
- Hygiene practices of employees, and restriction of any infected or ill employee from working with food.
- Construction and installation of equipment for maximum safety.
- Adequate ventilation, especially in cooking and dishwashing areas.
- Safe temperatures of dishwashing machines.
- Safe water sources; adequate hot and cold running water.
- Proper disposal of sewage and wastewater.
- Adequate numbers of toilets, sinks and separate handwashing sinks.
- Clean, covered interior trash receptacles, and exterior dumpster facilities that are properly constructed and enclosed.
- Insect, rodent and animal control (with written records available for inspection).
- Floors, walls, ceilings washable and in good repair; working floor drains in food preparation areas; lighting adequate and fixtures shielded in case of bulb breakage.
- Toxic items (like cleaning materials) properly labeled and stored.
- Proper storage of both clean and soiled linens, dishtowels, etc.
- A no-smoking policy, or designated smoking areas, which must be clearly marked.
- If a grease trap is used, its clean-out records must be available to inspectors.
- Emergency procedures (Heimlich maneuver, etc.) must be posted prominently in many foodservice work areas, along with any permits the city, county or state requires of the particular type of business.[5]

It is a caterer's typical first reaction to view health inspections as either a nuisance or a threat, but neither is really the case—at least, not if you have a food safety plan in place that combines common sense, local laws, and ongoing training. It is more helpful to see an official inspection as another safety measure, some objective eyes that can take a look at what your employees are doing and make improvements and suggestions. More about dealing with inspectors is provided later in this chapter.

Transporting Foods Safely

Foods that are prepared at a commissary or central location to be served at some other place create their own unique health and safety challenges. They must be stored, transported, handled, displayed, and served in a safe and sanitary manner. This means that you must be sure to:

- Prechill any foods that are to be served cold before you transport them. Keep them at a temperature of 41 degrees Fahrenheit or below, both for storage and for service.
- All food, serving equipment, and utensils must be carried in tightly covered containers or securely wrapped packages to protect them from contamination. Use insulated carriers packed with ice or frozen gel-packs for cold foods. For hot foods, preheat to temperatures above 140 degrees Fahrenheit and pack the hot containers snugly into carriers to hold the heat in during transport.
- Always store cooked foods separately from raw and/or ready-to-eat foods.

- Have your dairy delivery person bring perishables like milk directly to the event site in a refrigerated truck.
- If fresh drinking water is not available on-site, you must bring your own water supply.
- Be sure there is enough electrical power at the site for the cooking and holding equipment you plan to use.
- Label all food containers with their contents, storage requirements, and cooking or reheating instructions so there is no confusion at the event site.
- Pack food thermometers so internal temperatures can be checked upon arrival.
- Use the same personal hygiene standards "on the road" that you do in the commissary (regarding the use of hair nets, protective gloves, hand-washing practices, etc.). In case a hand sink or traditional hand-washing setup is not available at an event site, always bring instant hand sanitizers and antibacterial kitchen wipes for work spaces and utensils. These can be found in any supermarket, or visit the website www.handi-dandi.com.
- Clean and sanitize all insulated carriers between uses.
- Clean and sanitize the delivery vehicles regularly too.

More Sanitation Tips

Refrigeration. Refrigerator temperatures should range between 38 and 40 degrees Fahrenheit. These may vary according to local regulations. Refrigerators should be clean and sanitized inside and out. Condensation should never drip on foods, and fans should be kept clean.

Equipment and Food Surfaces. From cutting boards and work tables to your largest mixer, everything in your kitchen should be washed, rinsed, and sanitized after each use—as frequently as possible. To thoroughly clean some types of equipment a sanitizing solution is required to be pumped through them. Manufacturers usually provide both cleaning instructions and cleaning product recommendations. An example follows:

> After cutting up raw chicken, for example, it is not enough to simply rinse the cutting board. Wash, rinse, and sanitize cutting boards and utensils in a three-compartment sink, or run them through a warewashing machine. Make sure employees know which cleaners and sanitizers to use for each job. Sanitizes used on food contact surfaces must meet local or state department codes conforming to the Code of Federal Regulations (21CFR178.1010).[6]

The Code of Federal Regulations is the U.S. Food and Drug Administration's master document of food safety laws. Most health department rules and standards are based on this document. For stationary equipment, the National Restaurant Association's Educational Foundation recommends the following steps:

1. Turn off and unplug equipment before cleaning.
2. Remove food and soil from under and around the equipment.
3. Remove detachable parts and manually wash, rinse, and sanitize them, or run them through a warewasher, if permitted. Allow them to air-dry.

4. Wash and rinse fixed food contact surfaces, then wipe or spray them with chemical sanitizing solution.
5. Keep cloths used for food-contact and non–food-contact surfaces in separate, properly marked containers of sanitizing solution.
6. Air-dry all parts, then reassemble according to directions. Tighten all parts and guards. Test equipment at recommended settings, then turn it off.
7. Resanitize food-contact surfaces handled when putting the unit back together by wiping with a cloth that has been submerged in sanitizing solution.[7]

Dish Machines. Proper water temperatures are part of the story; an adequate rinse cycle is the other part, to keep guests from tasting (and ingesting) dish detergent. If there's a presoak or prewash cycle, the water temperature should be at least 120 degrees Fahrenheit. Wash water temperature should be 140 to 180 degrees Fahrenheit (for chemical or "low temp" machines, 120 degrees). Final rinse water should be 180 to 200 degrees Fahrenheit (165 degrees for stationary rack, single temperature machines; 120 degrees for chemical or "low-temp" machines). And for all cycles, sufficient water pressure is required—at least 20 pounds per square inch.

Cleaning and Pest Control. Off-premise catering facilities must be cleaned regularly, in accordance with established cleaning procedures. All utensils and equipment must be stored at least 6 inches above the floor. Spills should be wiped up immediately. When floors are being mopped, warning signs should be posted. Many caterers use a cleaning and sanitizing setup with two color-coded buckets, green for detergent and red for sanitizing solution. A white cloth is used with the detergent; a blue disposable cloth for the sanitizing agent. A discard bin for soiled cloths makes them easy to toss without reusing. Dispensing systems for the cleaning chemicals are handy, and they save money by dispensing the proper product in the correct amount, thus preventing waste.

Pest control is a huge priority for sanitation, and the best method is to leave it to the experts. Hire a professional, licensed pest control operator who can develop an ongoing pest control program that includes prevention, repairs, pesticides and/or traps, and related training for your people about what they can do to assist in the program, day to day. Find out more about commercial pest control at these websites: www.orkin.com; www.pestworld.com; and www.pctonline.com.

To reduce the chances for chemical contamination of foods, poisonous or toxic materials may not be stored near food preparation and serving areas and must be clearly labeled. Detergents, sanitizers, polishes, chemicals used for maintenance, insecticides, and rodenticides are permitted in foodservice areas, but only if storage and labeling requirements are followed.

Trash. Garbage should be deposited in garbage cans lined with heavy-duty plastic bags and removed frequently from the commissary. It should be deposited in containers or dumpsters outside, preferably in a lockable enclosure. There should be enough covered containers to hold all garbage and refuse, and separate containers for recycled items. (About 70 percent of restaurant kitchens participate in recycling programs. They can generally save you some money on trash pickup fees.) Dumpsters with sloped fronts should be equipped with safety legs to keep them from accidentally tipping forward. The trash area should be lit, so that employees can see where they're going if they are taking trash out after dark.

At off-premise event locations, especially outdoors, be sure the trash receptacles are convenient, but locate them away from food prep or cooking areas so as not to invite insects.

✕ Handling Customer Complaints

Off-premise caterers are not immune to foodborne illness outbreaks; therefore, they should know what to do if a crisis arises. Food poisoning is less likely to occur at an à la carte restaurant, where each guest chooses from a variety of dishes; food poisoning at an off-premise catered event usually involves many people eating the same foods.

When someone complains, alleging a food-related illness, it is very important to determine the facts (versus the opinions). A telephone caller should always be referred to the catering company owner, who should have a preprinted sheet of questions so that he or she will know what to ask the caller. Exhibit 12.1 is a sample of this type of form.

Anyone calling with such a complaint should be taken seriously. Samples of any foods in your commissary that may be suspect should be kept, *never thrown away*, and certainly not reused. Employees who were at the event should be interviewed, and all supplier records of where raw materials were purchased should be kept. In fact, one of your suppliers may be at fault and may have to recall some products. Some caterers may wish to conduct an investigation using an independent laboratory. It's good to know, well in advance of when you'll need them, what laboratory testing resources are available in your area. Your state health department and food processors in your area are good places to inquire.

An off-premise caterer should never immediately admit liability or offer to pay anyone's medical bills. Instead, show concern by saying, "I'm sorry you're not feeling well"—never anything like "I'm sorry our food made your sick." You can show dismay, but certainly not guilt. When the information has been obtained with the use of your preprinted question sheet, it is very important to notify your insurance carrier, who will generally pursue an investigation or settlement as appropriate. Even if a customer threatens to sue, or acts on that threat, you should continue to be polite. Just remember, you and your company have rights too, and you are entitled to a proper defense against what may be an inflated or spurious claim.

However, a valid complaint from a concerned guest can alert you to a possible problem with your food-handling methods or with the raw materials purchased from a supplier. Make sure your suppliers are informed if you receive complaints that involve their products. They may need to recall a hazardous product from the market.

Occasionally, you will be part of a recall or even perhaps a full-blown outbreak of a foodborne illness. In these rare cases, caterers are advised to hire a public relations firm skilled in crisis management. Trying to deal with the news media yourself can cause further damage if, as happens in so many instances, you are asked

⊠ Exhibit 12.1 *Call Sheet for Incoming Complaints of Illness or Injury*

1. TELL the caller you "have a few questions that need to be answered to confirm all the facts." Ask for the person's patience in answering each question as completely as possible.

Date and time of call _____

Who received the call? _____

Name of person who is calling _____

Contact numbers for this person _____

Name of person who is ill (or injured)_____

Does this person have any known illnesses or allergies? _____
_____

Describe the problem _____
_____
_____

Is there a particular item (a dish, specific food or beverage) you are complaining about?
_____

Date and time of the meal (or food) eaten _____

List the exact symptoms, and when they appeared _____

Did this person eat anything after the suspect meal? _____

What, and when? _____
_____

Has this person seen a doctor for the problem? (If so, when?) _____
Was there a diagnosis?_____

Name and phone number of doctor _____

Have you reported this to anyone else? (If so, whom?) _____

Do you still have any of the product (leftovers) in the original container? _____

May we send someone out to pick it up for testing? _____

Address _____
_____

_____   _____
Signature of person who took this report   Date and time

2. THANK the caller for his or her concern.

3. TELL the caller the complaint will be investigated, and that if the catering company has any further questions, someone from the company will call him or her.

4. DO NOT PROMISE ANYTHING other than that the company "will look into the complaint."

FOLLOW-UP ACTION

This complaint given to: _____

For follow-up investigation on (date and time) _____

Date of follow-up action: _____

What was done? _____
_____
_____
_____

Further contact with caller was made (date and time): _____
_____

"leading questions" or quoted out of context in interview situations. Your objective at this point is to minimize the losses and save the business. Protecting your business is worth every penny you will spend on professional public relations.

✕ *On-the-Job Safety*

Each year there are more than 250,000 on-the-job accidents in the foodservice industry that, on average, mean 35 lost workdays while the employee recovers. The majority of these are slip-and-fall accidents, but there are also muscle strains, burns, and cuts aplenty. So it's important to do whatever possible to make the workplace safe and comfortable for employees. Even at off-premise sites, a caterer must be able to quickly recognize unsafe conditions and take corrective action immediately.

Here are some standard practices that should reduce accident risks for both employees and clients:

- Floors must be kept clean, dry and in good repair. Spills should be wiped up immediately, and "caution" and "wet floor" signs should be used as appropriate.
- Dance floors at party sites must be checked for cracks in which a woman's heel could get caught. Honoring requests from clients and guests to make the dance floor "slicker" can result in a serious slip and fall. Floors should be smooth, but still provide traction.
- There should be adequate lighting in all areas where guests and employees walk, including parking lots. Dimly lit walkways at off-premise sites should be lit with temporary lighting. Employees never should be permitted to run, and they should be cautioned to use extreme caution when working at off-premise site with which they are not familiar. Better yet, there should be enough time in the set-up phase of an off-premise event for a short "walk-through" tour of the space for the staff members who will be working there.
- Employees should be instructed in correct lifting and transporting methods. When lifting, it is best to lift twice, first mentally and then physically. By lifting mentally, one thinks, "Is the item too heavy or too bulky to see around? Is the path clean, and is there a place to put the load?" Lifting heavy objects should be accomplished with these steps:
    1. Establish solid footing, and check to see that the floor is dry and clean.
    2. Stand close to the load, and spread feet to shoulder width.
    3. Place one foot slightly in front of the other to establish a focal point for the weight of the load.
    4. Keep the head over the body, and bend at the knees to reach the load.
    5. Grip the load with the whole hand, not just the fingers, and pull the load close while it is still on the ground.
    6. Tighten the stomach muscles. Arch the lower back in by pulling your shoulders back and sticking your chest out.
    7. Lift slowly, keeping the load close to the body with the legs taking the weight of the load.

8. To set the load down, reverse the procedure.

   Lifting belts are highly recommended for employees who are responsible for loading, unloading and receiving area duties. They should be stored in the receiving area and also carried routinely in the catering delivery vehicles.

■ Only staff trained to operate specific machinery should be permitted to use it. They should follow these procedures:

1. Use equipment only for its designated use.
2. Make sure the plug is disconnected and visible before disassembling, repairing and/or cleaning the equipment.
3. Use equipment only with its safety guards in place.
4. Remove jewelry, avoid loose clothing and restrain hair. Wear protective goggles, gloves, or other suitable clothing for that task.
5. Turn off the equipment if you get distracted.
6. Use proper tools to feed food into the equipment—not hands!
7. Never operate equipment with loose wires or damaged switches or plugs.
8. Report any maintenance problem immediately to management.

■ Knives should always be kept sharp, since dull knives easily slip off foods and can cut the person using them. Be sure everyone knows how to use knives correctly—tips like cutting away from the body, and cutting foods with fingers curled under. If a knife falls, don't grab for it—get out of the way! Knives should never be used to open containers, and they should be stored in a knife rack.

■ Anyone who has a cut or sore must keep it covered with a clean, dry bandage that would prevent any possible leakage or contact with food, dishes or utensils. As we've mentioned, the bandage is *in addition to* wearing gloves.

■ Burn prevention tips:

1. Remove lids from pots, pans, kettles (chafing dishes) carefully, allowing steam to escape away from the face and hands.
2. Use dry, flameproof potholders
3. Turn the handles of pans inward on the range so that pans cannot be knocked off. Make sure the handles are not placed too near the heat.
4. Move heavy or hot containers with enough help and know where the containers are going before picking them up.
5. Be careful when filtering, changing (discarding) shortening in fryers. Wait until the grease cools before handling.
6. Keep stove tops and hoods free of grease.
7. Keep oven doors closed when not in use.
8. Do not clean ovens and stoves until they have cooled.
9. Keep papers, plastic aprons, and other flammable materials away from hot areas.[8]

Also keep beverages away from fryer stations, because the cold beverages, if spilled into the hot grease, can cause a major eruption of the grease. Deep fryers should not be set up in high-traffic areas. And it is imperative to train inexperienced fry cooks—they have been known to reach into hot grease with their hands for an accidentally dropped article!

■ Ovens, broilers, and grills fueled by large propane tanks should never be used indoors or in any area lacking adequate ventilation. In some parts of the country, caterers also need special permits to use butane fuel and Sterno indoors. Check with the local fire or health department about such regulations.

■ Folding tables and chairs should be checked for damage before each use. Folding table legs should be locked in place to ensure that the table does not collapse while in use. Chairs should be inspected for splinters, loose or missing screws and bolts, and other unsafe conditions.

■ All cords should be taped down and covered with floor mats or some other protective covering so that staff and guests do not trip on them. Orange cords are common because they're the most visible. Warning signs should be placed in areas where staff members and guests could possibly trip.

■ The service staff should be trained in proper tray-carrying procedures. Injuries to guests caused by careless staff members have resulted in million-dollar lawsuits.

■ When working with charcoal, charcoal lighter fluid should be sprayed on the coals prior to lighting. It should never be sprayed on charcoal that is partially ignited, because the flame can travel up the stream of fluid and cause a severe burn or explosion.

■ Flaming drinks and tableside flambés should be avoided, as there have been numerous burn injuries reported by guests and waitstaff. The best policy is simply not to offer these types of items.

■ Fire extinguishers must be located near each potential fire source. Smart off-premise caterers also carry at least one fire extinguisher in each catering vehicle. All staff members should know how to use them.

First Aid and Emergency Procedures

The law does not require off-premise caterers to provide emergency assistance, but it does not forbid them from taking emergency action. No establishment or employee will be held liable for civil damage for an action that could be expected of any reasonably prudent person under similar circumstances.

First aid kits should be located in all catering commissaries and at all off-premise locations. All catering staff should be trained in the Heimlich maneuver, and some states require that an instructional sign with the Heimlich steps be posted in a conspicuous place in the catering commissary. Having at least some staff members trained in cardiopulmonary resuscitation (CPR) techniques is not required, but is an excellent idea and can be part of your employee training regimen.

When emergencies arise, the caterer or event manager must remain calm, determine the seriousness of the problem, and quickly decide whether to call for help. Meanwhile, the accident victim must be made as comfortable as possible, and basic first aid must be administered in accordance with a first aid guide, which you should *always* keep in each catering vehicle:

■ For burns, first remove whatever is causing the burn; use cool, running water to sooth *minor* burns; never apply ointments, sprays, antiseptics, or home remedies; and seek medical assistance in case of serious burns.

■ For wounds, first rinse with clean running water; apply pressure with a clean towel or napkin; using a first aid kit, apply a water-resistant bandage (covered with a plastic glove, for hand wounds); and have severe wounds treated by medical personnel.

A written accident or incident report must be completed for all accidents. Make your own form or ask your insurance company for one. Copies of these reports may go to most, or all, of the following:

- Your own insurance-related files
- The employee's personnel file with your company
- The catering company's Worker's Compensation insurer
- The Occupational Safety and Health Administration (OSHA)
- The claims agent for your general business insurer

After an accident (and as promptly as possible, within reason), it is important to ask the injured person exactly how he or she thinks the accident happened. Obtain witness reports and inspect the scene for conditions—lighting, cleanliness, wet or dry floors, fallen objects, outdoor weather conditions—that may have contributed to the accident. Note the condition of the person's shoes and clothing. Be alert for signs of alcohol or drug use. When a mishap like this occurs, you've got to think fast but remain calm. It is absolutely never advisable to:

- Argue with the injured person over the cause of the accident
- Reprimand any employee at an event site
- Offer to pay all medical expenses
- Admit any type of responsibility
- Mention insurance coverage
- Discuss the accident with strangers, at the site or afterward
- Permit photographs by anyone other than your own, or your insurance company's, representatives

Fire can cause serious accidents, deaths, and major property damage. Off-premise caterers should train their staff members to think fire safety and follow these procedures:

- Frequently check gas appliances for proper maintenance, and always check for a gas odor before lighting a match (which may signal a gas buildup).
- Be sure that all cigarettes and cigars are extinguished before putting them in the trash.
- All smoke alarms should be properly maintained.
- Grease to be discarded, oily rags, and other flammable or combustible materials should not be stored in the catering commissary.
- Power cords should be checked for damage, and water should never be splashed around electrical outlets.
- Hoods and exhaust filters should be cleaned at least weekly, and hot ductwork at least twice a year by a professional company. (Your insurance company, in most jurisdictions, will send an inspector to look at your fire protection system at least annually, if not every six months.)

Fire extinguishers are classified by the types of fires they are designed to put out, and rated by the size of fire they can extinguish in a single use. Use only extinguishers that have the Underwriters Laboratories (UL) or Factory Mutual (FM) approval logo on them. The most common extinguisher classifications are:

- Class A—Cloth, paper, wood, some types of plastic
- Class B—Flammable liquids
- Class C—Electrical equipment
- Class D—Combustible metals
- Class K—Commercial cooking-related fires

There are also "clean agent" fire extinguishers that can be used on fires around computers and other more sensitive types of mechanical equipment. Older fire extinguishers may not be effective and may even cause injuries. Those containing carbon tetrachloride or soda acid are no longer considered safe and should be discarded. Consult local fire and/or health department authorities for the number and types of extinguishers required, their correct placement, and maintenance requirements. You are also responsible for having an evacuation plan in case of fire, both for the commissary and at off-premise sites. Most local fire departments are happy to offer suggestions and participate in employee safety training.

✕ Government Agencies and Regulations

The foodservice industry receives a lot of assistance, and a lot of oversight, from a wide range of government organizations. Here are just a few you may deal with:

- Your local health department may be a city or county agency. This is the department that sends out health inspectors to check safety and sanitation conditions periodically, often unannounced.
- The health department of your state may become involved if an outbreak of food-borne illness has been reported.
- There are a number of federal agencies that deal with food-related issues. Their functions can range from tracking and investigating illness outbreaks, to inspecting meat, eggs, seafood, and imported foods, to upholding safe workplace laws. These agencies include the following:
  - U.S. Food and Drug Administration (FDA)
  - U.S. Department of Agriculture (USDA) and its subagencies, like the Food Safety Inspection Service (FSIS)
  - Centers for Disease Control (CDC) and its subagencies, like the Foodborne Diseases Active Surveillance Network (FoodNet)
  - Environmental Protection Agency (EPA)
  - National Marine Fisheries Service
  - Occupational Safety and Health Administration (OSHA)

Most of these agencies' regulations are enforced by state and local health departments. Off-premise catering managers must be acutely aware of health and safety regulations. Inspectors can cite, fine, and even close a food-related business for failure to comply with these requirements. It's a good idea to ask in advance for a blank copy of an inspection form so that you'll know what the inspectors look for and can work on total compliance. Also take a look at the Internet websites for these agencies. Most have a wealth of food safety and compliance-related information.

Federal OSHA inspectors look for different sorts of things than local health inspectors—accessibility of fire extinguishers, adequate hand railings on stairs, properly maintained and utilized ladders, proper guards and electrical grounding for food-service equipment, proper use of extension cords, lighted passageways that are free from obstructions, readily available first aid supplies, and so on. Again, fines are levied for serious violations.

So what happens when the inspector shows up at your commissary? It's important not to lose your cool, but to maintain a mutually respectful relationship with any inspector. The best kind of business you can be is one that is well-organized and receptive to his or her requests. Here are some tips for accomplishing this:

- Always be polite and professional, and instruct your staff to do the same.
- Ask questions; ask for the inspector's assistance or opinion. Don't make excuses.
- Don't be defensive or argumentative.
- Accompany the inspector as he or she tours your facility.
- Correct any violation immediately, if you can, right in front of the inspector who points it out.
- Never offer food, discounts, or any type of favor to the inspector.
- Be honest and to the point when you are asked questions.
- It's okay to converse and make small talk with the inspector. It makes the situation a little more comfortable for everyone.

Periodically, you may want to hire a food safety consultant to help you plan and improve your food safety practices in a variety of ways. These experts can save time in finding areas of improvement and can offer a fresh perspective. With their calibrated probe thermometers and flashlights, they'll check areas most commonly missed during cleaning—potato wedgers, can openers, ice machines, shelves under prep tables, floors under the food prep counters, mop/broom closets, and walk-in cooler fans. Using an outside consultant demonstrates to your staff, your customers, and your local health department that you take food safety seriously. For more information on food safety specialists, visit these websites: www.nsf.org, www.apha.org, and www.fcsi.org

✕ Security Procedures

Especially since the September 11 terrorist attacks in 2001, there has been an increasing focus on security in most industries. Today's caterer not only needs to be concerned with employee and guests thefts, but must also perform rigorous security checks prior to catering certain events. According to Carl Sacks of Event Creators, caterers who cater high-security events should:

- Do employee background checks on all job applicants.
- Photograph all employees in digital format that can be e-mailed to a third party to verify identity.
- Create picture ID cards for full-time and delivery employees.
- Identify their catering trucks with prominent logos.

- Send out all deliveries with proper paperwork.
- Send staff members to events dressed and ready to work, with no duffel or garment bags.
- Allow plenty of extra setup time, because of the high level of scrutiny expected and the resultant delays.

The U.S Federal Bureau of Investigation reports that in 2002, there were 420,637 robberies, costing their victims $539 million in stolen cash and property. Robberies that occurred in commercial locations, like restaurants and bars, accounted for almost 15 percent of these incidents, and off-premise caterers are not immune. Those who handle large amounts of cash are particularly vulnerable.

The costs for security systems—closed-circuit televisions, time-delay safes, and perimeter alarm systems—are high, but they will deter at least some burglars and embezzlers and lower insurance premium costs. You can examine some of your options on the website of the National Burglar and Fire Alarm Association, at www.alarm.org.

Other loss prevention tactics include depositing excess cash in a safe, varying your cash-handling routines, counting money only in a locked office, and never admitting any unauthorized personnel into the catering commissary. Put internal controls into place: The person who counts the end-of-day cash cannot deposit it without verifying the total with the company owner or another preauthorized employee. Keep a written record of all people who have keys to your building(s) and vehicle(s), and get those keys back when they leave your employ for any reason.

Many robberies are triggered by security leaks from current employees or committed by former employees who learn the security system, then quit and return to rob the business. However, almost 43 percent of robberies happen on the street, when someone going about his or her business is stopped by a stranger with a weapon. Another 13 percent happen at residences. In the 1990s, Round Table Pizza's San Francisco locations began posting a list of safety tips for their delivery drivers. These are still excellent advice and can be adapted for catering staff members as well:

1. Enter and exit the restaurant through the front entrance after dark.
2. Drop excess cash after every delivery run in a secured drop-box located in the delivery area.
3. Carry only a minimum bank, no more than $20 or $30. This bank might include two $5 bills, 10 $1 bills and a few dollars in change. Order takers should tell delivery customers that drivers will not accept bills larger than $20 for payment of food.
4. Always carry a cellular phone or two-way radio.
5. Always lock vehicles and leave headlights and emergency lights on, and use a flashlight for a night delivery. After exiting the vehicle, scan areas around the house, especially in darkened areas to the sides of the home.
6. Use extra caution in case of darkened homes or areas. If the situation seems threatening, do not make the delivery. Call the restaurant and have [the restaurant] phone the customer again, requesting [he or she] leave the front light on.[9]

It's not just money that disappears from catering companies. Controlling in-house theft of food products, tableware, and other items is another concern of every caterer.

Some caterers use security cameras, and others spot-check bags, purses, and employee lockers. When hired, employees should be informed about how their activities will be monitored and asked to sign a statement acknowledging that they know and understand this policy.

Another pesky problem is that guests at catered events seem to love to take off with "souvenirs." Your staff members should be alert for these sticky-fingered guests. A South Florida caterer recovered eight Champagne flutes from a female guest's purse, when alerted by an observant staff member who saw her stuff them into the oversized handbag.

This is just one reason that an inventory of equipment at the end of each catered event is a must. As we mentioned in Chapter 2 in our discussion of catering contracts, clients should be made aware that if there are excessive losses of napkins, flatware, or glassware, they will be billed for these losses. The same goes for table linens damaged by spilled wax or burns from client-provided candles or sparklers.

✕ *Insurance Coverage*

According to Anthony Marshall, former dean of the Florida International University School of Hospitality Management:

> Responsibility for accidents at an off-premise event makes matters even more sticky. The bottom line is that if someone is hurt, they're not going to care. They'll sue everybody involved whether they own the facility or they're the caterer. That person isn't going to get into the hassle of who's liable; they want compensation. A common defense taken by facility owners is to ask the caterer, or anyone involved in putting on the function, to indemnify them against any losses. This can be handled easily by purchasing insurance specifically for that event.[10]

When purchasing insurance, the off-premise cater should evaluate the size of the potential loss, the probability of the loss, and the resources to meet the loss if it should occur. Minor risks can be absorbed with the use of deductibles, but major risks should be covered. A good basic rule is to never risk more than you can lose.

Off-premise caterers should cultivate a good relationship with several reputable insurance brokers regarding the following types of insurance. Some of these may not apply to every caterer, or may apply only in some situations; others are required by law:

- **Property or business property insurance**—This includes everything owned by you in your business. It covers losses that are the results of fire and/or water damage, and theft.
- **Business interruption insurance**—This is a type of property insurance that covers expenses (salaries, rent payments, taxes, interest, utilities, and lost profit) in case your business must close temporarily because of a fire or other disaster.
- **"Property of Others" insurance**—This applies if you use anything routinely in your business that belongs to someone else—leased equipment, for example.
- **Liability insurance**—This covers the caterer's liability for injuries or damage that occurs either on the caterer's property or off-premise at event sites. It may

also include product liability (in case of a foodborne illness) and liquor liability (in case of alcohol-related accidents). An off-premise site often requires the caterer to include that specific site on his or her policy (as an "additional insured") for an event. Liability coverage is an absolute requirement in the catering industry. Get as much as you can afford.

- **Personal injury insurance**—This gives caterers the funds to protect themselves against libel, slander, defamation, and false arrest.
- **Glassware insurance**—Covers breakage of dishes and glasses.
- **Vehicle insurance**—In addition to the catering company's vans and cars, be sure the policy covers employees who are using their own vehicles on company business.
- **Equipment insurance**—Covers damage to equipment while it is being transported and during its use at off-premise events.
- **Food spoilage insurance**—Covers losses incurred when refrigerators and freezers fail. If your area is known for power outages, you'll want to have this coverage.
- **Workers' Compensation insurance**—This insurance is required by law and is typically administered by your state insurance commission. If you don't pay for coverage, your business can be shut down. "Workers' comp" covers employees for job-related accidents and injuries.
- **Health insurance**—This policy pays a portion of medical bills after the employee has paid a certain amount (the *deductible*). Some policies include vision care and dental work; others do not. The monthly cost of the insurance (the *premium*) is lower for policies with high individual deductible amounts.
- **Disability insurance**—This pays at least a portion of a person's income when he or she is unable to work for a long period of time after an injury or accident.
- **Umbrella coverage**—This is an extra option that gives a company more coverage than the standard, general liability limits—hence the name, "umbrella." It is designed to protect a business from an extraordinary loss. Your insurance agent or broker can discuss its appropriateness for a particular business.

The other type of coverage you may want to consider is bonding your employees, especially those who will be handling funds. There are several types of *fidelity bonds*. Their goal is to absolve the employer from legal responsibility for the dishonest acts of bonded employees. Depending on the bond, these acts can include everything from theft and forgery, to destruction of property, to outright disappearance of the employee. A bond can cover one person, all employees, or only those persons in particular job titles. The cost of bonding varies widely, depending on the type of coverage and number of bonded individuals.

Speaking of costs, David Talty, an insurance broker and lecturer at Florida International University, says it is common knowledge in the insurance industry that the cost of insurance has highs and lows that run in two- to three-year cycles. It is always best to buy insurance when costs are lower. Talty also advises:

> Be objective when purchasing insurance. Obtain bids, treat the various agents with respect and demand that they provide the best possible product at the lowest possible cost.

An insurance broker's job is to assist off-premise caterers in determining the right coverage and then to shop all of the insurance carriers available that underwrite off-premise caterers. It is always best to find a broker who represents a large number of carriers. Always insist on a strong and reputable insurance carrier with a high rating.[11]

It is always best to obtain bids from three or more brokers; you might also look into the various insurance programs offered by associations, like your state restaurant association or the National Association of Self-Employed Persons (NACE). Where insurance is not available, or if it is inordinately costly, restaurant owners sometimes pool their resources and become their own insurers. You may be able to participate in such a group.

✖ Conclusion

Although topics like insurance and workplace safety are mundane—and foodborne illness isn't exactly appetizing, either—we cannot sufficiently stress their importance in today's litigious society. Mistakes in these areas can cost an off-premise caterer his or her reputation and livelihood. Yet most of these problems are surprisingly easy to avoid, with the assistance of your local health and fire departments and your insurance carriers. You owe it to your customers and employees to ensure that the highest standards of sanitation and safety are being met, day in and day out.

Notes

1. Joan Oleck, in *Restaurant Business*, September 1, 1993.
2. The National Assessment Institute, *Handbook for Safe Food Service Management.* Copyright 1994. Reprinted with permission of Prentice-Hall, Englewood Cliffs, New Jersey.
3. *ServSafe Essentials, Third Edition.* Copyright 2004. Reprinted with permission of the National Restaurant Association Educational Foundation, Chicago, Illinois.
4. *Design and Equipment for Restaurants and Foodservice: A Management View.* Copyright 1999. Reprinted with permission of John Wiley & Sons, Inc., Hoboken, New Jersey.
5. *Developing Guidance to Expedite Food Product Recalls to Mitigate or Contain a Purposeful Continuation of Commercially Distributed Food.* Copyright 2002. Reprinted with permission of the University of Florida Department of Food Science and Human Nutrition, Gainesville, Florida.
6. *ServSafe Essentials, Third Edition.* Copyright 2004. Reprinted with permission of the National Restaurant Association Educational Foundation, Chicago, Illinois.
7. *ServSafe Essentials, Third Edition.* Copyright 2004. Reprinted with permission of the National Restaurant Association Educational Foundation, Chicago, Illinois.
8. *Restaurants & Institutions* magazine, © 1992. A publication of Reed Business Information, a division of Reed Elsevier, Inc. All rights reserved.
9. *NACE News*, the National Association of Catering Executives newsletter, Louisville, Kentucky.
10. *Restaurants & Institutions* magazine, © 1992. A publication of Reed Business Information, a division of Reed Elsevier, Inc. All rights reserved.
11. Personal interview with David Talty, Florida International University.

Chapter 13

Accessory Services and Special Requirements

This chapter addresses some services and requirements that are critical to your business success as an off-premise caterer. Most clients rely on the caterer's expertise in these areas as they plan special events and, in bidding situations, caterers with the most knowledge in these areas will gain the business. The clients know they can rely on them not only for good food and service, but for putting on an event that is socially correct and unique, even if it is a common type of event, such as a wedding or a bar mitzvah.

We encourage you to read as much as possible elsewhere about the topics covered in this chapter, but remember that experience is the best teacher. You will gain confidence when you resolve to learn as much as possible from each event you cater. Take detailed notes, observe, and evaluate the suppliers you use for accessory services during events.

Accessory Services

Accessory services are those additional services that contribute to the overall success of a catered event. They include:

Music and entertainment
Flowers, balloons, and décor
Photography and videography
Lighting and audiovisual services

Ground transportation and limousines
Valet parking
Fireworks and lasers

No, none of these services are technically part of your business. But the professional off-premise caterer must be knowledgeable in each of these areas, because most clients will rely on your judgment when planning for the use of these services. They realize that wonderful food and service at a wedding reception can be completely overshadowed by an inappropriate band, an impossible parking situation, or inadequate sound or lighting. At minimum, caterers need to know whom to recommend for these services. Out-of-town clients often depend on the caterer to recommend and book all accessory services. Local clients usually choose to engage at least some of their own services, but they may still come to you for advice. The key point in either case is to be able to recommend *only* those suppliers who are professional, dependable, and can meet the needs of each particular client.

Before specifically discussing each area of accessory services, let's consider how you, as the off-premise caterer, should charge for your expertise in these areas. It's a somewhat controversial topic in the industry. The most common practices—and justifications for them—are as follows:

- Some caterers charge nothing extra at all for making recommendations—they give clients a list and let them do the selecting and hiring. These caterers feel they make their money from the food, and that clients are entitled to the best possible prices on the other services.
- Others receive a small commission or referral fee from the supplier who gets the business. These caterers feel that they are, in effect, acting as sales representatives for the suppliers and that they are entitled to the referral fee.
- Many caterers hire the accessory providers, then mark up their services slightly and add them to the overall invoice for the event. Their feeling is that they spend time screening, contracting, and paying the providers and that they are, in effect, responsible for the performance of their services. The amount of markup will vary, depending on each specific situation. Such things as overall budget and the amount of profit to be made on other areas of the party (food, beverages, rental equipment, etc.) will affect the markup.

Off-premise caterers must base their policies on their own unique situations. For the most part, a good caterer who has been in business for any length of time has developed excellent working relationships with certain accessory suppliers. They have created a select team of winners who work well together to produce superb events. How the client is billed for these services depends largely on how the caterer feels about charging for that professional expertise.

Music and Entertainment

Music is the "heartbeat" of a party. It can transform spectators into participants and can truly make or break some types of events. A deejay playing the songs everyone loves to hear will certainly make the party more enjoyable. However, we recall at least one large party that was ruined when the party planner hired a Michael Jackson impersonator to perform for a group of soft drink company executives, when, at that time, Michael was promoting a competitor's soft drink.

There are three general types of music:

- Background music, a good choice during cocktail hours and dinner parties
- Music for dancing, best after dinner
- Music for listening, usually at events where the entertainer is the "show" and people are there to see that specific person or band

Music at catered events can range from background music provided by clients' stereos to the live sounds of large show bands. Harps and string quartets produce excellent background music and are always appropriate for wedding ceremonies. Deejays play a wide variety of prerecorded music at economical prices. Some deejays are also personalities who entertain between songs by "chatting up" the audience and acting as master (or mistress) of ceremonies. Party bands are always popular, with their wide range of "cover tunes" that appeal to all age groups.

Before a client decides to hire musicians, an off-premise caterer should offer this advice:

1. Be sure that the music fits the event. A string quartet at a country-western party is not appropriate. All too often, people make musical selections because they "know somebody who's in a band" or because somebody's relative offers to play for free. Big mistake, if the type of music doesn't fit the crowd.

2. Absolutely go to hear and see the group in advance. Any band worth hiring has a CD of its music, which should also be shared with the clients, but they need to see the performers in action if at all possible.

3. Music should appeal to the group as a whole, rather than just satisfying the clients' own personal tastes. Included in the musical equation should be the purpose of the event, the average age of those in attendance, the range of ages, the region of the country where the guests live, and where the party will be held.

4. Always obtain and sign a written contract that includes these essentials:

The exact price for a certain amount of performance time

A specified time by which setup will be completed (i.e., long before the guests arrive)

The start and end times of the performance (not the event!)

Scheduled break times (how often, and how long)

The exact location of the party

The type of party

The type of music to be played

The names of the musicians who will be playing (some leaders have a number of different groups playing under the same name) and their instruments

The musicians' attire (dress code, or not?)

Overtime charges, and who is authorized by the client to approve them if the event runs long

Cancellation charges, deposit amounts, and payment terms

A guarantee of work (that the musicians will be there, will perform, etc.)

5. There may be other areas to outline. Common concerns that should really be spelled out in the contract include:

Where instrument cases and personal belongings will be kept

Whether the musicians can bring guests and/or potential clients who wish to hear them

Whether they will be fed at the event

Whether they can drink alcohol during the event

Whether there is a changing and/or break area

Insurance requirements, depending on the venue

Be sure the entertainers have directions to the event site. A general rule that applies to every event is that music should be playing when the guests arrive. Strings may play softly as guests assemble for a wedding ceremony; rock music may be blasting as guests arrive for an outdoor barbecue; trumpets may herald guests' arrival at an upscale dinner at a prestigious location; mariachis may greet guests at a Latin-themed event; the orchestra might be belting out an upbeat tune as guests enter the ballroom for dinner. According to Lester Lanin, noted New York band leader, the preferred number of musicians varies, depending on the size of the group at an event:

GROUP SIZE	NUMBER OF BAND MEMBERS
125	5–7
250	7
500	12
750	12 + strings
1,000	15–20

Off-premise caterers should be familiar with certain terms when dealing with musicians and their agents.

- "Pre-heat" means cocktail hour music.
- The term "noncontinuous" varies from city to city, but it generally refers to the time musicians will play and the duration of their breaks. Usual examples are play for 40 minutes and rest for 20 minutes, or play for 45 minutes and rest for 15 minutes. (Too bad the caterers don't get breaks like this, eh?)
- Continuous" means there will be music throughout the evening—either no breaks, or very short ones lasting no more than 5 minutes. The musicians in larger bands and orchestras will break at different times throughout the party.

No matter who hires them, the off-premise caterer is the one responsible for working the musicians' requirements into the event. This means determining the amount and costs of seating, staging, and tenting. How many extra chairs will they require? How about music stands? (They should bring their own.) Portable stages can be expensive, and so are tents—but most performers with electrical equipment (sound board, amplifiers, etc.) will not play if they are unprotected from rain and other elements.

The cost of musical entertainment depends on several factors, including the size of the band or group; the season, night of the week, and time of day; and other regional factors.

Whenever live human beings are hired to perform an important service—like entertaining—problems are bound to arise. A savvy off-premise caterer is always prepared. Carolyn Prear, CSEP, president of Eclectic Events International in Toronto, Canada, offers these additional tips:

- Always have a back-up plan in case of cancellation.
- Consider cancellation insurance for major acts.
- Don't "beat the entertainers down" on pricing. However, if the budget needs to be trimmed, ask them to accommodate you.
- For major acts, review the "rider" to the contract, which covers things such as dressing rooms, meals, and other amenities.
- Choose a corporate entertainment agent for major acts. An agent can negotiate better prices, as well as handle the other details (insurance rider, travel arrangements, pre-performance sound check, etc.) The best agents are licensed by the American Federation of Musicians, of the U.S. and Canada.[1]

Flowers and Décor

Off-premise caterers are often consulted about floral design and the use of other items to decorate an event site. One of the reasons you are hired is typically because you have a sense of design and décor, not just great recipes—you can make a party look as good as the food tastes! Some caterers choose to create their own floral designs, which can be a highly profitable part of the business, rather than referring the work to others. Other caterers recommend floral designers or work regularly with a few they know and trust.

As with music, off-premise caterers who can prove they understand design and décor will be perceived more favorably by prospective clients than those who seem to have no clue about these important details.

When it comes to floral design, there are a few basics with which you should be familiar:

1. Floral centerpieces should never be more than 14 inches high, or they should be elevated on stands so as not to obstruct guests' views of each other across tables.

2. For upscale events, a few exotic flowers are much nicer than a larger number of inexpensive blooms such as carnations, mums, and daisies.

3. When budgets are limited, a large, striking arrangement at the entrance is much more effective than a number of smaller arrangements placed around the party area.

4. For weddings and receptions, the emphasis should be on the reception flowers and bouquets, rather than those at the church, because guests will enjoy them much longer at the reception than at the church.

5. The florist the clients select should always visit the party site first, before preparing a proposal and price estimate.

6. Whenever possible, the flowers used at a ceremony should be reused on buffet tables or in other areas at the reception site.

7. Off-premise caterers and their clients should be aware of extra charges typical of florists, such as delivery and setup fees. Also, as with wedding cake fixtures, arrangements must be made between caterers, clients, and floral designers for the safe handling, storage, and return of items like mirrors, special vases, and arches after the event is concluded.

8. When selecting flowers for catered affairs, there are a few surefire choices:
- For scent, use roses, gardenias, narcissus, and tuberoses.
- For height, use gladiolas, wildflowers, snapdragons, larkspur, and flowering branches.
- For color, use tulips, gerbers, lupine, irises, alstromeriums, ranunculuses, and anemones.
- For economy use sweet william, heather, miniature carnations, and Queen Anne's lace.

9. Always look for florists who understand the needs of the off-premise caterer as well as the client, and will stick to the budget.

10. Clients should always have a plan for distributing the flowers upon the conclusion of events. Some hold drawings for them, hiding stickers under the chairs or placing a small bow on a piece of flatware to signify who "wins" an arrangement. At charitable events, the centerpieces can be sold to benefit the organization. When flowers are left behind, off-premise caterers should control their distribution, rather than simply let the staff take them at random. In many cases, caterers can reuse the flowers "as is" or rearranged for another event the following day. Under no circumstances should the staff be allowed to remove floral arrangements from the tables until approved by the off-premise caterer or party supervisor.

11. Live plants such as areca palms and ficus trees add dimension to certain off-premise locations. They work well to disguise tent poles, act as a backdrop for the stage and musicians, fill in otherwise empty or awkward-looking corners of rooms, and line entrances to create an aisle-like effect.

In terms of prices, some off-premise caterers recommend that the budget for flowers should be approximately 10 percent of the food cost for an event. Smart caterers and their clients also realize that flower prices change dramatically according to the time of year. Flowers are usually less expensive during spring and summer and most expensive between Thanksgiving and Christmas. Roses are extremely expensive around Valentine's Day and Mother's Day unless ordered months in advance. Many florists refuse to do weddings or other catered events during these holiday weeks because that's when they are swamped with traditional holiday business.

Contracts for florals and décor are relatively simple, but they should include:

- Who will show up, when they will show up, and where they will show up.
- Will they stay until you approve the work?
- A complete listing of everything that is required. This includes the small items, such as flowers to garnish the hors d'oeuvres trays and the fern around the wedding cake. Never assume.
- The size, shape, color, number, and types of flowers for each arrangement, as well as where they will go.

- Deposit and cancellation terms.
- Does the designer guarantee his or her work? What happens if, at the last minute, you or the clients are not pleased?

Aside from using florals and plants, the décor of a party, wedding, or event can be enhanced with ice carvings, balloons, and props. Caterers are limited only by their imagination when it comes to decorating. Both brides and corporate planners are becoming increasingly interested in the "looks" of their parties, and this trend is expected to continue. Creative caterers can separate themselves from their competitors by offering in-house floral and other décor services that they control, instead of leaving them to contractors.

In most markets caterers can arrange for ice carvings in all shapes and sizes. These work well for cold food presentations, particularly raw bars, so it is important to know a couple of vendors who can provide this service.

The use of balloons is an inexpensive way to decorate. Balloon centerpieces and arches add color, excitement, and a festive feel to any party and provide a good way to fill up a large room on a moderate budget. "Balloon walls" can be used to hide a person or products—on a stage or platform, for instance—cued to explode all at once to reveal what's behind them. Again, these are services that some caterers provide, and some subcontract to others.

Many caterers have accumulated all sorts of props to enhance buffets, dining tables, and the event itself. We know one South Florida caterer who travels to Europe each summer, buying items to enhance her displays and create a unique look.

A variety of machines may be employed to produce special effects. Scent machines can produce up to 1,300 different scents. Bubble-, snow-, and fog-making machines can enliven any party. Visit snowmasters.com to learn more about these special options; bulbco.com offers both effects machines and custom lighting equipment.

Photographers and Videographers

Off-premise caterers should establish relationships with several good photographers and videographers. These professionals may be recommended to clients, and, in turn, most of them will also provide the caterer some good photos and videos from the caterer's events to show prospective clients.

In our experience, the best photographers and videographers for events are those who are calm, efficient, and have a sense of humor. They are able to keep things moving so that the pace does not "bog down." It is important that guests are not left sitting, awaiting their dinner, while a photographer is still shooting photos. A professional photographer will want to know from the clients how they wish the event to be remembered. The photographer can shoot dozens of "candids" of guests as they enjoy the event or focus on more formal, group shots—or both. Décor and other details should not be ignored. We know of one married couple who spent a tidy sum on a beautiful custom-decorated cake but have not a single photo of it; the photographer showed their faces as they were cutting the cake, but didn't bother to get the cake itself in any of the pictures! If there are certain people who "must" be in the photos, the client (or the caterer) should be able to point them out during the event.

Off-premise caterers should advise prospective brides and other clients wishing to use a photographer to evaluate a photographer's work by:

- Visiting the photographer's Internet website.
- Reviewing complete albums of work, rather than the best shots from a number of albums. By doing so, they can visualize the photographer's style from start to finish.
- Selecting a particular photographer, rather than a large studio that will simply send out one of its "associates" with a camera.
- Inspecting photographs for sharp shadows in the background (not good), and looking for detail in areas such as the wedding cake icing and the wedding gown (good).

Additional tips come from Randie Pellegrini of the California-based catering firm Cordially Invited and Los Angeles wedding photographer Joe Buissink:

- Do a walkthrough of the wedding and reception site with the photographer prior to the wedding to determine where the formal shots will be made.
- Be sure to go over the timeline of the wedding with the photographer, and be sure the photographer is aware of any photo restrictions in the church or temple, as well as rules at the reception site—where to park and unload, where to plug in equipment, etc. (Older, historical sites sometimes have limited power, and circuits can easily be overloaded.)
- Be sure to pay the photographer ahead of time.
- Be sure the flowers arrive before the photographer.
- If a hair and make-up person has been hired, make sure [he or she stays] through formal shots in case touch-ups are needed.[2]

When it comes to negotiating a contract with a photographer, the late Michael Pecora, of Signature Gardens and Signature Grand in South Florida, used these guidelines, which he was gracious enough to share with us before his death in May 2003:

- Who will show up, when will they show up, and how long will they be there?
- What are the arrangements if more time is needed?
- How many photos will be taken?
- Are charges by the day, the hour, or the event?
- What type of film will be used, and will it be professionally processed?
- What are the deposit and refund policies?
- When will the proofs be ready and, after you select the photos, when will the album be ready?
- What will the photographer do if the photos are not delivered on time? (Long delivery times are often an indication of cash flow problems.)
  - Be sure to get the price list for "extra" prints in advance.
  - How does the photographer guarantee his or her work?
  - Be sure you determine who owns the copyrights to the pictures. Discuss in advance the photographer's right to use your photos in albums and on his or her website.

Lighting and Audiovisual Assistance

Lighting is among the most-often overlooked elements at catered events. The beautiful food displays are inadequately lit, or dangerous steps and other obstacles are barely visible. If an event is to be held after dark, it is imperative that the off-premise caterer visit the site during that time to accurately assess the situation and lighting needs.

Good lighting is truly "invisible." It can highlight attractive features, hide flaws, and provide for guests' safety, all without calling attention to itself. Many off-premise caterers handle some of their own lighting, and others work with lighting specialists.

Off-premise caterers should at least have "a basic knowledge of lighting, so as to be able to professionally assist clients in this area," says South Florida lighting specialist Stephen Pollock. Pollock and Nicole Pierce Fraser, director of business development for Media Stage (Sunrise, Florida, and Bayamon, Puerto Rico), offer these illuminating tips:

1. Theatrical-type light fixtures can work wonders for buffets. These fixtures are easily mounted, adjustable, and can hold colored gels (a gel is a film placed over the bulb to make the light a certain hue). They can be purchased or rented and can provide illumination ranging from soft, diffuse lighting to a hard-edged, focused pattern. This type of lighting can also be created by pipe-and-base, a weighted base with an upright pipe and light source attached to it. Most people don't pay attention to where the light originates—they just notice that it's there.

2. For buffet lighting, a good instrument is the 6-inch *fresnel light*, which puts out a soft light that can be narrowed to a spotlight or "flooded" to wash a wide area with light. The perfect color for lighting food is generally a "no-color" pink, which is a pale pink that is almost white, but adds a rosy glow to a buffet. Buffet centerpieces can be lit with another color, such as a lavender. It is best to light buffets from the front, top, and back whenever possible.

3. Lighting is only as good as the power sources available. You usually cannot illuminate a whole room by plugging into a simple wall outlet. Using separate circuits in other rooms, or even renting an electric power generator (be sure it's a silent model), can solve this problem.

4. Caterers should also be sure that additional lighting sources have dimmers on them, so that the lighting can be adjusted to fit the mood.[3]

Exhibit 13.1 is a lighting glossary prepared by Stephen Pollock. It is also important to be familiar with the terminology used regarding "conventional" and "intelligent" lights. Many people throw these terms around without knowing what really they mean.

- **Conventional lights** have no motors and do not move once they are installed and focused. Of course, their colors can still be changed by changing the gel colors.
- **Intelligent lighting** (which can be motorized or computer programmed) is more expensive, but is essential for events that require high-impact lighting. These

---

❌ *Exhibit 13.1* *Lighting Terms*

Fresnel—A lighting instrument named for the fresnel lens it uses to produce a diffused, soft-edged beam. The spacing between the lamp and the lens can be adjusted to alter the beam spread, from soft to flood.

Gobo—A template inserted into a focusable lighting fixture that defines the pattern of the light as it is projected. Gobos can be made of either metal or glass; metal gobos give a "two-color" look (black and one other color), and glass gobos can provide more color. Glass gobos provide a great look for empty walls and entrances.

Leko—This device contains an adjustable lens that allows a beam to be focused with either a soft or hard edge. A group of internal shutters allows the beam to be cropped, and many lekos have an adjustable iris to allow a variation of the beam's diameter. Lekos can accommodate a "pattern holder" (containing a gobo) for projection of a specific image. Lekos are used for specific lighting situations, like buffets or podium spots. Keep in mind that they must be mounted somewhere.

Par light—Short for "parabolic aluminized reflector" light. Unlike fresnels and lekos, the reflector and lens are built right into this lamp. Par lamps are available ranging from very narrow spotlights to wide floodlights. These are fairly inexpensive and versatile. By simply changing the gel color, you can change the whole mood of a room. They work well for uplighting and can be set on the ground or floor, to point upward.

Pin beam—A small, 25-watt lamp that projects a narrow beam of light up to 20 feet. It is often used to light banquet tables and can make a simple centerpiece look stunning. (Keep in mind that the pin beam must be mounted directly over the centerpiece in order to avoid an angled beam that may cast undesirable shadows.) Pin beams are also used to highlight mirrored balls and dance floors.

Wash—A broad, even, soft form of lighting over all (or part of) a room or stage. It is created by a group of floodlights, set up to provide general illumination in one or more colors. More than one "wash" can be set up to cover an area, blending multiple colors attractively.

---

lights work well to highlight people in the room (at an awards program, for example) or for doing "ballyhoo effects" at the entrance to create a mood. They also work well when directed at people when they are dancing and having fun.

Frequently, off-premise caterers are asked to provide audiovisual equipment such as podiums, microphones, slide and overhead projectors, movie screens; VCR, DVD, or CD players; rear-screen projectors, computers for PowerPoint, or other, similar programs, and so on. A caterer should establish relationships with one or more audiovisual (A/V) suppliers and provide this additional service to clients. Many caterers add markups to their costs for this equipment, creating additional profits in exchange for the time it takes to deal with these matters. Others simply recommend reliable audiovisual equipment suppliers to their clients and prospective clients. Hotels often have their own A/V people and equipment, and clients are charged by the hotels to rent this service for events held in their facilities.

Don't think of audiovisual technology as something to be used only for speeches and presentations. It can be used for many aspects of special events: to enhance a theme with music or visuals, to add a personal touch to wedding receptions or birthdays with photo montages of the person(s) being honored, and so on. Technology changes constantly, and off-premise caterers should at least be familiar with the basics of the latest advances in these areas, so as to be able to recommend enhancements to their clients.

Ground Transportation and Limousines

Occasionally, off-premise caterers are asked to arrange ground transportation for clients, usually for out-of-town corporate clients or for wedding parties at destination wedding locations who require transportation to and from the event site. They may also schedule transportation for wedding couples on the day of the ceremony— limousine service, a horse and carriage, a trolley or rickshaw ride for the wedding couple and their guests. In Dallas, Texas, the city's trolley system even allows children's birthday parties on moving trolleys.

In our experience, it is better to be familiar with transportation vendors and to make informed recommendations than it is to actually book these services. Most caterers have learned that their time should be devoted to the event itself, rather than worrying about whether the buses or limousines arrive on time. You should also advise the clients using buses for transportation to event sites as to the following:

- Be sure there is a "greeter" to meet the guests, both as they board the bus and disembark.
- Each bus driver must have a map with detailed directions to the event. (We've seen buses full of guests get lost and arrive an hour late!)
- Refreshments should be on board if the trip will be longer than 20 minutes.
- Movie star look-alikes, fortune tellers, magicians, or palm readers can provide entertainment during longer trips.
- Taking Polaroid pictures of the guests can be a fun and welcome addition.
- Written or verbal travel guides along the way will create interest.
- An end-of-party pickup time should be reconfirmed so that the transportation is present when guests are ready to leave the party site. (Some guests like to leave early, so it's important to have at least one bus for early departures.)

When recommending ground transportation providers, the main criteria are dependability and reliability. You may also keep on file the types of transportation each company can offer. For instance, there are now "stretch" limousines that seat up to 16 passengers, and most come equipped with a telephone, television, and beverage service. According to Lynn Campanile of Bayshore Limousines in South Florida, Lincoln Town Cars are popular, partly because of their comfort and "conservative" look. However, it's fun to have vendors that offer things like Hummer limousines or "stretched out" Ford Excursions. And in Texas, the limo with a set of "Texas Longhorns" affixed to the front is practically a staple. For weddings, many couples prefer elegant vintage cars like the Rolls Royce and Mercedes Benz. As their caterer, you must be prepared to offer options!

Valet Parking

From time to time, off-premise caterers are asked to assist clients with valet parking services. Many locations do not lend themselves well to self-parking, and clients may wish to provide valet service as an accommodation to the guests.

When recommending valet parking companies to clients, caterers should investigate the following:

- Is the company properly bonded and/or insured?—$5 million is a good minimum for broad-spectrum liability insurance. Harm done to a vehicle while the valet is driving is the responsibility of the valet service. Theft or vandalism that occurs when the car is parked is usually not covered.
- How does the service handle claims, and how long does the claims process take?
- Does the service carry a business license and a valet permit to operate in the municipality where the party is to take place?
- Are the people who work for the valet company clean-cut, well-groomed, and immaculately attired?
- Are the valet attendants courteous? These are usually the first people guests talk to when arriving at an event. The first impression should always be outstanding.
- Is there a policy on tips for the attendants?
- Can the company provide references or letters of recommendation? Be sure to call the references.
- If possible, observe the company in action. Is there is a long wait for cars, do they provide sufficient staff, and how well do they treat the vehicles?

The number of valet parking staff necessary depends on these factors:

1. The number of expected vehicles. On average, there will be two to three people per car.
2. How will they be arriving? Will they "trickle in," as is common before a wedding ceremony? Or will there be a "tidal wave" of cars as most of the guests arrive at the same time for a wedding reception?
3. How far do the valet attendants need to take the cars to actually park them?

Professional valet companies will evaluate each situation and be able to recommend an adequate number of parking attendants to service an event. When waiting in line for your car to either be parked or returned to you, one minute always seems like ten. Keeping this in mind, it is usually better to have too many, rather than too few, valet parking attendants.

The valet attendants should assemble at the party site one hour in advance of the arrival of the first guests. Their appearance should be checked by the off-premise caterer, and the details of the event should be discussed. The valets should be provided with a written script, just a couple of lines, telling them exactly how to welcome the arriving guests. For example, they might say, "Welcome to the Smith wedding reception! Please be sure to take your valuables with you, and follow the sidewalk to the reception."

Some interesting little perks can be included by valet parking services. We've seen them wash car windows (at no charge to the guests, of course) while the guests are at the event. Another idea is to provide a party favor for each vehicle, a surprise farewell gift as the guests depart. For Saturday night events, a complimentary copy of the following Sunday's local newspaper can help create a favorable impression.

Fireworks and Lasers

Ted Walker, president of Add Fire Inc. in Miami Shores, Florida—one of the nation's leading fireworks firms—says, "The use of pyrotechnics [fireworks] can cause the level of excitement of any event to heighten and continue throughout the event. There are three ways to maximize the use of fireworks: outdoor aerial display, outdoor ground displays, and indoor pyrotechnics."[4]

Most people are familiar with outdoor displays. These are launched from the ground, produce their effects high in the sky, and require a large amount of room. Outdoor ground displays—meaning fireworks that are not shot into the air like an aerial shell—are normally used in conjunction with aerial displays to add "dimension" to the overall production. They can be custom-made to call specific attention to a logo, trademark, or business phrase or message. A ground display offers a greater arena for aesthetic demonstration and can safely be placed not only on the ground, but on a hot air balloon, helicopter, stadium wall, mountainside, ocean float, or cruise ship. Visit the website addfire.com for a look at what can be done—presenting a company's logo, all in fireworks, for instance.

Fireworks companies will inspect the site for safety and aesthetic positioning of the fireworks in the environment, secure the necessary permits, and provide insurance and bonds as required. The local fire inspector may request a "trial run" before the event, which fireworks companies are accustomed to providing. This should be part of the contract and included in the overall cost.

Today a variety of flameless "fireworks" made specifically for indoor use can add color and excitement to events without the fire hazard. These release streamers and confetti for up to 90 seconds at a time and can be "choreographed" to music. The website x-streamers.com is a good place to check these out. Another related product that's popular for indoor use is the Glitzzz Super Sparkler. These are great in birthday or anniversary cakes and can also be hidden in centerpieces and activated remotely. The manufacturer's website is sparktacular.com.

Laser light shows can also add excitement to a catered event. Laser light is a solid beam of light that, when coupled with computer choreography, creates complex and colorful visual displays that can be synchronized to music. Indoor lasers, which include models such as variscan, dualscan, and smartscan, look like lasers but are less expensive. When this type of laser is used with a smoke machine, the audience can't tell the difference between this and a "real" laser. The website lasernet.com is one place to get more information.

✕ *Themes and Theme Parties*

Most types of gatherings—from weddings to charitable auctions to cocktail parties—can just be more fun if the client or caterer has a theme to unify all aspects of the event.

Think of a theme as the "umbrella" that encompasses every aspect of the event. Each part or "rib" of the umbrella is an important part of keeping it together:

- **Invitations**—Be certain they include details of any special dress expected of guests.
- **Transportation to the event**—To get them in the mood for what's to come.
- **Décor**—Really focus on the entrance(s) to set the tone; for very large events (500 guests or more), place large props well above eye level.

- **Atmospheric touches**—Use fog, lighting, soundscaping, and/or scents to help create a mood.
- **Food and beverage menus**—Carry through with any ethnic cuisine, color scheme, or fabric print for linens, tableware, buffet displays.
- **Music and entertainment**—Select appropriate musicians or entertainers for the event or, at least, get the band to dress in costume, in the spirit of the event.
- **The "script" for the event**—Who says what, when? Toasts, announcements, award presentations can all be written with the theme in mind.
- And, of course, costumes for staff and/or guests make it especially fun.

Often, the event itself dictates the theme, whether it's a party for a particular holiday, a birthday (ask about the guest of honor's hobbies, special foods, job, etc.), an anniversary, or another lifetime milestone. But when it doesn't, the off-premise caterer should be a fountain of ideas for interesting themes to fit any situation.

A great book for theme ideas is *Pick a Party* by Patty Sachs (Meadowbrook Press). This is a virtual party "bible," with 145 innovative themes, organized with a comprehensive, easy-to-use chart designed to help caterers find the appropriate themes for various occasions: life events and holiday celebrations; the Academy Awards, Super Bowl, Kentucky Derby, and Mardi Gras; and Las Vegas casino, Hawaiian luau, and Caribbean beach parties, to name a few. You can also find theme ideas on the Internet. Here are a few recommended sites: designsofdistinction.com, ararental.org, party411.com, and themepartiesnmore.com.

Popular magazines are also excellent sources of theme ideas. *Bon Appetit, Good Housekeeping, Sunset, Southern Living,* and *Better Homes & Gardens* are full of recipes and home hostess–related suggestions that can be adapted for catering. You can rent movies related to a theme, and hit the "pause" button once in a while to closely observe the décor, dress, props, and backdrops. Guests may be more likely to relate to Hollywood's version of reality than to reality itself!

Themes come from everywhere. Consider these sources:

- Popular books, classics or current bestsellers
- Geographic concepts: the New England clambake, the Wild West barbecue and square dance, the California Surfin' party (the authors' favorite!)
- Heritage events: Kwanzaa, Cinco de Mayo, Obon, Chinese New Year, Bastille Day, Santa Lucia/Festival of Lights
- Historic periods: Roaring '20s, Fabulous '50s, Ancient Greece or Egypt

Before you get carried away with any theme, however, you must be certain it fits the client's original needs and purpose, including the client's budget, and the demographics of the prospective guests. Here are some other tips:

- Look for venues with built-in themes—museums, historical sites, etc.
- Consider accessibility by cars, motor coaches, or boats/yachts.
- Consider the flow of guests within the space, and allow plenty of room for the props.
- Always have a backup plan in case of inclement weather.
- Find out whether there are scheduling conflicts with competing events.

If there's a downside to theme parties, it is that planning and executing them is so time- and labor-intensive, requiring total immersion for the caterer. You would be well advised to charge accordingly for these services. This includes research and development time, time spent meeting with clients, the cost of the costumes, props, and décor, and all the other "extra" elements, as well as employees' time to round them up. This expense is over and above the costs of food, beverage, tables, chairs, linens, china, glassware, flatware, and staffing. The good news is that if a particular theme works well for you with one group, it can be used again with others.

✖ *Kosher Catering and Bar/Bat Mitzvahs*

Kosher is a term that applies to all foods that observant Jews will eat or use that meet the specifications and requirements of the Dietary Laws, which date back to the Old Testament. The *kashrut* is the series of Jewish laws that deal with how these foods must be prepared; it is an ancient Hebrew word that means "fit," or "correct."

As provided with the kind assistance of Eric Kaufman of Executive Catering in Miami, here are the basics that distinguish kosher foods from nonkosher:

1. Kosher animals must have both split hooves and chew their cud—meaning that they almost "double digest" it. It goes from the stomach back into the mouth to be chewed again, and is then finally digested.

2. Kosher fish must have fins and scales. For example, salmon is considered a kosher fish; sturgeon is not. Shellfish are not kosher.

3. Animals and birds must be killed in a specific manner by a *shochet*, a kosher butcher. Therefore, animals killed for sport are not kosher. In the case of kosher beef, only the forequarters are normally used.

4. All meats are "koshered" by being soaked and salted before cooking, because kosher practitioners are not permitted to eat blood. If any egg has a blood spot, it cannot be used. Animals that are seriously diseased or injured in a major organ at the time of slaughter are not acceptable for kosher use. For example, animals that have scar tissue on their lungs, even if they are healthy at the time of slaughter, are not to be used. You may hear the term *glatt kosher; glatt* means "smooth"; it refers to the lung cavity being entirely smooth, which makes it clear that there are no problems with the lung itself. The term is sometimes used to indicate that those responsible for the food have taken extra care to make sure the food is kosher. Animals are inspected by a special rabbi called a *mashgiach* before they are slaughtered by the *shochet*.

5. Meat and dairy products may never be "mixed" together. If any dairy product, such as lactose sugar, lactic acid, or whey, comes in contact with the meat during cooking, the dish is no longer kosher.

6. Kosher food items must be stored and cooked apart from nonkosher foods.

A couple of excellent websites provide insight into these practices and the religious laws behind them: us-israel.org and jewfaq.org/kashrut. It would be worth your while to become familiar with these stringent dietary requirements, which are not at all impossible for caterers to work with.

> The mashgiach also plays the role of the overseer during the food preparation stages, ensuring that dairy and meat are never mixed together in the same bowls, ovens, sinks, etc. The mashgiach also checks to see that any food to be used is distinguished by proper kosher symbols.[5]

The following are ideas for kosher menus:

- **Breakfast:** Chopped eggs, herring, blintzes, bagels, lox, whitefish, cream cheese (a basic dairy-based breakfast)
- **Lunch:** Knish (a traditional baked, stuffed packet of bread dough), Waldorf salad, brisket with prune sauce, duchess-style potatoes, steamed broccoli and baby carrots, fresh fruit salad for dessert
- **Dinner:** Smoked salmon mousse appetizer, Boston bibb salad with raspberry dressing, Chicken Veronique, any steamed vegetable, a poached pear with mint sauce for dessert.

It's important to note that when fish and meat dishes, including poultry, are presented on the same menu, they are never served on the same plate, during the same course, or with the same utensils.

> A true kosher kitchen will have at least two sets of all cooking tools, serving utensils, sinks, and dishwashers to ensure the mix of items such as meat and dairy does not occur. However, one general exception to the rule is glassware, though many strict kosher Jews also choose to avoid this. . . . Machines cannot be lubricated with pork-based oils or whale oils. If so, they are no longer kosher.[6]

And remember, kosher is not a cooking style, and "kosher style" does not mean the same thing as foods that have been properly prepared as kosher. These foods may taste and look like traditional Jewish foods, but they do not meet the high kosher standards required by the Dietary Laws.

A *bar mitzvah* is performed in a temple or synagogue on the Sabbath near the date of a Jewish boy's 13th birthday. For a girl, the celebration is called a *bat* or *bas mitzvah*. This is a major event in a young person's life, celebrating the beginning of adulthood. The key word to describe foods served for such an event, hosted by the child's parents, is "abundant!" And the menu must be selected to please both the teen and the adults.

Today's bar mitzvahs are exciting events. They can be quite lavish, and they're generally theme-oriented. Some feature deejays who play songs the kids hear on the radio, high-energy dance tunes to get everybody onto the dance floor, video games, laser lights, fog machines, roving video cameras that capture guests and flash their images on a big screen, and various themes, depending on what is popular with kids at the time.

In addition to visiting the websites we mentioned, if you plan on a Jewish clientele, you might subscribe to *Kosher Outlook: The Magazine for Kosher Living* (1444 Queen Anne Road, Teaneck, NJ, 07666) or *Kashrus* (P.O. Box 204, Brooklyn, New York, NY 11204). Both magazines focus on Jewish food products and preparation techniques. The website JewishLink.net is also helpful, with links to information about traditional music, art, and much more, in addition to kashrus expertise.

✕ *Weddings and Receptions*

In the past decade, the amount of information available on weddings and receptions has grown 1,000-fold, primarily due to the wedding-related Internet websites like theknot.com and weddingchannel.com, to name just two. There's good news and bad news about this wealth of information—the bad news is that caterers, bridal couples, and their parents can be totally overwhelmed and overloaded by what they can find! The good news is that a good caterer, with patience and persistence, can help sort through the clutter and aim the bewildered wedding party in the right direction.

Weddings are big business for caterers, and some are known specifically for their wedding expertise. For most of us, weddings occupy the weekends and corporate events are mainly held during the week. It's a profitable niche, but you have to be the right kind of person for this peculiar type of stress—infinitely patient, very understanding, and knowledgeable about the many wedding traditions and etiquette. Some caterers choose to take classes specifically geared for wedding planners, just to become familiar with all the pomp and ritual. Check the website of the International Academy of Wedding Consultants, Inc. (academyofweddings.com) for some very comprehensive, weekend-long class options.

This kind of background is important, because today's brides are looking for one-of-a-kind venues, complete with exotic foods for their once-in-a-lifetime fantasy day—and, often, they can afford it. They expect first-class "hand-holding" (attention to every detail), explicit time lines, production value, food tastings, cutting-edge or elegant venue choices, and streamlined flowcharts.

We classify the three major "negatives" about a wedding as bad food, bad music, and a bad flow of events. Successful weddings have layouts that flow smoothly—the movement of the wedding party and guests is very important. A wedding can quickly turn into a disaster when things don't go as planned. Most mishaps are predictable and/or preventable, but timing is critical and every activity must be planned in advance. Caterers also need to know how to handle simple but inevitable timing-related situations: What if the guests arrive early at the reception? What if the bride and groom arrive incredibly late? What if the relatives change the itinerary altogether, before the newlyweds even get there? What if the florists or musicians don't show up on time?

Most of these situations can be handled by meeting with family members and vendors in advance to ensure a smooth flow. If a wedding planner is not involved, it is often up to the caterer to orchestrate a full rehearsal in advance, with all key players in attendance and every detail checked and double-checked. Communication is the key to ensure a great wedding day experience for everyone involved, so the off-premise caterer must understand that the time spent with bridal couples and their families will far exceed the amount of time spent in planning a corporate event.

Wedding Time Lines and Traditions

Wedding plans begin with the engagement. Normally, the bride's family determines the number of guests, but should consult with the groom's family before determining this number. Usually, only close friends and family are invited. Business acquaintances are not invited unless the wedding is to be extremely large.

The caterer should be able to assist a couple in suggesting sites, not only for the wedding and reception, but for also engagement parties and the rehearsal dinner. Younger couples may never have planned a catered event before, and their parents may be only slightly more experienced in this area. They will usually welcome—and expect—your ideas for interesting locations or your professional "take" on those they are already considering. Later, they will rely on you for suggestions about music, photography, vows, clergy, flowers, the wedding cake, and even the knife to cut it with. Many off-premise caterers assume the role of wedding consultant, handling myriad details for the bride. Just be sure your fees reflect this labor-intensive role. It is one thing to cater a reception, and quite another to plan a full wedding weekend for a busy bride.

Even in these modern times, there is an incredible amount of tradition associated with weddings. Do not expect your clients to know it! You should become familiar with wedding protocol for both Christian and Jewish ceremonies, and with basic etiquette issues, in order to assist couples and their families with the actual ceremonies. There are dozens of, shall we say, interesting situations nowadays: For instance, the parents of the bride are divorced, may or may not have remarried others, and may or may not be speaking to one another. People may want their children and friends involved in the ceremony. The bride and groom may practice different religions and want to incorporate both faiths. And what about same-sex marriages? Caterers who know how to handle these delicate circumstances further demonstrate their value to prospective clients.

Exhibits 13.2 through 13.7 depict not only the order for processionals and recessionals, but also where to stand during the ceremony for both Jewish and Christian weddings. These exhibits are from *How to Manage a Successful Catering Business, Second Edition,* by Manfred Ketterer (Hayden Book Co., 1991), reproduced with the permission of the publisher. Exhibit 13.7 shows where people typically stand in a receiving line and how the wedding party is seated at the bride's and parents' table during the wedding reception. In our experience, very few receptions today include formal receiving lines—but again, you'll want to be familiar with the protocol.

The Wedding Reception

Of course, very little is "typical" when it comes to the modern wedding. People get married as they skydive, scuba dive, or stand barefoot on the beach. No matter what the setting, they still need to eat. Budget-minded couples may decide not to have a full meal for guests after the wedding, opting instead for nice hors d'oeuvres, cake, and Champagne. But the traditional, more formal receptions still include a cocktail time with hors d'oeuvres and drinks, during which guests mingle and socialize (while the posed wedding party photos are being taken). The main meal is served when the bride and groom join the reception, sometimes preceded by a "first dance" and a Champagne toast.

The proper toasting procedures are:

- The best man toasts the bride and groom,
- The groom toasts the bride and her family,
- The fathers toast the bride and groom, and
- The bride and groom toast each other.

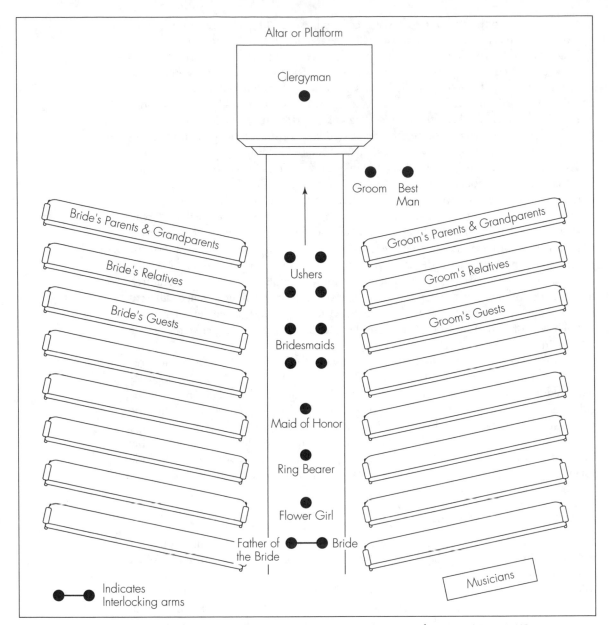

Exhibit 13.2 *Processional for a Christian Wedding (Source: How to Manage a Successful Catering Business, Second Edition, by Manfred Ketterer. ©1991. This material is used by permission of John Wiley & Sons, Inc.)*

If the couple plans on serving an expensive premium Champagne for the toast (rather than a nice-but-less-pricey sparkling wine), it's best to do the toasting before the meal so the guests are able to appreciate it. We've seen half-full glasses of incredible bubbly sit unused on tables at the end of the evening, because the toast was done at the same time as the cake cutting, near the end of the reception. Serve the

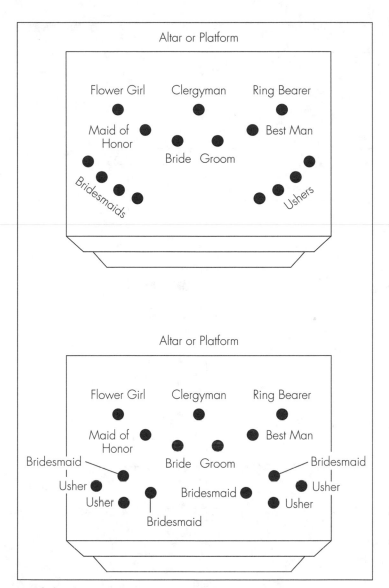

Exhibit 13.3 *Positioning of a Bridal Party for a Christian Wedding (Source: How to Manage a Successful Catering Business, Second Edition, by Manfred Ketterer. ©1991. This material is used by permission of John Wiley & Sons, Inc.)*

good stuff first—and if you're using the less expensive sparklers, the toast can be delayed until after dinner with the wedding cake, when taste buds are saturated and most guests are full. For receptions where Champagne is served only for the toast, it is best to save the toast until the time of the cake cutting, so that guests will be less likely to go to the bar for refills and be refused additional Champagne.

Off-premise caterers are frequently asked to place party favors on guest tables, provide a separate gift table (although most guests do not bring wedding gifts to the

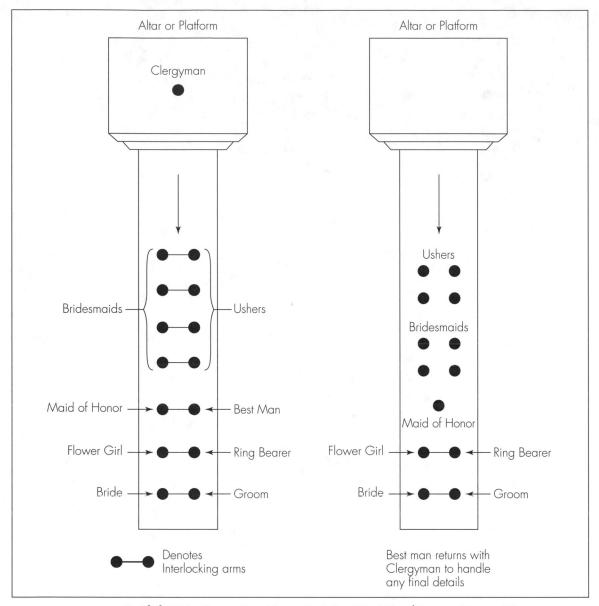

Exhibit 13.4 *Recessional for a Christian Wedding (Source: How to Manage a Successful Catering Business, Second Edition, by Manfred Ketterer. ©1991. This material is used by permission of John Wiley & Sons, Inc.)*

reception and it is considered poor etiquette to do so), and provide an escort table on which the seating cards can be placed.

The main meal can be a seated, served meal, a buffet, or an arrangement of food stations—or it may contain elements of all of these. There can be food stations during the cocktail reception, for example, then a preset first course, followed by a

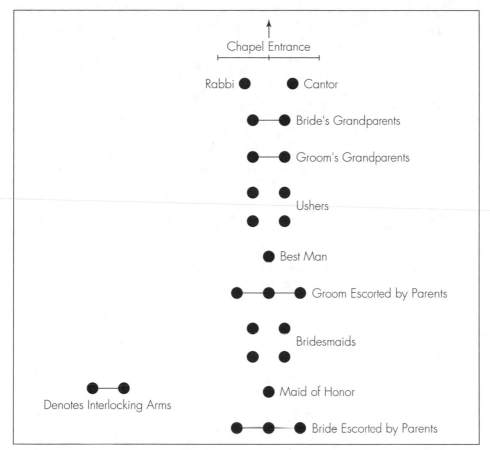

Exhibit 13.5 *Processional for a Jewish Wedding (Source: How to Manage a Successful Catering Business, Second Edition, by Manfred Ketterer. ©1991. This material is used by permission of John Wiley & Sons, Inc.)*

buffet. Again, think "flow"—what will keep the guests happy, interested, and involved in the festivities?

When the meal is finished, it is best to offer dancing before the cake cutting. This allows guests a chance to move around after the meal and ensures that they stay in the spirit of the event. According to Jerry Wayne, popular musician and band leader in South Florida:

> The music mix can be magical to the success of the wedding. For most weddings, there are guests of all age groups, and wedding bands must be able to bridge the gap between dancers who love Cole Porter, George Gershwin and show tunes, yet lure the young at heart onto the dance floor with today's hits and old time rock and roll.[7]

To achieve this magical mix, band leader Simon Salz provides his prospective clients with a Wedding Music Planner, which he has graciously allowed us to reproduce as Exhibit 13.8. It pins down all the information the musicians need to do

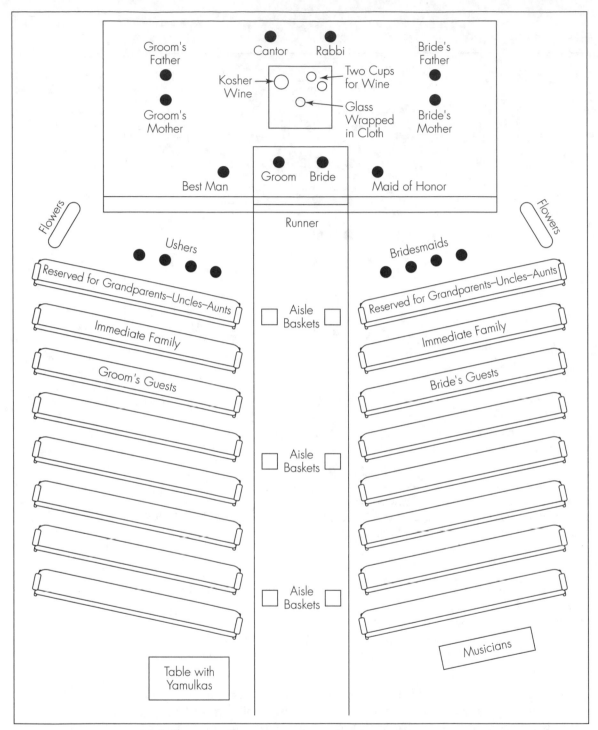

Exhibit 13.6 *Positioning of a Bridal Party for a Jewish Wedding (Source: How to Manage a Successful Catering Business, Second Edition, by Manfred Ketterer. ©1991. This material is used by permission of John Wiley & Sons, Inc.)*

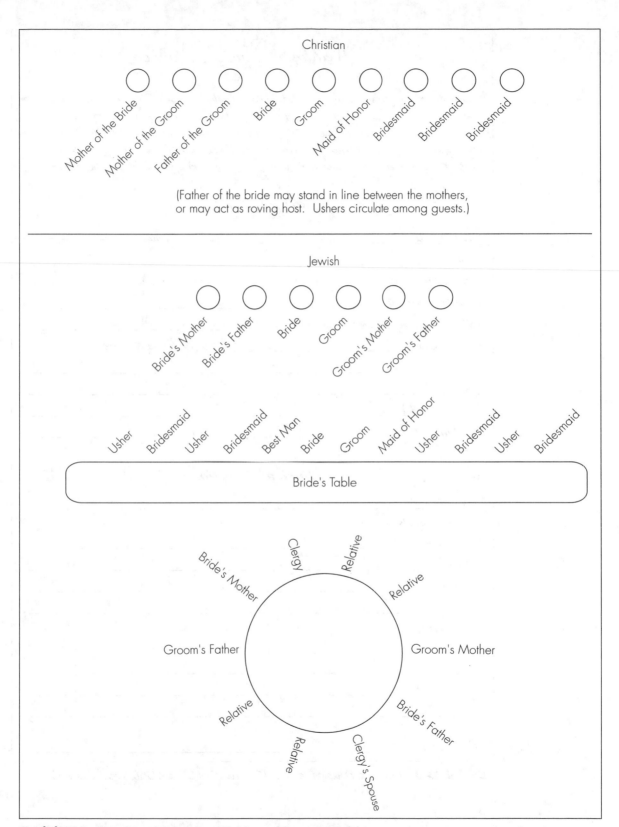

Exhibit 13.7 *Receiving Lines, Head Table and Parents' Tables*

Wedding Music Planner

Music plays an important role at your wedding, setting the atmosphere and providing memories for many years to come. Each family has its own unique tastes in music—as well as pieces that have special meaning for the participants. This planner is a guide to the musical decisions you will be making as well as a way to gather the information needed to provide fitting music for each part of your event. Once completed, this planner will be invaluable in making your special day 'note' perfect.

The Wedding Ceremony

Wedding Date _____ Start Time _____ Approx. Length of Ceremony _____

Location _____

Approx. # of Guests _____ Will a sound system be needed for the music? __ no __ yes

Attire for Musicians _____

Religion/Ethnicity/Style of Wedding Ceremony _____

Instrumentation _____ Will you want a vocalist? __ M __ F

Special Musical Requests _____

_____

Music to Avoid _____

Prelude: Start Time _____ Approximate Length _____

Musical Selections

Prelude _____

Processionals —

    Bridal Party _____

    Groom _____

    Bride _____

    Other: _____ _____

Ceremony

    When in service?

    _____ _____

    _____ _____

    _____ _____

Recessional _____

Exhibit 13.8 Wedding Music Planner (Courtesy of Simon Salz Productions.)

The Wedding Reception

Bride's Name _____ Groom's Name _____

Time of Reception: from _____ to _____

Location of Reception _____

Type of Music Preferred During Cocktail Hour _____

Type of Music Preferred During Dinner _____

Type(s) of Dance Music Preferred (check as many as you like):

___ Big Band/Swing   ___ Latin   ___ Rock/Pop   ___ Ballroom   ___ Line Dancing

___ Klezmer/Jewish   ___ Country   ___ Disco   ___ R&B   Other: _____

Instrumentation _____

Persons To Be Introduced for Grand Entrance:

Name   Relationship

_____   _____

_____   _____

_____   _____

_____   _____

_____   _____

Upon Entrance of Newlyweds, Introduce Them As _____

Song for First Dance _____

Other Important Songs _____

_____

Songs or Things to Avoid _____

_____

Please indicate who will be brought up to dance after the bride and groom. It is traditional to invite up the parents, then the wedding party, and then the rest of the guests. As this is not always the case, we need to know your preference.

_____

_____

_____

When will the toast be given? _____ Who will give it? _____

Will you have a cake cutting? _____ A bouquet/garter toss? _____

Other rituals, announcements, or events _____

_____

NOTES:

Exhibit 13.8 (continued)

their part at both the ceremony and the reception. (Learn more about music options at simonsalz.com.)

Wedding Cakes

If the Champagne toast is not done before the meal, it should be done immediately before the wedding cake is cut. The bride and groom cut the first piece of wedding cake together, using a special, decorated cake knife. The cake table setup is especially important for the caterer, who should provide a plate, napkin, and two forks for the couple to use. Here's how it's supposed to go: First, the bride feeds a bite of cake to the groom, then the groom feeds a bite of cake to the bride. This symbolizes their willingness to share each other's lives. After this, the catering staff cuts and serves the rest of the cake to the guests. A nice additional touch is to serve fresh fruits or another, lighter dessert on the same plate as the cake. This creates a more visually interesting plate, satisfies those guests who choose not to eat wedding cake, and generates a bit of additional profit for the caterer.

The top layer of the cake is saved for the couple to eat on their first-year anniversary, although some eat it on their first-month "anniversary." A wonderful touch is for caterers to provide a cake box with name and logo, which will remind the couple of the caterer every time they open their freezer during the first year of their life as husband and wife. (Yes, marketing is everywhere!) An interesting alternative, suggested by Staten Island caterer Frank Puelo, is to send a freshly made miniature wedding cake to the couple on their first anniversary. At some receptions, there is a "groom's cake" in addition to the wedding cake. (Historically, the groom's cake was the original wedding cake, but today it is a classy alternative, often a chocolate or spice cake, to the white wedding cake.)

Most off-premise caterers do not produce their own wedding cakes, but they should align themselves with one or more bakers who are known for their excellent-quality wedding cakes. Pastry chefs and cake decorators are taking bold steps to design cakes that practically leap off the table—real edible works of art, which can reflect the couple's professions, hobbies, and/or whimsical personalities. We've even seen them made of Krispy Kreme donuts, cupcakes, cannolis, and mini-cream-puffs. So much is going on in this field that it's impossible to do justice to the topic here. We suggest these websites for fantastic wedding cake ideas and photos: sylviaweinstock.com, anapazcakes.com, iceboxcafe.com, mikesamazingcakes.com. Another excellent source is *The Bridal Planning Book: Behind the Scenes*, by Michael Pecora, available on this website: thesignaturegrand.com. For many years, Pecora ran the two very successful banquet halls at the lavish Signature Grand in Florida, and his book contains more than 20 pages about wedding cakes.

Some caterers ask for a referral fee, and others receive a wholesale price for the cake, then charge the client retail. Some charge a cake-cutting fee, in addition to charging for the cake itself. When ordering wedding cakes, couples should be prepared to tell the caterer or the baker the following:

- The number of expected guests
- The desired color and flavor of icing and trim

- The flavor of the filling and the cake
- What they wish to have on top of the cake
- The particular style of cake they like, if any (flowers, pillars, rolled fondant icing, fresh fruit as garnish, mirrored bases, etc.)

As the caterer, you will be asked for your advice, so you should be able to show the couple photos or the websites of the bakers. In your own selection of vendors, it's important to sample the cakes. Are they flavorful, attractive, moist? The most frequent complaint about wedding cakes overall is that they are "dry." The couple should also be encouraged to sample the cake selections. Bakers who offer various flavors— carrot cakes, mocha, white chocolate, liqueurs, and fresh fruits—are always in demand.

If the caterer is not at all involved in the cake order, he or she should at least find out well in advance who the baker is, so that if the cake does not arrive on time, the caterer or event manager can call the baker without disturbing the bridal couple or their families.

If the cake is to be decorated with fresh flowers, it is smart to rely on the florist who is hired for the wedding to supply the cake flowers, rather than the baker. This ensures that the flowers at the reception all "work together" and are fresh and color-coordinated.

Details, such as delivery times and the return of pillars and mirrors used underneath the cakes, should be coordinated between the baker, the couple, and the off-premise caterer to avoid confusion and losses.

Final Reception Details

After the cake cutting, dancing usually resumes. Then, as the event draws to a close, the bride tosses her bouquet to the single women in attendance and the groom removes the symbolic garter from the bride's leg and tosses it to the eligible bachelors. As the bridal couple depart, guests frequently throw birdseed, flower petals, streamers, or something similar. Every facility—even outdoor locations, like city parks— have rules about what is (and is not) allowed to be tossed, and caterers must absolutely know these regulations. Some facilities do not permit any items at all to be tossed. If birdseed or flower petals are thrown, the off-premise caterer should immediately make sure that they are swept up to avoid someone's slipping.

At the end of the reception, off-premise caterers should have the following items clean, packed, and ready for the couple or family to take with them:

- The cake top packed in a clean, attractive box
- Any leftover foods or wedding cake, as prearranged
- Toasting goblets, cake knives, and any other accessories provided by the couple for use at the reception
- The guest book and pen in their original boxes

To avoid dealing with money on the night of the reception, off-premise caterers should provide wedding couples an invoice in advance, so that they simply need to bring the balance due in an envelope to the reception. Why ruin a romantic evening by having to discuss finances before the couple depart on their honeymoon?

For this reason, more and more caterers require payment in full as much as one week in advance of the wedding, along with a credit card number as a precaution in case there are additional last-minute charges for alcohol, staff overtime, extra guests, and so on. Of course, these should be included on a printed invoice and mailed to the clients so they are not surprised by additional charges when they see their credit card statements a month later.

Working with Wedding Planners

Caterers, as a group, have truly mixed feelings about working with wedding planners, as a group. Care must be taken to make sure that the responsibilities of each are clearly outlined—and not overstepped—in planning large, elaborate weddings. Like caterers, some wedding planners are better than others. The best ones are professional, well-organized, and competent, allowing you more time to devote to what you do well—that is, providing excellent food and service.

The Association of Bridal Consultants (bridalassn.com) and International Academy of Wedding Consultants (academyofweddings.com) are two first-rate sources to rely on when inquiring about the credentials of wedding planners or recommending planners in a particular geographic area. Each organization provides training and a certification process and asks members to adhere to certain professional and ethical standards.

Many consultants not only charge the bride for their time, but also expect some form of referral fee or commission from the catering company. Ethically, however, the consultant is also required to inform the bridal couple about how his or her fees are earned. Remember, if you are asked to pay a referral fee to a wedding consultant, he or she must let the clients know about this. A consultant who accepts such a fee is also, technically, liable if the caterer (or any other supplier) does not live up to the clients' expectations.

Wedding planners are obligated to provide the best possible service, at the best possible price. It can be a good working relationship, because a wedding planner can relieve the caterer of a lot of time-intensive details—from making and placing place cards at tables, to negotiating contracts with other vendors. A good wedding consultant will bring you prequalified clients, saving you time and making you money. When things go wrong, as they sometimes do, a competent planner will work with you to correct the situation and, under no circumstances, will he or she tell the harried bride about near misses and minor mishaps.

What a professional wedding consultant expects from you is the ability to be a "team player" in the wedding preparations. This means being helpful, responding to requests in a timely manner, and keeping your ego in check. After all, weddings are a true team effort. And the real "stars" are the bride and groom—not the planner or the caterer.

Today's Trends

As bridal couples become increasingly knowledgeable and sophisticated, caterers who want their business must keep up with current trends. Here are some ideas that are currently popular:

- Serve "signature drinks"—mojitos, martinis, perhaps a custom cocktail (a "Lycheetini" for a bride from China is one example we've seen).
- Use all-inclusive pricing, a package that includes the food, beverages, rental equipment, staff, floral décor, music, wedding cake, photography, and videography. The package can then be added to and customized as needed.
- Allow brides to place family photos around the reception room to personalize the setting. Wedding photos of parents, grandparents, and other relatives work well, along with photos of the bridal couple from infancy on. Some companies will make short video montages of these photos, set to music.
- Miami wedding planner Helen Fong takes a Polaroid photo of each wedding guest as he or she arrives, then pastes it into an oversized guest book. Guests write personal messages next to their pictures.
- Many caterers provide a "lady-in-waiting" to assist the bride on the wedding day.
- Afterglow stations are hot! These, as we've mentioned previously, include espresso, cappuccino, and other coffee drinks, along with cognacs, cordials, and liqueurs. The "coffee-making" function of this station can be subcontracted, which can free up your staff for other duties.
- Bathroom baskets packed attractively with the necessary grooming essentials show that all details have been covered.
- Laser-printed menus cost little, yet they add a classy, professional touch.
- Theme and destination weddings are popular. Smart caterers learn all they can about the customs and cultures of couples who are from foreign lands or want to include their family heritage in their celebration.
- Holding a food tasting prior to a wedding is a great way to spend time with the bridal couple, learning about their wants, needs, and desires, as well as an excellent time to "up-sell" to more elegant food and services.
- We've noted more brides request an "intermezzo" course. One of our most popular is Ginger Pear Sorbet, served in a hollowed-out pear. We place each serving on four rose petals that form a simple, enveloping garnish, as the petals "wrap" themselves around the base of the pear.
- Thanks to Martha Stewart and others, more brides seem to want long banquet tables that seat scores of guests, rather than the typical 60- or 72-inch rounds. A 66-inch round is becoming increasingly popular, which seats ten guests a bit more comfortably than the 60-inch table but takes up less room than a 72-inch table.
- Dove and butterfly releases—after the clergyperson says, "You may kiss the bride"—have been around quite a while, but are still a hit.

✕ Conclusion

The more you cater, the more you read, and the more events you attend as a guest yourself, the better you will become at building your "arsenal" of themes, services, and vendors to help you make these events a reality. We put a lot of information on weddings in this chapter, partly because these are often catered events, but also because overall expertise in catering them is in short supply. Part of your business is building trust with clients and co-workers, and you never know when a beleaguered bride, church employee, or vendor's assistant will ask *you* how something is supposed to be done. If you can save the day with the correct answer, why not know it?

Notes

1. Carolyn Prear, CSEP, president of Eclectic Events International, Toronto, Canada, in *Special Events* magazine, July 2001.
2. Randie Pellegrini, principal, Cordially Invited, and Joe Buissink, wedding photographer, Los Angeles, California, in *Special Events* magazine, October 1997.
3. Stephen Pollock, lighting specialist, Fort Lauderdale, Florida, and Nicole Pierce Fraser, director of business development, Media Stage, Sunrise, Florida, in personal conversations with the authors.
4. Ted Walker, president, Add Fire, Inc., Miami Shores, Florida, personal interview with author.
5. *NACE News*, publication of the National Association of Catering Executives, Columbia, Maryland (nace.net), May 1993.
6. *NACE News*, publication of the National Association of Catering Executives, Columbia, Maryland (nace.net), May 1993.
7. Jerry Wayne, *Jerry Wayne's Private Party Band*, Miami, Florida. (jerrywayne.com)

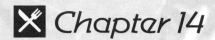 **Chapter 14**

Budgeting, Accounting, and Financial Management

Okay—now let's make all these great food, décor, and party ideas into a business! If you think organizational skills are required to put a wedding together, just wait until you try doing your first-year taxes. Off-premise caterers who understand the financial aspects of their business will definitely increase their chances of success in this challenging field. They need to know how to prepare budgets, produce accounting records, analyze financial reports, implement cost control techniques, deal with banks, and limit tax liabilities and understand how computers and software programs can assist them.

Successful caterers know how the revenues and expenses from catered events flow through the business records and end up as profits or losses. They understand the difference between "profit" and "cash." Those caterers who fail to understand their business "by the numbers" will simply be more likely to fail over time. So, in addition to knowing these basics, we suggest that you take an accounting class or two. Another excellent resource for the business owner or manager who is not an accountant by nature is *Finance and Accounting*, by Suzanne Caplan, part of the Adams Media "Streetwise" series (Adams Media Corporation, 2000). Subtitled *How to Keep Your Books and Manage Your Finances without an MBA, CPA, or a Ph.D.*, it teaches the reader just that.

✖ *Preparing a Budget*

No one should even consider starting an off-premise catering operation without first preparing a budget to determine the feasibility of the business venture. Off-premise caterers have lost millions of dollars by not first projecting their sales, then relating these sales to actual overhead expenses. Together, these steps form a basic budget.

A budget is a plan for operating a business expressed in financial terms. It includes sales and expenses, which are projections based on whatever information is available to you: past performance, current prices, future forecasts, and the like.

One of the most common mistakes made by a new caterer is committing to large overhead expenses (such as rent, utilities, and equipment financing) without first determining how these expenses will relate to the projected sales. This caterer takes on large financial obligations, assuming that large sales will follow. When these sales fail to appear, or materialize more slowly than the caterer expected, the expenses exceed revenues and the business often has no chance to catch up.

For example, a start-up off-premise caterer with no guaranteed sales or previous experience would probably be foolish to assume a $2,000 monthly lease and a $1,000 monthly payment for equipment financing. As a general rule, these two expenses should never exceed 10 percent of monthly sales, which means in this case that the caterer would need to average monthly sales of $30,000. A more realistic amount would be $300 to $500 per month for these expenses, as the required revenues would be significantly less and obviously more achievable.

For the purpose of illustrating basic accounting principles, we've created a fictitious caterer, aptly named the Hypothetical Catering Company. This person is starting a small off-premise catering business from a small kitchen equipped with basic kitchen equipment and utensils. Hypothetical Catering pays an annual rent of $5,000 ($417 a month), is financing the business with personal savings, and plans to rent the necessary front-of-the-house equipment from a local rental company. All examples and exhibits in this chapter refer to this "company," and readers are cautioned at this point not to use these exhibits and examples as "gospel." They are not. Nor should they assume that the various revenues, expenses, and profits are absolute numbers to be emulated by all off-premise caterers. Again, they are not. Every off-premise caterer operates differently. The purpose of our example is simply to relate financial theory to reality.

The first step in developing a budget is to project sales based on past performance and projected future performance. Obviously, start-up caterers will have no past performance to evaluate, so they must make "educated guesstimates" about their projected sales. When estimating upcoming sales, it is better to err on the conservative side. Your projections should be based on your own best estimates of the following:

- Number of events you expect to cater
- Average selling price of each event
- Seasonal variations
- National and local economic indicators
- Competitive factors
- Industry trends

Start by making these projections for a full year, then breaking them down by month. For example, a start-up off-premise caterer who will focus on outdoor events in the Southern United States will generate more sales in the cooler months (those with more pleasant weather) and fewer sales in the scorching hot months. This caterer, who projects $100,000 in first-year sales, could realistically have these monthly sales projections:

January	$2,000 (first month in business)
February	3,000
March	8,000 (pleasant weather conditions)
April	6,000
May	9,000
June	5,000 (warmer months begin)
July	2,000
August	4,000
September	3,000
October	10,000 (weather begins to cool down)
November	15,000 (reputation is building)
December	33,000 (excellent holiday season)
First year total	$100,000

Why is it necessary to project sales on a monthly basis? Isn't it adequate to simply project them for the year? The answer is "No!" Bills must be paid monthly, no matter what the profit for a particular month, and a start-up business must plan accordingly to have enough operating capital (cash) on hand. In our example, it is more than likely that Hypothetical Catering will lose money in the months of January, February, July, August, and September, but generate a profit in the other months. In those months of overall loss, the business will be unable to pay its expenses from revenues; therefore, operating capital (cash) will be needed. A detailed discussion of this subject follows later in this chapter.

The next step in preparing a budget is to estimate expenses. The four main expense categories are:

- Cost of sales (food cost; also called "cost of goods sold")
- Payroll and related costs
- Direct operating expenses
- Administrative and general expenses

There is a detailed discussion of these expense categories in the section "Chart of Accounts" in this chapter. For now, we offer a brief definition and description of each of them.

Cost of Sales. This is estimated by reviewing past performance results for this category, as well as two factors:

- Your menu pricing strategy, which means what you will charge for each item. This figure should always include a percentage of profit.
- Current prices of raw materials and ingredients.

For example, an off-premise caterer whose overall pricing strategy is to triple the basic cost of the food should achieve a $33\frac{1}{3}$ percent cost of sales, as depicted here:

Food cost for dinner is $5 \times 3 = \$15$ (per person)

$5 divided by $15 is the cost of sales percentage = $33\frac{1}{3}$ percent

Here are a few markup factors and their associated food cost percentages:

MARKUP FACTOR	PROJECTED FOOD COST/COST OF SALES
5	20%
4	25%
3	$33\frac{1}{3}$%
2.5	40%

Most off-premise caterers operate with cost-of-sales figures between 20 and 40 percent. For budgeting purposes in this chapter, we use $33\frac{1}{3}$ percent in our examples.

Payroll and Related Costs. Payroll taxes, unemployment taxes, and other costs directly related to payroll vary from caterer to caterer. Unlike the cost of sales, which can vary based on the caterer's volume of business, payroll costs have some components that are fixed and others that are variable. For instance, most caterers employ one or more employees on a permanent basis, who come to work and must be paid regardless of the level of business. These people's paychecks are essentially "fixed payroll." Successful caterers know that the fewer employees in this category, the better. When business drops off in slower seasons, these employees must still be paid, and a large fixed payroll can quickly erode profits and create huge losses. So every off-premise caterer should strive to keep payroll costs in check by keeping permanent employees at a minimum, staffing events with part-timers who work only when needed. These are "variable payroll" costs, and they should make up the bulk of your payroll expense.

Ideally, payroll and related costs as a percentage of sales should stay constant, rather than fluctuate as sales increase or decrease from month to month. Off-premise caterers generally operate with payroll and related costs between 20 and 35 percent.

At this point, it is critical to note that operators with high food cost percentages should have lower labor cost percentages, and vice versa. An off-premise caterer with a 40 percent food cost and a 35 percent labor cost will not stay in business long. Caterers should strive for a combined cost-of-sales and payroll percentage of 50 percent or less if they are to maximize profitability.

The next budgeting step is to compute actual payroll and related expenses based on available information. Assume that Hypothetical Catering employs a cook who works an average of 30 hours per week at an hourly rate of $9 and a helper who works 20 hours per week at an hourly rate of $7. Together, these two employees earn $410 per week, or $21,320 annually. This caterer's related costs (employer's FICA expense, unemployment taxes, and other expenses that are directly related to payroll) add another 20 percent to the payroll, which increases the total to $25,584:

$21,320 \times .20 = \$4264$

$4264 + \$21,320 = \$25,584$

A shortcut to obtain the same result is to multiply $21,320 by 1.2, which will yield the same answer.

Hypothetical Catering often hires additional staff for parties. This additional staff, *including related costs*, is 10 percent of total revenue.

Direct Operating Expenses. These include the costs of doing daily business, for such things as supplies, to transportation, utilities, and advertising. Of course, they vary greatly among businesses. Within this category, some operating expenses are fixed; others are variable.

Administrative and General Expenses. These may seem like operating expenses, but they are classified differently. They are the "office expenses" of your business—the costs of things like letterhead and business cards, telephone, insurance, repairs and maintenance to the building, and rent payments if you're leasing an office or kitchen space. Again, these amounts vary greatly, depending on the company.

In both of these categories, costs should be kept at a minimum in order to attain maximum profitability. A complete explanation of operating and administrative expenses follows later in this chapter, but for our budgeting illustration, we'll assume our fictitious caterer tries to keep both administrative and general expenses at $800 per month.

Armed with all this knowledge, it is now possible to complete an annual budget by month for our Hypothetical Catering Company.

REVENUE	COST OF SALES	PAYROLL EXPENSE	OPERATING AND RELATED EXPENSES	ADMINISTRATIVE AND GENERAL EXPENSES	PROFIT/LOSS
$ 2,000	$ 667	$ 2,332	$ 800	$ 800	($2,599)
3,000	1,000	2,432	800	800	(2,032)
8,000	2,667	2,932	800	800	801
6,000	2,000	3,032	800	800	(632)
9,000	3,000	2,590	800	800	1,810
5,000	1,667	2,632	800	800	(899)
2,000	667	2,332	800	800	(2,599)
4,000	1,333	2,532	800	800	(1,465)
3,000	1,000	2,432	800	800	(2,032)
10,000	3,333	3,132	800	800	1,935
15,000	5,000	3,632	800	800	4,768
33,000	11,000	5,432	800	800	14,968
$100,000	$33,334	$35,442	$9,600	$9,600	$12,024

In this example it is interesting to note that most of the profit is made in December, which means that, in effect, there is negative cash flow during the rest of the year. Hypothetical's owner would be unable to extract any cash from the business until the end of the year, unless he or she was able to receive large advance deposits on future business, which is quite unlikely in the case of a first-year caterer.

It is also apparent that, on a monthly basis, this caterer does not generate a monthly profit until sales reach about $8,000. This is the *break-even point*, which is discussed later in this chapter.

Is $12,024 an acceptable profit for a first-year caterer? This depends entirely on the caterer. Is Hypothetical Catering a part-time or full-time venture? Was this caterer unhappily employed for a number of years and is now just happy to be on his or her own? What are the caterer's other financial obligations? Are there savings from which to draw until the business becomes more successful?

✖ *Start-Up Expenses*

As pointed out earlier in this text, the best way to start an off-premise catering business is by utilizing an existing foodservice facility that operates for other purposes, such as a restaurant, club, or hotel. However, there are some instances in which an individual may wish to rent a commissary to use exclusively for off-premise catering.

How much will this cost? There are many factors that will affect this calculation, so our estimate for a 2,000-square-foot commissary shows a range of figures. These are annual figures for a business with projected gross annual sales between $400,000 and $1,000,000 per year:

Advance rent and security deposits	$ 3,000–5,000
Equipment and fixtures	50,000–100,000
Leasehold improvements	10,000–20,000
Licenses and permits	1,000–2,0000
Marketing expenses	1,000–10,000
Utility and phone deposits	500–1,000
Accounting and legal services	500–2,000
Pre-opening payroll	2,000–5,000
Supplies and uniforms	1,000–2,500
Prepaid insurance	2,000–5,000
Miscellaneous other expenses	1,000–3,000
Total Start-up Costs	$72,000–155,500

These figures arc simple, rough estimates of what it might cost to lease and set up a catering commissary. Each situation will be different, and ours for this book is strictly hypothetical. The figures are not meant to be used for anything other than discussion purposes within this text.

✖ *Cash Budgets*

We've talked about estimating income and estimating expenses, but neither of these estimates accounts for cash flow. They simply record revenues and expenses and do not take into account when the actual cash is received.

A *cash budget* accounts for the actual flow of cash in and out of the catering business. Income from a catered event is recorded on the day the event occurs but, for the same event, the cash flow could be different.

For example, assume that Hypothetical Catering books a party for March 15, with a total price for the event of $1,000. This caterer requires a $250 deposit, which is received on January 15. Another $250 is paid on February 15, and the balance is paid on the day of the event. In this particular situation, cash is received during three months of the year, yet the sale (revenue) is not recorded until March 15. This is one way in which cash flow differs from basic budgeting.

A second budgeting difference occurs on the expense side. The off-premise caterer purchases food and supplies on credit and does not need to pay for them until the 10th of the following month. In this example, suppose that the food and supplies that must be bought for the event will cost the caterer $250. However, this caterer need not pay for them until the 10th of the following month.

What about payroll costs? They are generally paid within one week of the party date and, although they do have some effect on cash flow, their impact is minimal in terms of this discussion.

What other factors separate income and expense budgets from cash budgets? Prepaid expenses, such as insurance fees and utility deposits, are accounted for differently. Many off-premise caterers finance their insurance premiums, paying anywhere from one-fourth to one-half of the policy's premium amount in advance, then financing the rest over a 6- to 10-month period. In the case of a $3,000 annual insurance policy, it will show on the income and expense budget as a monthly expense of $250 for all 12 months of the year. However, in the cash flow budget, it must be recorded the way the caterer chooses to pay it. The actual cash flow could be a big payment of $1,000 on January 1, and the remaining $2,000 in 10 payments of $200 over the next 10 months. The cash budget would show this as follows:

MONTH	OUTWARD CASH FLOW
January	$1,000
February through November	$200
December	None

Another major difference between cash and revenue budgeting occurs with the purchase of major equipment and fixtures. In our example of start-up costs, Hypothetical Catering Company needs $50,000 worth of equipment to get started. For cash budgeting purposes, assume that half this amount can be paid in advance and the remaining balance is to be financed over three years.

The cash flow statement would show outward cash flow of $25,000 in January, and equal amounts of outward cash flow during the next 36 months for the remaining $25,000 that was financed, plus interest charges.

However, the income and expense budget would show different figures—equal to the amounts that can be depreciated under federal and state laws. (For an understanding of depreciation and the rules pertaining to it, an off-premise caterer should definitely seek the professional advice of a Certified Public Accountant (CPA) and an attorney.) Assume for now that the law allows this caterer to depreciate the equipment over a five-year period. In that case, the monthly depreciation amount would be the price of the equipment ($50,000) divided by its "useful life" (60 months), which equals $833.33 per month. The income and expense budget would show a cost of $833.33 per month for equipment.

Start-up off-premise caterers *must* project their cash flows annually, with the first year of operation being the most important. Now let's take the example (with first-year sales expected to be $100,000) and determine the cash needs for Hypothetical Catering, using a basic cash budget system that projects cash receipts and payments on a monthly basis.

Cash receipts include:

Cash sales
Collection of accounts receivable
Advance deposits for future parties

Cash payments include:

Food purchases (cost of sales)
Payroll and related expenses
Direct operating expenses
Administrative and general expenses
Owner's draw (amount of money the owner takes from the business)
Prepaid expenses (such as insurance)
Start-up costs

In order to produce a cash flow statement here, some assumptions must be made:

■ That all clients pay advance deposits equal to one-half the total bill during the month prior to the party; all remaining balances are due the day of the party.
■ That the cost of goods sold (cost of sales) and operating expenses are paid in the month following the event.
■ That administrative and general expenses, and payroll and related expenses, are paid in the same month as the event.
■ That our caterer does have a $3,000 insurance policy and is paying it off with one-third ($1,000) in January and the rest in ten equal monthly payments of $200 from February through November. (Any interest charges for not paying the policy in full are included in the $3,000 total.)

Our example does not include any start-up expenses, but these can vary significantly—from zero to six-figure amounts. To keep it simple, this example addresses cash flow from operations. Let's take a look at the books:

JANUARY CASH RECEIPTS

Revenue	$2,000 (all of the month's sales revenue)
Advance deposits	1,500 (half of February's sales revenue)
Total Receipts	$3,500

JANUARY CASH EXPENSES

Cost of Goods Sold	-0- (all on credit, to be paid in February)
Operating expenses	-0- (all on credit, to be paid in February)
Payroll and related	2,332
Administrative and general	1,550 (adjusted for prepaid insurance)*
Total Disbursements	$3,882

*This figure was determined by increasing the $800-per-month charge for administrative and general expenses by $750, because it was necessary to prepay $1,000 of the insurance premium. Therefore, the cash disbursement was $750 more than the budgeted amount.

CASH BALANCE AT END OF MONTH (JANUARY)

Receipts	$3,500
Disbursements	3,882
Cash balance at month's end	(382)
(without considering beginning cash balance)	

So in January, the records indicate a loss of $2,599, but things don't look so bad from a cash flow standpoint, because Hypothetical Catering Company received some advance deposits and did not have to pay some major expenses (cost of goods sold and operating expenses) until February. In terms of cash flow, the negative number was only $382.

Now let's see how it goes in February:

FEBRUARY CASH RECEIPTS

Revenue	$1,500 (remaining half; the first half was received in January)
Advance deposits	4,000 (half of March's sales revenue)
Total Receipts	$5,500

FEBRUARY CASH EXPENSES

Cost of goods sold for January	667
Operating expenses for January	800
February payroll and related	2,432
February administrative and general	750*
Total Disbursements	$4,649

*As in the previous example, the cash disbursement for administrative and general expenses is actually only $200, which is $50 less than the budgeted amount.

Cash increase during February	$851
Cash balance at beginning of month	(382)
Cash balance at end of month	469

Again, despite a loss, a positive cash flow was achieved. If you'd like to practice, just continue this exercise throughout the year and project the positive and negative cash flows for the remaining ten months.

The point is that it's very important to understand the inherent differences between cash flow accounting—which keeps track of cash as it flows in and out of the business—and your income and expense accounting, which is a true measure of the profitability of a business. Both are important. However, without positive cash flow, you will be unable to remain in business.

✗ Break-Even Points

All off-premise caterers must know their break-even points—that is, the amount of revenue necessary for the business to "break even," posting neither profit nor loss. At the break-even point, revenue equals expenses.

To calculate a break-even point, costs must be divided into two types, fixed and variable. Fixed costs are a specific dollar amount, while variable costs are a percentage of revenue, because they will go up or down depending on how busy you are. Referring to our Hypothetical Catering Company, we can separate these costs as follows:

VARIABLE COSTS

Cost of goods sold	$33\frac{1}{3}$% of revenues
Payroll and related (for part-timers)	10% of revenues
Total Monthly Variable Costs	$43\frac{1}{3}$% of revenues

FIXED COSTS

Fixed monthly payroll (for employees)	$2,132
Operating expenses	800
Administrative and general expenses	800
Total Monthly Fixed Costs	$3,732

There are a number of methods for determining the break-even point, some of which are extremely sophisticated, using techniques with names like "regression analysis." In this case, though, simplicity is the key. One formula that can be used is:

Fixed costs ÷ contribution margin = break-even point

The *contribution margin* is the difference between 1 and the variable costs. In this case, it would be:

$$1 - 43\frac{1}{3}\% = 56\frac{2}{3}, \text{ or } .5667$$
$$(1.0 - .4333 = .5667)$$

Using this formula, our break-even point can be calculated as follows:

$3,732 (fixed costs) ÷ .5667 (contribution margin) = $6,585

The break-even point for this caterer for any given month is $6,585. This figure can be verified by taking a look back at the projected profit and loss chart we made for Hypothetical Catering for the year. The financial projections for April show a loss of $632 on sales of $6,000, whereas the figures for March reveal a profit of $801 on sales of $8,000.

The break-even point is really just a target at which to aim. It gives you some indication of the level of revenue it will take to turn a profit. Potential investors and bankers will ask for this information as well. It's also important to note that your break-even point can change over time, so you should recalculate it a couple of times a year. Costs tend to inch up, and the break-even point will reflect this. In addition to controlling costs, you may have to consider raising prices if your projections show you're not meeting the break-even point, month after month.

✂ *Accounting for Revenue and Expenses*

The purpose of this section is to introduce you to a basic accounting system that can be implemented by off-premise caterers on a daily basis. Today, there is no need to engage a costly accountant to keep the most basic business records. Most of your accounting needs can be computerized, but you still need to understand what you're inputting into the system and why. The basics are easy to learn and can quickly be taught to a qualified staff member.

Knowing how to do the books does not eliminate the need for a CPA, particularly for year-end tax preparation, but it does provide a structure for documenting daily revenues and expenses, and for producing the records a CPA will require to handle your tax needs. This can save thousands of dollars in expensive accounting fees.

Perhaps the most critical part of a good accounting system is that records be kept on a daily basis and always input into the computer on a timely basis. Record revenue and expenses every day, while they are current and fresh in your mind. When small business owners don't keep their financial records up to date, nothing good can come of it—bills and/or taxes are not paid on time, and penalties and/or interest charges may be levied.

The end results of all record keeping for a particular time period are the Income Statement and the Balance Sheet. These two documents show an off-premise caterer the company's financial status for that time period. The Income Statement shows the net profit or net loss. The Balance Sheet is essentially a snapshot of the financial status of the business as of a particular date. More about both of these documents shortly.

This accounting system is not double-entry bookkeeping, and it does not replace the expertise of a good CPA, but it does provide the off-premise caterer with accurate figures that can be used to better manage the business.

Accounting Journals

The basic components of this accounting system are *journals,* which are ledgers used to record various financial transactions—sales, expenses, and so forth. The "name" of the journal typically describes the type of information recorded there. By using these basic accounting components, the caterer can easily prepare both income statements and balance sheets by simply recording totals and major figures from these journals. Let's talk about some of the basic types of journals.

Sales and Cash Receipts Journal. This is used to record sales and cash receipt information as it occurs. It can be as simple as a columnar accounting pad with sufficient columns to record the various categories of revenues and cash receipts, as well as any service charges, sales taxes, and gratuities. Examples of revenue and cash receipts headings include:

Advance deposits
Food sales
Labor charges
Beverages, setups, mixers, wine corkage fees
Rentals and equipment
Flowers and décor
Music and entertainment
Parking and valet services
Photography and video

Service charges
Gratuities
Sales taxes
Total amounts paid

Many of these columns are used only when the caterer actually provides or subcontracts for these services—for music, parking, floral design, photography, and so on. When the clients directly pay these vendors, there is no need for a caterer to record the transactions, since they do not affect the financial affairs of the catering business.

When a figure is written into a journal (or typed, in the case of a computer program), it is called *posting* to the journal, and the figure is called a *journal entry*. The source documents for posting to this journal are the copies of invoices provided to clients, and receipts for the advance deposits received from clients. (Please note that it is best to also keep a separate Advance Deposit Journal in addition to the Cash Receipts Journal so that advance deposits can be quickly located without going through page after page of journal entries.)

To illustrate this procedure, Exhibit 14.1 shows a sample invoice for an off-premise event, and Exhibit 14.2 provides a sample page from Cash Receipts and Sales Journal. These two exhibits show how sales are posted from the invoice to the journal.

Petty Cash Journal. The purpose of this journal is to record expenses paid for out of petty cash—and there is nothing "petty" about it. Every off-premise caterer pays for miscellaneous (usually small) expenses from petty cash. A last-minute purchase at the supermarket is an example of a petty cash expense. Although these expenses are not large amounts, they add up quickly, and petty cash can be the least "secure" of your finances, easily pilfered if you don't keep an eye on it. Petty cash is not meant to pay for major purchases. Off-premise caterers wishing to establish a petty cash fund should first write and cash a check, made payable to cash, for the amount of the fund. Most such funds range from $100 to $1,000, depending on the size of the business and the expected uses. Petty cash should be kept separate from personal cash.

Off-premise caterers should retain receipts for all petty cash purchases, and the total value of these receipts, added to the remaining cash in the fund, must always equal the total amount of the fund. For example, if your petty cash fund is $500 and there is $300 in cash in the petty cash box, there should be $200 worth of receipts.

Once the petty cash fund is depleted to a point where it should be replenished, the receipts are posted to the Petty Cash Journal (as shown in Exhibit 14.3), and a replenishment check is written that totals the exact amount of the receipts. The journal is simply a summary of all petty cash purchases, with a total for each type of expense. The fund should always be replenished at the end of each accounting period to ensure that all expenses are accounted for in the same period.

It must be emphasized that all petty cash receipts must be marked "Paid" once they have been reimbursed from the petty cash fund, to prevent fraudulent reuse at later times by a dishonest person.

⊠ *Exhibit 14.1* *Sample Invoice for Off-Premise Catering and Other Services*

January 15, 20___
(Date of Invoice)

(Name of Client)
(Address of Client)

INVOICE FOR OFF-PREMISE CATERING SERVICES ON JANUARY 15

30 DINNERS AT $15 PP	$450
30 BEVERAGE SETUPS, MIXERS, ICE AT $2 PP	60
STAFFING	200
FLORAL DÉCOR	100
RENTAL EQUIPMENT	400
TOTAL PRICE	$1,210
20% SERVICE CHARGE	242
6% STATE SALES TAX (VARIES BY STATE)	87.12
TOTAL CHARGE FOR EVENT	$1,539.12
LESS: ADVANCE DEPOSIT PAID	(600.00)
BALANCE DUE	$ 939.12

NOTES

1. In this example, sales tax is charged on the service charge, which is the law in most states.
2. It is highly recommended that off-premise caterers be paid in full no later than the day or night of the event, rather than extending credit. Even the largest corporations have ways to pay for things if required. Astute caterers will advise all clients that they require payment in full upon the completion of the event.
3. One way to do this easily, without disturbing the client on the night of the event, is to submit an invoice in advance of the event and ask the client to bring a check in that amount. (Some caterers require payment in full prior to the day of a wedding reception. This is a much smoother procedure than disturbing a bride or her mother near the end of a wedding reception to write a check.) Additional charges for extra guests or other unexpected costs can be invoiced.
4. Invoices may be prepared on preprinted invoice forms, or simply on the caterer's letterhead paper. It is highly recommended that invoices be prenumbered for control purposes, to ensure that all invoices are accounted for and reconciled to cash receipts.
5. Math and other errors in invoices can be extremely costly and embarrassing. It is difficult to go back to a client one month after the party and ask for additional money due to an invoice mistake. Overcharges can be embarrassing and can give some clients the impression that the off-premise caterer is deliberately overcharging.
6. In the preceding example, state sales tax was charged on the service charge. What about charging sales tax on tips that the client pays? In most states, sales tax on gratuities need not be charged only when the following conditions are met:
❑ The gratuity or tip is 100 percent voluntary.
❑ All of the gratuity is distributed to employees.
❑ These two conditions are stated in the contract.

Exhibit 14.2 Sample Page from a Cash Receipts and Sales Journal

DATE	PARTY NAME	FOOD SALE	BEV. SALE	STAFF	FLOW	EQUIP.	MUSIC	SERVICE CHRG.	SALES TAX	TOTAL	ADV. DEP.	AMOUNT PAID
1-1	JAMES										600	600
1-15	JAMES	450	60	200	100	400	—	242	87.12	1539.12	939.12	
1-25	PEREZ	900	—	400	100	400		260	93.60	1653.60	1653.60	
1-29	SMITH										1500	1500
TOTAL		1350	60	600	100	400		502	180.72	3192.72	3192.72	4692.72

NOTES:

1. Each column can be set up easily on columnar accounting paper.
2. Posting to this journal is made directly from the invoice.
3. The Amount Paid column is completed only upon receipt of payment.
4. At the end of the month, each column is totaled, and most of the totals are posted to the Income Statement for the month.

⚒ Exhibit 14.3 *Sample Petty Cash Journal*

			Account to be Charged				
Date of Purchase	Food	Beverage Mixers	Supplies	Laundry	Postage	Office Supplies	Total
1-15	25	25					$ 50
1-15			75				75
1-15				25			25
1-20					25		25
1-20						25	25
1-25	25	25					50
Total	$50	$50	$75	$25	$25	$25	$250

NOTES

1. The total figures from the columns in the Petty Cash Journal can be used to post expense to the Cash Disbursements Journal.
2. $250 is the amount reimbursed by a check from the general checking account payable to cash for the petty cash fund. The fund must be reimbursed at the end of the accounting period.

Advance Deposit Journal. This journal simply lists the client's name, the amount and date of the deposit, and the date of the event. It is used in conjunction with the Sales and Cash Receipts Journal. It's handy, because it simplifies the search when you're preparing final invoices for clients and want to make sure they're getting proper credit for what they've already paid. Moreover, in preparing a balance sheet, the total amount of advance deposits is listed under "Liabilities," because the off-premise caterer has yet to perform the necessary service and is "liable" for performance.

Occasionally, clients forfeit an advance deposit. Forfeited advance deposits should be shown as "Other Income" on the financial statement. If the deposit is to be used for a future party, this must be noted in the Advance Deposit Journal, along with the final date that it can be used.

Let's say, for instance, that a client plans an event for March 15 and gives the off-premise caterer a $500 deposit. On March 1, the client cancels the party but the caterer agrees to apply the deposit toward any other event the client may book with the caterer until December 31 of the same year. This is noted in the Advance Deposit Journal and applied to any party held during the year; or if it remains unused, it is listed as Other Income on the December financial statement. This, and other sample journal entries, are shown in Exhibit 14.4.

Cash Disbursements Journal. The purpose of this journal is to record all cash disbursement and expenses. An excellent system for small business operators is a "pegboard" or "one-write" check writing and record keeping system. These systems often include provisions for writing and recording payroll checks, although most

---

✖ *Exhibit 14.4* Sample Advance Deposit Journal

Date of Deposit	Name of Client	Date of Event	Amount of Deposit
1-1	James	1-15	$ 600*
1-29	Smith	2-14	1500
Other entries			
2-15	Rapp	3-15	500

(On 3-1 party canceled—deposit valid until 12-31)

*Once a party is completed, and the deposit has been credited on the final invoice, a straight line may be drawn through the listing to reflect credit. For example, on January 15, after the James party, a straight line is drawn through the entry to indicate proper crediting.

---

caterers are usually better off engaging a computerized payroll firm for the payroll function to ease the bookkeeping load.

The pegboard system simply imprints a duplicate copy of each check as it is written directly on the journal page, and there are sufficient columns for headings showing the nature of the expenses. As each check is written, the amount charged to each account may be recorded at the same time. At the end of each journal page, and at the end of each accounting period, the columns are totaled and posted to the income statement summary.

The form for this type of journal includes space for the following entries:

Date of check
Check issued to
Amount of check
Check number
Bank balance
Date and amount of deposits into account

The form also contains columns for recording many different categories of expenses, on the reverse side of the page.

Invoices from suppliers are the basic input documents, which trigger the cash disbursement process. There are a few basic rules to follow when processing invoices:

- Invoices should be turned in to the accounting office daily, rather than being allowed to build up and become a huge paperwork chore. When processed daily, they are easier to handle and errors can be corrected on a timely basis, rather than 20 or 30 days after the receipt of the merchandise.
- All invoices should be checked for errors in arithmetic. Special attention should be given to returned merchandise and/or merchandise that was on an invoice but not received.
- Once they are checked, most bookkeepers and accountants file the invoices by vendor or supplier name until they are due for payment.

- At the end of the month, all invoices from each vendor or supplier are totaled and compared with the monthly statement sent by that vendor. Differences are discussed until there is a mutually satisfactory resolution.
- Off-premise caterers should always pay bills on time, but there is no need to pay them early—unless there are special circumstances or a discount is offered for early payment.

Payroll Journal. As indicated previously, off-premise caterers are advised to engage a payroll company for the preparation of payroll checks, journals, federal and state payroll tax reports, and individual earnings records. This work is very detailed and time-consuming and can be more efficiently handled by firms specializing in this type of work at surprisingly inexpensive prices. For more information on payroll processing services, visit the website adp.com. Costco also has a payroll service for small businesses; find out more at costco.com.

✂ Chart of Accounts

All sources of revenue and expense are listed in a *Chart of Accounts*. Each type of account has a number, which is assigned by you or your accountant. Accounts that are used for recording revenues and expenses may include the following:

Revenue Accounts
Food Revenues
Beverage Revenue
Equipment Revenue
Floral and Décor Revenue
Music and Entertainment Revenue
Revenues from Other Services (as appropriate)
Sales Tax Collected

Expense Accounts
Cost of Sales Accounts
 Cost of Sales—Food
 Cost of Sales—Beverage
 Cost of Sales—Equipment
 Cost of Sales—Floral and Décor
 Cost of Sales—Music and Entertainment
 Cost of Sales—Other Services (as appropriate)
Payroll and Related Costs
Direct Operating Costs
 Uniforms
 Laundry
 Replacement Costs
 Supplies
 Transportation
 Licenses and Permits

> Miscellaneous
> Advertising and Sales Promotion
> Utilities
> Sales Tax Reimbursement to State

Administrative and General Expenses

> Office Supplies, Printing, and Postage
> Telephone
> Data Processing Costs
> Dues and Subscriptions
> Insurance
> Fees to Credit Organizations
> Professional Fees
> Miscellaneous
> Repairs and Maintenance
> Rent and Lease Expense

Here's a brief explanation of the revenues and expenses included in each account:

Food Revenue—All sales of food. Some off-premise caterers use this account to record the entire bill for an event, including both food and staff. Others create a separate account for what they charge for staff at events.

Beverage Revenue—All sales of mixers and bar setups (when the client provides the alcohol and the caterer provides the mixers, etc.); or, in those states where caterers are licensed to sell alcoholic beverages, the revenue from alcoholic beverages and mixers.

Equipment Revenue—All revenues from rental equipment and other equipment provided by the caterer. Of course, if clients deal directly with rental firms for equipment, this account is not used. Off-premise caterers who own equipment and rent it to clients would use this account to record the revenue.

Floral Décor, Music and Entertainment, and Other Revenue—All revenues from vendor-related services, if and when they are provided by the caterer.

Food Cost—All food purchases, less adjustments for inventory fluctuations and employee meals. (A detailed explanation of this account is given later in this chapter.)

Beverage Cost—All costs of soft drinks, bottled water, ice, juices, fruit and other garnishes used for drinks served from bars or beverage stations.

Equipment Cost—All costs for equipment rentals.

Floral Décor, Music and Entertainment, and Other Costs—All costs for engaging vendors and/or purchasing flowers and décor items used for parties and events.

Payroll and Related Expenses—All wages paid to employees (including vacation pay, sick pay, and holiday pay), the employer's share of FICA (Social Security) expense, federal and/or state unemployment taxes as applicable, employee meal costs, and the costs of any other employee benefits. (*Please note:* The cost for Workers' Compensation insurance is not included in this account, but in the Insurance account, because it is a form of insurance.)

Direct Operating Expenses

Uniforms—All costs related to uniforms—purchase or rental, cleaning and repairs, and related items, like name badges.

Laundry—All costs for the laundering of table linens, napkins, towels, aprons, and other linens, whether you use a laundry service or do it yourself.

Replacements—All purchases of china, glassware, flatware, tables, chairs, platters, trays, pitchers, serving dishes, chafing dishes, kitchen utensils, and serving utensils.

Supplies—All purchases of items such as Sterno, charcoal, mesquite, cleaning products and polishes (including brooms, mops, brushes, and pails); toothpicks, doilies, and all other paper products; trash can liners, aluminum foil and plastic film, matches, disposable dinnerware, utensils, containers, and other applicable supplies.

Transportation—The costs involved in transporting foods and supplies to the party site. This may include leasing or renting vehicles, or depreciation of owned vehicles, as well as vehicle operating expenses (fuel, oil, repairs, and maintenance).

Licenses and Permits—Costs for all federal, state, city, or county licenses required to operate the off-premise business, along with any special permits and/or inspection fees for particular events.

Miscellaneous—All costs for minor purchases that are not included in any of the other direct operating accounts, but are directly related to serving the customer.

Advertising and Promotion—All costs for advertising in any medium (TV, radio, newspaper, magazine, trade journal) except help-wanted ads; costs of producing brochures and menus, direct mail, signage; donations, expenses for entertaining clients, referral fees, complimentary food or other services, and any other expenses directly related to promoting or creating sales.

Utilities—All costs for electricity, light bulbs, water, sewage, waste removal, propane, natural gas, and the like. (Remember, in this case, telephone service is not a "utility.")

Sales Taxes—Amounts paid to local and state governments for sales taxes.

Administrative and General Expenses

Office Supplies, Printing, and Postage—All costs for printed matter that is not related to advertising or promotion. This includes accounting forms, letterhead, catering forms and invoices, office supplies, and all postage except what is used for advertising and promotion.

Telephone—All costs for telephone equipment rental, portable and vehicle phones, monthly service charges, long distance charges, and other telephone charges.

Data Processing—All costs for data processing, including preparation of payroll checks and reports, mailing lists, and so forth.

Dues and Subscriptions—Costs for dues paid for memberships in business organizations and subscriptions to trade papers and magazines.

Insurance—Includes costs of all business insurance as described in this text, including Workers' Compensation, and all costs for health, life, and disability insurance paid by the off-premise catering firm for its employees.

Fees Paid to Credit Organizations—If you take credit cards (which are discussed later in this chapter), this account includes the fees paid to credit card companies.

Professional Fees—This may include legal fees, accountant's fees, engineering firm fees, consultants' fees, etc.

Miscellaneous—All costs for any minor charges of an administrative nature. Monthly bank charges go here, for instance.

Repairs and Maintenance—All costs for painting and decorating, repairs to all equipment, and maintenance of grounds. Other charges to this account are charges for building alterations that are not considered "improvements," such as plastering or upholstering. Costs for maintenance contracts for signs and equipment are also included here.

Rent and Lease Expenses—All fees paid to the off-premise caterer's landlord for use of the premises, plus any payment of local taxes or insurance made by the tenant under the lease terms, such as property taxes and sewer taxes.

✕ *Income Statement Summary*

The Income Statement Summary is a worksheet used to summarize and calculate certain expenses prior to preparation of the Income Statement for the accounting period. (An accounting period is usually either one month or three months.) Most expenses can simply be posted directly from the Cash Disbursements Journal to the Income Statement; however, some expenses—things like cost of sales, payroll and related expenses, and prepaid insurance—require some intermediate calculations before posting to the Income Statement. Let's examine these calculations in detail as they relate to the Income Statement Summary.

Cost of Sales Calculation for an Income Statement Summary

The basic formula for computing cost of sales is:

The value of your beginning inventory
Plus (+) purchases
Less (−) the value of your ending inventory
Less (−) employee meals and other credits
Equals (=) cost of sales

How do you get the inventory figures? As a caterer, you take inventory by counting everything you have in stock for the type of inventory you're doing (dishes, food, equipment, etc.) and then can calculate the value of that inventory. This may be done weekly, monthly, quarterly, or annually. Exhibit 14.5 is a sample inventory sheet that allows room for four inventories (on four different dates) on a single page. This reduces paperwork and the time spent in preparing a new page for each inventory period.

Most inventories are multipage forms, with enough pages to list all the items to be inventoried or counted. Each of these pages is extended and totaled. *Extension*

⊠ **Exhibit 14.5** *Sample Inventory Page*

ITEM DESCRIPTION	DATE_____			DATE_____			DATE_____			DATE_____		
	QTY	PR	EXT	QTY	PR	EXT	QTY	PR	EXT	QTY	PR	EXT

PAGE TOTAL
FOR PERIOD _____   _____   _____   _____

Note: In this sample:
QTY = AMOUNT OF INVENTORY ON HAND FOR A PARTICULAR ITEM.
  PR = UNIT PRICE FOR THE ITEM.
EXT = EXTENDED VALUE, WHICH IS THE QUANTITY MULTIPLIED BY THE UNIT PRICE.
For example, an off-premise caterer takes inventory and counts 10 pounds of sliced bacon, at a cost of $1.75 per pound. This caterer would simply multiply 10 pounds times $1.75, and calculate an extended value for bacon of $17.50.

means multiplying the number of units of an item by the unit cost. The figures are totaled by adding all of the extensions on each page. Once each page is totaled, a "grand total" (or total inventory value) is obtained by adding all the individual page totals. The grand total is posted to the Income Statement Summary. The ending inventory for one month becomes the beginning inventory for the following month. For example, the inventory taken on January 31 is both the ending inventory for January and the beginning inventory for February.

Taking inventory is time-consuming, and for many off-premise caterers whose businesses and inventories are small, the time could be better spent in other areas. But for larger caterers, with large fluctuations in monthly revenues and expenses, and for those who need to keep a very careful eye on costs, the inventory process is essential.

At this juncture, let us assume that our hypothetical off-premise caterer took an inventory at the end of January and calculated an inventory value of $200. How does this figure relate to the cost of sales calculation on the Income Statement Summary?

INCOME STATEMENT SUMMARY CALCULATIONS—JANUARY

Beginning inventory for January	$ 0000
Food purchases for January	897
Less: Ending inventory for January	(200)
Less: Cost of employee meals for January	(30)
Cost of food sales for January	$ 667

INCOME STATEMENT SUMMARY CALCULATIONS—FEBRUARY

Beginning inventory for February	$ 200
Food purchases for February	1,140
Less: Ending inventory for February	(300)
Less: Cost of employee meals for February	(40)
Cost of food sales for February	$1,000

Payroll and Related Cost Calculations for an Income Statement Summary

Once the cost of sales is calculated for food, the next step is to calculate the payroll and related costs for the accounting period. This procedure is also best done on the Income Statement Summary, as it involves a number of figures. Here's the formula:

Gross wages
Plus (+) employer's share of FICA expenses
Plus (+) federal and state unemployment taxes
Plus (+) cost of employee meals
Plus (+) cost for any other employee benefits
Equals (=) total cost for payroll and related expenses

Let's use this formula to calculate the payroll and related costs for January, using our hypothetical caterer's numbers:

Gross wages	$1,777
Plus (+) employer's share of FICA at 7.65%	136
Plus (+) federal and state unemployment taxes*	100
Plus (+) cost of employee meals	50
Plus (+) cost of worker's comp insurance	100
Total payroll and related costs	$2,163**

*Unemployment tax laws vary from state to state. Off-premise caterers are responsible for adhering to both state and federal unemployment tax laws.

**Also note that this amount is slightly less than the budgeted amount for January ($2,332), because the total cost for unemployment, FICA, and employee meals was less than 20 percent of the gross payroll for the month.

Prepaid Expense Calculations for an Income Statement Summary

Off-premise caterers frequently prepay expenses for insurance and other major expenses. They may pay their total annual insurance premium in January, for instance, but because the insurance is in effect for the whole year, this expense should be spread out over the entire 12-month period to present the most realistic picture of the company's finances. If it was "charged" in total on January's books, this would totally distort the financial results by overstating the January loss, and either understating losses or overstating profits in future months. This topic was addressed earlier in the "Cash Budgets" section of this chapter. The correct calculation would be:

Total cost for insurance for year	$3,000
Expense per month (divided by 12)	250

Please note, however, that even with this calculation of the true monthly expense, you can choose to handle the actual payment of the expense a little differently. Our fictitious caterer made a $1,000 insurance payment in January, one-third of the total amount due. Then, the remaining months (through November) show a $200 disbursement as the remainder is paid off.

There may be other calculations unique to particular off-premise caterers that can be done on the Income Statement Summary. Once these are complete, work can begin on preparing the Income Statement.

✕ The Income Statement

A properly prepared Income Statement depicts a company's profit or loss, as well as other key numbers, for a particular period. The period may be a month, a quarter, or a year. Completing this statement is an excellent way to measure the financial health of an operation. Exhibit 14.6 is a sample Income Statement for our hypothetical off-premise caterer.

Here's a short explanation of each Income Statement entry:

Food Revenue—Includes food sales and the labor (staff) charges, service charges, and sales taxes related to food sales.

Beverage Revenue—Includes beverage sales (both alcoholic and nonalcoholic) and the sales of related items, like mixers and ice. It also includes labor charges, such as bartenders' wages, service charges, and sales taxes related specifically to alcohol and other beverage sales.

Equipment, Floral, and Music Revenue—Includes any money, service charges, and sales taxes charged for providing these services.

Total Revenue—The total of the preceding revenue categories.

Food Cost of Goods Sold—An amount already calculated on the Income Statement Summary, which can be taken directly from that summary.

⊠ *Exhibit 14.6* Income Statement

Year Ending December 31, 20__

	Food	Beverage	Equipment	Floral	Music/Ent.	Total
Revenue	$90,000	$5,000	$10,000	$3,000	$2,000	$110,000
Cost of Sales	30,000	1,500	8,500	2,500	1,800	44,300
Gross Margin	$60,000	$3,500	$ 1,500	$ 500	$ 200	$ 65,700
Payroll & Related	25,000	1,000				26,000
Direct Activity Profit	$35,000	$2,500	$ 1,500	$ 500	$ 200	$ 39,700
Direct Operating Expenses						
Uniforms	500					
Laundry	500					
Replacements	1,000					
Supplies	3,000					
Transportation	1,000					
Licenses	200					
Miscellaneous	500					
Adv and Promo	2,000					
Utilities	3,000					
Total	$11,700					$ 11,700
Administrative & General Exp						
Off Supp/Print	500					
Telephone	2,000					
Data Proc	1,000					
Insurance	3,000					
Fee to Credit	-0-					
Professional Fees	500					
Miscellaneous	100					
Repair/Maint	1,000					
Rent/Lease	5,000					
Total	$13,100					$ 13,100
Net Profit/Loss	$10,200	$2,500	$ 1,500	$ 500	$ 200	$ 14,900

Beverage Cost of Goods Sold—The total purchases of both alcoholic and non-alcoholic beverages. (Larger catering operations may wish to adjust these figures through the Income Statement Summary, just as they do with the Food Cost of Sales.)

Equipment Cost of Sales—The total of all amounts paid to rental companies for equipment rentals made on behalf of clients; and/or the cost of purchasing small, incidental equipment for rental to clients; and/or the depreciation and amortization of major equipment and supplies that are purchased to be rented to clients.

Floral and Music Cost of Sales—The amounts paid to florists and musicians for their services when provided by the off-premise caterer.

Total Cost of Sales—The total of the preceding Cost of Sales categories. Gross Margin figures are computed by deducting the cost of sales from the revenues for each department.

Payroll and Related Expenses—Taken from the Income Statement Summary for each department.

Direct Activity Profit—The amount that remains after deducting payroll and related costs from the gross margin.

Operating Expenses and Administrative and General Expenses are posted to the Income Statement from the totals for these accounts in the Cash Disbursements Journal.

The totals of these expenses are then subtracted from the Direct Activity Profit to determine the profit or loss for the accounting period.

Please note in Exhibit 14.6 that all of the Operating Expenses and the Administrative and General Expenses are charged to the food account. In theory, some of these expenses are directly attributable to the other accounts; however, for an operation of this size—generating $110,000 in annual revenues—in our opinion, this is not necessary.

✖ The Balance Sheet

Off-premise caterers should be familiar with Balance Sheets in order to gain a clearer picture of their business. Whereas an Income Statement shows the revenue and expenses of a company for a certain period of time, the Balance Sheet shows the company's assets, liabilities, and net worth—as we mentioned, a snapshot of its financial condition. When total liabilities are deducted from total assets, the resulting figure is called the *net worth* of the company on that specific date.

Assets are things of value that are owned by the business. For an off-premise caterer, assets would include:

- Cash
- Amounts due from clients (your *Accounts Receivable*)
- Food and other types of inventory
- Prepaid expenses (such as insurance)
- Fixed assets (land, buildings, improvements to a building, vehicles, major kitchen and operating equipment)

Accumulated depreciation on the fixed assets is deducted from their value, a task best left to your accountant. Accumulated depreciation is the total of all depreciation charged to the business for income tax purposes. The laws governing how this is done, and how much depreciation is allowed over a certain time period, are strict and thorough.

BILL'S TIPS FOR FINE-TUNING YOUR FINANCES

Using QuickBooks is an excellent way to keep track of your financial affairs. It's worth the minimal financial investment, as well as the investment in time to learn how to use it. QuickBooks is a popular computer accounting program with an "audit trail" feature that you should always leave on.

At least once a year, complete a Balance Sheet. It will be required for federal income tax purposes.

Take a complete annual inventory each year of all your physical assets, such as equipment and computers. Also take monthly inventories of your food and beverage supplies. Inventory only the case lots and large items, and use estimates for open containers and goods in process. The larger the catering firm, the more important this is, because items have a way of disappearing.

Do a "cost-out" of each event—that is, look back at all the figures to determine the costs of food, staffing, and other direct expenses. Aim for a gross margin of 50 percent after all direct operating expenses are deducted from revenues.

Look into having prices from your major food and beverages suppliers downloaded directly into your computer for costing and inventory purposes.

Have some form of control over party hours at event sites. A portable time clock helps, as does having a third party verify hours. Dishonest party supervisors have been known to put in "ghost employees" who never work, but are paid.

It's imperative to reconcile each checking account monthly. With online banking, this can even be done on a daily basis. In addition, the petty cash fund should be reconciled at least once a month.

Keep in mind that the conditions for fraud and embezzlement are need, opportunity, and failure of conscience. Smart caterers keep their eyes open regarding employees who have financial problems, and they also eliminate or reduce temptations for theft.

Take a hard look at fixed expenses. Many are not necessarily "fixed" and can be reduced. Take utility costs, for example. Visit the websites energystar.gov and restaurant.org for just a few of many energy-saving ideas. Score.org also has suggestions for reducing fixed expenses.

Half of most caterers' advertising budgets are often wasted. The trick is to determine which half! Have a tracking system in place to determine where your business originates, and eliminate those advertising expenses that do not produce results.

Get at least three bids on liability, property, and Workers' Compensation insurance each year. A reliable resource for insurance quotes is candcinsurance.com.

A couple of times a year, revisit each and every administrative and general expense and look into ways of reducing each one. Sometimes simply by asking for a lower fee, you can get it. (Of course, this does not apply to your local electricity provider, but you can definitely negotiate things like cellular phone rates.)

Liabilities are obligations. For a caterer, these would include:

- Outstanding loans
- Advance deposits from customers (for events yet to occur)
- Amounts owed to vendors (your *Accounts Payable*)
- Accrued payroll (amounts owed to employees as of a certain date)

The difference between the amounts of assets and liabilities is called *equity*.

A simple example of the Balance Sheet for the Hypothetical Catering Company at the end of its first year of operation could be as follows:

BALANCE SHEET
HYPOTHETICAL CATERING COMPANY
FOR THE PERIOD ENDING DECEMBER 31, 2005

Current Assets

Cash		
In the Bank	$5,000	
In Savings	2,000	
Total Cash	$7,000	
Accounts Receivable		
Due from Clients	1,000	
Total Accounts Receivable	1,000	
Inventories		
Food	500	
Total Inventories	500	
Prepaid Expenses	–0–	
Total Current Assets	$8,500	
Fixed Assets	–0–	
Total Assets	8,500	

Liabilities and Equity

Current Liabilities		
Accounts Payable	$1,000	
Accrued Payroll	500	
Advance Deposits—Clients	1,000	
Total Current Liabilities	$2,500	
Long-Term Liabilities	–0–	
Total Liabilities	$2,500	
Equity	$6,000	
Total Liabilities and Equity	$8,500	

✗ Analyzing Financial Statements

In addition to knowing where to put the numbers on financial statements, our caterer must also understand how to analyze the data on the Income Statement, Balance Sheet, and other financial records, so they'll be useful for making good management decisions. In fact, the primary reason your financial reports must be accurate and timely is so that they can be of maximum use to you.

Analyzing Income Statements

Income Statements should include year-to-date figures, which are essentially totals of the results for the year. These totals help to make sense of the month-to-month fluctuations in revenues and costs and can be easily compared with year-to-date figures for prior years to see how the business is growing (or not). You can also compare year-to-date totals with the amounts you have budgeted to see whether you are meeting your budget projections.

Percentage comparisons are done for revenues and expenses to see how well the caterer is controlling expenses. Percentage comparisons are handy because they take into account fluctuations in revenues. For example, the cost of sales figure for food one month might be $1,000, and the following month, $2,000. Does this mean that food costs are rising and becoming excessive? Not necessarily! It depends on the amount of food revenues. If food costs are budgeted to be about 33 percent of sales, and sales for these two months are $3,000 and $6,000, respectively, then things look fine. However, if sales in the second month are only $5,000, this means that food cost has jumped to 40 percent of sales, and the caterer needs to investigate and perhaps take corrective action.

Another way to compare is to look at a particular month, the same month in the previous year, and the month immediately before it. (Example: May 2005, May 2004, and April 2004.) With the three sets of figures in front of you, check them carefully. Are sales increasing or decreasing from the prior year and/or the prior month? How do they compare with budgeted amounts? If sales are up from the prior periods, were prices raised, or were more guests served?

Yet another comparison is to divide total sales during a period by the number of guests served to determine a *check average*. Restaurants do this frequently to determine spending patterns (an average amount spent per guest), as well as how well their servers are selling "extras" like desserts, drinks, and appetizers to increase the check average.

The *payroll percentage* is another key. This is computed by dividing food, payroll, and related costs by food revenues to come up with a percentage. Seasonal operators will see large variances in their payroll percentages between busy and slow seasons. Many off-premise caterers experience large swings in monthly revenues, which will affect this percentage greatly if key staff members are kept on the payroll during the slow season.

Prime cost is the term used for the combined cost of food and payroll. Many operators use this as a guideline. They realize that if their food costs are high, then their payroll costs must be low, or vice versa. An off-premise caterer who operates with a 40 percent food cost will not stay in business long with a 40 percent labor cost. The total of 80 percent prime cost is simply too high to generate a profit. Successful off-premise caterers operate with prime costs in the range of 40 to 65 percent.

It's tempting to analyze only the food and labor costs, since these are your biggest expenses in the catering business. But don't neglect direct operating costs and administrative costs, which should be compared in the same manner. You need to know if any of these expenses are too high or too low, and if so, what changes can be made to adjust them.

Of course, the most important figure is the net profit or loss amount. When people talk about a business's "bottom line," this is it—and, for many, it represents the true measure of success. How much did they earn after all expenses were paid?

And how much is "enough?" The answer depends on the individual caterer. In general, profit percentages for off-premise caterers are greater than those reported by restaurants. But profits also vary greatly from month to month for caterers with highly seasonal businesses. During slow periods, losses are common; during peak seasons, profits are generous. It takes a hardy and committed businessperson to ride the financial rollercoaster.

Analyzing Balance Sheets

Balance Sheets for off-premise caterers also reveal operational successes and failures. Let's look over several of the figures on a typical Balance Sheet and consider what they might indicate, businesswise.

The first place to check is the cash in the operational (business checking) account. Is there enough to pay all the bills on time? If there is more than enough, excess cash should be deposited into interest-bearing accounts to generate a little more income. Is there too little? If so, is the Accounts Receivable amount high (meaning that clients are not paying you on time), or are your payment terms too lenient? Other common reasons for too little cash are:

- The business is not profitable in the long run.
- The owners are withdrawing too much cash from the business.
- Inventories are too high.
- The business is experiencing one of its seasonal fluctuations.

Some caterers who experience seasonal cash fluctuations obtain lines of credit from their banks from which to draw during slow seasons and pay back when business improves. Others borrow money in the form of loans. Still others, who are well established and know that during certain seasons there will be a lack of cash, can ask their clients for larger advance deposits for events during those times. This is very effective, because the caterer doesn't have to pay any interest expense, but it may (in some cases) require giving the clients a slight discount on the events in exchange for the higher deposits.

Accounts Receivable should be practically nonexistent or, at least, kept at a minimum. Many businesses "age" their Accounts Receivable by separating them into time frames:

- Current (due and payable within 30 days)
- Less than 30 days past due
- 31–60 days past due
- 61–120 days past due
- More than 120 days past due

The longer accounts are past due, the less likely you'll be able to collect them, so astute caterers will not allow their accounts to become past due. Of course, there are always those rare and unpleasant situations when a check bounces or a caterer is duped into granting credit before realizing the debt will be almost impossible to collect. Some off-premise caterers establish a reserve account for this type of situation by expensing small amounts each month to the operation as "bad debt" expense. This transaction does not involve cash. It is nothing more than a paper entry, charging a small expense against profits each month and making an offsetting charge to a re-serve account or bad debt account. By doing this, if there is a bad debt, the finan-cial statement for the month is not distorted by it. A CPA can tell you more about this procedure and its impact on a company's federal income taxes.

Food inventory turnover is determined by dividing the Food Cost of Goods Sold for the month by the end-of-month food inventory value. If the Hypothetical Cater-ing Company has $10,000 of Food Cost of Goods Sold for a month, and the ending food inventory for the same month is valued at $1,000, this caterer's food inventory turnover is 10 ($10,000 divided by $1,000). The higher the food inventory turnover figure, the better—as long as there are sufficient amounts of foods on hand with which to operate efficiently. Restaurants operate with inventory turnovers of 3 to 5, but most off-premise caterers should have higher turnovers. Astute off-premise cater-ers monitor their inventory contents and promote or discount items that have been in stock for long periods of time—as long as they are still fresh, of course.

It is well understood among experienced off-premise caterers and restaurateurs that low inventories help reduce theft and pilferage. Thieves are more likely to steal from large inventories, thinking that a disappearance is less likely to be noticed, than from smaller inventories.

Another Balance Sheet analysis compares current assets to current liabilities. This comparison is known as the business's *current ratio*. A ratio of 2 to 1, in which current assets are twice as large as current liabilities, is considered good. For off-premise cater-ers, a current ratio of 1 to 1 is also acceptable, because inventories and receivables are generally low, meaning that a large portion of the current assets consists of cash.

✕ Controlling Costs

Controlling costs is a daily function of all successful off-premise caterers. These busi-ness owners operate with their eyes wide open, always looking for waste, inefficiency, and other problems that can adversely affect profitability. Some hands-on measures that smart caterers take include:

- Checking trash cans for product that has been discarded accidentally. You'd be surprised at how much flatware and other items are carelessly tossed!
- Counting all rental equipment before and after each event
- Learning to schedule intelligently—scheduling enough staff to complete the job ac-curately and on time: not too few people so that everyone needs to rush, and not too many standing around waiting for something to do.
- Monitoring utility costs; turning appliances and lights off when not in use, or in-stalling timers or motion detectors on lights in some rooms.
- Buying labor-saving devices (computers, kitchen equipment) that will reduce daily payroll expenses. Portable electric time clocks can be purchased for off-premise events.
- Inspecting all areas for safety hazards and correcting them promptly.
- Carefully examining each operating cost and administrative and general cost at least quarterly to determine if there are any savings that can be made.

■ Involving the staff in safety and cost-saving measures by encouraging and rewarding their ideas and suggestions.

Of course, this list could go on indefinitely, but simply being present at all events, watching and working alongside your employees, will do wonders to reduce costs. In addition to hands-on techniques, there are several types of forms that caterers have developed to suit their own needs for projecting, analyzing, and controlling costs. Many of them are computerized. Let's examine three types of forms that can be very effective tools for projecting and controlling costs.

The Pre- and Post-Event Cost Form

A Pre- and Post-Event Cost Form, shown in Exhibit 14.7, is completed at the time the first proposal is submitted to a potential client, updated as changes are made to the original proposal, and finalized upon conclusion of the event with actual expenses. It's almost a "mini" Income Statement, as it includes projected revenues, food costs, equipment costs, labor and related costs, and operating costs, then contrasts them with what was actually spent in each category. The results can reveal errors made in pre-costing and planning the party, or the wisdom behind a successful and profitable event. Either way, it can assist the off-premise caterer in improving his or her profitability.

Daily Income Statement and Report

Another form that many larger off-premise caterers use is a Daily Income Statement and Report (see Exhibit 14.8). Its advantage is that it provides caterers with daily or weekly results, giving them timely information to use in correcting problems, rather than waiting until the end of the month or the quarter.

This report is completed by recording information from client invoices, supplier invoices, time cards and/or time sheets, bank deposits, and checks written. Daily estimates can be used for expenses such as rent, utilities, and insurance—typical business outgo that occurs regularly and without much variation from day to day.

The form allows space for daily activity postings, as well as a "Month to Date" column. The Month to Date column averages out the results from all previous days in the month (which can vary tremendously from day to day), and the end-of-month totals can be compared with the Income Statement for the month. Variances between the two statements can be reconciled at this point.

Ideal Food Cost Calculation Technique

Many off-premise caterers do not truly know whether their food cost percentage is too high, too low, or on target. They know how their results compare to their budgets, prior years, and prior months, but when it comes to knowing exactly what their food cost should be, they do not know. Because different menu items are sold with different food cost percentages, they need a formula from which to calculate the "ideal" food cost percentage, taking this into account.

⊠ Exhibit 14.7 *Pre- and Post-Event Cost Form*

Name of Client: _____

Date of the Event: _____

Minimum Number of Guests Expected: _____

Type of Cost	Projected Cost	Actual Cost
Food Cost—List Each Menu Item		
_____		
_____		
_____		
_____		
_____		
_____		
_____		
_____		
_____		
_____		
_____		
_____		
Total Food Cost	_____	
Labor Cost Calculations—List Costs for:		
Food Preparation at Commissary	_____	
Labor Cost for Delivery/Return	_____	
Supervisory Payroll	_____	
Kitchen Payroll	_____	
Front-of-the House Payroll	_____	
Total Payroll	_____	
Add: Estimate Benefits %	_____	
Total Payroll & Related	_____	
Rental Equipment Expense	_____	
Direct Operating Expenses	_____	
Supplies	_____	
Transportation Vehicle(s)	_____	
Linens	_____	
Uniforms	_____	
Other	_____	
Total Operating Expense	_____	

Calculation for Event Profitability

Revenue		Projected	Actual
Food/Payroll			
Equipment			
Other			
Total			
Less Expenses			
Food Cost of Sales			
Equipment Cost			
Payroll and Related			
Other			
Total			
Operating Profit			

Another problem is that revenues from various menu items change from month to month. For example, the Hypothetical Catering Company sells two popular meals, a chicken dinner and a steak dinner. The chicken dinner sells for $15 and has a 30 percent food cost, and the steak dinner sells for $20 and has a 40 percent food cost. What food cost should the owner look for? It depends on the number of sales of each menu item. For example, if almost all sales during the month are chicken dinners, and the menu is designed for the chicken to generate a 30 percent food cost, then the food cost for the month should be 30 percent. If it is 35 percent, the caterer may have a cost control problem. But if most sales are steak dinners, and the food cost at the end of the month is closer to 40 percent, everything should be fine.

However, most caterers will sell some chicken dinners and some steak dinners. How can the ideal food cost be calculated? The answer is simple. It starts with the caterer determining what percentage of total sales is chicken and what percentage of total sales is steak. This is done by dividing the sale of a particular type of dinner by the total amount of food sales:

Total food sales for the month	$5,000
Sales from steak dinners	1,000
Sales from chicken dinners	4,000

Steak dinner sales as a percentage of total food sales:

$$1,000 \div 5,000 = .20 \ (20\%)$$

Chicken dinner sales as a percentage of total food sales:

$$4,000 \div 5,000 = .80 \ (80\%)$$

Then, the ideal food cost formula is to multiply the percentage of total sales for each menu item by the food cost percentage and, finally, to total these extensions. Let's try it.

⊠ Exhibit 14.8 *Daily Income Statement and Report*

Date _____

	This Date	Month to Date
Revenues (Posted from client invoices)		
Food		
Beverages		
Equipment		
Florals		
Music and entertainment		
Other		
Total revenue		
Cost of sales (Posted from vendor invoices)		
Food		
Beverages		
Equipment		
Florals		
Music and entertainment		
Other		
Total cost of sales		
Cost of sales percentage of revenues		
Gross margin (Revenues less cost of sales)		
Food		
Beverages		
Equipment		
Florals		
Music and entertainment		
Other		
Sales tax		
Total gross margin		
Gross margin percentage of revenues		
Payroll (Posted from time cards and time sheets. Calculate hours worked times hourly rate plus estimate for benefits.)		
Payroll and related percentage of revenues		
Activity profit (Deduct payroll from gross margin)		
Activity profit percentage of revenues		
Operating expenses (Caterers may use estimates or post figures directly from supplier invoices.)		
Uniforms		
Laundry		
Replacements		
Supplies		
Transportation		
Licenses		
Miscellaneous		

	This Date	Month to Date
Advertising and promotion		
Utilities		
Sales tax submission to state		
Total operating expenses		
Operating expense percentage of revenues		
Administrative and general expenses (Caterers may use estimates or post figures directly from invoices as appropriate.)		
Office supplies, printing, and postage		
Telephone		
Data processing		
Dues and subscriptions		
Insurance		
Fees to credit organizations		
Professional fees		
Repairs and maintenance		
Rent and lease expense		
Total administrative and general		
Administrative and general expense percentage of total revenues		
Net profit/loss (Activity profit less operating expenses and administrative and general expenses)		
Net profit/loss percentage of total sales		
Other information		
Bank balance		
Beginning balance		
Plus: Deposits this date		
Less: Checks written this date		
Ending bank balance		
Accounts receivable		
Accounts receivable beginning balance		
Less: Paid on account		
Plus: Charges to accounts		
Ending accounts receivable balance		

Steak dinner food cost percentage times percentage of total food sales (40 percent):

$$.40 \times .20 = .08 \ (8\%)$$

Chicken dinner food cost percentage times percentage of total food sales (30%):

$$.30 \times .80 = .24 \ (24\%)$$
$$\text{Total of extensions} = .32 \ (32 \text{ percent})$$

This is a simple example of how the calculation is made, so let's try something a little more challenging, determining an ideal food cost for an off-premise caterer who sells six different dinners, all at different food costs, as follows:

TYPE OF DINNER	FOOD COST	PERCENT OF SALES	EXTENSION
Chicken	25	20	.050
Roast Beef	30	15	.045
Italian	20	10	.020
Seafood Platter	35	20	.070
Broiled Fish	25	10	.025
New York Strip Steak	35	25	.0875
Totals		100%	.2975

Ideal Food Cost = 29.75%

For off-premise caterers with licenses to sell alcoholic beverages, this same formula can be adapted to beverage sales. It can be very useful, because there often are large variances between costs for different types of liquor, beer, and wine. For example, martinis generally have higher cost of sales percentages than draft beer, making it difficult to determine the overall cost of sales based on various sales levels for these drinks.

✕ *Computers in Catering*

Today's caterer cannot compete in the marketplace without a computer—or several! At the very least, computers simplify the process of preparing proposals, menus, and contracts. You may not recall the days of typewriters and carbon paper, but we do. Now, when we make a mistake, we can hit the "Backspace" or "Delete" key and keep going.

Most caterers maintain templates of sample menus, proposals, and contracts in their files, which can simply be customized to meet the needs of different clients. Caterers also keep track of their clients, staff, suppliers, and others using very basic lists and forms that can be created in Outlook, Microsoft Word, Microsoft Works, or ACT for Windows.

Some caterers purchase catering software programs to help them manage certain facets of their operations. Most of these software programs are designed for one of three areas of the business:

Sales and Service—These types of programs focus on keeping you organized as a manager. Electronic functions keep track of bookings (and eliminate accidental double bookings), maintain customer and vendor databases, and provide "trace file" functions that automatically remind the caterer to confirm guest counts, finalize menus, obtain deposits from clients, and ask about new business from a client who hasn't recently been "active." The software also contains form letters that may be customized for your business or a particular situation.

Back–of–the–House Management—These programs can help a caterer make sufficient staffing assignments, day-to-day or before an event; track accessory services; and keep vendor and supplier records. They contain customizable forms for various functions or departments of the company, as well as layout or design features that can be used to plan parties, weddings, and other special events.

Revenue and Cash Flow—Features of these programs include cost and profit analyses, menu management and pricing functions, and bookkeeping features that allow the caterer to manage Accounts Receivable.

Despite all the advantages of specialty programs, they are not absolutely necessary. We have operated successfully for years without specialty software, using only the basic Microsoft Office programs and ACT for Windows. In fact, it is our opinion that many caterers probably invest in expensive software that they either do not utilize or underutilize. Remember, the idea is not to spend more on the software than you save on the efficiencies it may create.

Other caterers rely too heavily on the software's pricing program, rather than taking market conditions into consideration that certainly impact prices. Some spend hours entering data. Indeed, they know exactly how many dill pickles they have in their walk-in cooler, when perhaps simply going into the walk-in and seeing for themselves would be far more cost-effective!

The bottom line here is *buyer beware.* Be sure you're going to save money and improve a process or task before becoming bogged down with computer software programs that may not work for you.

Clearly, computers and specialized software programs are here to stay, and they are becoming better and less expensive. Some sell for less than $1,000. For readers looking for more information on these options, we offer the following list of software suppliers along with their website addresses:

BSynergy.net	www.synergy-intl.com
CaterEase Software	www.caterease.com
CaterMate	www.catermate.com
CaterPro	www.caterprosoftware.com
CaterTrax	www.catertrax.com
CaterWare	www.caterware.com
Caterxpert	www.caterxpert.com
CookenPro Commercial	www.cooken.com

A final tip: When considering a major software purchase, it is better to change (which usually means upgrade) your system to fit the software, than to try to change the software to fit your system. Adapting a particular new program to an outdated system is asking for trouble. It can be expensive, sometimes not very effective, and certainly time-consuming. And by all means, if you need help learning to use a program, or your computer(s) in general, take a course and pay for your key office employees to do the same.

✕ *Managing Money*

In your catering career, you will no doubt have to deal with banks and bankers. And in so doing, it is wise to adhere to a few simple but important rules.

1. Pay all bills on time. Never pay bills early unless there is a cash discount offered for early payment. There is clearly no advantage to early payment, and definitely a disadvantage when money paid early could possibly be earning interest in an interest-bearing account.

2. That brings us to Rule 2: Place any excess cash (that is, whatever is not needed for day-to-day operations) into interest-bearing accounts. There is no reason not to take advantage of every opportunity to generate additional income. Off-premise caterers should pay particular attention to this during very busy times of year, like Christmas, when money can pile up quickly in general accounts.

3. Do not extend credit to clients or vendors. Off-premise caterers are in the catering business, not in the banking business to offer short-term loans. Caterers dealing with large corporations and organizations that say they take weeks to process invoices should develop the practice of billing early (in advance of an event) for the estimated amount of the party, or at least a large percentage of the expected total due, and ask that the bills be paid in full prior to the day or night of the event. Any remaining smaller balances can be invoiced after the event.

4. You should under no circumstances issue a check when there are insufficient funds in the bank to cover it. It is almost always better to approach creditors first and tell them of your financial difficulties, with a plan in mind to share with the creditors as to exactly how you intend to pay the bills. A good rule for a checking account is that the balance on any given day should average no less than 30 percent of the total amount of the checks written during the month. For example, if you write $10,000 worth of checks during the month, the business checking account should maintain an average checking account balance of $3,000 at all times.

5. Always establish a personal and trusting relationship with a banker. At some point, a problem or need will arise when a caterer will require a loan, or some other special service, from the bank. It is far better to deal with an individual at that bank with whom you have established a relationship, than to hunt for someone and have to explain your situation if there is a problem.

6. All checking accounts must be reconciled (balanced) once a month, immediately upon receipt of the bank statement(s). Any delay can result in compounding of errors and undue hardship in trying to unravel the financial disarray. Errors made by customers and banks can result in embarrassment when a supplier returns a check because of insufficient funds. One of the worst things a caterer can do is to let bank statements accumulate and then try to reconcile many months at one time. Instructions for reconciling bank statements are on the back of most bank statements. Use them!

7. Bank deposits should be made on a daily basis. As soon as money is received, it should be deposited. It is not good policy to pay bills directly from cash receipts. Payment by check, or from the petty cash fund, leaves a better audit trail.

8. In catering companies with two or more owners, two signatures should be required on checks that exceed a certain dollar amount. Moreover, one owner should be responsible for approving the invoices; the other owner should sign the checks.

Selecting a Bank

Off-premise caterers should shop for a bank the same way they shop for other vendors and suppliers, and place their primary business accounts with a bank that can make the largest overall contribution to the business even if it is not conveniently located. When searching, caterers should ask for references from other business owners and suppliers and look for a bank that understands the foodservice industry—not all of them do. Caterers must also feel comfortable as individuals when dealing with the bank and the bankers. If these criteria are met, chances are you've found the right bank.

Loan Applications

When off-premise caterers need to borrow money, they should first look to the financial institution where they keep their general, payroll, and other checking accounts. The chief problem with many banks is that they have very conservative lending practices, particularly for foodservice businesses.

When requesting a loan, good accounting work is mandatory, and copies of your company's bank statements should be provided along with the actual loan request. This helps to establish a relationship. Off-premise caterers should provide accurate and realistic figures and should be prepared to answer bankers' inquiries about these figures. Astute bankers know that it is a sure sign that someone is not on top of his or her business when they ask a question and the loan applicant responds with, "I need to get with my accountant and get back to you."

Off-premise caterers who need assistance in completing loan applications and financial projections can contact local offices of the Small Business Administration (SBA—on the Internet at sba.org). or the Service Corps of Retired Executives (SCORE—on the Internet at score.org). Their expertise can be tapped for a small fee, or even at no cost in some cases. The SBA and SCORE can also assist with things like deciding what type of business you want yours to be—sole proprietorship, corporation, limited liability partnership, or another type. A third place to go for expert assistance is a Small Business Development Center (SBDC). There are about 900 of them in the United States, federally funded and often affiliated with college campuses.

Lenders consider the following factors when making loan determinations:

1. **Character**—Experience in catering, special skills, honesty, integrity, and willingness to pay back the loan promptly.

2. **Capacity**—The actual ability of the applicant to pay back the loan with interest. To prove this, you must show projected Income Statements, Balance Sheets, and Cash Flow Statements for three to five years.

3. **Capital**—Loans to off-premise caterers must be personally guaranteed by the owner. If you're the owner, you must decide which of your personal assets (if any) you are willing to risk.

4. **Collateral**—Since foodservice equipment depreciates quickly and has no particular value to lenders, many banks require that personal property be put up as collateral, which will be seized if the loan is not paid back. Examples of personal property are home equity and personal savings accounts.

Prudent lenders will look at the first year's financial statements (for someone already in business) and may ask to see projections for the next three years of operation. They won't lend you a bundle—more like 8 to 10 percent of the business' total revenue. For example, an off-premise caterer who projects $750,000 in business during the next three years could perhaps obtain a loan for $60,000 to $75,000, with payback terms over the next three years.

SBA-guaranteed loans may be granted to entrepreneurs who cannot qualify for commercial loans. These loans offer an extended payment schedule of 7 to 8 years, but they have a reputation for being difficult to obtain and involving lots of paperwork. You can find local SBA offices in many cities, or check out the website, sba.org.

Aside from applying for bank loans and SBA loans, off-premise caterers may look to credit unions, real estate developers, private investor groups, limited partnerships, and even friends and family members to help finance their start-up businesses. We must caution, however, that borrowing should be kept at an absolute minimum in order to maximize profits and cash flow. It is difficult and stressful to start out a business saddled with obligations of monthly debts and/or high interest to repay.

✖ *Credit Card Processing Services*

More and more caterers are accepting credit card payments for catering services. It's a convenience for the client, but can be a rather expensive proposition for the caterer, because credit card companies charge a processing fee that varies from 2 percent to as much as 7 percent or more. And it's amazing how a credit card processor with an advertised rate of 2.5 percent can quickly double this fee with "special charges"— transactions fees, monthly fees, and miscellaneous other fees. You will want to check your credit card processing statements monthly to be sure the processing company isn't hitting your business with some of these extra charges.

The cost of this "convenience" should also be taken into consideration when setting your prices. A gross margin of 2 to 7 percent on each party is very significant and must be included in the pricing structure, or you end up losing a small percentage on every transaction paid for by credit card. For more information on credit card processing, visit these Internet websites: bancardboulder.com and costco.com. Caterers who chose not to accept credit cards on a regular basis, but find themselves in need of credit card processing occasionally in order to book a client, should take a look at paypal.com, another service that offers credit card processing at fairly modest fees.

✕ *Federal Taxes*

What would business be like in the United States if there were no federal taxes? Most likely, almost all businesses would be more profitable and, certainly, would require less paperwork. However, taxes are a way of life, and business owners face more than their fair share. The major tax laws that affect off-premise caterers relate to payment of:

> Federal income taxes (both corporate and personal)
> Social Security (also known as the Federal Insurance Contributions Act, FICA)
> Medicare taxes
> Federal unemployment taxes (FUTA)

There are also a number of state and local taxes on sales, payroll, income, and so on. These change often, so there is no substitute for the services of a good Certified Public Accountant (CPA) to assist you with them. This text is meant only as an overview of the touchy topic of taxes, containing general information that is relevant at the moment, as we're writing this. For federal tax questions and forms, the Internal Revenue Service website (irs.gov) is a gold mine of information.

Most off-premise caterers are incorporated and must file a corporate income tax return at the end of the year. A *year* means either a calendar year or a fiscal year. If based on a calendar year, the tax return is due no later than March 15 of the following year.

It is imperative to report income and expenses properly on the income tax form! Overstatements of expenses and/or understatements of income can ultimately ruin a successful business. The penalties for errors and omissions are substantial, and the cost for professional tax preparation assistance is small as compared with the consequences if the report is done incorrectly. This is serious business, involving interest, penalties, and even prison terms in some cases, if the IRS decides that information was given fraudulently to avoid paying taxes.

However, there is nothing wrong with taking full advantage of the legal deductions allowed by the tax laws. Here are a few of the tax deductions that catering businesses often overlook:

- Employers' payments for educational expenses—either their own or their staff members' attendance at classes and seminars
- Magazines, books, audio and video tapes related to business skills
- Bank and/or credit bureau service charges and fees
- Gifts to vendors and clients
- Casual labor and tips
- Casualty and theft losses
- Home office expenses

- Commuting miles between home and work
- Business-related computer services charged to personal accounts and/or credit cards
- Parking, meters, tolls, and cab fares related to business
- Postage
- Participation in, or attendance at, trade shows
- Telephone calls away from the business
- Contributions to SEP and Keogh accounts (self-employed retirement plans)

Your CPA can surely add to this list as well. As you prepare for year-end taxes, it is time to take a hard look at your expected profit. If it's high, that is a mixed blessing in terms of taxes. Consider:

- Purchasing equipment and loading up on stock
- Paying vendors in advance on accounts due
- Delaying client billing until the beginning of the next accounting period

If your profits are lower than expected, consider:

- Arranging with key vendors to delay payment until the beginning of the next accounting year
- Reducing your own pay as company owner for a month or two
- Asking key clients for larger advance deposits

Being tax-savvy and taking these steps can improve your profits and show your banker improved results.

Tax Withholding

Employers are required to pay one-half of the Social Security (FICA) and Medicare taxes for their employees. The other half is withheld from employees' paychecks by you, as their employer, and paid quarterly to the IRS. The maximum wage base for payment of Social Security tax is $60,600; however, all wages are subject to the Medicare tax.

Like any other self-employed person, off-premise caterers must also pay the full amount (both the employer's and the employee's halves) of Social Security and Medicare taxes on their own wages that they receive from the catering firm. You may be able to reduce the amount of Social Security tax you pay if you're married and your spouse happens to work outside the business and pay FICA at that job.

Off-premise caterers are also required to pay federal unemployment insurance (FUTA) for their staff, as well as state unemployment tax. Amounts of the state taxes vary among the states; normally, the amount of federal unemployment tax is reduced by the amount paid to the state.

What happens to the money you withhold from employees' paychecks for FICA, Medicare, and FUTA? There are very specific federal rules about this, with which your CPA will be familiar. These monies must be deposited at certain intervals into banks; then the banks forward the money to the U.S. Treasury. Sometimes a business owner who is short on cash may be tempted to use these withheld wages for business expenses, postponing their federal deposit until cash flow improves. We know business owners who have been jailed for this, and/or whose companies have been shut down for not making their federal payments. It is a violation of federal law, and the penalties are severe. We hear business owners say that although the IRS will allow delinquent taxpayers to negotiate payment plans for what they owe, it is better to borrow money to keep the taxes current than to have to deal with the IRS when they fall behind. In our view, this is true.

✗ Conclusion

Finances may be the last topic of this text, but it is by no means the least important. Financial knowledge is the key to business success, and a profitable bottom line is the end result of good management. Fancy menus, beautiful linens, and flawless parties must generate profit—otherwise, their presentation is in vain.

It is as important to understand the financial workings of your business as it is to understand the desires of your prospective customers or the intricacies of food preparation in a commercial kitchen. If this means getting some more business-related training before you embark on a full-fledged off-premise catering career, by all means, get it. Your future success will most definitely depend on it.

Index